Reforming Empire

Reforming Empire

Protestant Colonialism and
Conscience in British Literature

❊   ❊   ❊   ❊   ❊   ❊

Christopher Hodgkins

University of Missouri Press
Columbia and London

Copyright © 2002 by
The Curators of the University of Missouri
University of Missouri Press, Columbia, Missouri 65201
Printed and bound in the United States of America
All rights reserved
5 4 3 2 1   06 05 04 03 02

Library of Congress Cataloging-in-Publication Data

Hodgkins, Christopher, 1958–
    Reforming empire : Protestant colonialism and conscience in British literature / Christopher Hodgkins.
      p. cm.
    Includes bibliographical references and index.
    ISBN 0-8262-1431-2 (alk. paper)
    1. English literature—Protestant authors—History and criticism.   2. Imperialism in literature.   3. Protestantism and literature.   4. Conscience in literature.   5. Colonies in literature.   I. Title.
PR408.I53 H63 2002
820.9'358—dc21   2002028947

∞™ This paper meets the requirements of the
American National Standard for Permanence of Paper
for Printed Library Materials, Z39.48, 1984.

Designer: Jennifer Cropp
Typesetter: Bookcomp, Inc.
Printer and binder: The Maple-Vail Book Manufacturing Group
Typeface: Bodoni Book

For permissions see p. 289.

Frontispiece: *The Boyhood of Raleigh* (1870) by Sir John Everett Millais, © Tate, London 2002. Note the high Victorian view of Tudor imperial origins: Millais represents the young expansionist having his imagination fired by an exotically dressed sailor (perhaps Iberian) telling far-flung tales to the earnest English boys. Note also the subtle and ironic memento mori: the grounded and listing toy ship in the lower left corner seems to foreshadow the eventual undoing of Ralegh, and perhaps of the imperial vision.

For Hope

My face in thine eye, thine in mine appears,
And true plain hearts do in the faces rest;
Where can we find two better hemispheres,
Without sharp North, without declining West?

Contents

Acknowledgments ix

Introduction: Binding Ties 1

One. Once-and-Future Kings
The "Matter of Britain" and Protestant Imperial Recovery from John Dee to *Cymbeline* 10

Two. The Uses of Atrocity
Satanic Spaniards, Hispanic Satans, and the "Black Legend" from Las Casas to Milton 54

Three. Stooping to Conquer
Heathen Idolatry, Protestant Humility, and the "White Legend" of Drake 77

Four. The Nubile Savage and the Soulless Slave
Imagining Race from Pocahontas to the Colonial Color Line 113

Five. Prophets against Empire
Countertraditions, 1516–1815 137

Six. "Hollow All Delight!"
Countertraditions, 1815–1945 191

Afterword: Moravians in the Moon 241
Bibliography 249
Index 267

Acknowledgments ❈ ❈ ❈ ❈

This book was conceived in two places on one day more than seventeen years ago: in a graduate seminar room at the University of Chicago and then in a Hyde Park movie theater. In my "Renaissance Intellectual Texts" seminar, Janel Mueller and Richard Strier were introducing us to Richard Hakluyt's *Principal Navigations, Voyages, Traffiques and Discoveries of the English Nation*, and we had come to the account of Francis Drake on the beach in northern California, humbly refusing the worship of the awed natives and then boldly claiming all of their lands and services for Queen Elizabeth. A few hours later, as I relaxed at a showing of John Huston's film version of Rudyard Kipling's "The Man Who Would Be King," I suddenly realized that I was seeing Drake's encounter ironically revisited. "We're not gods," says Michael Caine as the opportunistic Peachey Carnehan to an awestruck Saeed Jaffrey as Billy Fish, "we're Englishmen, which is the next best thing." But when Peachey's comrade in deception, Danny Dravot (Sean Connery), later plays a god in earnest, he loses his empire and his head. To me, this intersection of Elizabethan imperial piety, late Victorian fable, and modern film irony suggested that for centuries, the British lived with a fearful tension between their professed metaphysical modesty and their frequent colonial expansionism.

This 1985 conception began a long gestation. Marriage and children, a doctoral dissertation and a book on George Herbert, moves from Chicago to Michigan to North Carolina—all intervened before my Drake-Dravot convergence grew into a serious research project in the early 1990s. I decided that I would survey the rise and decline of the British Protestant imperial imagination from the beginning to the end of the British Empire, from Tudor days to modern times. Along the way

x Acknowledgments

I have examined archival materials in libraries from the Huntington to the Newberry and from the Folger to the British and Bodleian; I have presented papers at conferences from Puerto Vallarta to Montreal, from Miami to Lisbon to London (and from Raleigh to Manteo to Chapel Hill); I have visited Drake's Bay, Drake's Roanoke Island landfall, and Drake's Devonshire estate—not to mention Fort Raleigh, Jamestown, the Plymouth Harbor steps, and Dr. Johnson's study. In short, I have had the quasi-imperial pleasure of covering a great deal of intellectual, chronological, and geographical territory, and not surprisingly I have many debts to acknowledge.

The oldest of these debts are to those who nurtured and encouraged this project at the earliest stages. After Chicago and graduate school, two years as a visiting assistant professor of English at Calvin College put me among colleagues with a lively interest in the Reformation and British literature; among them Edward E. Ericson Jr. and John Netland (once-and-future department heads, respectively) have been particularly helpful in responding to queries and reading drafts. A 1990 summer NEH seminar on the "Protestant Imagination" at Ohio State University under the direction of John N. King immersed me in Protestantism not only as a system of belief and thought but also as a system (sometimes in spite of itself) of iconography, myth, and legend. Since my arrival at the University of North Carolina at Greensboro in 1991 and my beginning this book in earnest, the developing text has enjoyed an extraordinary amount of attention from colleagues in many literary periods: Robert Kelly, Charles Tisdale, and Denise N. Baker in Arthurian and medieval; Russ McDonald in Shakespeare and Tudor-Stuart; James E. Evans and Jennifer Keith in the "long eighteenth century"; Donald Darnell and Kelley Griffith in earlier American; SallyAnn Ferguson in African American; Marilyn May Lombardi in romantic; Randolph Bulgin and Mary Ellis Gibson in Victorian; Robert Langenfeld, Keith Cushman, and Gail McDonald in late Victorian and modern; Yumna Siddiqi in postcolonial; and Christian Moraru in theory. Two outstanding department heads, James E. Evans and Denise N. Baker, have unfailingly encouraged and supported this project through many grant, leave, and travel proposals and have endured its growth, like Marvell's vegetable love, vaster than empires and more slow.

Other UNCG colleagues have been helpful as well, particularly historians Santa Arias, Jodi Bilinkoff, Robert Calhoon, Phyllis Hunter, Colleen Kriger, and Paul Mazgaj; Beverly Maddox-Britt and Charna Howson of the Office of Research Services; Michael Kloepfer in our computing services office; and our outstanding Jackson Library staff, particularly William Findley, Nancy Fogarty, Nancy Ryckman, and Mark Schumacher. My research assistants Kim Puchir, Adam Cox, Pamela Whitfield, and Travis Mulhauser have borne many a book and clerical burden, and four different undergraduate and doctoral seminar groups on the "British Imperial Imagination" have served as lively sounding boards for my developing ideas.

Beyond UNCG, many other scholars and critics over the years have generously read drafts or offered substantial responses to or advice on this project. Among these are James Alsop, David Alvarez, Reid Barbour, Wayne C. Booth, Deborah Bowen, Richard W. Clement, Alan C. Dessen, June Dwyer, Simon Edwards, Susan Van Zanten Gallagher, Stephen J. Greenblatt, Margaret Hannay, Richard Hardin, Kenneth Hodges, Jeffrey Hush, Bruce Johnson, Noel Kinnamon, Jeffrey Knapp, Laura Lunger Knoppers, Jameela Lares, Roger Lundin, Debra Meyers, Mona Modiano, Steven Mullaney, Jeffrey Powers-Beck, Anne Lake Prescott, Luz Elena Ramirez, Leland Ryken, Brenda D. Schildgen, Michael C. Schoenfeldt, Debora Shuger, Joseph H. Summers, William Tate, Mark Valeri, Miland Wakankar, and John N. Wall. I am particularly grateful to the two outside readers of my manuscript for the University of Missouri Press, J. Martin Evans of Stanford University and John D. Cox of Hope College. Their thorough and remarkably constructive suggestions are inscribed throughout. It goes without saying that all remaining mistakes, oversights, solecisms, and infelicities are mine and mine alone; but I suppose that I should say it anyway, and hereby do. I ask my reader's patient correction of the faults that remain.

At the University of Missouri Press itself, I have for a second time been pleased to work with the courteous, frank, and helpful staff, including Beverly Jarrett, Clair Willcox, Jane Lago, Karen Renner, and Beth Chandler. Susan Brady's careful copyediting has relieved many of my textual worries. I owe a debt of thanks to Daniel W. Doerksen, the coeditor of our forthcoming essay collection, for bearing with my delays as I complete this manuscript.

As to financial assistance, I am thankful to UNCG for three faculty grants supporting my travel to the Huntington Library and the British and Bodleian Libraries in the spring and summer of 1992; to the Andrew W. Mellon Foundation for a grant enabling me to spend the wonderful summer of 1995 at the Huntington; and to the Pew Charitable Trusts and particularly the Pew Evangelical Scholars Program for a year of paid research leave during 1998–1999. As to hospitality, I am warmly grateful to my brother and sister-in-law Craig and Diane Hodgkins, and to my sister and brother-in-law Catherine and Christopher Logue, for housing and feeding me in the spring of 1992, and I thank my fine friends Richard and Nancy Hand of Leatherhead, Surrey, for all the homely English comforts during my first research summer in the United Kingdom. I thank my brother Charles Hodgkins for advice on copyright permissions and for his good-humored perspective. Speaking of perspective, I am pleased that my parents, Norman and Eleanor Hodgkins, have always maintained a sincere interest in my work; that my daughters, Mary and Alice, have grown from infancy to tall loveliness during the writing; and that my preschool son, George, busy with so many urgent projects of his own, nevertheless sometimes condescends to ask me about mine. For help with indexing, I thank Mary and also my wife, Hope, who has been my best reader and in every sense my closest. I dedicate this book—and life after this book—to her.

Reforming Empire

Introduction

Binding Ties

For a bag of pepper [the Jacobean traders] would cut each other's throats without hesitation, and would forswear their souls, of which they were so careful otherwise; . . . It seems impossible to believe that mere greed could hold men to such steadfastness of purpose, to such a blind persistence in endeavor and sacrifice. To us . . . they appear magnified, not as agents of trade but as instruments of a recorded destiny, pushing out into the unknown in obedience to an inward voice. . . . They were wonderful. —*Joseph Conrad,* Lord Jim

The strength of empire is in religion. —*Ben Jonson,* Timber, or Discoveries

The latter end of his commonwealth forgets the beginning.
—*William Shakespeare,* The Tempest

In his brooding modern fictions that saw the coming end of empire, Joseph Conrad nevertheless remembered its early modern beginning. He ironically eulogized the Jacobean pepper traders; he evoked Drake's *Golden Hind* and Ralegh's Eldorado; and he told his imperial tales through a man with the Faustian name of "Marlow." Conrad also remembered, even while portraying the gross materiality of earthly conquest, that empire was in some uncanny way ultimately a matter of the spirit—"something you can set up, and bow down before."[1] Significantly, the foreign-born Conrad—Polish, Catholic, infidel—came from

---

1. Joseph Conrad, *Heart of Darkness*, 29 (*Golden Hind*); 61, 66 (Eldorado); 32 ("bow down").

well outside the charmed circle of British Protestant imperialism; yet better than most insiders he conjured up the bright and dark angels of the empire, in order to name them and to stand both in awe and in judgment.

Though "[a]ll Europe contributed to the making of Kurtz," the education and ancestry of this "emissary of light" were "partly in England," and "his sympathies," Marlow assures us with mock patriotism, "were in the right place."[2] So Conrad's apocalyptic voice raises vital questions about his adopted country and its colonial project. Was there a distinctly British way of imagining colonial possession? And how did the Britons conceive of their eventual dispossession, the latter end of their commonwealth? What bound them together in this long project of binding other peoples under? And yet what bound them back, restrained them, and eventually undid the imperial ties?

This book answers each of these questions by focusing attention on British religion. For four centuries, the strength of the British Empire—and also its weakness—was in religion; specifically in the Protestant imagination that gave the empire its main paradigms for dominion and possession but also, paradoxically, its chief languages of anti-imperial dissent. From the Elizabethan Richard Hakluyt's *Principal Navigations* and Edmund Spenser's *Faerie Queene* to Rudyard Kipling's "The Man Who Would Be King" and Evelyn Waugh's *Black Mischief*, English literature about empire has turned with strange constancy to religious themes of worship and idolatry, atrocity and deliverance, slavery and service, conversion, prophecy, apostasy, and doom. David Armitage asks whether it is possible for political historians "to discern any precise and undeniable [Tudor-Stuart] Protestant contribution to the ideological origins of the British Empire"; he concludes that, apart from "a common anti-Catholicism" and John Locke's "agriculturalist argument" for possession, Protestantism contributed no such thing. British imperial ideology, he writes, "remained fissured and unstable as much because of, as in spite of, the contribution of Protestantism." Armitage is right, though rather circular: his point is that Protestants had no pope. The Reformation began by opposing the world-imperial "disposing powers" of the papacy, upon which the Iberian Catholic empires had based their claims. Having no Vatican, says Armitage, the reformed powers in Europe, England, and Scotland had trouble articulating any right to universal, "catholique" imperial possession; such claims seemed "Romish," and the reformers had done—so they believed—with Rome.[3]

---

2. Conrad, *Heart of Darkness*, 39, 86.
3. David Armitage, *The Ideological Origins of the British Empire*, 64, 66, 98–99.

However, I will show that by the end of the Tudor-Stuart era, English Protestantism's literary imagination had made essential and enduring contributions to a shared sense of British destiny, of liberatory mission, and of moral exceptionalism. These contributions went well beyond mere antipopery, though they subsumed it. Early modern Protestants reformed the Arthurian chronicles and claimed the *translatio imperii* (transfer of empire) from the Caesars; they proposed to free the subject peoples of rival empires from spiritual and political bondage; and they refused the worship offered by adoring natives in order to merit possessing their lands—all expansionist paradigms and tropes that remained potent through the Victorian era. Yet Tudor times also saw the genesis of Protestant imperial unease and guilt: what Armitage calls the empire's ideological "fissures" and "instability" were no mere accidental side effects but rather constituted an enduring and often deliberate anti-imperial countertradition. As much as some British Protestants might labor to make London the new Rome, the pluralism and protest inherent in Protestantism could never be fully colonized. What the one hand built up, the other hand often sought to pull down.

There is nothing new in recognizing that religion and empire are closely intertwined. Indeed, it has been nearly sixty years since Louis B. Wright, in *Religion and Empire*, argued for the centrality of "piety and commerce" to the first wave of English overseas expansion between 1558 and 1625. Wright's historicist thesis—that Protestantism gave the English their sense of spiritual and geographical destiny in this watershed period—is true as far as it goes, which, as I will show, is quite far indeed.[4] But a newer historicism has emerged over the past two decades that has both appropriated and eclipsed the old, nowhere more than in the study of empire; some of the more prominent examples from the past decade are Stephen J. Greenblatt's *Marvelous Possessions*, Richard Helgerson's *Forms of Nationhood*, Jeffrey Knapp's *An Empire Nowhere*, David J. Baker's *Between Nations*, and Joan Pong Linton's *The Romance of the New World*.[5] These studies, all associated with the overlapping new historicist and cultural materialist projects, have usefully taught us to look past and indeed beneath the official orthodoxies of early modern England to concrete and contingent

---

4. Louis B. Wright, *Religion and Empire: The Alliance between Piety and Commerce in English Expansion, 1558–1625*.

5. Stephen J. Greenblatt, *Marvelous Possessions: The Wonder of the New World;* Richard Helgerson, *Forms of Nationhood: The Elizabethan Writing of England;* Jeffrey Knapp, *An Empire Nowhere: England, America, and Literature from "Utopia" to "The Tempest";* David J. Baker, *Between Nations: Shakespeare, Spenser, Marvell, and the Question of Britain;* Joan Pong Linton, *The Romance of the New World: Gender and the Literary Formations of English Colonialism.*

ethnic, economic, and sexual particulars—that is, to the assumed bedrock of race, class, and gender.

These important literary and cultural studies recapitulate Wright's thesis, though now in a minor key. That is, they generally assume the complicity of Protestant (and of course Catholic) orthodoxy in imperial expansion, while focusing their interpretive attentions on the heterodoxies that questioned or opposed that project from the cultural margins.[6] There is no doubt an enormous amount to be learned at those margins, and from the heterodoxies that in fascinating ways anticipate the orthodoxies of our own age; but, as Debora Shuger has observed, "the trouble with this division of beliefs into orthodox and subversive is that so-called subversive ideas keep surfacing, however contained, within the confines of orthodoxy."[7] When "conservatives" talk like "radicals," perhaps the anomaly is not in the speaker but in our terms.

So this book attends to aspects of the British imperial imagination that are neglected or subordinated by both the old and new historicisms. I aim to revisit Wright's thesis with new questions and new evidence in order to understand more fully how Protestant religion helped the English to imagine, take, and hold a British Empire; but I also seek to explain how that same religion compelled many of the English, from the time of the empire's beginning, to foresee and desire its end. From the start, English Protestantism offered not only support for expansionism but also substantial resources for anti-imperial opposition. So, with Anne Barton, I dispute the common new historicist claim that "what looks to us like subversion in the art of the past . . . is merely something orthodoxy makes strategic use of in order to sustain itself."[8] On the contrary, there is much within orthodoxy—in this case, Christian orthodoxy—that made real subversion possible.

This book, then, is clearly historicist; like other analyses of cultural poetics, it is concerned with reading culture as well as with reading poems, plays, stories, and novels, and it attends often to nonliterary textual artifacts, asking of them literary questions about genre, language, metaphor, plot, and characterization. Furthermore, in dealing with these diverse sources this book departs from the older positivist historicism that refused to acknowledge an influence that could

---

6. Anthony Pagden's extensive work on comparative imperialisms, while more purely historical than literary, makes similar assumptions about the relations between religion and colonial expansion. See especially his *Lords of All the World: Ideologies of Empire in Spain, Britain, and France c. 1500–c. 1800*.

7. Debora Shuger, *Habits of Thought in the English Renaissance: Religion, Politics, and the Dominant Culture*, 1.

8. Anne Barton, "Perils of Historicism," 54.

not be literally documented. For instance, this study assumes that in a print culture as circumscribed as Tudor-Stuart England's, a robust intertextuality existed; thus even in the absence of direct reference or quotation, strong substantive parallels and similarities between texts are sufficient to warrant attention as probable influences, especially in the works of encyclopedic figures like Spenser, Shakespeare, Milton, or Swift.

However, *Reforming Empire* does not share certain other new historicist and cultural materialist assumptions. In addition to seeing the possibility of real cultural dissent coming from within the "dominant culture," I also seek to treat religion more fully on its own terms. The human impulse to worship—to organize life around invisible hopes, fears, and certainties—is so ancient, culturally persistent, and pervasive that it cannot be reduced to or adequately explained by the race-class-gender categories. Certainly religious considerations interpenetrate profoundly with ethnic, economic, and sexual ones; but religion has its own imagination, its powerful languages of symbol and story, its unique moving force. Thus it possesses a sphere that, while interdependent with other spheres at the boundaries, is independent at its center. So if, as Shuger has argued, religion was the principal category in which sixteenth- and seventeenth-century authors thought through a whole range of vital concerns, certainly this must be true for the origins of empire as well.[9]

If this book modifies the methodology of some colonial and postcolonial studies, it modifies the chronology of others. Many scholars of the empire have, like Shakespeare's Gonzalo, made the latter end of their commonwealth forget its beginning.[10] David Armitage notes how reluctant many contemporary historians and political scientists have been to treat seriously and substantially the empire's Tudor-Stuart origins. Armitage suggests that this resistance "is symptomatic of a more lasting unwillingness to consider ideologies of empire as part of political theory or the history of political thought."[11] While no one can reasonably fault recent literary scholarship for a similar indifference to ideology, it is nevertheless strangely true that most leading critical work on the literature of British imperialism does little to connect the early modern to the later empire. In his *Poems of Nation, Anthems of Empire*, Suvir Kaul rightly acknowledges that "it is indeed possible to trace . . . a discursive and ideological continuum

9. Shuger, *Habits of Thought in the English Renaissance*, 6.
10. William Shakespeare, *The Tempest*, 2.1.160–61, in *The Complete Works of Shakespeare*, 4th ed., ed. David Bevington (New York: Longman, 1997). All further quotations of Shakespeare will be from this edition; citations will be made parenthetically by act, scene, and line numbers, unless otherwise indicated.
11. Armitage, *Ideological Origins of the British Empire*, 4.

between the voyages of Raleigh and the exploits of Kitchener," though Kaul's focus is still on the "long eighteenth century."[12] Indeed, most influential literary studies of that later empire—particularly Martin Green's *Dreams of Adventure, Deeds of Empire,* Patrick Brantlinger's *Rule of Darkness,* Lewis Wurgaft's *The Imperial Imagination,* and Edward Said's *Culture and Imperialism*—locate its beginnings in the eighteenth or nineteenth centuries.[13] So in its chronological scope, *Reforming Empire* bridges this divide, tracing early modern Protestant imperialist themes, images, and vocabulary as they persisted and filtered into the fiction and poetry of the modern era. I focus not only on the Renaissance and Reformation ideologies that accompanied English colonization and anti-colonialism; I also pursue these threads through the empire's Augustan growth to its Victorian climax and twentieth-century end.

My project begins by asking what special powers the religious imagination brought *to* empire and brought to bear *on* empire. The etymology of "religion" features its force of binding—"re-ligare." To unite, to subjugate—for these two binding functions, England's Tudor-Stuart colonialists relied on the imagination of a reformed Christianity that was, ironically, born in protest against papal bondage, and that celebrated its own resistance to the transatlantic empire of "popish" Spain. Thus English Protestant imperialism contained its own opposite: a paradoxical anti-imperial strain, a religion of self-restraint, a binding *back* by the conscience. Though this conscience often was neutralized or conscripted to legitimize conquests and pacify the conquered, it often found memorable and even fierce literary expression.

Basing my argument on these three kinds of religious binding—unification, subjugation, and self-restraint—I divide the book into three main sections: the first about the origins of England's myth of imperial destiny and its sense of exceptionalist reforming righteousness; the second about religion-based rationales for colonizing native peoples; and the third about the bad conscience that

12. Suvir Kaul, *Poems of Nation, Anthems of Empire: English Verse in the Long Eighteenth Century,* 21–22.

13. Green traces the imperial imagination to the early eighteenth century with Defoe; Brantlinger, Wurgaft, and Said treat it mainly as a nineteenth-century phenomenon. See Martin Green, *Dreams of Adventure, Deeds of Empire;* Patrick Brantlinger, *Rule of Darkness: British Literature and Imperialism, 1830–1914;* Lewis Wurgaft, *The Imperial Imagination: Magic and Myth in Kipling's India;* and Edward Said, *Culture and Imperialism.* Even Donald Greene, in an otherwise fine exploration of Samuel Johnson and empire, overstates the case by claiming that the Seven Years' War of 1756–1763 "did indeed bring the British Empire into being" by adding Canada and India to Britain's possessions. See Donald J. Greene, "Samuel Johnson and the Great War for Empire," 39. Yet as I will discuss in chapter five, Greene's subject, Samuel Johnson, more correctly traced the beginnings of the empire back to Elizabeth I.

haunted England's imperial project from its beginnings with forebodings of its end and of wrath to come. Along the way, I pay particular heed to the tensions and negotiations between voices of exceptionalism and of conscience. Significantly, we will see that English Protestantism was at its most anti-imperial when it was, like many of the first reformers, at its most Augustinian—that is, when it understood empire not mainly as a vehicle for the ingathering of far-flung souls but rather as a profitless temptation to gain the world at the price of one's soul, and of other souls far and near.

Chapter one, "Once-and-Future Kings: The 'Matter of Britain' and Protestant Imperial Recovery from John Dee to *Cymbeline*," is the first of three chapters to focus on religion's power to bind *together*. In it, I argue that late Tudor and early Stuart nationalism reimagined the political implications of being fully and finally post-Roman—that is, postcolonial *because* postpapal. The revival of native identity and the related rejection of "popery" powerfully shaped the kingdom's own claim to the *translatio imperii*, the inheritance of Caesar's mantle. Fitfully under the early Tudors and emphatically after the Reformation, English writers recovered and reinvented the "British" identity. Key texts include Dee's writings, Spenser's *Faerie Queene*, and Shakespeare's *Cymbeline*.

In chapter two, "The Uses of Atrocity: Satanic Spaniards, Hispanic Satans, and the 'Black Legend' from Las Casas to Milton," I discuss the second unifying element, the power of a common religious enemy in Catholic Spain. Drawing on Hakluyt's *Principal Navigations*, I demonstrate that his expansionist prophecies were informed by the conviction that England's imperial struggle was not merely against flesh and blood but above all against profound spiritual evil, incarnate in the papal Antichrist and his Spanish legions. On the way from Las Casas's indictments of Spain's conquistadors to *Paradise Lost*, I survey antihispanicism from Ralegh's quest for El Dorado to late Cromwellian opera.

Chapter three, "Stooping to Conquer: Heathen Idolatry, Protestant Humility, and the 'White Legend' of Drake," is an examination of the third crucial unifying element in British imperial religion: Protestant moral exceptionalism. To Francis Drake's 1579 encounter with the adoring natives of northern California, as first reported by Hakluyt, I trace the enduring British "White Legend"—countering Spain's "Black Legend"—that pious restraint merits possession. I find this paradigm at work from Shakespeare's *Tempest* and Defoe's *Crusoe* to the ironic adventure tales of Kipling and Conrad.

My argument in chapter four, "The Nubile Savage and the Soulless Slave: Imagining Race from Pocahontas to the Colonial Color Line," turns to religion's second major imperial role, that of subordinating colonized peoples. Discussing the much-mythologized 1614 marriage of Pocahontas to John Rolfe, I show that biblicist and classicist elements in the British imperial imagination fused during this arguably "preracist" period, making it briefly possible to celebrate "mixed" marriage. But these "preracist" themes coexist with "protoracism" in the same biblical and classical paradigms. I trace the transition to the very different situation existing by the 1680s, when the color line became impermeably fixed in antimiscegenation and other laws. Focal texts include Jonson's *Masque of Blackness*, sermons on Virginia, varied colonial correspondence and statutes, Aphra Behn's *Oroonoko*, and William Byrd's *Histories of the Dividing Line*.

In chapter five, "Prophets against Empire: Countertraditions, 1516–1815," I take up what might be called Britain's own "Black Legend" by exploring two persistent English strains of binding religious conscience. The first of these countertraditions was the more clearly anti-imperial: the Christian humanist critique that opposed empire building not only for oppressing the colonized but also for disastrously weakening the colonizer. The second countertradition—that of Protestant imperial "trusteeship"—was not flatly opposed to empire yet sought, often effectively, to ameliorate its worst evils. These countertraditions feature some of the most robust voices in English literary history, including More, Daniel, Herbert, Milton, Swift, Johnson, Burke, Blake, and Austen.

I follow these oppositional themes from the height to the end of the empire in chapter six, "'Hollow All Delight': Countertraditions, 1815–1945." Between the Napoleonic and Crimean Wars, an uneasy alliance developed between evangelicals and utilitarians in support of imperial "trusteeship." Though their shared program for reforming the conduct of empire was remarkably successful, it unintentionally provided a metaphysical justification for the next wave of expansion under the later Victorians. Yet as the century turned, these metaphysical certainties were being shaken by Darwinian doubt, with secular imperialists shouldering aside Christian sentiment in favor of Saxon racial destiny. Increasingly, religion came to be seen as a source of folly, trouble, and dread, with the doctrine of "trusteeship" increasingly exposed as hollow or even homicidal. Key writers include Browning, Tennyson, Seeley, Kipling, Conrad, Forster, and Waugh.

Finally, in the afterword, "Moravians in the Moon," I consider Anglicanism's final break with empire. If the imperial anxieties of Victorian Protestantism had been palliated with hope of bringing light to the dark places, by the late 1930s Britain's Protestant imagination was undergoing a conversion of its own, turning against its old imperial romance. Instead, as represented by the influential apologetics and fiction of C. S. Lewis, English "mere Christianity" was returning to the Augustinian and Christian humanist critique of empire.

A final word on method: to appropriate an ecclesiastical metaphor, the approach to theory throughout this book is ecumenical, indeed latitudinarian. We can admire and learn from many theoretical schools to the extent that they raise new questions, consider neglected evidence, and yield fresh readings, but generally we should shy away from those that begin to answer their questions in advance. Richard Strier has written of literary texts—indeed all texts—as "resistant structures," built to complicate, counteract, and even defeat the reader's a priori schemes.[14] Similarly, whether reading primary or secondary materials, we should assume that a writer's intentions matter—especially if we are writers ourselves. This is what it means to practice charitable reading: not enshrining authorial intent nor glossing over difference, contradiction, stupidity, and wickedness, but instead exercising care and *caritas* with texts, refusing merely to bully or bend or break them to our interpretive will. Especially when reading things that we expect to offend us ethically, politically, or aesthetically, we ought to observe Wittgenstein's dictum, which I take to be only a slight hyperbole: "Don't think, but look."[15] It is the closest thing to a hermeneutic Golden Rule.

---

14. Richard Strier, *Resistant Structures: Particularity, Radicalism, and Renaissance Texts*, 1–2.
15. Ludwig Wittgenstein, *Philosophical Investigations*, 31e; as in Strier, *Resistant Structures*, 2.

One

Once-and-Future Kings

The "Matter of Britain" and Protestant Imperial Recovery from John Dee to *Cymbeline*

Remembering [for colonized peoples] is never a quiet act of introspection or retrospection. It is a painful re-membering, a putting together of the dismembered past to make sense of the trauma of the present. —*Homi K. Bhabha,* The Location of Culture

O Glastonbury, Glastonbury, the treasurie of the carcases of so famous, and so many persons . . . how lamentable is thy case now! howe hath hypocrisie and pride wrought thy desolation! . . . yet that Apostolike Joseph, that triumphant British Arthur . . . doe force me with a certaine sorowful reverence, here to celebrate thy memorie. —*John Dee, in Richard Hakluyt,* Principal Navigations, *1.18*

Renowmed kings, and sacred Emperours,
Thy fruitfull Offspring, shall from thee descend;
Braue Captaines, and most mighty warriours,
That shall their conquests through all lands extend,
And their decayed kingdomes shall amend:
—*Merlin to Britomart, Edmund Spenser,* The Faerie Queene *3.3.23 (italics mine)*

In my end is my beginning. —*motto of Mary Stuart, Queen of Scots*

It is remarkable that Homi K. Bhabha's words about colonial and postcolonial memory, reflecting on the twentieth-century end of European empires, should apply so justly to the British Empire's sixteenth-century beginnings.[1] Much as an Indian visiting the Taj Mahal in 1947 might feel mixed grief and hope at former Mogul greatness, so Dr. John Dee, antiquarian to Queen Elizabeth I, could write in 1577 of his "sorrowful reverence" at the sight of King Arthur's Glastonbury "tomb." In both cases, what had been might be again; the departed empire, which treachery had divided and ruined, might be celebrated and restored by regenerative mourning. Such acts of "memorie," whether "re-membering" Akbar's India or Arthur's Britain, invoke unique yet eerily similar tragicomic myths, with their religious or quasi-religious nationalisms, their nativist celebrations of vernacular language and culture, their grim rehearsals of alien oppression and atrocity, and their bright hopes of reforming righteousness.

In this chapter I propose that imperial Britain began, more or less, in the imagination of a "postcolonial" England. In the first of three chapters to focus on religion's power to bind *together*, I examine Protestantism's role in reviving the myth of a unified "Britain" and an ancient "British Empire." This revival enabled the religious reformers to define themselves as inheritors of that lost empire who were "re-forming" it in multiple ways—recovering it, improving it, expanding it, and converting it to "godliness." If we wish to know why, in the midst of Elizabeth's reign, the English Reformation warms to the "Matter of Britain," the answer is that late Tudor and early Stuart nationalism reimagined the political implications of being fully and finally post-Roman—that is, postcolonial *because* postpapal. Protestants saw the recently rejected papists as having prolonged for a millennium the worst aspects of Roman imperial rule. Thus to Elizabethans and Jacobeans a renewed "British" identity promised not only a rationale for a unified island kingdom but also a sphere of international influence that could counteract the Vatican and unify Europe (and newfound America) under a non-Roman catholicity.

My warrant for this answer lies in reading Tudor-Stuart imperial advocates like John Dee and Richard Hakluyt not so much as harbingers of modernity but rather as revivers and reformers of an authorizing antiquity. In other words, I will consider Elizabethan and Jacobean imperialism in relation to the humanist, and particularly the Protestant, dictum *ad fontes* ([return] to the sources), which makes empire building for them, in Dee's own potent phrase, "this Brytish discovery and *recovery* enterprise" (italics mine).[2]

---

1. Homi K. Bhabha, *The Location of Culture*, 63.
2. William H. Sherman, *John Dee: The Politics of Reading and Writing in the English Renaissance*, 151.

More specifically, I ask what it meant for the part-Welsh queen of England in 1577 to hear Dee call her Arthur's descendant and a British empress, and for her to read in the 1590s of Spenser's Britomart and her seer's glass and of Merlin's mirror. And what did it mean for the Scottish King James VI to ascend the English throne in 1604 and, claiming Arthurian descent, to rename his combined kingdoms with their ancient title of "Great Britain"? And what did it mean for James in 1610 to view Shakespeare's *Cymbeline*, a tragicomedy of British resistance and eventual submission to imperial Caesar, set at the time of Christ's first coming?

This Tudor-Stuart project of expansive imperial recovery clearly meant that, like the early Protestant humanists before them, English writers from Dee and Hakluyt to Spenser and Shakespeare returned to "ancient" textual sources, recovering and reinventing the Matter of Britain. Yet as they did so, these writers combined often discordant elements that represented complicated responses to their own colonized past: medieval accounts of an inherited Trojan imperial identity intertwine with classical accounts of a native noble savagery. In the former, devolutionary view, British civility and empire preceded Rome's imperial conquest; indeed, Geoffrey of Monmouth's Arthur, like Malory's, can claim that "mine ancestors did of yore obtain possession of Rome."[3] In the latter, tutelary view—derived from Tacitus through the Henrician antiquarian Polydore Vergil—hardy British wildness was seasoned and trained by Roman imperial discipline but also was seduced and undermined by Roman dissipation.

However, for all of these writers, the potential and apparent conflicts between these alternative pasts are secondary to their shared belief in an imperial restoration coming for their island; both versions looked forward by looking back to imperial Rome, when Trojan nobility and British savagery had been redeemed by a Christianity that was both imperial and *pre*papal. Thus, in an Elizabethan feat of creative anachronism, both British Arthur and British Constantine become prototypical "Protestant" emperors, foreshadowing Britain's reformed and reforming empire to come.

Rex Quondam

"Once there was a King." So commence fairy tales, ballads, chronicles, tragedies, romances—and empires. Early modern British imperialism begins

---

3. Geoffrey of Monmouth, *The History of the Kings of Britain*, trans. Sebastian Evans (New York: E. P. Dutton, 1958), 9.16.206. All further citations of this edition will be indicated parenthetically in the text by *HKB* followed by book, chapter, and page number.

in antiquarian hope: its founding agents paged eagerly backward in chronicles of an imagined former end, seeking warrants and portents of a new beginning, a returning King. But at the heart of Christian hope is a returning King of Kings, and this was especially so for early Protestant Christians. They saw themselves as rescuing their churches from papal usurpation of Christ's royal prerogatives in advance of his imminent coming. These reformers also saw themselves as disciples of Augustine, whose scathing attacks on Roman conquest in *The City of God* warned against confusing human kingdoms with those of Christ.[4]

This otherworldly loyalty helps to explain why some early English reformers had little use for the promised return of their island's own *rex quondam*, Arthur, King of Britain, or indeed for the Matter of Britain in general. Indeed, the initial wave of reform made Arthur the target of violent iconoclasm: his Glastonbury Abbey "tomb," a shrine since 1278, was destroyed in the Dissolution of the Monasteries in 1539.[5] Probably the best-known comment by an early English Protestant on the ancient legends of the island comes from Roger Ascham in *The Schoolmaster*, and it is stingingly negative. Writing in the 1560s, Queen Elizabeth's beloved tutor and Latin secretary warns that the subject matter of Sir Thomas Malory's *Morte Darthur* came from days "when papistry as a standing pool covered and overflowed all England," that it was "made in monasteries by idle monks or wanton canons," and that "the whole pleasure of [the] book standeth in two special points—in open manslaughter and bold bawdry."[6]

Yet little more than a decade later, we find the enthusiastic Protestant preacher Richard Hakluyt ignoring such strictures and turning to British antiquities compiled by another of the queen's advisors, John Dee. Dee, like Ascham, was a Protestant Cambridge man, though with a difference: for Dee—cosmographer, mathematician, antiquarian, oculist, physician, astronomer, alchemist, and astrologer—was thought by some contemporaries to be Merlin reincarnate; and this hermetic polymath also coined the phrase "British Empire."[7] For four decades, Hakluyt was to invoke Dee and Dee's chief chronicle source, the

---

4. Augustine, *The City of God against the Pagans*, 147.
5. The plaque at the Glastonbury site reads: "In the year 1191 the bodies of King Arthur and his Queen were said to have been found on the south side of the Lady Chapel. On 19th April 1278 their remains were removed in the presence of King Edward I and his Queen to a black marble tomb on this site. This tomb survived until the dissolution of the Abbey in 1539." Notably, King Edward "Longshanks" had Arthurian ambitions; having conquered Wales by 1284, he attempted to unify the island by subjugating Scotland, an attempt frustrated by William Wallace and Robert Bruce. See Kenneth O. Morgan, ed., *The Oxford History of Britain*, 154–59.
6. Roger Ascham, *The Schoolmaster* (1570), 68–69.
7. See, under "British," definition 2, *The Oxford English Dictionary*.

twelfth-century Benedictine Geoffrey of Monmouth, for a warrant of astonishing reach: England's continuing right to King Arthur's transatlantic empire, which supposedly had stretched, on the eve of Mordred's rebellion, from Greenland to the gates of Rome.[8] These claims, which Dee advanced in his *General and Rare Memorials*, Hakluyt then pressed insistently in his own cosmographical compilations, particularly his voluminous *Principal Navigations* (1589; 1598–1600).[9]

What accounts for the change in attitude from Ascham's icy contempt to Dee's and Hakluyt's warm embrace? How does the Protestant revival of these legendary, "monkish" materials transform the nation, and Protestantism, and the materials themselves? How did textual discovery become a pretext for geographical discovery—and possession? The textual discoveries of former kingdoms were, during the Renaissance, as exciting as geographical discoveries of living ones; Richard Schoeck has suggested that "the illumination of an ancient author [was] as stirring as the voyages of Vespucci, or Drake, Raleigh, and Frobisher."[10] So, argues William H. Sherman, paper conquest generally preceded actual English exploration and empire. Specifically, Dee's famous program of "spatial or geographical reconnaissance"—his collecting of discovery data and his making of maps—was preceded by his program of "historical" and "textual reconnaissance," or "the collection of precedents for territorial (re)possession and for empire itself." Thus, before Hakluyt's *Divers Voyages* (1582) and *Principal Navigations*—containing mainly sixteenth-century exploration accounts—comes Dee's *General and Rare Memorials* (1577), which reproduces British and English antiquities to convince Queen Elizabeth of her ancient imperial titles. And even Hakluyt's copious *Principal Navigations* devotes its first volume to bringing "Antiquities smothered and buried in darke silence, to light" (*PN* 1.39). Indeed, as Sherman notes, in terms of practical colonial possession, "as long as Elizabeth reigned—and for some time after—the British Empire remained a textual affair."[11]

---

8. John Dee, *The Private Diary of Dr. John Dee, and the Catalogue of his Library Manuscripts*, 4; see also Sherman, *John Dee*, 187. This warrant was further bolstered in Dee's mind by a later Celtic connection of Madoc, the exiled Welsh prince who supposedly had discovered America in 1170; see Sherman, *John Dee*, 91, 185, 187, 188–89.

9. John Dee, *General and Rare Memorials pertayning to the Perfect Arte of Navigation*; Richard Hakluyt, *The Principal Navigations, Voyages, Traffiques and Discoveries of the English Nation* (London, 1903–1905), 1:398–445. All further citations of this edition will be indicated parenthetically in the text by *PN* followed by volume and page number.

10. Richard Schoeck, "Renaissance Guides to Renaissance Learning," 241.

11. Sherman, *John Dee*, 151, 152.

However, before saying "*merely* a textual affair," we must recognize the kind of text invoked by the likes of Dee and Hakluyt. For by referring to antique British territorial claims as described in Geoffrey of Monmouth's *History of the Kings of Britain* (c. 1136), these Elizabethan cosmographers are not simply invoking some bare chronology of legal precedent. They also are *evoking*—conjuring with what was in their day already one of earth's richest myths. Significantly, the myth took shape in the immediate context of colonial subjection. Geoffrey was a Welsh-Breton cleric writing about seventy years after the Norman Conquest, and his *History* seems intended to support Norman imperial ambitions: he promulgates Merlin's supposed prophecies about the end of Saxon rule, and he raises hopes of a British/Celtic restoration with Norman help.[12] So the *History* has always had what we might call strong postcolonial implications: as Michelle R. Warren writes, it is "a fantasy of empire and the ambivalence of colonial desire because it portrays the forgotten empire of a marginalized people in reaction to an urgently present colonial dynamic."[13]

Geoffrey stirs these longings at the start with a *rex futurus:* Trojan Brutus, or Brute. The great-grandson of Aeneas, he is exiled from recently conquered Italy for accidentally killing his father, Silvius—thus emblematically overthrowing the Romans in their common ancestor (*HKB* 1.3.6). Brutus gathers a band of Trojan refugees in Greece and, guided by the goddess Diana's oracle, passes the Pillars of Hercules and conquers the western island of Albion, renaming it "Brutain" or "Brytain" after himself. Then, centuries before the Latins founded the city of Rome, Brutus builds the future London as the former Troy—"Troynovant." Thus is the Trojan end their beginning, and Brutus the first British *rex quondam* in a long line.

After this opening, Geoffrey narrates—and largely invents—nearly two millennia of chronicle history, from Brutus's portentous division of his kingdom among his three jealous sons to Cadwallader's final retreat from the Saxons, and concludes with that *rex quondam*'s divine vision of future British restoration. In between, the epic catalogue of royal names includes many familiar to modern ears: Hudibras, Lear, Cordelia, Gorbodog (Gorboduc), Lud, Cymbeline, Constantine, Uther Pendragon, and, above all, Arthur. Significantly, one pair of royal brothers more obscure to us, Brennius and Belinus, was especially important to the Tudors, and to Geoffrey's Arthur himself: as supposed conquerors of Rome

---

12. Hugh A. MacDougall, *Racial Myth in English History: Trojans, Teutons, and Anglo-Saxons,* 7–10.

13. Michelle R. Warren, "Making Contact: Postcolonial Perspectives through Geoffrey of Monmouth's *Historia regum Britanniae,*" 116.

in the days of the Republic, they are cited by Arthur as a precedent on the eve of his planned attack on the imperial city (*HKB* 9.16.206).[14]

Among Geoffrey's royal rolls, the Arthurian materials are overwhelmingly preeminent; if we include Merlin's preparatory prophecies and actions, they comprise nearly half of the book. To the reader whose Arthurian knowledge comes mainly through Chrétien de Troyes and Malory, Geoffrey seems alternately familiar and strange: as in the romances, Geoffrey's Arthur is born in fulfillment of Merlin's prophecies after the adulterous coupling of his father, Uther, with Gorlois's wife, Igerna (Ygraine), and his conception is engineered by Merlin's magic. And, as in the romances, Arthur assumes the throne in his youth, unifies the island kingdom, marries Guenevere, and rules magnanimously under the sign of the cross. Yet Guenevere proves unfaithful, and Modred (Mordred) raises a rebellion in which he and Arthur are both mortally injured, though Arthur is borne to the Isle of Avalon for the healing of his wounds.

However, many of the most famous elements associated with later French and English romances are missing from Geoffrey's account: Arthur's obscure childhood with Sir Ector, the Sword in the Stone, the witchery of Morgause and Morgan le Fay (Modred here is Arthur's nephew, not his incestuous son), the residence in Camelot, the Round Table and its Knights, the Grail Quest, even Lancelot himself (Guenevere's illicit liaison is with Modred). Indeed, missing is most of the "bold bawdry" of which Ascham complained. As to the "open manslaughter," it is conducted not in the individual chivalric service of ladies but rather in concerted territorial conquest. Furthermore, rather than portraying a dispirited king seeking spiritual renewal through a semimagical eucharistic relic, Geoffrey gives us an Arthur who exudes religious and military confidence, ever expanding Christendom along with his beneficent sway. By the end of book 9, Britain has become "Lady of thirty realms" (*HKB* 10.7.222): all the pagan "Northern Islands" from Greenland to Iceland, the Orkneys and Ireland, then heathen Scandinavia and Lapland "even unto Russia," then Denmark, Flanders, Germany, and Gaul.

Climactically, book 10 is devoted to Arthur's overthrow of Roman power in Europe, which Geoffrey understands as a *restoration* of earlier British sovereignty and as the fulfillment of Diana's oracle to Brutus:

> [In Britain] by thy sons *again* shall Troy be builded;
> There of thy blood shall Kings be born, hereafter

---

14. In fact, at the time of Henry VIII's epochal divorce from Katharine of Aragón, he supported his antipapal claim to supreme imperial jurisdiction in England by asserting Brennius's Roman conquest. MacDougall, *Racial Myth*, 17.

Sovran in every land the wide world over.
(*HKB* 1.11.18; italics mine)

Having defeated the Roman Procurator Lucius in Burgundy, Arthur sends the commander's corpse as a defiant "tribute" to the Roman Senate, promising to follow and take Rome in the spring. Only the treason of his wife and his nephew back in Britain can divert Arthur's attention and abort his otherwise inevitable victory (*HKB* 10.13.232). It is these intoxicating *quondam*s that Dee and Hakluyt seek to transform into *futuri* in the late Elizabethan imagination—both the queen's and her people's.

Elementing the myth: antiquity, catholicity, particularity, tragedy

For these Tudor archival activists, the Matter of Britain held a number of complementary practical attractions. First, the myth of *rex quondam* offered an authorizing and notably *multilayered* antiquity. This layering is especially evident when Geoffrey's Arthur rebuffs Roman demands for tribute by turning the tables with the claim that "mine ancestors did of yore obtain possession of Rome" (*HKB* 9.16.206). Here are, prima facie, two layers already: the twelfth-century monk Geoffrey calls on Arthur, who himself calls on his generalized forebears. More of these ancestral layers are then enumerated as Hoel King of Brittany—a member of Arthur's council—rises to announce that in Uther's son "the prophecies of the Sibyl . . . are witnessed by tokens true, that for the third time shall one of the British race be born that shall obtain the empire of Rome. Already are the oracles fulfilled as to . . . the two illustrious princes, Belinus and Constantine [who] have worn the imperial crown. . . . And now in thee have we the third" (*HKB* 9.17.207). As in a hall of mirrors, each framed object of restorationist hope in turn casts our eyes further back and further in to a previous hope: from sixth-century Arthur to fourth-century Constantine, son of the British princess Helena and the first Christian emperor; then from Constantine to pre-Christian Belinus, British conqueror of republican Rome (*HKB* 5.6–7.94–96; 3.9.54–56).

Indeed, there are more layers yet. Implicit in the mention of the Sibyl is Brutus, British founding father of "Troynovant," and as noted, a restoration of Trojan empire in his own right. So for Queen Elizabeth to read Dee's and Hakluyt's hopeful words that "we may . . . valiantly recover and enjoy . . . this Imperiall British monarchie" (*PN* 1.17) is for her to see far more than a territorial or jurisdictional claim; it is to view her own crowned image as in a seer's glass, reflected backward in frame after glittering frame, and to see that her crown is old Priam's. It is also to hear a celestial voice say that she is both the fulfillment of prophecy and herself a prophecy of further fulfillment. It is as if three episodes of *The Faerie Queene* were met in one, and Britomart were to gaze at her imperial ancestors and offspring in "Merlin's Mirrour."[15] Indeed, Dee's diary proudly tells of how, more than once, "the Quenes Maiestie" appeared at Dee's Mortlake house to view her future in his seer's crystal, to her "great contentment and delight."[16]

Second, in addition to providing the authorization of deep antiquity, the Matter of Britain, and especially its Arthurian core, had (and has) since its beginnings demonstrated a durable catholicity, a widening appeal across borders and cultures. Who knew not Arthur? "Renowned shall he be in the mouth of the peoples," prophesied Geoffrey's Merlin, "and his deeds shall be as meat to them that tell thereof" (*HKB* 7.3.139). From British and English chronicles to Norman, Breton, French, and German romances, to Malory's culminating redaction, the peoples of medieval Europe had embraced and naturalized the tales in myriad ways. Only the songs of Charlemagne and his knights enjoyed anything like the same widespread fame—and these too generated restorationist hopes. Indeed, one need not be a structuralist or a devotee of Joseph Campbell's monomyth to note the remarkably global persistence of returning-king legends in general and of Britain's in particular, a persistence suggesting something like universal, catholic appeal.[17]

Undoubtedly Dee and Hakluyt write as universalists. They announce explicitly from the outset that what they seek in these antiquities is indeed a kind of all-encompassing and transformative knowledge. In Dee's words, again quoted by Hakluyt, the aspiring cosmographer strives "to find himself *Cosmopolites,* a citizen and member of the whole and only one mysticall citie *universall,* and so consequently to meditate of the Cosmopoliticall government thereof, under the King almightie" (*PN* 1.16). Furthermore, in this call for a divinely supervised cosmopolitanism one can hear Dee's desire—in the divided aftermath of the Reformation—to recover an ecumenical world citizenship not reliant on papal authority, a political and spiritual catholicity independent of Roman Catholicism. So I will refer to the transcultural appeal of Britain's dynastic mythology mainly in terms of this practical catholicity—practical both in the sense of its

---

15. Edmund Spenser, *The Faerie Queen*, in *The Poetical Works of Edmund Spenser*, ed. J. C. Smith and E. de Selincourt (London: Oxford, 1952), 2.10, 3.2, 3.3. Unless otherwise noted, all further citations will be to this edition and will be made parenthetically by book, canto, and stanza number. Here the citations are to book and canto number.

16. Dee, *Diary* 4, 9–10. Characteristically, however, Dee does not tell even his diary just what Elizabeth saw there.

17. Joseph Campbell, *The Hero with a Thousand Faces*.

having had such a broad reception history by the 1570s and in the sense of its particular usefulness to early English Protestant imperialists.[18]

And indeed the empire builders value the Bruto-Arthurian past not only for the supposed antiquity of its authority and the clear catholicity of its fame but also, third, for the very particularity of its claims. However general or transcendent the appeal of returning kings and recovered glories, this most celebrated once-and-future lineage was—in origin as well as nomenclature—irreducibly British. Celtic titles of men and women, of specific rivers and mountains, coasts and regions, castles and towns—these words anchor the chronicles in a recognizable geography; they give these airy nothings a local habitation and a name. In fact, in a culture as Christian, and especially as biblicist, as late Tudor England's, the scandal of such particularity was far less than in our age. Taking incarnationalism in a different direction from their masters Augustine and Calvin, Dee and Hakluyt reason that if the Divine Word Himself could become flesh in a village far off to the east, why might not a divine political ideal be incarnated, more or less, on their island in the west in order for its gospel to spread from there around the world?

So, immediately after his praise of cosmopolitanism, Dee makes clear that God's particular instrument for the achievement of a "Cosmopolitical government" is potentially very close to hand:

> if this Brittish Monarchie would heretofore have followed the advantages which they have had onward, they might very well, [ere] this, have surpassed by justice, and godly sort, any particular Monarchie els, that ever was on earth since mans creation. . . . But yet . . . there is a little lock of Lady Occasion flickering in the aire, by our hands to catch hold on, whereby we may yet once more (before all be utterly past, and for ever) discreetly and valiantly recover and enjoy . . . the godly prosperity of this British Empire under our most peaceable Queene Elizabeth. (*PN* 1.16–17)

Most notable about this passage are the following: that Britain once held much of the world in its hand and might again; that Dee's urgent admonition to grasp Lady Occasion by the forelock is couched in a lament for past opportunities squandered; that this chance for imperial recovery comes "yet once more" only, after which "all be utterly past, and for ever"; and that for Dee, the term "Brittish Monarchie" is practically identical with his famous coinage, "the British

---

18. Indeed, as Hugh A. MacDougall writes, long before the Reformation—even in the twelfth and thirteenth centuries—expansionist Anglo-Norman monarchs like Edward I had invoked Geoffrey's *History* as "a claim useful in the promotion of a national church less subject to the control of Rome." MacDougall, *Racial Myth*, 14.

Empire." This conflation of "monarchy" with widening "empire" implies an organic, acorn-to-oak relation between throne and territorial expansion; it also assumes the Trojan ur-oak that had dropped the ancient British acorn in the first place. From smaller things—Geoffrey's Arthur is first of all a "duke of battles," the "Boar of Cornwall," and then king of all "Ynys Brydain"—grow greater things, as he becomes king by right and conquest of all the "Northern Islands" and then of the entire Roman world (*HKB* 7.3.139, 10.13.232; *PN* 1.6).

Or nearly so. For, as Dee's lament implies, integral to this myth of imperial recovery is a fourth crucial element: the memory of catastrophic loss on the brink of triumph. Antiquity, catholicity, particularity—all of the elements that the myth supplies are alchemized into ideological gold by this tincture of tragedy. In order to enlist their queen and their countrymen in their "discovery and recovery enterprise," Dee and Hakluyt evoke moments of national peripeteia, of past empire evilly divided and cut off. "O Glastonbury, Glastonbury," Dee cries out, "the treasurie of the carcases of so famous, and so many persons . . . how lamentable is thy case now! howe hath hypocrisie and pride wrought thy desolation! . . . yet that Apostolike Joseph, that triumphant British Arthur . . . doe force me with a certaine sorowful reverence, here to celebrate thy memorie" (*PN* 1.18). Heaviest in memory is of course Arthur's fall, just short of plucking the unsurpassable conqueror's crown of Rome itself.

Furthermore, such recollections of imperial demise are also, like the British lineage, many-layered. Arthur's fate puts Dee in mind of "very many other . . . mighty princes" of Britain, whose sad fortunes were brought on by their own dotage, by princely treachery, or by corporate sin (*PN* 1.18). Although Dee does not enumerate, Arthur's undoing recapitulates other tragic divisions and subjugations of the kingdom back to Brutus himself: the founder's foolish, Lear-like schism of Britain into tracts for his three antagonistic sons, Locrine, Albanact, and Camber; Lear himself, splitting the recently reunited island again between the vicious Goneril and Regan at the expense of Cordelia, thus renewing civil war (though won, in Geoffrey's version, by Cordelia); Gorbodog (Gorboduc), whose fratricidal sons, Ferrex and Porrex, bring an end to Brutus's dynasty; Cassibelaunus, who twice rebuffs the invasions of Julius Caesar but then provokes his nephew Androgeus to the treason that gives Caesar victory; and finally Cadwallader, last of British kings, driven into exile when God, in his wrath against national apostasy, gives the island over to Saxon invaders until Merlin's prophecies are fulfilled and the British remnant is spiritually restored (*HKB* 12.17.262).

This oft-mirrored turn from triumph to disaster—which in the cases of Gorboduc and Lear gave the English stage its first and its greatest native tragedies, respectively—serves Elizabethan imperialism in two ways: first, as I will show in my concluding chapter, it presents a kind of national memento mori, a reminder of the dangers of hubris and the frailties of greatness; but second, and more immediately, it provides a means of enlisting the present in fulfilling the betrayed destiny of the past. A heritage of tragic loss can confer moral or spiritual grandeur on its heirs, at least in the minds of those heirs themselves. Such imaginations may presume that Britain's great heart has endured in captivity and will return in power once it has turned from over-reaching, division, and apostasy. Then the new generation, bold in renewed purity and reformed faith, will rise, undo the follies, schisms, and sins of their fathers, and repossess the island and the earth.

Certainly this sort of regenerative nostalgia was not unique to England. There are especially strong resemblances between British foundation myths and those of other European nations, among them England's chief rivals: France, with its legendary Francio, son of Hector; Portugal, descended from the wandering Trojan Lusus; Spain, tracing its Gothic line back to Gothelus; and of course Rome, which had first colonized the imaginations of these peoples, teaching them to cast a restorationist eye back to the light in Troy.[19] England's adversarial emulation of Spanish imperialism will form the substance of my next chapter. Here it is sufficient to note that in one famous year, 1492, the supposed descendants of Gothelus completed the reconquest of their peninsula, expelled their "infidels," and set out to win the Indies. However fanciful in origin, the restorationist idea had undeniable material consequences.

Similarly, in 1604, Scotland's King James ascended the English throne, consolidated the two crowns, secured a Protestant succession, and, as we have noted, restored the ancient Celtic name of the island, citing his own Arthurian ancestry. Entering London, he was eulogized as a *rex futurus* come to right the primal wrong and close the circle of time: some of his happily apocalyptic new subjects sang that the kingdom was "By *Brute* divided, but by you alone, / All . . . again united and made One."[20] Two years later, the first Jamestown colonists sailed to plant yet another Troy in the wilderness of Virginia.

Arthurian Eclipse and Recovery

However, despite its deep antiquity, transnational catholicity, national particularity, and purifying sense of tragedy, the Matter of Britain had not always

---

19. MacDougall, *Racial Myth*, 8. See also A. C. Hamilton, ed., *The Spenser Encyclopedia*, 113, "Britain, Britons."
20. David M. Bergeron, *English Civic Pageantry, 1558–1624*, 85.

appealed to the English Protestant imagination. As noted, some early English humanists, especially the Protestant humanists, looked largely with disdain on what seemed to them a quintessential vestige of those middle times between the loss of biblical and classical light and their recent recovery. To quote Roger Ascham more fully:

> In our forefathers' time, when papistry as a standing pool covered and overflowed all England, few books were read in our tongue, saving certain books of chivalry . . . made in monasteries by idle monks or wanton canons; as one for example, *Morte Darthur,* the whole pleasure of which book standeth in two special points—in open manslaughter and bold bawdry; in which book those be counted the noblest knights that do kill most men without any quarrel and commit foulest adulteries by subtlest shifts. . . . Yet I know when God's Bible was banished the court and *Morte Darthur* received into the prince's chamber.[21]

Clearly Ascham identifies Malory's version with "popery": the Frenchified *Morte Darthur,* with its romanticized focus on adultery and single combat, suits "Romish" decay and "monkish" idleness.

Indeed, for much of the earlier sixteenth century, the myth of British imperial recovery was in eclipse at court. Sydney Anglo has shown that fifteenth-century England had experienced sporadic revivals of British primitivism, but that such claims were more concerned with national consolidation than with imperial expansion. During and immediately after the dynastic wars, Yorkists, Lancastrians, and especially the early Tudors sought to parlay their varying Welsh connections into an Arthurian pedigree. The most notable burst of Arthurianism came in 1486, the year after Richard III was defeated, Henry VII was crowned, and Malory was printed: the new king chose Winchester, home of the supposed Round Table, for the birth of his first son, whom he named "Arthur," tracing the infant's lineage back to his namesake.[22] Yet significantly, the first Tudor king—still new to the throne and carrying wartime debt—chose not to emulate Arthurian expansion. When two years later Christopher Columbus, through his brother, approached Henry VII proposing that he increase his empire with a westward voyage of discovery to the Indies, Henry showed little interest.

Furthermore, as memories of the Wars of the Roses receded and Tudor rule grew secure, Brutophilia waned; when Prince Arthur married Katharine of Aragón in 1501, only one known mention was made of his British ancestry, and, predeceasing his father, he was necessarily disqualified as *rex futurus.*

---

21. Ascham, *The Schoolmaster,* 68–69.
22. Sydney Anglo, "The *British History* in Early Tudor Propaganda," 28–29, 40.

Subsequently Arthur's hardier brother, Henry VIII—with one notable exception to be discussed below—gave little official attention during his long reign to the Matter of Britain. Indeed, Henry VIII's Italian-born historian, Polydore Vergil, questioned the very historicity of Arthur, a skepticism seconded by fellow humanist John Rastell. So, as Anglo writes, "the Early Tudor use of the *British History* should be regarded . . . as an early efflorescence and subsequent decline."[23]

How then did this quintessentially medieval myth, suffering from humanist skepticism, "popish" associations, and decades of official neglect, undergo a revival during England's increasingly Protestant 1570s and 1580s? Was this revival simply a justifying superstructure built on the material base of reviving English nationalism? Or was there something that the reformed religion of *sola scriptura, sola fide,* and *sola gratia* (Scripture alone, faith alone, grace alone) found intrinsically congenial in the promise of *rex quondam, rexque futurus*? In other words, was there not only an ideology of empire after the fact but a metaphysics of empire before the fact?

The first step toward understanding the symbiosis between British imperial recovery and England's Protestant Reformation is to distinguish between differing strands of the *rex futurus* myth. When Ascham attacks the godless bawdry of Arthurian story, he is, as I have noted, attacking what is to his mind something medieval, with a French title and popish morals designed to seduce and feminize the youth of England. Malory's severe defects, to Ascham's mind, result from his source and style being *outlandish* rather than *native*, and *old* rather than *ancient*. The latter difference is especially important to the Protestant humanist, who saw the medieval as merely temporary, a rotten wooden facade collapsing under the condemning weight of time, whereas he saw great survivals of antiquity as monuments of ageless stone, timelessly durable in their truth.

So when Dee and Hakluyt invoke the British past, they stress its authorizing antiquity. What this means textually is that they turn not to Malory but to Geoffrey, stressing Arthur the conqueror of Rome rather than the Arthur of Lancelot and Guenevere, the diachronicity of genealogies back to Brutus rather than the anachronicity of knights on the Grail Quest—that is, stressing the ancient rather than the merely antique. The publishing history confirms this shift: after Dee's references of 1577, Geoffrey's full *History* comes into print in 1587, at about the time that Malory is going out of print, a hiatus that would last for nearly two centuries.[24]

---

23. Ibid., 33, 35, 40.
24. Howard Maynadier, *The Arthur of the English Poets,* 343.

Having noted this telling shift in preferred textual sources, I also would like to consider more deeply certain key Protestant doctrines in order to make clear the developing links between religious reformation and imperial recovery. Thus it is necessary to look behind the emphatic Protestant *solas*—*sola scriptura, sola fide,* and *sola gratia*—to their implied *nons*. For the reformers to say that saving truth is known *only* through the Scripture was also to say that it is *not* known through mere church tradition or papal pronouncement. For them to assert that salvation comes *only* through faith was also to assert that it comes *not* through sacraments mediated by papally authorized priests. For Protestants to claim that forgiveness is given *only* by God's sovereign grace was also to claim that it is *not* given in return for ritual penitence imposed by Rome. In other words, one thing that all of these apparently exclusive *solas* share in their historical moment is their rejection of Rome's claim to universality, which, as we have already seen, involves Protestants in a search for some alternate form of post-Roman catholicity.

So the "practical catholicity" of the Bruto-Arthurian claims appeared as a godsend to Elizabethan documentary imperialists—by selectively quoting Geoffrey's *History* they were able to construct a plausible alternative Christian cosmopolitanism with the British rather than the Roman church as first among equals. Geoffrey's accounts portrayed British Constantine and Arthur swaying the entire Roman world at a time when, according to the Protestants, there were as yet no popes—for the reformers held that under Constantine, the bishop of Rome ruled *with* rather than *over* other bishops.[25] Such a general precedent appealed greatly to English Protestants whose Luthero-Calvinist belief in a universal, invisible church coexisted with their anxiety that the all-too-visible armies and galleons of Spain would encircle and snuff the Reformation. Might not God protect his reformed ministers of sovereign grace by restoring a British sovereign to his gracious *imperium*?

---

25. For instance, John Calvin argues against papal supremacy by noting that Constantine handled a particular ecclesiastical dispute by referring the parties first to a panel of bishops and then, after their decision, referring the appeal to the bishop of Arles. "We therefore see," Calvin asserts, "how far the Roman pontiff then was from that supreme dominion." John Calvin, *The Institutes of the Christian Religion,* 4.10.1128–29. In Calvin's view, even by the time of Gregory the Great (590–604 A.D.), the papacy did not claim the absolute supremacy that it came to hold by the ninth century.

Dee and Hakluyt are citing Geoffrey's *History* selectively, of course; Geoffrey was no antipapalist. Indeed, he claims that Christianity came first to Britain when King Lucius appealed to Pope Eleutherius, who sent Fagan and Duvian to convert and baptize the king and people in 156 A.D., 150 years before Constantine. *HKB* 4.19.86–5.1.88.

It is here, at the intersection of Christian catholicity and British particularity, that some further reference to contemporary postcolonial theory is illuminating. Stephen Slemon writes that one way of defining the postcolonial is as "the name for a condition of nativist longing in post-independence national groupings."[26] For although Roman legions had left Britain in the fifth century, Elizabethans felt very deeply that the most pernicious vestige of Rome's colonial occupation— the caesaro-papism of the Roman church—had not been put off the island conclusively until 1558. To understand more fully the revulsion of these late Tudor writers at "popery," one must take into account that they associated it with all that was degraded and corrupt in the culture of old imperial Italy—so, as we will see in *Cymbeline*, good Romans like Caius Lucius have Latin names, while bad Romans like Iachimo have Italian ones. Thus, when Ascham reminds his readers of the contemptuous Italian saying that *"Inglese italianato è un diavolo incarnato,"* he is saying more than his literal translation about Italianate Englishmen becoming "devils in life and condition."[27] He also intends us to hear the condescending sneer of the imperial center at the pretender from the colonial margins.

Thus, if viewed as an expression of England's particular "nativist longing" less than twenty years "post-independence," Dee's Arthur appears as a model post-colonial liberator. His "first coming" restored the political self-determination of the island and successfully demonstrated the marginality of the former imperial center; his Tudor "return"—in the form of Elizabeth's reviving sphere of British dominion—will consolidate the spiritual liberation of the people and guarantee a wider and wider realm for divine grace to save other peoples from Romanist abuse.

Yet, as we have already observed, this hoped-for demise of one universal-particularist claim—Rome's—required the assertion of another—Britain's. What may seem like a flat and hypocritical contradiction would not have seemed so to Dee and Hakluyt. We have already observed that Christian incarnational theology could, at least theoretically, reduce the scandal of particularity. If the Creator could be both God and a Palestinian Jew, then one Roman bishop might be Christ's supreme Vicar, or one Book his supreme authority, or one king and kingdom his chosen instrument. When, on grounds provided by that one Book, the Reformation rejected the Roman bishop's title *pontifex maximus*, it was denying both his priestly and his quasi-imperial functions claimed from the Caesars. The old sacrificial priestly authority the reformers understood to

---

26. Stephen Slemon, "The Scramble for Post-Colonialism," 45.
27. Ascham, *The Schoolmaster*, 66.

belong to Christ alone, while they devolved the mediatory priestly authority, in varying degrees, on national and regional churches, on congregational councils and pastors, and on individual believers. However, the Reformation left the legatee of Caesar's transnational imperial authority unstable and indefinite.

Indeed, as I will discuss more fully in chapter five, the first stage of Reformation scripturalism frowned on imperial expansionism, preferring to keep its internationalism spiritual rather than political. The early reformers allied themselves with national and local princes, and with vernacular language and culture, over against the rejected universalism of Rome—its exclusively Latin language and its ultramontane bonds and laws. This was especially true in England, where the first Henrician phase of the Reformation was not mainly theological or doctrinal but administrative and cultural: Parliament and the bishops voided the power of the pontiff, made the king supreme head of the church, and published an English Bible. Significantly, this form of English Erastianism claimed, like Dee's Arthurianism, to restore the natural rights of a native monarch—in this case his right to govern *his* national church. Thus Henry VIII's headship is celebrated as a sovereignty *recovered,* not created; in ecclesiastical matters Henry is a kind of *rex futurus,* and the bishop of Rome a usurping foreign prince.[28] Thus we find, in the 1540s and 1550s, writers like John Leland and Bishop John Bale celebrating Arthur as a Protestant hero for driving Roman power from the island.[29]

As the next generations of English Protestantism became increasingly theological and doctrinal, especially under the influence of Calvinist Geneva, the momentum grew to purge the national church of more and more Roman vestiges—surplices, ceremonies, rites, and customs. Ironically, the impetus of Protestant nativism sometimes made for paradoxical apologetics. When the decidedly anti-Calvinist prelate Lancelot Andrewes, bishop of Winchester, sought to defend the preservation of many church rituals attacked by Puritans, he took pains to demonstrate their ancient British, pre-Roman pedigree—that is, their derivation from the druids. Strangely, it mattered not to Andrewes that these rites were pagan in origin; what mattered for his argument was that they long predated the introduction of papal religion into the island.[30]

Internationally, English defiance of papal authority was bound eventually to force confrontations that would highlight the need for some warrant counter-

---

28. G. R. Elton, *The Tudor Constitution: Documents and Commentary,* 355–56; J. J. Scarisbrick, *Henry VIII,* 272–73.

29. Keith Thomas, *Religion and the Decline of Magic,* 427.

30. Lancelot Andrewes, *A Learned Discourse of Ceremonies Retained and Used in Christian Churches,* 2–4, 12–13.

balancing the pope's transoceanic claims. Significantly, it was English Protestant mariners who precipitated the first material challenges to papal globalism. In the 1560s and early 1570s, seagoing cousins John Hawkins and Francis Drake flouted the Tordesillas line—drawn through the poles by Pope Alexander VI in 1493 to divide the Earth into Spanish and Portuguese hemispheres—by sailing to the Caribbean for trade and for plunder. In chapters two and three, I will discuss, respectively, English capitalization on Spain's "Black Legend," and Drake's own quasi-Arthurian legend ("If the Dons sight Devon, I'll quit the port of Heaven").[31] However, most notable in this context is that Drake was allied with and influenced by Dee and shared, though on more pragmatic grounds, Dee's urgent desire for a Protestant *cosmopolis* that would erase papal boundaries. According to William H. Sherman, Dee consulted repeatedly with Drake, and when Drake left England in 1577 on the voyage that would become his famous circumnavigation, he probably had with him Dee's newly printed *General and Rare Memorials*, which invited the queen to renew Arthur's rights across the ocean—certainly one of history's most portentous collaborations between theory and practice.[32]

So we see how certain Protestant distinctives—love of a pure, "primitive" antiquity, belief in a pre-Roman catholicity, and respect for vernacular particularity—seem eventually to have meshed with answering elements in British kingly lore. A fourth element is, in its possible relation to Protestant theology, the most problematic and yet the most intriguing: the tragic kingly downfall, which makes the hoped-for restoration both necessary and possible. I began by noting that British imperialism began in hope, but it was also born in fear: the same Geoffrean chronicles that repeatedly promise a new beginning also point anxiously ahead to a latter end in which prophetic promise is hard to distinguish from apocalyptic threat. How did these accounts of a tragically truncated former empire appeal to Protestantism's sense of pervading sin—and of restorative repentance?

First, there is the quasi-biblical structure of Geoffrey's *History*. This is not surprising, since the writer was a churchman, but the degree to which the British chronicle echoes the narrative trajectory and the providentialist mindset of the Old Testament king books would have both attracted and reassured many Elizabethan Protestant readers. Unlike Virgil's founding epic, *The Aeneid*, and like the Hebrew kingly chronicles, Geoffrey's *History* presents not only the rise but also the fall of the kingdom. Like the Jews, the British are a chosen nation, a

---

31. John Sugden, *Sir Francis Drake*, 12, 323.
32. Sherman, *John Dee*, 177.

people set apart, called out by divine oracles and established in their promised land; yet they swell with pride, flout God's laws, and so in the end He gives them over to the hand of their heathen enemies—but with a promise of repentance and return. Furthermore, at the heart of both Israelite and British holy histories are the extended, exemplary stories of especially great kings (David, Arthur), their comings foretold with full prophetic color, their victories spreading order and godliness through an ever-wider empire until excess, adultery, and family treachery bring ruin.

There are of course important differences between Geoffrey's Arthur and the biblical David: Arthur personally lacks David's moral complexity, being essentially a victim of others' sins, and he also lacks David's inward spirituality, being mainly a valiant, magnanimous, but unreflective holy warrior. This difference in characterization makes Arthur's fall more an object of tragic pity and restorationist zeal than a spur to psalmic reflection on cleansing the secret sins of one's own heart. Thus Geoffrey's portrayal displays the moral exceptionalism that undergirds much imperial conquest, British or otherwise. Yet such exceptionalism is to some degree counterbalanced by the moral complexity of Geoffrey's *History* as a whole, which narrates a generous amount of British evil and, finally, British exile by God's immediate, wrathful hand. "Woe unto us, miserable sinners!" laments King Cadwallader, the last of the line. "[O Saxons, n]ot your valor drives us forth, but the might of Him that is over all, the God whom never have our people been slow to offend" (*HKB* 12.15.260–61).

Besides such moral exempla, there is a second, related reason that the sinful fall of old Britain might finally have fired Elizabethan Protestants with imperial hopes. This reason is implied in Cadwallader's lament and made explicit to him soon after by a prophetic Voice promising "that the people of the Britons should again possess the island by merit of their faith" (*HKB* 12.17.262). There would be something strangely reassuring to a late Tudor Protestant in hearing that his island's past glories ended not because of an overwhelming outside enemy invader but rather because of spiritual infidelity within the camp. Such a statement suggests that, after all, the Britons were inferior only to themselves, that nothing could defeat native British might but British weakness and God's own chastening hand.

Even more suggestively, the sign of this impending providential reversal is the "merit" of restored British "faith" ("*per meritum sue fidei*" in the original Latin).[33] Although Geoffrey could hardly have had the reformers' *sola fide* in mind, the

---

33. Geoffrey of Monmouth, *The Historia regum Britanniae of Geoffrey of Monmouth*, 533.

coincidence of his phrase with the renewed late Tudor emphasis on salvation through faith could, in many Elizabethan eyes, be read as a prophecy that the island's Protestant Reformation would set in motion the divine machinery of imperial recovery. Indeed, I will show that for Edmund Spenser, this is precisely what it means. This promise reverses Job's tragic outcry: the Lord hath taken away, and the Lord will give.

Reforming Merlin: John Dee and Revisionary Typology

Such a prophecy requires a prophet, and there is never any textual doubt over who plays Elijah to Arthur's second coming: "God had willed the Britons should no longer reign in Britain before that time should come whereof Merlin had prophesied" (*HKB* 12.17.262). In a purple burst of apocalyptic prophecy at the heart of Geoffrey's *History*, Merlin reads out the future to the doomed British King Vortigern, predicting Arthur's first coming, his conquests of "the islands of the Ocean" and "the forests of Gaul," and his fierce threat to "the house of Romulus" just before his "doubtful end" (*HKB* 7.3.139). Then, vague "ages" later, returns the glorious "Boar of Cornwall," reconquering the home island and then sweeping east across the continent:

> Cadwallader shall call unto Conan [past king of Brittany]. . . . then shall gush forth the fountains of Brittany and shall be crowned with the diadem of Brutus. Wales shall be filled with gladness and the oaks of Cornwall will wax green. The island shall be called by the name of Brutus and the name given by foreigners shall be done away. From Conan shall issue forth the warlike Boar that shall try the sharpness of his tushes within the forests of Gaul. . . . even unto furthest Spain shall sweep the swiftness of his career. . . . Then shall the Boar of commerce arrive in the land, who shall recall the scattered flocks unto the pastures they have lost. (*HKB* 7.3.142–43)

I have already noted how both Henry VII and his great-great-grandson James I invoked Merlin to verify themselves as the long-lost British King. Both claimed descent from Cadwallader, and Henry, as earl of Richmond, had launched his successful bid for the throne from a Breton exile, landing in Welsh Milford Haven on his way to defeating that other Boar, Richard III, at Bosworth Field. Indeed, King James felt his Celtic claims so strongly that when he restored to the island "the name of Brutus"—"Great Britain"—he did so over the objections of the House of Commons, a portent of future Stuart parliamentary relations.[34] Also

---

34. Thomas, *Religion and the Decline of Magic*, 416–18.

notable about this prophecy is its emphasis not only on British reunification but also on territorial and commercial expansion—which, along with Merlin's other prognostications of a religious reformation, constitute what would become a kind of imperial trinity.

If a quasi-biblical typology enabled Tudor-Stuart interpreters to read Merlin as an Elijah crying in the preimperial wilderness, such a typology also allowed for a contemporary Briton to play John the Baptist to Merlin's Elijah, preparing the way for a British messiah. Into this role stepped John Dee. Like Hakluyt of Welsh blood, Dee was passionate about his Cambrian identity, naming his firstborn "Arthur" and writing his own ancestors and offspring marginally into his copy of *The Laws of Hywel Dda,* thus claiming descent from Welsh kings.[35] He believed that the time of the Saxons was ending, and that he was born to restore Britain to itself.

Much has already been written of the paradoxical Dee, as scholarly cosmopolitan and as ur-imperialist, as magus and as early scientist.[36] I wish to complicate these paradoxes further by noting their religious dimensions: for at Cambridge in the 1540s young Dee was tutored by the influential Protestant humanist John Cheke; he was, even in later years, apparently a sabbatarian; and his diaries reveal, interwoven with his sometimes bizarre physical and metaphysical experiments, a wide lifelong streak of Protestant providentialism.[37] William Sherman has labored effectively to rescue Dee from the label of mere magician and finds in Dee a man undertaking a veritable constellation of roles and animated by a powerful sense of religious mission.[38] Dee does significantly resemble Spenser's Merlin, Marlowe's Faustus, and Shakespeare's Prospero, to all of whom he has been linked as a model. However, Dee is above all that a remarkable kind of Renaissance figure who seems from a modern viewpoint to be an agent of transition between irreconcilable epochs and ideologies, but who seemed to himself to be seeking—and often finding—a *discordia concors* among them.

Given his variety of roles, it is worth noting that Dee first acquired his magician's reputation at Cambridge by creating stage effects for a Trinity College dramatic production—a fact that is especially suggestive when we consider that he has been linked as a model not only with Spenser's Merlin but also with

---

35. Sherman, *John Dee,* 108.
36. In addition to Sherman, *John Dee,* see Frances Yates, *Giordano Bruno and the Hermetic Tradition,* and Peter J. French, *John Dee: The World of an Elizabethan Magus.*
37. Dee, *Diary,* 18, 25, passim.
38. Sherman, *John Dee,* 4–5, 23, 99–100.

those Renaissance stage magi, Doctor Faustus and Prospero.[39] Dee kept this theatrical flair all of his life, becoming known as a "character" and presenting his projects and his antiquities to anyone with the authority, wealth, or practical ability to actuate them, from the queen, Burghley, Walsingham, Ralegh, Archbishop Whitgift, and Sir Philip Sidney to Hakluyt, Hawkins, Gilbert, Drake, Cavendish, and Hariot. For Dee, as for the humanist movement in general, the way back was the way forward, "recovery" the key to progress, but he saw both scientific and metaphysical advance as dependent on spiritual reform. In particular, Dee saw patriotic British nationalism serving the cause of Protestant internationalism—as when his diary delightedly records a visit in 1583 from Sidney and the Polish Protestant prince and ambassador Albert Laski, through whom Sidney had hopes of establishing the Reformation in eastern Europe, where Dee traveled soon after.[40]

Thus Dee's archival recovery project required accommodating the Matter of Britain, especially Merlin and Arthur, to Protestant biblicism. We have already seen how the British legends' antiquity, universality, particularity, and tragic sensibility could resonate with the Reformation; it remains to explore the extent to which this revisionary typology actually adopted *rex futurus* and his prophet into the Protestant fold. For such a retroactive project there were ample and venerable precedents in Christian interpretation of the Hebrew Bible: Old Testament characters from Melchizedek to Moses to David were reread in the New Testament as prophecy personified, prefiguring Jesus and, disciples before the fact, "following" him. Furthermore, classical and extrabiblical figures had long been seen to prefigure Christ, from Hercules' rescue of Alcestis to the son of the "Virgin" in Virgil's so-called "Messianic Eclogue." In a case similar to the "reforming" of Geoffrey, early Protestant Bishop John Bale assimilated the medieval chronicler Bede to the Reformation, numbering him among the "mighty Eliases" [Elijahs] of proto-Protestantism.[41]

It is in this typological vein that a number of English reformers before Dee and Hakluyt had converted Merlin and Arthur from anti-Romans to anti-Romanists, and indeed Lollard and other sectarian interest in Geoffrean prophecy had moved Counter-Reformation authorities to place Merlin's supposed writings on the *Index Librorum Prohibitorum*. They had some cause, it appears: early Protestant Bishop Richard Cox believed that Merlin, in his prophecies to Vortigern,

---

39. *The Dictionary of National Biography*, 5:721b; the production was of Aristophanes' *Peace*. For Dee compared with Faustus and Prospero, see Sherman, *John Dee*, 16, 51.

40. Dee, *Diary*, see index (for his varied contacts); 20, 21 ff. (Sidney and Laski); Malcolm William Wallace, *The Life of Sir Philip Sidney*, 296.

41. John Bale, *Select Works of John Bale*, 137.

had predicted Henry VIII's Dissolution of the Monasteries; the aforementioned Bale also believed Merlin to have foretold the entire Reformation; and the authors of *The Mirrour for Magistrates,* published in the second year of Elizabeth's reign (1559), praise "learned Merlin whom God gave the spirit to know and utter princes' acts to come."[42]

The most extensive crystallization of such reinterpretations by a Tudor-Stuart Protestant is Thomas Heywood's *Life of Merlin* (1641), in which the Elizabethan playwright turned mystic chronicler toward the end of his life. This book combines a brief biography based on Geoffrey's Merlin materials, a chronological history of Britain from Brutus to Vortigern, and Heywood's own running commentary on Merlin's prophecies and their fulfillments up to the reign of Charles I. Heywood takes pains to note instances of "prophetical poets and seers among the gentiles"; indeed, Merlin is discovered to have sympathetically predicted, among other things, the Henrician Reformation, Protestant suffering under Queen Mary's tyranny, Queen Elizabeth's godly rule and love of Scripture, and the miraculous exposure of the Gunpowder Plot. Most significantly for my present argument, Heywood links this march of fulfillment and Reformation with the promise of further colonial expansion: he calls Brutus's conquest of Albion "the first foundation of our British *Colony*" and "the first *Plantation* of this Island," and he speaks similarly of Great Britain's further "*Plantations* . . . in Virginia, [and] Bermudas or Summer Isles."[43]

Reforming Arthur: Protestant Imperial Typology in *The Misfortunes of Arthur* and *The Faerie Queene*

Arthur himself is subject to increasing narrative and religious reformation in the course of his later Tudor revival. The earlier Protestant praisers of Arthur—Cox, Leland, Bale, most prominently—jettisoned the suspect elements of French romance to celebrate him in nativist terms as an anti-Roman champion. Elizabethan chroniclers Raphael Holinshed and John Stow continued largely in this nativist line, though the latter's recusancy kept him from advancing the fuller doctrinal agenda of the Reformation—Stow's Arthur drives

---

42. For the *Index,* Cox, Bale, and the *Mirrour,* see Thomas, *Religion and the Decline of Magic,* 408–9 and notes.

43. Thomas Heywood, *The Life of Merlin* (1641), 39–41, 248–50, 264–67, 280, 283–87, iii, title page, 287.

out Roman political power, but as in Geoffrey he still bears "the image of Our Lady" upon his shield.[44]

Arthur's revival also brought Geoffrey's tragic vision to the stage in *The Misfortunes of Arthur*, promising a national purification not merely political but also spiritual. In February during the Armada year 1587–1588, with the renewed Romanist threat nearing its highest pitch, the play was performed for the queen herself at Greenwich Palace.[45] The work of many hands—most prominently those of Thomas Hughes and Francis Bacon—this Senecan revenge tragedy portrays Arthur as an implacable and successful anti-Roman warrior who nevertheless suffers for the fault his father made in conceiving him. The avenging ghost of Gorlois, cuckolded and murdered by Uther, appears in the first scene to cry for "reuenge / on ruthlesse *Brytaines* and *Pendragons* race," predicting that "*Mordred* shall be the hammer of my hate" (1.1.25–26, 50). Combining the imperial conqueror of Geoffrey with the personally flawed hero of romance, this Arthur's fall is a spectacle warning against moral and imperial over-reach, even in a good cause—Arthur has been excessively violent in battle and indulgent to the wicked Mordred (here his bastard son).

Yet the sting of the play's tragic reversal is largely removed in the final scene: Gorlois reappears, now appeased, to announce future British revival in a time of renewed righteousness under Elizabeth:

> Sinne hath his pay: and blood is quit with blood. . . .
> *Brytaine* . . . in thee some glorious starre must shine,
> When many yeares and ages are expirde
> Whose beames shall cleare the mist of miscontent . . .
> For *Brytaine* then becomes an Angels land,
> Both Diuels and sprites must yeelde to Angels power,
> Vnto the goddesse of the Angels land. . . .
> And with foresight of her thrice happie daies,
> *Brytaine* I leaue thee to an endlesse praise.
> (5.2.3, 11, 18–20, 23–25, 30–31)

The Angel/Angle pun serves to strengthen Gorlois's sense of happy inevitability, since Elizabeth not only revives British rule but also overcomes ancient Anglo-

---

44. Robert Huntington Fletcher, *The Arthurian Material in the Chronicles*, 268–71; John Stow, *Annales, or, a Generall Chronicle of England . . . Continued unto 1631*, 54. Holinshed follows Geoffrey closely for most of the pre-Arthurian story, but in the Arthurian period he does so only in the matter of Arthur's northern conquests, his anti-Roman campaigns, and his last battle.

45. Brian Jay Corrigan, ed. *The Misfortunes of Arthur: A Critical, Old-Spelling Edition*, 1–3.

British enmity, all by means of an "angelic" purification of the island and of her people. Here tragic catharsis promises to reform not only Britain's temporal state but her spiritual state as well.

Without doubt the most radical reformation that Arthur undergoes in Tudor times, and by far the most important, is found in Spenser's *Faerie Queene*. Indeed, from its first printing in 1590 until the republication of Malory in the early nineteenth century, it was Spenser's version of Arthur that informed most other treatments of the British king. And yet his Arthur is so profoundly altered that one critic has commented, "*The Faerie Queene* is a great poem, but not a great Arthurian poem."[46] Such a judgment depends, of course, on what one considers to be incidental and what essential to the tradition. Spenser freely discards many traditional elements because for him at the heart of the Matter of Britain is its assurance that spiritual regeneration is both the cause of and the reason for imperial restoration.

For this reason, many particulars crucial to the Geoffrean or Malorian texts are absent in Spenser's. Though *The Faerie Queene* is a romance, gone are the romance elements of Morgause and Morgan, Camelot, the Round Table and the Grail Quest, Lancelot, Percival, and Bedivere (indeed the only traditional knight to appear at all is Tristram). Conversely, though the poem abounds in chronicle, gone also are vital chronicle elements, including Arthur's illegitimate begetting, his marriage to Guenevere, and, most important, the very presence of Mordred.

Some of these omissions might be understood as deferral rather than as flat exclusion—after all, Spenser presents Arthur as a young prince, not yet as a king, and his adventures as the prehistory of the famous deeds that someday will fill the blank pages of *Britons Moniments*. But it is that very blank—so arrestingly introduced at the House of Temperance in the ninth and tenth cantos of book 2—that illustrates most strikingly what Spenser and his intended Elizabethan audience considered truly essential in the Arthurian tradition: that it promises imperial renewal only after national repentance, and mainly for the purpose of spreading that spiritual renewal. It is this focus that determines what Arthuriana Spenser includes and what he excludes.

Crucial inclusions and exclusions are both on display in book 2, as Arthur reads in "a chronicle of Briton kings, from Brute to Vthers rayne." The studious prince peruses something very much like Geoffrey's history, mostly unaltered, for sixty-seven stanzas, through King Aurelius Ambrosius. Then, not yet aware

---

46. L. R. Galyon, "Spenser, Edmund," in *The Arthurian Encyclopedia*, ed. Norris J. Lacy, 522.

of his own ancestry, he turns the page (so to speak) and finds this piece of *textus interruptus:*

> After him *Vther*, which *Pendragon* hight,
>   Succeeding

This jolting break in the narrative's forward motion is followed without punctuation or caesura by

>   There abruptly it did end,
> Without full point, or other Cesure right,
> As if the rest some wicked hand did rend,
> Or th'Authour selfe could not at least attend
> To finish it: that so vntimely breach
> The Prince him selfe halfe seemeth to offend,
> Yet secret pleasure did offence empeach,
> And wonder of antiquitie long stopt his speach.
>   (2.10.68; italics mine)

Here Spenser brings together, in potent combination, a proto-imperial tableau displaying in miniature the full appeal of the Matter of Britain to the Elizabethans. Here is the authorizing "antiquitie" of the chronicle with its quasi-scriptural power of evoking wonder; the universal empire encoded in the punning reference to "Cesure/Caesar"; the particularly British provenance and destiny of that empire; and, most important, the sense of outrage at "some wicked hand" that has robbed the narrative and Arthur—who is indeed the nation personified—of their proper imperial ends. Spenser's most brilliant effect lies in transforming the anacoluthon on the page into a kind of wound inflicted by treachery and calling for redress, a textual bloody shirt to wave at the somnambulant reader and wake him to action.

And yet the stanza ends by stressing not Arthur's righteous rage but rather his even stronger "secret pleasure" and "wonder," leading into the next stanza's enraptured patriotic outburst, as he

>   At last quite rauisht with delight, to heare
> The royall Ofspring of his natiue land,
> Cryde out, Deare countrey, O how dearely deare
> Ought thy remembraunce, and perpetuall band
> Be to thy foster Childe, that from thy hand
> Did commun breath and nouriture receaue?
> How brutish is it not to vnderstand,

> How much to her we owe, that all vs gaue,
> That gaue vnto vs all, what euer good we haue.
> (2.10.69)

Spenser here heightens Arthur's passionate sincerity by having him speak paradoxically as still merely Britain's "foster Childe," not yet fully aware of his royal nativity but nevertheless deeply loyal and grateful for British nurture. Of course, as the double entendre on "Childe" implies—its feudal meaning is that of an heir apparent—he is inwardly sensing his high birth, while the pun on "brutish/British/Brutus" suggests that he is intuiting his connection not only to a royal but to an imperial destiny. As Merlin will soon tell Britomart in book 3, and as his historical referent John Dee had told Elizabeth since the 1570s:

> Renowmed kings, and sacred Emperours,
> Thy fruitfull Offspring, shall from thee descend;
> Braue Captaines, and most mighty warriours,
> That shall their conquests through all lands extend,
> And their decayed kingdomes shall amend:
> (3.3.23)

Here is the full promise of *rex futurus*, coming again to restore Britain's universal *imperium*. What Artegall will be to Britomart in fulfilling the temporal chronicle, Arthur will be to Gloriana/Elizabeth, conceiving an immutable empire through the Virgin Queen.

However, in his modest piety Arthur does not count Gloriana, nor his coming equality with Caesar, as things to be grasped—not yet, at least. As I will show in chapter three regarding Drake's legend, it is humble and pious restraint that merits possession, in Arthur's case of crown, kingdom, and empire. His pursuit of glory, and of the Faerie Queene herself, is founded on this rejection of presumption and pride. It is intriguing to consider that Spenser's pupil, Milton, may have been under the influence of these stanzas when, in *Paradise Regain'd*, he has the youthful Jesus turn over the Hebrew prophecies to see that they spell his name.[47]

I have been arguing that the Arthurian core of this doubtfully Arthurian poem reveals what was truly indispensable for Spenser and his intended readers in the Matter of Britain. The poet can jettison most of the Arthurian romance elements from his romance and many of the traditional chronicle elements from his chronicle. For him, the essence of Bruto-Arthurianism is its promise that imperial restoration both follows and furthers spiritual regeneration.

---

47. John Milton, *Complete Poems and Major Prose*, 487–88.

This is why, even if we allow for a certain degree of deferral in the poem—so that Spenser's princely prehistory might be seen as preparing Arthur for some of his traditional exploits—it is still hard to imagine Spenser's Arthur developing into a flawed or tragic figure. In other words, it seems unlikely that the Prince Arthur who appears and disappears throughout Spenser's first six books could, in the latter uncreated six or after, abandon Gloriana for a Guenevere or conceive a Mordred, much less fall prey to him. Such a denouement would seem like sheer authorial fiat; Arthur's momentum and trajectory are all the other way. Being a chivalric romance, *The Faerie Queene* of course has many such colorful betrayals, abandonments, misbegettings, and falls; but Arthur, as Spenser's figure of ideal fulfillment, is the reconciler, the unifying perfecter of all virtues into a general "magnificence" or "magnanimity," divine grace as deus ex machina, the *rex futurus* who will never be past.

Sovereign grace and gracious sovereignty

Understanding Arthur's ideal typological status can also help us better to grasp the strong link between Arthur's spiritual and imperial significations. Spenser seems to assume that his reader possesses some sympathy with the enterprise of British imperial recovery and with its religiously Protestant impulses. And, in fact, concepts of royal sovereignty and divine grace were especially intertwined in the early English Protestant imagination: the catchphrase *sola gratia* was frequently expounded by the reformers in terms of God's kingly prerogative or "sovereign grace," while Christian kings and queens had long been addressed as "gracious sovereign" and been said to rule "by the grace of God." Perhaps most tellingly, the initial English Reformation under Henry VIII had made the king "supreme head" of the church, and while Elizabeth had softened the formulation to "supreme governor," spiritual and temporal sovereignty remained closely connected. Thus it is not accidental that Arthur, Spenser's allegorical ideal of coming imperial magnificence, is also, in the poem's spiritual allegory, his chief character representing irresistible divine grace.

Admittedly, some controversy attends the claim that Arthur allegorically enacts Protestant *sola gratia*. We of course have Spenser's own word in the poem's introductory letter to Ralegh that "in the person of Prince Arthur I sette forth magnificence . . . which vertue . . . is the perfection of all the rest."[48] A critic

---

48. Edmund Spenser, *The Faerie Queene*, ed. Thomas Roche Jr. (New Haven: Yale University Press, 1981), 16.

like Gordon Teskey treats this statement as excluding all other allegorical roles for Arthur, particularly the role of divine grace.[49] But surely Spenser need not be taken so exclusively on this point? Both John N. King and Darryl Gless have demonstrated in some detail how Arthur bodies forth irresistible grace. In canto 8 of book 1, Redcrosse lies imprisoned by his own compounded sins in the bowels of Orgoglio's castle, totally unable to free himself. Arthur's first intervention in the poem, notes John N. King, shows him here as "an agent of divine grace, [who] rescues Redcrosse and makes it possible for the knight to 'witness' to his own faith as a Protestant saint."[50] In fact, this rescue allegorically reenacts the Reformation of the English church, liberating its patron saint, George, from the wiles of the Roman/Babylonian whore Duessa on her apocalyptic beast. Arthur's approaching bugle blast (1.8.3–4) represents grace's irresistibility as music opening every iron castle gate, and, in the fight before the castle walls, Arthur defeats Duessa's seven-headed beast by revealing the "blazing brightnesse" of his invincible diamond shield (1.8.19–20).

This irresistible shield, writes Gless, is Arthur's "decisive weapon." Significantly, like its bearer, it has been "reformed" by Spenser. In Geoffrey of Monmouth, and even as late as Stow's *Chronicle*, the shield bears the mediating image of the Blessed Virgin; here, it is sheer ineffable light representing, says Gless, "the divine glory unmediated, a direct intuitive vision made possible and rendered transcendently potent by the grace that justifies." Uncovered in the presence of the wicked, the shield "produces first a paralyzing terror akin to despair; it then reduces proud enemies to what they in essence are, dust, ashes, 'nought at all.' "[51]

Moreover, after this debut, the shield's next appearance in the poem destroys enemies who are not only spiritual but also strongly political. Specifically, the shield figures crucially in the eighth canto of book 5, when Arthur and his half-brother, Artegall, defeat Souldan and Adicia in an episode representing England's divine deliverance both from Marian tyranny and from the Spanish Armada. These historical references to "Bloody Mary" and Philip II are clearly marked: the couple's shared rule "by tortious powre and lawlesse regiment," their idolatrous hatred of good Queen Mercilla ("Mercy"—another avatar of Elizabeth), and the galleonlike loftiness of Souldan's war-chariot (5.8.30, 19, 28).

---

49. Gordon Teskey, "Arthur in *The Faerie Queene*," in *The Spenser Encyclopedia*, ed. A. C. Hamilton, 71.
50. John N. King, *Spenser's Poetry and the Reformation Tradition*, 212; see also 208–12 passim.
51. Darryl J. Gless, *Interpretation and Theology in Spenser*, 130, 131–32.

But it is Arthur's shield that provides the crucial referent linking historical and divine. Nearly overborne by Souldan's immense killing machine, Arthur unveils the searing light, and as "God's Wind" scattered the Armada of 1588, the shield forces Souldan's "fierie-mouthed steeds" to drag his huge chariot high and low until he is left, like so much flotsam, "Torne all to rags, and rent with many a wound, / That no whole peece of him was to be seene, / But scattred all about, and strow'd vpon the greene" (5.8.37–38, 42). After this victory, the two brothers continue to expand their Arthurian sway: in cantos 10 and 11, Arthur liberates "Belge" (the Netherlands) from Spanish tyranny; and in canto 12, Artegall, alone for his finale, comes to the aid of reform in France (Sir Burbon) and Ireland (Irena).

It is crucial to recognize that in both book 1 and book 5, Arthur's spiritual status as bearer of God's sovereign grace fully interpenetrates his historical-political status as royal head of the church and as restorer of a gracious British sovereignty. In book 1, the allegory of Redcrosse's individual redemption by grace dovetails with the historical allegory of national reformation and introduces the theme of how Saxon England will be inducted into the larger cause of British imperial recovery. In book 5, personal and national salvation give place to international salvation, as resurgent Britain is by canto 12 well begun in the work of reconstituting Arthur's old European *imperium*, imagined here as a sphere of benevolent influence inimical to "lawlesse regiment."

It is also important to note that book 5 belongs to Artegall, the knight of justice, and that just before the fight with Souldan in canto 8, Artegall meets Arthur for the very first time. This meeting occurs in confused circumstances that stress both their spiritual-religious difference and their historical-political equivalency in the allegory—that, in other words, Artegall (justice) is not Arthur (grace), and yet he is Arthur's equal, "Art-egall." As each intervenes to rescue an endangered damsel, each on first sight assumes that the other is a "Paynim," and they fight to an absolute draw until the rescued damsel, Samient ("Sameness"), reconciles them and moves them to unite forces against Souldan and Adicia in defense of Mercilla (5.8.1–24). Here justice and grace—so often seen as opposites—embrace and then combine their mutually necessary powers against idolatrous, oppressive evil.

So we can see how for Spenser, the essence of the *Artus redivivus* myth is in its promise that imperial restoration is both the result of spiritual reformation and a precondition for the spread of further spiritual reform—the Britons shall again come into their possession "by merit of their faith." Arthur's idealized "empire" means not an invasive tyranny but rather a sphere of protection from such tyranny, a protection provided by a divinely appointed strength that is irresistible and magnificent in the perfection of its virtues, and that is gracious in the doing of all its justice. Spenser's Arthurianism, stripped of all that he considered accidental, is conquering mercy personified, aggression sublimed and sanctifying, sword and cross reconciled, *rex futurus* under *rex caeli*.

"Salvagesse sans finesse": British Savagery, Roman Civility, and the Alternative Myth of the *Translatio Imperii*

But what, after all, of Artegall? If Arthur needs only to discover his own glorious past in order to realize his yet more glorious future, this cannot be said of his decidedly un-ideal half-brother. On the contrary, Artegall first appears in book 4 as an ignorant and bloodthirsty woodland savage and blunders his way through a series of sometimes comic administrations of justice. He undergoes the triple humiliation of capture by an Amazon, forced transvestism, and rescue by Britomart, his betrothed; and, according to Merlin's prophecy, he is doomed to death by unspecified treachery. Artegall's trajectory points to an alternative myth that both counters and complements Arthurian imperial revivalism: the myth of the *translatio imperii*, of the British savage transformed by Roman civility in preparation for inheriting the mantle of empire.

This myth of the domestic savage enjoyed a marked revival in later Elizabethan and early Stuart England. Whether due to an increased awareness of African and American "savages," or because native English rusticity seemed threatened by unprecedented urbanization and possible invasion, the period between 1570 and 1620 saw a wave of renewed interest in England's hardy and violent pagan past. Significantly, this revival—and to some degree Artegall himself—had its intellectual roots in the anti-Arthurian historiography of Polydore Vergil, court antiquarian to Henry VIII. In his *Anglica Historia* (1534), the Italian humanist Polydore rejected the imperial claims of both Brutus and Arthur as mere fable, earning him the condemnation of patriotic English writers like John Leland and John Bale. But Polydore was no anti-imperialist; rather, he assured King Henry of his right to the imperial crown through the indisputably historical line of Constantine the Great. Constantine's bold British blood from his mother, Helena, had been, as it were, subdued and disciplined by that of his Roman father, Constantius, and purified by Constantine's Christian conversion. In making this claim, Polydore received some English support from John Rastell, but, as we have seen, it was Dee's and Hakluyt's Arthurianism, still looking to Geoffrey's *History*, that dominated the first wave of Elizabethan imperial recovery.[52]

52. Denys Hay, *Polydore Vergil*, 157–58, 199 (anti-Arthurian); 96–97 (Constantine); 30 n. 3 (Rastell).

It was left for William Camden to pick up and advance the alternative standard that is represented by Artegall. In his *Britannia* of 1586, Camden proposes, as Debora Shuger has written, "a radically different model of English prehistory." She notes that instead of the traditional "devolutionary scheme, which portrays early British history as the gradual decline of an advanced Trojan civilization, *Britannia*'s opening chapters narrate British origins as the slow and bloody civilizing process that followed Roman colonization."[53] As Shuger's persuasively revisionist article shows, it is this tutelary model—of violent "white barbarism" overcome and pacified by Roman order and cultivation—that is the proper interpretive context for Spenser's *View of the Present State of Ireland.*

Shuger demonstrates that Camden and Spenser present ancient Albion in terms that we might call Hobbesean: pre-Roman Britain, like pre-British Ireland, was thought to be dominated by Caucasian barbarians or "Scythians" (read northern Europeans). Camden and Spenser portray this culture as pervasively violent (the Britons would rather fight than plow); hence they had no agriculture (they were pastoralists and hunters); they had no cities (they lived in isolation); they had no justice-bearing central government (the common folk were enslaved to a ruthless aristocracy); and this aristocracy preferred arbitrary lawlessness to ordered government.[54]

So, as Shuger shows, Spenser's program for Ireland is no more "genocidal" than Camden's portrait of Roman colonization in Britain: in neither case is the object the destruction or even the decimation of the common people; rather it is their liberation from a corrupt, barbarian, warrior aristocracy and their reorganization into a productive agricultural and urban society. One may abhor Spenser's Machiavellian reasoning and yet admit that its object is not extermination but "civility." It is significant, then, that Artegall's first two appearances in *The Faerie Queene* emphasize the stark contrast between what he will become and what he presently is. In 3.2.24–25, Britomart's first sight of her future mate comes as a vision in "Merlin's myrrhour," and his ideal image there is of civil and chivalrous perfection, a "comely knight, all arm'd in complete wize," clad in "*Achilles armes, which Arthegall did win.*" Yet in his first actual appearance soon after, at Satyrane's tournament in book 4, Artegall is the image of the crude barbarian warrior:

> For all his armour was like saluage weed
> With woody moss bedight, and all his steed
> With oaken leaues attrapt, that seemed fit

---

53. Debora Shuger, "Irishmen, Aristocrats, and Other White Barbarians," 496.
54. Ibid., 499–501.

> For saluage wight, and thereto well agreed
> His word, which on his ragged shield was writ,
> *Saluagesse sans finesse*, shewing secret wit.
>
> (4.4.39)

Artegall's French motto—"wildness without refinement"—condenses the *translatio imperii* myth into a pithy phrase; he is almost entirely in the rough, with very little diamond in view. His behavior at the tournament confirms this judgment, as he cuts his way wrathfully through all the Knights of Maidenhead until unhorsed by the chaste, restrained, and civil power of Britomart herself. Though neither future mate yet recognizes the other, we recognize how profoundly Artegall's savage energy needs taming.

After this initial encounter, the process of Artegall's refinement is long and arduous. His first real sight of Britomart's beauty two cantos later begins the process of softening his vengefulness (4.6.12–22), but when he returns as Spenser's Knight of Justice in book 5, his interventions, though well-meaning and at times clever, are at first crude and cruel. With the help of his pitiless page, Talus, who represents the simplistic eye-for-eye principle of justice, Artegall sentences the murderous Sangliere to bear his victim's head about like a "rated Spaniel" tied to its stinking kill (5.1.28); he dismembers and drowns the beautiful but corrupt princess Munera, despite her "holding vp her suppliant hands on hye" (5.2.25–27); and he allows Talus to push the nihilistic "Gyant" off a cliff without hearing his full discourse (5.2.48–50).

It is only after Artegall's humiliating imprisonment by the Amazon Radigund and his subsequent rescue by Britomart (5.7.37–42) that Artegall's savage vengeance is humanized and humbled into a truer justice. Significantly, Britomart has by this time been confirmed as the bearer of Christian empire: in a vision she sees herself wearing an ecclesiastical "Mitre" that is transfigured into an imperial "Crowne of gold" (5.7.13). The implication is that Roman-style martial discipline is not enough to prepare the British savage for empire; a Constantinian conversion is necessary, too. After this transforming vision, Britomart is able not only to rescue Artegall but also to change him into something approaching her ideal of just and compassionate manhood. Remarkably, it is only after this personal reformation that Artegall for the first time meets his half-brother, Arthur, and is able to join him in enforcing reformed Protestant justice throughout Europe—in the above-mentioned episodes of Souldan and Adicia (Philip II and Bloody Mary—5.7), Belge (the Netherlands—5.10), Duessa and Burbon (Mary Queen of Scots and Henry of Navarre—5.11), and Irena (Ireland—5.12). Once Spenser has civilized and christened the British savage, he makes him complement rather than contradict the logic of restored Arthurian empire.

However, if Spenser could, like Camden, portray pre-Roman Britain as dark and bloody ground, he also evokes other versions of this *translatio imperii* myth that were more nostalgic and elegiac. "Salvagesse sans finesse" can imply loss as well as gain; "finesse" can mean not only "refinement" and "civility" but also "guile." Commentators as early as Tacitus in the first century A.D. had admitted that *Romanitas* brought to Britain a loss of innocence: he reports that though the Britons originally were valiant and hardy warriors, when they learned Latin and donned the toga, "gradually they gave in to the attractions of vices, porticoes, and baths, and the elegance of banquets. And this was called civilization among those who did not know better, although it was part of slavery."[55] We have already seen that in the 1560s a Protestant humanist like Roger Ascham, despite his eloquent defense of Latin learning, could echo Tacitus in abominating Latin culture's effeminizing effects on English youth.

Significantly, these same assumptions about savage nobility unite the otherwise polarized polemics of Stephen Gosson and Philip Sidney in their *School of Abuse* and *Defense of Poesy*. Writing in 1579, the antitheatrical Gosson nominally conflates ancient Britons with Englishmen and then celebrates the antique virtues. "Consider with thyself, gentle reader, the old discipline of England [Britain]," Gosson writes;

> mark what we were before and what we are now. . . . [Dio Cassius, the Roman historian] saith that Englishmen could suffer watching and labor, hunger and thirst, and bear of all storms with head and shoulders. They used slender weapons, went naked, and were good soldiers. They fed upon roots and barks of trees, they would stand up to the chin many days in marshes without victuals, . . . the men in valor not yielding to Scythia, the women in courage passing the Amazons. The exercise of both was shooting and darting, running and wrestling and trying such masteries as either consisted in swiftness of feet, agility of body, strength of arms, or martial discipline.[56]

That Gosson blames the degradations of his own weak piping time of peace on the malign influence of poets and players is of course true but beside my point; for Philip Sidney—even in opposing Gosson and defending the "virtue-breeding delightfulness" of poetry—shares with Gosson the same ideal of a primitive, even savage virtue. In fact, two of Sidney's chief positive examples of poetic influence are the "barbarous and simple Indians" of America and the "true remnant of the ancient Britons" in Wales, for whom he has real hopes of spiritual improvement because in their native nobility both groups revere

---

55. Tacitus, *Agricola, Germany, Dialogue on Orators*, 11, 18.
56. Stephen Gosson, *The School of Abuse*, 34.

poets.[57] Indeed, even Camden, though coolly skeptical of Geoffrey's *History*, can be found praising the ancient Britons' "manlike courage and warlike prowess" and their courageous resistance to Roman invasion.[58]

So it is that Artegall, Spenser's barbarous ancient Briton, represents not only the positive reformation and civilizing of the island's ancient culture but also the danger of its emasculation. Significantly, in his pivotal combat with Radigund, Artegall is bested not by her fighting skill but by his own weak will (5.5.17)—a circumstance analogous to Spenser's earlier account of Rome's having originally conquered Britain through the help of British traitors (2.10.48–49). More important, Radigund triumphs over Artegall by requiring him, like Hercules, to "be dight / In womans weedes, that is to manhood shame"; she hangs "his warlike armes . . . on high" and breaks his sword; and she seats him in a "long large chamber, which was sield / With moniments of many knights decay" where he is locked away "spinning and carding" (5.5.20–22). Thus, while trapped in Radigone, Artegall reenacts Tacitus's account of colonized British decadence: seduced into temporary weakness, he needs to be awakened by a higher love and restored to his true manhood. Significantly, then, Britomart's rescue of him not only humbles Artegall's warrior pride and refines his sense of justice, but it also restores him to true male dignity, rearming him for battle (5.7.40–41).

Yet however well Artegall is prepared by this transformation, he still does not function well alone—as we have observed, it is only by working in concert with Britomart and later with Arthur that Artegall is able fully to succeed at bringing justice. In fact, by the end of book 5, Artegall is separated again from Arthur, and although he rescues Irena (Ireland) from Grantorto (the monstrous incarnation of the old Irish aristocracy), his reforms are cut short as he is recalled to the Faerie Court under a cloud of slander (5.12). So as a reformed British wild man, Artegall allegorically indicates that neither *salvagesse* nor *finesse*, neither native might nor acquired civility, will be enough to acquire and hold imperial sway. For Spenser, this tutelary myth of the *translatio imperii*, while important, is in the end ancillary to the recovery of lost Bruto-Arthurian glory.

British Crosses: *Romanitas*, Romance, and Proto-Christian Conversion in *Cymbeline*

If, for Spenser, it is Arthur and not Artegall who clearly remains first among equals, Shakespeare's rendering of British antiquity in *Cymbeline* (1610) is more

---

57. Ibid., 273.
58. William Camden, *Remains Concerning Britain*, 14.

ambiguous. Like Spenser, Shakespeare crosses the Bruto-Arthurian and the anti-Arthurian myths in this hermetic romance. But much more than Spenser, Shakespeare unravels both of these rival British myths and thoroughly reweaves them, creating a dazzling—and often bewildering—composite. The binding thread of this recombinant myth is what Lila Geller calls "pre-Christian Christianity"—the Renaissance humanist notion of a paganism virtuous and humble enough to recognize and embrace its own coming obsolescence in a new dispensation of divine grace.[59] The play is set at a crossroads in British history: old Britain is both resisting and yielding to Roman discipline and dissipation, and the cosmic order is crossing a threshold at the time of Christ's birth. The play presents us with ancient Britons both as fallen Trojans (the deceived Posthumus and the decadent Cloten) and as noble savages ("Polydore"/Guiderius and "Cadwal"/Arviragus); but whether the British pagan is a degenerate son of Brutus or a crude yet hardy woodsman, it is only when he embraces his "cross" by submitting to a Jehovan Jove that he proves worthy to inherit the mantle of empire.

Nevertheless, while religion and empire are profoundly interwoven in the play, the ethos of "pre-Christian Christianity" requires that the particular religious connections be left implicit, and that making these connections be left mainly to the audience. This implicitness about religion is also deeply involved with the play's extreme aesthetic self-consciousness—what Judiana Lawrence calls its combination of "assent to the aims of ethical romance and a critical analysis of its means."[60] One of the play's great pleasures for its original Jacobean viewers—King James included—would have been in seeing through a glass darkly and perceiving the secret hand of God (and the playwright) reshaping their ancestors and themselves for imperial glory.

So it is that Shakespeare keeps his play silent where his chronicle sources have much to say about Cymbeline as a harbinger of Christ. Both Lila Geller and Robin Moffit observe that in *Cymbeline* Shakespeare makes no overt reference to the event, as he does in *Hamlet* (1.1.164–70) and (arguably) in the contemporaneous *Antony and Cleopatra* (4.6.5).[61] In contrast, Shakespeare's chronicle sources for *Cymbeline* focus almost exclusively on the link between Caesar and Christ: John Stow's *Chronicles of England* (1580)—like Geoffrey of Monmouth's *History* and Raphael Holinshed's *Chronicle* (1577)—tells us

---

59. Lila Geller, "*Cymbeline* and the Imagery of Covenant Theology," 249.
60. Judiana Lawrence, "Natural Bonds and Artistic Coherence in the Ending of *Cymbeline*," 459.
61. Geller, "*Cymbeline* and the Imagery of Covenant Theology," 241; Robin Moffit, "*Cymbeline* and the Nativity," 212–13, 215.

almost nothing of King "Cvnobelinus" except that "[i]n the xiiij year of his raigne Christe our sauioure was borne in *Bethlehem* of *Juda*. . . . When Caesar Augustus the seconde Emperoure, by the will of GOD hadde stablished moste sure peace throughe the Worlde."[62] For Shakespeare's sources, King Cymbeline achieves his peculiar prominence through self-effacement: he interests them not as an active king in his own right but as a passive site of intervention for a new religious and political order that will bring universal peace.[63] "Cvnobelinus" must decrease; the coming kings—earthly and heavenly—must increase.

About these particulars of religio-imperial fulfillment *Cymbeline* remains remarkably reticent. And yet this reticence is in no way absence or negation. As Geller, Emrys Jones, and Alexander Leggatt all have observed, the play's *explicit* romance of national conversion to proto-imperial *Romanitas* depends profoundly on its *implicit* romance of conversion to proto-Christian humility; and for the early Jacobean court that connection would have been relatively easy to make.[64] This is why, as I will show, Jupiter's appearance in the play (5.4) so strongly suggests Jehovah or God the Father: this Jove is a monotheistic, providential deity who ordains "crosses" to purify the faith of Imogen and to redeem her bewitched father, lost brothers, and erring husband—and through them, the nation. He is the divinity who in the end shapes the most astonishingly multiplied set of conversions, reversals, and revelations found anywhere in Shakespeare.

All of these religious cruxes, crosses, and textual collisions intersect in Shakespeare's romancing of the Matter of Britain—specifically, as he counterposes the two rival myths of British imperial destiny that we have been observing. On the side of the devolutionary Trojo-Britannic myth, *Cymbeline* evokes both the tragedy and the restorationist hope of Geoffrean chronicle history. Posthumus Leonatus descends—in both senses—as the end of a mighty line, his name suggesting both its fall to near extinction and its derivation from ancient native strength. His father, we are told, fought against the Romans "with glory and admired success," while his older brothers "Died with their swords in hand"; his father then died of the consequent grief and his mother "deceased / As he was born" (1.1.32, 36, 39–40). This association with a virtuous but fatal past is augmented when Posthumus is exiled by King Cymbeline for marrying the

62. John Stow, *The Chronicles of England, from Brute vnto this present yeare of Christ 1580*, 17, 35.
63. For Geoffrey, see *HKB* 4.11.79–4.12.80; for Holinshed, see Raphael Holinshed, *Holinshed's Chronicle as Used in Shakespeare's Plays*, 228–29.
64. Emrys Jones, "Stuart *Cymbeline*"; Alexander Leggatt, "The Island of Miracles: An Approach to *Cymbeline*." Further citations of these articles will appear parenthetically.

long-suffering princess Imogen, named for "Innogen," the wife of Brutus, the exiled Trojan founder.[65] Significantly, Posthumus's supposed return from exile at Milford Haven in Wales (3.2, 3.4) associates him with the Milford Haven landing of Henry Tudor in 1485, on his way to restoring "Arthurian" rule at Bosworth Field. Thus the potential for a restoration of the noble Trojan line is, for the time being, thwarted by the king's blind insistence that Imogen marry his new queen's son, the egregious Cloten.

Cloten represents another kind of Trojan degeneration. He is, we are told, "a thing / Too bad for bad report" (1.1.17–18), mentally and morally deracinated, a fop whose insular nationalist bombast represents a perversion of "sceptered-isle" patriotism. Insulting the noble Roman Caius Lucius, emissary from Augustus Caesar, Cloten airily proclaims that "Britain's a world / By itself," and in his maladroit mouth the famous protective "moat" surrounding the island becomes a potentially effeminate personal garment: "if you seek us afterwards in other terms [by invasion], you will find us in our saltwater girdle" (3.1.13–14, 78–80). Due to his mental effeminacy, Cloten can in the end be "redeemed" only by decapitation; yet, strangely and significantly, without his "clodpoll" head, his still-virile body is indistinguishable from Posthumus's and is mistaken for that by Imogen herself (4.2.120–24, 186, 299–335). Ironically, these two opposite forms of British manhood have more in common than either realizes.

This same double evocation of Trojan fall and potential restoration is found in the name of "Cadwal," which the embittered exile "Morgan"/Belarius gives to Prince Arviragus after abducting him to Wales in infancy. According to Geoffrey, Cadwallo and Cadwallader are the last two kings in the Trojo-Britannic line, yet we have seen that after his defeat by the Saxons, Cadwallader retires to Rome and prophesies a British restoration out of Wales once the nation's suffering and faith atone for their sins (*HKB* 12.15–17). As "Cadwal," Arviragus unknowingly represents the old Trojan glory, exiled until it learns both proper humility and proper pride: on the one hand, Belarius commands both princes to

> . . . Stoop boys; this gate [of their Welsh cave]
> Instructs you how t' adore the heavens and bows you
> To a morning's holy office: the gates of monarchs
> Are arched so high that giants may jet through
> And keep their impious turbans on . . .
> (3.3.2–6)

65. Indeed, the Oxford editors of the play have reverted to spelling her name "Innogen" throughout—see, for example, the Oxford text in William Shakespeare, *The Oxford Shakespeare*.

Yet on the other hand Belarius soliloquizes with some satisfaction that even though he has kept the princes ignorant of their royalty, blood will tell:

> . . . though trained up thus meanly
> I' th' cave wherein they bow, their thoughts do hit
> The roofs of palaces, and nature prompts them
> In simple and low things to prince it much
> Beyond the trick of others.
>
> (3.3.82–86)

Significantly, after being trained in the rudiments of natural religion by Belarius, the princes are in fact brought back into their royal destiny by the intervention of their sister, Imogen, as "Fidele" (4.2); as in Cadwallader's prophecy, the British kingdom is restored "by faith" (*HKB* 12.17.262).

Yet Shakespeare tightly interweaves this myth of Trojo-Britannic fall and restoration with its opposite: the tutelary noble savage myth is powerfully evoked in the name of "Polydore," given by Belarius to the abducted prince Guiderius. Henry VIII's court antiquarian Polydore Vergil was, as we have seen, the most outspoken anti-Geoffrean historian of the Tudor era, proposing instead of Brutus and Arthur a *translatio imperii* through the Christianized Brito-Roman Constantine. In keeping with this myth of savage virtue, Shakespeare gives both of the rusticated princes a crude woodland piety and courage, but their ignorance must be corrected and their manners reformed before they can be ready to rule. Again, it is Imogen as "Fidele" who is the catalyst for their transformation: after "Polydore"/Guiderius has done the necessary but brutal business of beheading Cloten, he and "Cadwal"/Arviragus learn princely gentleness and compassion in mourning both Cloten and the supposedly dead "Fidele" with their exquisite song "Fear no more the heat o' th' sun" (4.2.258–81). By the end of the play, when they are fully reunited with their faithful sister and their repentant father, they have developed the needed balance between savage courage and civil restraint.

As we have seen, the meeting of the noble savage with Latin culture was thought to be a mixed blessing at best. Representing Roman virtue and civility in the play is the general Caius Lucius: he behaves with utmost courtesy to the rebellious Britons, fights bravely (if ineffectively), and passes the crucial moral test posed by "Fidele": he pities and protects the faithful youth (4.2). At a greater distance, beneficent *Romanitas* is personified in Augustus Caesar, whom even King Cymbeline admits had been his friend and benefactor when he had been schooled in Rome. On the other hand, representing Rome's luxury, dissipation, and Machiavellian evil is Iachimo; the very form of his name suggests Italianate decadence rather than classical rectitude. Moved by nothing beyond his own nihilism, Iachimo reprises Iago to Posthumus's Othello: for ocular proof of Imogen's adultery, he insinuates himself into her bedchamber, stealing her bracelet and observing her in naked sleep; then he uses the titillating "evidence" back in Rome to poison the exiled husband's mind against her (2.2; 2.4). With his satanic mixture of lust and venom, his ingenious play on Imogen's trust and Posthumus's male honor, Iachimo represents how British simplicity can be played upon and overcome by intricate Latin finesse. On the imperial level, as we have already noted, Spenser voiced the common view that it is Roman guile, not military victory, that enables the Caesars to conquer Britain.

Integral to all of this mythic interweaving is the fall and redemption of Posthumus himself. The play begins with a description of Posthumus's nativity, and with what Leggatt aptly calls the "outrageously idealized" praise of his character (191). Thus Posthumus is acclaimed for his classical virtue; he is identified with the myth of Arthurian return; he is compared to "a descended god" (1.6.169); and he shows himself mighty in battle, dressing as a "Briton peasant" to join with the young princes and Belarius in turning the tide against the invading Romans and rescuing King Cymbeline himself (5.1, 2). Yet, like Claudio in *Much Ado about Nothing*, like Othello, and like Leontes in *The Winter's Tale*, Posthumus turns with obscene ease against his loving and loyal woman. That Posthumus should fall so far and so hard into murderous paranoid jealousy powerfully enacts the insufficiency of pagan goodness: whether as a descendant of ancient heroes or as a hardy rustic, man does not live by virtue alone, but (as Protestantism would have it) by grace, and through faith—in this case, literally through the faithful and forgiving "Fidele."

As the play's central Briton *agonistes*, Posthumus, on the way to his personal reformation, also acts out the limits of pagan nationalism. It is out of suicidal despair over his benighted treachery to Imogen that he joins "Polydore," "Cadwal," and "Morgan"—"Two boys, an old man twice a boy"—in their successful patriotic stand against the Romans, and afterward he is so dismayed by his own survival that he changes back into Roman dress in the hope of summary execution by his countrymen (5.3.56, 68–80). Indeed, so crushed is Posthumus by guilt that it takes a literal deus ex machina intervention to restore his will to live. Imprisoned by the Britons, he sees in a dream vision the spirits of his dead family complaining, Job-like, to Jupiter on his behalf. Significantly, when Jupiter appears, the god explains that Posthumus's suffering was necessary not only for his own purification but also for national redemption:

> Whom best I love I cross; to make my gift,
> The more delayed, delighted. Be content.
> . . . .

> He shall be lord of lady Imogen,
>   And happier much by his affliction made.
> ....
> Then shall Posthumus end his miseries, Britain be fortunate and flourish in peace and plenty.
>
> (5.4.101–2, 107–8, 144–45)

Posthumus's "cross"—his agonizing divine test—precedes salvation for Britain, and in keeping with his name ("after burial"), it means new life out of assured death. Jove is the author of these marvelous "crosses," which in the economy of "pre-Christian Christianity" anticipate the island's conversion to the powerfully implicit Christian God. Following this heavenly vision, restorative grace begins to flow: Posthumus is almost instantly freed, and, while seeking to make his contrition to King Cymbeline in the play's last scene, he finds himself embraced, against all hope, by Imogen herself.

It is crucial both to the play's aesthetic method and to its imperial meaning that this marital reconciliation be part of a denouement renowned—and notorious—for its balletic complexity. The intricate conclusion is meant to produce a numinous sense of divine intervention in the affairs of individuals and of empires. Shakespeare's other romances—*Pericles, The Winter's Tale,* and *The Tempest*—are famous for their concluding spectacles of tragicomic revelation and reversal. But when it comes to the sheer number of "crossed" characters and delayed delights, act 5, scene 5 of *Cymbeline* is in a class by itself.

The scene begins as the evil queen dies confessing her attempts to poison Imogen and also Cymbeline; the king then curses her memory and turns to adopt Caius Lucius's British page, who is recognized by "Polydore" and "Cadwal" as the resurrected "Fidele," who in turn demands an explanation of Posthumus's ring worn by Iachimo, who confesses his plot against Posthumus, who steps forward to confess his proxy murder of Imogen and impatiently strikes down the interrupting "Fidele," who is revived by Pisanio, who reveals "Fidele" to be Imogen, who curses her supposed poisoner Pisanio, who explains that he unknowingly received the poison as a gift from the queen. And on it goes: wives proven unfaithful and faithful; sons identified by tokens and birthmarks; loyal servants exonerated; traitors, villains, and an erring husband repentant, forgiven, and restored—to a very grand total of twenty-five separate discoveries and recognitions, concluding with Cymbeline's universal proclamation that "Pardon's the word to all" (5.5.426).

This sudden superabundance of tragicomic comfort certainly strains credulity —indeed Cymbeline himself is dumbstruck through much of the scene—but that is one part of the point: like its king, Britain stands at the hinge of time, and the new Christian age of miracles breaks in on the old pagan world with incomprehensible strength. If the reversals were more reasonable in number or proportion, they would be less divine. The other part of the point is that all of these individual restorations and reconciliations are related to a larger national and imperial regeneration. Once Cymbeline has pronounced his general pardon, he hears a reading of Jupiter's prophecy—that Posthumus shall "end his miseries" and "Britain be fortunate and flourish in peace and plenty"—and takes this as his cue to connect the personal and the political. Further confounding reason, Cymbeline surrenders from a position of strength:

> My peace we will begin. And, Caius Lucius,
> Although the victor, we submit to Caesar
> And to the Roman empire, promising to pay
> Our wonted tribute, from the which
> We were dissuaded by our wicked queen,
> Whom heavens in justice both on her and hers
> Have laid most heavy hand.
> (5.5.463–69)

In this new economy of grace, the conqueror willingly stoops, yielding the trophy of nationalist victory not merely to Augustus himself but to the incalculable divinity who has been shaping all their ends. The implication is that if Britain's miraculous social and spiritual reconnections are to be maintained, arrogant and insular nationalism (personified by the queen and Cloten) must die and give place to a chastened and divinely ordained internationalism.

Yet by acknowledging the limits of local patriotism, Cymbeline paradoxically discovers that Britain's future will be unlimited. The play's final revelation is that when the conqueror stoops, he conquers more. The Romans receive his gracious submission with answering grace, as their soothsayer Philharmonus recounts his vision of Rome's imperial glory merging with—indeed disappearing into—Britain's:

> . . . for the Roman eagle
> From south to west on wing soaring aloft
> Lessened herself, and in the beams o' the sun
> So vanished; which foreshadowed our princely eagle,
> Th' imperial Caesar, should again unite
> His favor with the radiant Cymbeline,
> Which shines here in the west.
> (5.5.474–79)

As the play ends, "[a] Roman and a British ensign wave / Friendly together" (5.5.484–85), for the moment equal, but in time the Roman eagle will vanish in the British sun. So Shakespeare moves beyond the British self-effacement of his chronicle sources: in his version, Caesar must decrease, and the sons of Cymbeline must increase. One of those sons was King James I, claiming descent from Constantine and from Arthur, claiming the titles of Caesar and *rex futurus*, sitting in Shakespeare's audience—and on the restored throne of "Great Britain."

Even more than Shakespeare's other romances, *Cymbeline*'s spectacularly multiplied resolutions raise questions about the intersections between metaphysical, political, and aesthetic power. What power is it, after all, that can bring noble British savages to true Roman courtesy, a fallen "Trojan" and a depraved Italian to true repentance, a British king in happy submission to Rome, and the Roman authorities to endorse Britain's imperial future? There is an aesthetic problem here, since the audience or the reader may see the power of sheer authorial fiat at work. As Leggatt, Jones, and Lawrence all observe, many readers and viewers from Shakespeare's day on—including Samuel Johnson and George Bernard Shaw—have found *Cymbeline*'s divinity shaping far too many ends, displaying its artifice too overtly, and too flatteringly in King James's royal presence (Leggatt 208; Jones 99; Lawrence 440–41, 459).

But even if we grant the play's betrayals of logic, and indeed its shaping proximity to early Stuart imperial politics, we need not grant its aesthetic failure. Most members of a Jacobean audience would have perceived these improbabilities as a higher kind of mimesis; if the playwright seems to be playing God, it is because he is imitating not only human but heavenly action. The stage may threaten to crack under the load of signification, but that is because the little world that it portrays is being broken and remade. Indeed, the play pays its audience a great aesthetic compliment by inviting them to piece out its imperfections not only with their thoughts but with their very lives—hence its gesture outward to James as the living fulfillment of its imperial romance. Moreover, by making it so dramatically hard for the audience to suspend disbelief in the supercomplex denouement, Shakespeare may be highlighting both how difficult and yet how necessary is the will to believe when it comes to building nations and empires. Last, by so thoroughly interweaving Bruto-Arthurian and anti-Arthurian myth, *Cymbeline* performs early Stuart England's ambivalence about nationalism and empire: its harrowing of Posthumus warns that before the crown comes the cross; and its violations of ordinary logic gesture toward the extraordinary logic of heavenly grace.

Yet, for all of its aesthetic difficulty and moral complexity, *Cymbeline* ultimately presents Britain as destined for greatness. Constantine had seen the cross in a vision with the words *in hoc signo vinces* (under this sign, conquer); the British crosses of *Cymbeline*, like Constantine's, are signs of coming conversion and conquest. And in fact, even as Posthumus was agonizing in 1610 on a Jacobean stage, another "New Troy" was struggling into existence in Virginia. It was at Jamestown, as I will discuss in chapter four, that John Rolfe's 1614 marriage to the savage princess Pocahontas could be celebrated as a two-way exchange: raising the noble natives to reformed Christian civility, while restoring some of Britain's ancient warrior virility. By reviving and reforming the multifaceted Matter of Britain, English writers from Dee and Camden to Spenser and Shakespeare both imagined a common bond and laid a positive claim to a reunited island, a restored empire, and an expanding divine mission. But such common bonds alone generally do not build empires. We turn now to the necessary common enemy.

Two

The Uses of Atrocity

Satanic Spaniards, Hispanic Satans, and the "Black Legend" from Las Casas to Milton

And should I at your harmless innocence
Melt, as I do, yet public reason just,
Honor and empire with revenge enlarged
By conquering this new world, compels me now
To do what else though damned I would abhor.
—*Satan, John Milton,* Paradise Lost *4.388–92*

Whoever fights monsters should see to it that in the process he does not become a monster. —*Friedrich Nietzsche,* Beyond Good and Evil *4.146*

In October 1568, 114 English seamen, their ship badly damaged by a battle in the Gulf of Mexico, voluntarily stranded themselves on the coast of the Yucatán peninsula. They stepped ashore into what would become for the British one of their most luridly imagined hells: a howling tropical jungle, steaming with disease, crawling with exotic vermin, peopled with fierce tribesmen, and, worst of all, governed by Spaniards. Fifteen years later one survivor, Miles Philips, landed back in England alone, bearing on his body the marks of chains, the rack, and the lash, and bearing in his mind the kind of stories that haunt the hearer's sleep. These stories, which further blackened the already "Black Legend" of

Spain, he recorded for Richard Hakluyt, who included them in his 1589 *Principal Navigations* (9:398–445).

I have described how the archival enterprise of Hakluyt and John Dee revived and reformed an ancient British identity, and how it began to bind together a newly imagined Protestant "Britain" for the territorial recovery—and expansion—of a lost "Brytish Empire." The second unifying element that I now take up is the power of a shared religious enemy in Catholic Spain. Spain's imperial legacy came under much renewed scrutiny during the Columbian quincentennial of the early 1990s, and this scrutiny occasioned an outpouring of written comment—historical, political, anthropological, and literary. Of particular interest to scholars have been the writings of Bartolomé de Las Casas, colonial bishop of Chiapas in southern Mexico, implacable advocate of Indian rights, and voluminous recorder of Spanish atrocities.[1]

But historical and literary scholars are at an earlier stage in studying the alchemical process by which Elizabethan preachers like Hakluyt, as well as poets and playwrights, coined Las Casas's Black Legend into ideological gold. Stephen Greenblatt's book *Marvelous Possessions* attends closely to the mentalities of Spanish and English conquest, and Jeffrey Knapp's *An Empire Nowhere* sees England developing a peculiarly otherworldly expansionism justified by its sense of itself as pure and insular; however, neither scholar says much about English uses of the Black Legend itself. Richard Helgerson, in his ambitiously cross-disciplinary *Forms of Nationhood,* does observe that Elizabethan England necessarily defined itself and the character of its overseas expansion in terms of its relationship to Spain; but his discussion of the topic, while pithy and suggestive, is quite brief.[2]

This relative dearth of discussion is surprising, because Helgerson is right; we cannot adequately understand the British Empire or its literary productions unless we see them in the tremendous Spanish shadow that loomed so large at the empire's birth. Paradoxically, Spain's empire very nearly made British expansion impossible, and yet it created conditions that made British imperialism

---

1. Some of these works include: James Axtell, *Beyond 1492: Encounters in Colonial North America;* Greenblatt, *Marvelous Possessions;* Barnett Litvinoff, *1492: The Decline of Medievalism and the Rise of the Modern Age;* Marvin Lunenfeld, ed., *1492: Discovery, Invasion, Encounter;* Anthony Pagden, *Spanish Imperialism and the Political Imagination: Studies in European and Spanish-American Social and Political Theory, 1512–1830; Representations* 33, Special issue: "The New World"; Kirkpatrick Sale, *The Conquest of Paradise;* and Jerry M. Williams and Robert E. Lewis, eds., *Early Images of the Americas: Transfer and Invention.*

2. Knapp, *An Empire Nowhere,* 12–14; Helgerson, *Forms of Nationhood,* 181–87. See also Wright, *Religion and Empire,* vi.

feasible. Furthermore, Spanish threats made English colonization seem materially necessary; and above all, Spanish atrocity made the English response seem—to most Protestant imaginations, at least—spiritually righteous.

Indeed, Spain menaced the English Protestant imagination far longer than it menaced the English nation. As a case in point, I will examine one of the enduring literary fruits of *la leyenda negra:* that encyclopedic piece of Protestant imagining known as *Paradise Lost.* Composing 150 years after Las Casas first compared the conquistadors to demons, and nearly a century after the last serious Spanish threat to English interests, John Milton nevertheless chose to compare his Prince of Darkness to a conquistador. Throughout his epic, Milton amplifies Satan's audacity and atrocity with frequent, implicit parallels to Cortés's conquest of Mexico. These Spanish inflections afforded Milton special means to demonize the Devil. They also suggest the degree to which the British were able to transmute their own daunting imperial liabilities into ideological advantages and virtues, and even their anti-imperialist impulses into a divine mandate for a reforming empire.

The Enabling Enemy: Imagining Spanish Atrocity

Though England's colonial enterprise was rapidly expanding by the 1660s, a century earlier England's dreamed-of "empire" consisted of little beyond Dublin's pale. Spain's rich and vast American realms presented obvious obstacles to English overseas expansion. Yet, ironically, Spain's imperial conquests in other ways made Britain's transatlantic empire possible. It was, after all, the Spaniards who found the Americas when no one else was looking, amassing great bodies of cultural, geographic, and navigational information, not to mention incalculable fortunes in silver and gold. Such intelligence and treasure, when seized by pious spies and privateers like Hakluyt and Francis Drake, eased the way for English discovery and colonization.

Furthermore, Spain presented England with its most compelling material motive for empire building: national survival. In 1558, Elizabeth assumed the throne of a debt-ridden island kingdom lacking an adequate navy. By the early 1570s, she had been excommunicated by the pope, so that she lived under the growing threat of papally sanctioned overthrow, assassination, or Spanish invasion. Far from ruling the waves, the English by the early 1580s could fear that soon they might not rule their own island. Before the end of the decade England would indeed confront the overwhelming reality of the Armada, the largest invasion fleet yet assembled in history.

But while Spain shipped American gold by the galleonload to pay its mercenary armies and build its ships, the preacher Richard Hakluyt perceived the ideological uses of national adversity, arguing in 1582 that, under God's providence, England's status as imperial laggard might transmute into an opportunity; for, he noted, there yet remained "unpossessed . . . those blessed countries, from the point of Florida Northward," where strategic fortresses and settlements could be planted to hedge in King Philip's dominions, harrass them if necessary, and indeed roll them back. But these material motives cannot account adequately for the sense of national virtue permeating the voluminous Hakluyt. If the uses of adversity were sweet, the uses of atrocity were strangely sweeter. For while France had for much longer occupied the role of England's natural enemy, Spain came, after the Reformation, to occupy the spiritually vital role of *super*natural enemy. Informing Hakluyt's expansionist prophecies was the sense that this struggle was not merely against flesh and blood; above all it was against profound spiritual evil, incarnate in the papal Antichrist and his Spanish legions. Here again, England's status as imperial latecomer worked paradoxically to its advantage, for it inherited almost ready-made one of history's great propaganda bonanzas: Spain's Black Legend. Miles Philips's harrowing account of hellish life and flaming death in Spanish America merely confirmed recent British experience during the reign of Elizabeth's half-sister, "Bloody Mary"—herself the wife of Spain's Philip II—when Protestants were tortured, hung, dismembered, and especially burned publicly and in large numbers. And it complemented highly hispanophobic accounts of King Philip's harsh suppression of the rebellious Calvinist Netherlands. Similarly, for decades the English had imagined Spanish America as a vast slave camp under satanic rule, where life was cheaper than water.

Las Casas

Yet it had not long been thus. In the early years of the century, before Luther's schism, England had happily celebrated the "Spanish match" of Mary Tudor's uncle, Arthur, prince of Wales, and then her father, Henry VIII, to Mary's mother, Katharine, princess of Aragón. And, as I have noted, the demonized Spaniard was no English Protestant invention; for no one did more to create and disseminate the Black Legend of Catholic Spain than the ardent Spanish Catholic Bartolomé de Las Casas.

A former plantation owner whose father had sailed on Columbus's second voyage, Las Casas underwent a conversion in his thirties, became a priest in 1510, and renounced his Hispaniola *encomienda* in 1514. In the 1520s, he joined the Dominicans and began appealing to papal and imperial authorities, arguing that Spanish conquest amounted to deliberate genocide; for within forty years of Columbus's landing, the aboriginal inhabitants of the West Indies—whether through displacement, overwork, disease, or frequent systematic extermination—were virtually extinct.[3] Although Las Casas tends to exaggerate native meekness in order to magnify Spanish evil, he is nevertheless a compelling and often accurate chronicler of atrocities, sometimes spiking his narrative with Erasmian sarcasm. He writes that in Hispaniola

> the Spaniards entered . . . , and since forty years they have done nothing else . . . than outrage, slay, afflict, torment, and destroy them with strange and new, and divers kinds of cruelty, never before seen, nor heard of, nor read of. . . . They made bets as to who would slit a man in two, or cut off his head at one blow: or they opened up his bowels. They tore the babes from their mothers' breast by the feet, and dashed their heads against the rocks. . . . They made a gallows just high enough for the feet to nearly touch the ground, and by thirteens, in honor and reverence of our Redeemer and the twelve Apostles, they put wood underneath and, with fire, they burned the Indians alive. . . . [The killer] stirred up the fire, until they roasted slowly, according to his pleasure. I know his name, and know also his relations in Seville. I saw all the above things and numberless others.

In Mexico, in the town of Cholula, the "men calling themselves Christians" were welcomed by "all the lords of the land . . . and above all the priests, with great submission and reverence"; in response, the conquistadors assembled thousands from this welcoming party in a large courtyard. Then some armed Spaniards were stationed at the gates of the courtyard to guard them:

> thereupon all the others seized their swords and lances, and butchered all those lambs. . . . Two or three days later, many Indians who had hidden, and saved themselves under the dead bodies . . . came out alive covered with blood, and they went before the Spaniards, weeping and asking for mercy . . . : no mercy, nor any compassion was shown them. . . . More than one hundred of the lords whom they had bound, the captain commanded to be burned, and impaled alive on stakes stuck in the ground. . . . It is said, that while those five, or six thousand men were being put to the sword in the courtyard, the captain of the Spaniards [Cortés] stood singing.[4]

---

3. See Anthony Pagden's introduction to his translation of Bartolomé de Las Casas, *A Short Account of the Destruction of the Indies*, xvii–xxx, for a full biographical sketch.

4. Bartolomé de Las Casas, *A Very Brief Account of the Destruction of the Indies*, 312–19, passim. On the Erasmian echoes in Las Casas's writing, see Santa Arias, "Empowerment through the Writing of History: Bartolomé de Las Casas's Representation of the Other(s)."

Mutilation, mass rape, disembowelment, impaling of pregnant women, roasting, racking, tearing and trampling by horses, dismemberment by boar hounds—Las Casas's accounts of this "hellish tyranny" exfoliate into hundreds of numbing pages.

Such accounts had enabled Las Casas, by 1550, to persuade King-Emperor Charles V to forbid further conquest and, eventually, Indian slavery; but in anti-Spanish minds, the nation's guilt remained inexpungible. Las Casas first published his *Brevíssima relación de la destrucción de las Indias* (*A Short Account of the Destruction of the Indies*) in 1552 in Seville, and its contents quickly were taken, especially by Protestants, to confirm the wealth of horrendous rumors already circulating about New Spain.[5] As Las Casas's Flemish translator asks in 1578: "I pray you what right had the Spaniards over the Indians[?] . . . was there therefore any reason that [Spain] should for crying in the night, *There is a God, a Pope, and a King of Castile who is Lord of these Countries,* murder 12, 15, or 20 millions of poore reasonable creatures, created (as our selves) after the image of the living God?"[6] When a complete English translation, *The Spanish Colonie,* finally appeared in 1583, its running title at the head of each page was *The Spanish Cruelties*—"Spanish cruelty" already being an established English epithet. In this context of inflicted human suffering, "Spanish" served not as a mere ethnic marker but was transmuted to a measure of degree and a moral judgment; it had come to carry its own terrible hyperbole. "Spanish cruelty" brought to mind biblical habitations of dragons—the dark realms of Nebuchadnezzar, the groaning land of the pharaohs.

"Out of that thraldom": Miles Philips in the belly of the beast

From abominable New Spain, Miles Philips emerged in 1582, a prodigy of endurance, to tell his story (*PN* 9.398–445). Whether he intended it or not, Philips's account joins him in Hakluyt's larger project of documenting Spanish cruelty and building a case for liberatory British expansion. In concert with Hakluyt's Protestant biblicism, Philips's account often echoes the scriptural narratives of Joseph and Daniel, with Mexico a harsher Egypt or Babylon. But

---

5. H. C. Porter, *The Inconstant Savage: England and the North American Indian, 1500–1660,* 153.

6. Bartolomé de Las Casas [Batholomew de las Casas or Casaus (sic)], *The Spanish Colonie, or, Briefe Chronicle of the Acts and gestes of the Spaniardes in the West Indies, called the newe World,* leaf 3, verso.

in his epic longing for home and his protean wiliness in returning there, Philips seems as much a Devonshire Odysseus. By his own admission, he is not a martyr, but a survivor.

Philips had had the regrettable luck of landing in Mexico not long before the Inquisition was established in Spanish America, and, to this new bureaucratic institution hungry for casework, he and his marooned comrades became something of a pilot project. In a land of dark Mayans, Aztecs, and Castilians, the blond, heretic English could not hide long. They were imprisoned and questioned closely by the Chief Inquisitor for a year and a half. They were racked and chained while relearning Latin prayers and rehearsing Tridentine theology. A number of the more unyielding Protestants were burnt on Good Friday, 1575; the more prudent Philips crossed his fingers, swore allegiance to the pope, and watched his friends blaze. He then became overseer of Indian and African slaves building a church and observed their treatment by the Spaniards.

The ensuing story of Philips's tortuous homeward odyssey defies adequate summary. In the end, he lands home at Poole in February 1582 in the rather unlikely guise of a middle-aged cultural exchange student, having told the wary English sea captain in Majorca that he "had been 2 years in Spain to learn the language." At various points during his return, the reader finds him lurching through the Yucatán jungle in neck and leg irons; successfully impersonating a Spanish soldier, and later a native Granadan; mistakenly arrested as a colonial gentleman's runaway son; surrounded by wild beasts in Guatemala; brought for questioning before the perfidious viceroy of New Spain; nearly rescued by the circumnavigating Francis Drake in a sea chase off of Acapulco; refusing "many fair offers" of marriage to Mexican women; refused passage by an officious British ship's captain; working as a weaver in Seville; and all along hounded by Inquisitors, and befriended by kindly gentry, friars, Indians, and Africans.

For the monks, he has put aside Protestant animosity and developed grateful respect. Dominicans, Franciscans, Benedictines—nearly all "did very courteously use us," and many "do utterly abhor and mislike of that cruel Inquisition." For his fellow slaves, this former slaver expresses admiration, sympathy, and even shared outrage: he writes that "[I] had great familiarity with many of [the Mexicans], whom I found to be a courteous and loving kind of people, ingenious, and of great understanding, and they hate and abhor the Spaniards with all their hearts, they have used such horrible cruelties against them, and do still keep them in such subjection and servitude, that they and the negroes also do daily lay in wait to practice their deliverance out of that thraldom" (*PN* 9.430). Such a statement, like the whole of this engrossing memoir, is remarkably free of the overt Anglo-imperial boosterism frequent in Hakluyt's collections.

Nevertheless, Philips's harrowing reportage splices cleanly into Hakluyt's larger themes and purposes. Newfound America is, in both senses, appealing: appealingly lucrative, noble, and nubile (even in chains); and, crying out from those chains, it is appealing for deliverance. Imperial Spain is, on the other hand, unspeakable: duplicitous, dumbfoundingly cruel, prodigiously greedy, and pervasively loathed—even by many of its own gentlefolk and religious. If the time seems ripe for strategic English inroads "from the point of Florida Northward," the time also may be ripening for a liberating struggle in New Spain itself, the very belly of the beast.

Indeed, a promising precedent for such an English-led insurgency had already been set by Drake during his 1572 raids in Panama. There he formed a remarkably equal alliance with the *cimarrones,* or maroons, a loose-knit but much-feared confederation of escaped African slaves intent on terrorizing their former Spanish masters. With their substantial help (and with that of a French Huguenot pirate named Le Testu), Drake captured a two-hundred-mule train carrying bullion over the isthmus from Panama City to Nombre de Dios on the Gulf—a prize of about £40,000 in Elizabethan money.[7] Drake found common ground with his allies in their shared sense of injury at Spanish hands; Drake had lived, like Miles Philips, through an ambush at San Juan D'Ulua, and now he began to fulfill his personal threat of vengeance on the viceroy.

Liberating paradise: Ralegh in Guiana

Besides Drake's, probably the most famous anti-Spanish voice in England was that of Sir Walter Ralegh, who seldom neglected an opportunity to enlarge upon "the Spanish cruelties." Ralegh takes special pains to portray the English as restrained and virtuous liberators in narrating his own 1595 voyage up Guiana's Orinoco River in search of the ever-receding El Dorado. Actually, however, it was Ralegh's own self-restraint—or lack of it—that sparked his long and ultimately fatal attraction to Guianan gold. In 1592, Queen Elizabeth discovered that her powerful favorite had not only seduced but, perhaps worse in her view, secretly married one of her young ladies-in-waiting, Elizabeth Throgmorton. The queen's response was to imprison both Ralegh and his new wife in the Tower of London, and upon his release in 1594, Ralegh was adrift. Because he had possessed few material assets before winning the queen's affections fifteen years earlier, her

---

7. Sugden, *Sir Francis Drake,* 61–75.

disenchantment was tantamount to financial destruction. As Louis Montrose and Mary C. Fuller both note, one anonymous wag is said to have written that "All is alarm and confusion at this discovery of the discoverer, and not indeed of a new continent, but of a new incontinent" (Montrose 185–86; Fuller, *Voyages* 74).[8]

So Ralegh caught eagerly in 1594 at a slight sign of returning royal favor, a commission to prosecute a private strategy challenging Spain's hegemony in the Caribbean and South America. He was already noted, and notorious, as the sponsor of three failed attempts in the 1580s to colonize the coast of present-day North Carolina, but he had always managed in the past to parlay his losses into gains, and he saw his main, and perhaps his last, chance in "El Dorado." He sailed to Guiana in 1595, hoping to discover a storied empire of rich, remnant Incas eager for protection from Iberian invasion, or at least to find enough treasure in the Orinoco basin to restore himself to the queen's full graces. Instead, he returned to produce in 1596 his account of the expedition, *The Discoverie of the Large, Rich, and Beautiful Empire of Guiana,* which presented the queen with what he hoped would be three enchanting prospects: a promise of golden empire in a new Eden, the protection of that Eden from insinuating Spaniards, and the evidence that, as Montrose puts it, the "discovery of a new continent discovers him to be newly continent" (187).

Thus, in some of the most rhetorically supercharged passages in the narrative, Ralegh stresses the paradisal, ore-bearing abundance of the feminized Guianan landscape and the alluring prelapsarian nakedness of its female inhabitants. He also stresses, in contrast to the rapacious and lecherous Catholic Spaniards, the courteous and chaste restraint that distinguishes him and his fellow servants of the Protestant Virgin Queen. Indeed, the very approach to the inland empire is portrayed in lyric language that rolls back the thorns and thistles of Adam's curse and displaces them with the restored Garden of God. The land was, writes Ralegh, "the most beautifull . . . that euer mine eies beheld: and whereas all that we had seen before was nothing but woods, prickles, bushes, and thornes, heere we beheld plaines of twenty miles in length, the grasse short and greene, and in diuers parts groues of trees by themselues, as if they had been by all the art and labour in the world so made of purpose . . . the birds towards the

---

8. Louis Montrose, "The Work of Gender in the Discourse of Discovery"; Mary C. Fuller, "Ralegh's Fugitive Gold: Reference and Deferral in *The Discoverie of Guiana*"; and Mary C. Fuller, *Voyages in Print: English Travel to America, 1576–1624,* chap. 2, 55–84. Citations of these three pieces will be made parenthetically as "Montrose"; "Fuller, 'Fugitive'"; and "Fuller, *Voyages*."

euening singing in euery tree with a thousand seueral tunes."[9] Furthermore, this peaceable kingdom also has excellent military and mineralogical possibilities, "the ground of hard sand easie to march on, eyther for horse or foote . . . and euery stone that we stooped to take vp, promised eyther golde or siluer by his complexion" (Ralegh 82). Neither does this Eden lack for ripe and guileless Eves, of whom "we saw many hundreds, and had many in our power, and of those very yoong, and excellently fauored which came among vs without deceit, starke naked" (61). Summing up the virgin land in his narrative's most famous phrase, Ralegh promises that "*Guiana* is a Countrey that yet hath her Maydenhead. . . . It hath neuer beene entred by any armie of strength, and neuer conquered or possesed by any Christian Prince" (115).

The credit for Guiana's enduring "Maydenhead" Ralegh ascribes doubly to the Protestant English; first, for their chaste restraint in the face of temptations both sexual and material, and second, for their rescue of virgin Guiana from the lust and greed of Spain. Ralegh had introduced himself to the Indians as "the servant of a Queene . . . who was a virgin," and who was "an enemy to the [Spaniards] in respect of their tyrannie and oppression" (8). Accordingly, Ralegh praises the Virgin Queen's exceptionally chaste soldiers, swearing that although they were tempted to the sorest degree, "I neither know nor beleeue, that any of our companie one or other, by violence or otherwise, euer knew any of their women." Nor did the English violate the virgin land; they resisted temptations to open the natives' gold-filled graves and to steal their gold-laden canoes, and indeed declined to steal "so much as a *Pina*, or a *Potato* roote" (61).

Instead, Ralegh repeatedly asserts that Elizabeth has sent them as liberators and protectors because she, "having freed all the coast of the northern world from [Spanish] servitude," desires now "to defend the countrey of *Guiana* from their inuasion and conquest" (8). The Guianans already had tasted the deceit and atrocity of the Spaniards, who not only stole their gold but also "tooke from them both their wiues, and daughters daily, and used them for the satisfying of their own lusts, especially such as they took in this manner by strength" (61). Thus the natives are happy to aid Ralegh in attacking the Spanish stronghold at San José, which he burns "at the instance of the Indians" (8). In short, Ralegh's controlling narrative conceit is to present himself as both the discoverer of a new Eden and as the avenging guardian angel whose flaming sword will keep

---

9. Sir Walter Ralegh, *The Discoverie of the Large, Rich, and Beautiful Empire of Guiana*, ed. Sir Robert H. Schomburgk (1898; reprint, New York: Burt Franklin, n.d.), 57, 82. All further citations of this edition will be made parenthetically.

the ejected Spanish serpent out of the Garden. It is his exceptionally pious restraint—"before the maiestie of the liuing God" (61) and the majesty of his imperial queen—that merits possession.

It is this enduring dream of a liberating English conquest of America, of rolling back an empire that Las Casas had called "Moorish," "barbarian," "hellish," and "infernal"—indeed, of regaining lost paradises beyond the sea—that brings us to the chief literary fruit of this historicizing: namely, the question of John Milton's Satan as a conquistador.

Milton's Satan as Conquistador

How imperialist, or anti-imperialist, was Milton? Was he, as David Quint, Andrew Barnaby, and Diane Kelsey McColley argue, straightforwardly anti-colonial by the time he wrote his great epics in the 1660s?[10] That Milton held more divided views on colonialism is suggested by the rich pattern of parallels in *Paradise Lost* between Satan's overthrow of Eden and Cortés's conquest of what Milton calls "Rich *Mexico* the seat of *Montezume*."[11] This other "fall" the poet found rendered in sixteenth-century accounts by Las Casas, José de Acosta, and Francisco López de Gómara—all reprinted in English by Samuel Purchas in the 1625 edition of *Hakluytus Posthumus, or Purchas His Pilgrimes*.[12] Indeed, Milton's own nephew and student, John Phillips, produced in 1656 *The*

---

10. David Quint, *Epic and Empire: Politics and Generic Form from Virgil to Milton*; Andrew Barnaby, "'Another Rome in the West?': Milton and the Imperial Republic, 1654–1670"; Diane Kelsey McColley, "Ecology and Empire," 112–29.

11. John Milton, *Paradise Lost*, in *Complete Poems and Major Prose*, ed. Merrit Y. Hughes (Indianapolis: Odyssey, 1957), 11.407. Unless otherwise indicated, all further citations of *Paradise Lost* will be made parenthetically to this edition by book and line numbers.

12. Samuel Purchas, *Hakluytus Posthumus, or Purchas His Pilgrimes*. Hereafter I will cite Purchas parenthetically by volume and page numbers. There can be no doubt that Milton knew and read *Purchas His Pilgrimes;* the table at the end of his *Brief History of Moscovia* names the voluminous collection as a major source. See John Milton, *Complete Prose Works of John Milton*, 537–38. Furthermore, Robert Ralston Cawley notes the "incontrovertible evidence" of Milton's quotations from Purchas in his commonplace book. See Cawley's *Milton and the Literature of Travel*, 96–97. Cawley argues that Milton's unusual spelling of the Inca emperor's name in *Paradise Lost* (11. 406–10) indicates that the poet's source for these Mexican and Peruvian references is Purchas rather than his favorite geographical compendium, Peter Heylyn's *Cosmographie*. Regarding the Incas, one could make a related case from Purchas for Pizarro as another satanic model. I have focused on Cortés because he was the first and thus the prototypical conquistador, and because his exploits parallel Satan's more often—and for brevity's sake.

Tears of the Indians, his translation of Las Casas's *Brevíssima relación* (*A Short Account*).[13]

Milton's Mexican motif stops short of historical allegory like Spenser's in *The Faerie Queene*, and it coexists with a dazzling variety of other motifs; nevertheless, his stream of allusion does create a kind of reverse historical typology. Spanish methods of conquest both anticipate and fulfill Satan's strategy of assault on Eden: bold spiritual duplicity. Like Cortés, Milton's Satan succeeds against seemingly great odds by manipulating and mastering the native religious imagination through the crucial agency of a woman.

Milton and antihispanicism

It should be clear by now how anti-Iberianism would have come naturally to Englishmen of Milton's generation—born soon after Elizabeth's death in 1603, reared under James I and Charles I, and many like Milton eventually rising up against the house of Stuart after 1642 for more radically Protestant reform of church, state, and society. The early Stuarts usually suppressed anti-Spanish writings in order to pursue a policy of "détente" with Spain, yet, as William S. Maltby writes, "the majority of the English people were lying in enforced quiescence, awaiting the dawn of another day." Indeed, the spectacle of England's crowned head bowing so appeasingly toward Spain seems to have heightened England's suppressed hispanophobia, creating a deep longing for a renewal of their fathers' and grandfathers' Protestant crusade. After Charles I's crown and head fell under Oliver Cromwell's axe in 1649, that day came with a vengeance.[14]

Especially during the Cromwellian Protectorate of 1653–1658, antihispanicism would again receive official promotion and take arms as active foreign policy. And that policy was active indeed: in 1654 the Lord Protector, without any Spanish provocation, launched an invasion fleet against Spain's West Indian colonies, and in 1655 he issued *A Declaration . . . against Spain* that called for nothing less than a religious crusade to liberate all of Spanish America. As Cromwell's Latin secretary, Milton contributed his *Latin Manifesto*, arguing Cromwell's neo-Elizabethan case in the language of international learning.[15] The debt of these declarations to Las Casas is clear, and to complete the connection,

---

13. John Phillips, *The Tears of the Indians*.
14. William S. Maltby, *The Black Legend in England*, 114–15.
15. Ibid., 117–20.

in the next year Milton's nephew John Phillips translated Las Casas's *Brevíssima relación* (*A Short Account*) as *The Tears of the Indians.*

The military fruits of Cromwell's "Western Design" were disappointing, though not unimportant—in 1656, the English took Jamaica, continuing a process (begun with Barbados) that eventually brought much of the Caribbean under British rule. The literary fruits were, in Milton's case, rich, and in a few other cases, strange. One of the strangest is a Puritan opera, specially commissioned by Cromwell, entitled *The Cruelty of the Spaniards in Peru.* Written under special dispensation by the pardoned Stuart dramatist William Davenant and produced in London in 1658, it draws obviously on Las Casas's most sensational materials. Indeed, in one of its stage directions, it seems to epitomize the English image of the satanic Spaniard: the curtains open on captive Peru, revealing "Racks and other Engines of torment, with which the Spaniards are tormenting the Natives and English Mariners. . . . Two Spaniards are likewise discover'd, sitting in their cloakes, and appearing more solemn in Ruffs, with Rapiers and Daggers by their sides; the one turning a Spit, whilst the other is basting an *Indian Prince,* which is rosted at an artificiall fire."[16] Yet deliverance comes by the end of this opera: fulfilling Cromwell's wildest dreams, English troops storm in to the rescue like angels harrowing hell, dispatch the craven Spaniards, and receive the grateful allegiance of the liberated Peruvians.

Given Milton's active participation in a regime that found such uses for Spanish atrocity, it is necessary to recognize that his anti-imperial impulses, so powerfully expressed by Jesus in book 3 of *Paradise Regain'd,* had their limits. As J. Martin Evans writes in *Milton's Imperial Epic,* "Everything depended [for Milton] on the identity of the colonizer, the nature of the colonized, and the purpose of the colony."[17] In other words, Milton saw imperial expansion through a complex moral glass. While he believed that English rule also could be perverted to infernal ends, his antidote to evil empire was good empire, rather than none at all—for his God is an Emperor too.

"Glistering Spires and Pinnacles adorn'd": Ibero-American parallels

Many parallels between the Satanic and Iberian enterprises in *Paradise Lost* involve basic matters of setting and plot. David Quint has looked for analogues mainly to Portugal and the East, demonstrating that Satan's voyage in books 2

---

16. William Davenant, *The Cruelty of the Spaniards in Peru,* 19–20.
17. J. Martin Evans, *Milton's Imperial Epic,* 146, 147.

and 3 parodies Vasco da Gama's discovery of the sea route to India, as rendered by Luis de Canoëns in *Os Lusiadas*.[18] But Milton's allusions to Spain's western discoveries are equally suggestive. These begin with Satan's commission in Pandemonium. Speaking under the Vatican-like dome of Hell's capital, his lieutenant Beelzebub climaxes the hellish consult by proposing the "easier enterprise" (2.345) of an attack on the "happy isle" (2.410) of this "new world" (2.403).

> . . . here perhaps
> Some advantageous act may be achiev'd
> By sudden onset: either with Hell fire
> To waste his whole Creation, or possess
> All as our own, and drive as we were driven,
> The puny habitants, or if not drive,
> Seduce them to our Party . . .
> (2.362–68)

Beelzebub envisions a kind of geopolitical coup, one that we can recognize as analogous to Spain's American outflanking of its Islamic and Christian rivals at the end of the fifteenth century.[19]

Also, while Satan the navigator may resemble da Gama and Columbus, as a traveler he is even more like the wily Cortés. There is more at work in Satan's successful voyage than mariner's luck, skill, and perseverance; there is also, most essentially, interpersonal guile. In his crucial negotiations at the frontiers guarded by Sin, Death, and Chaos in book 2, Satan seems less like Columbus the earnestly persistent and more like Cortés the trickster.

First of all, both Satan and Cortés opportunistically stoke the fires of resentment and dissension. Cortés's chaplain, Gómara, writes that, upon reaching the Mexican coast, Cortés found Montezuma's outlying imperial vassals ripe for rebellion and sought their aid and direction. The Indians of Cempoala and of Tlaxcala further inland were "not well affected to Mutezuma, but readie, as farre as they durst, to entertayne all occasions of warre with him" (Purchas 15.509).

---

18. Quint, *Epic and Empire*, 253–56; see also James H. Sims, "Camoens' *Lusiads* and Milton's *Paradise Lost:* Satan's Voyage to Eden."

19. Advancing the intriguing claim that Cromwell served as a model for Satan, Robert Thomas Fallon associates this passage with the Protector's Western Design and English hopes during the 1650s to seize Spain's possessions in the New World. However, as Fallon admits, "Satan's expedition enjoys more success than did Cromwell's"—indeed, so much more that, I would argue, the original Spanish conquerors are the more plausible referent here. See Robert Thomas Fallon, *Divided Empire: Milton's Political Imagery*, 130.

Similarly, in *Paradise Lost,* Sin and Chaos, while nominally subject to God "th' Ethereal King" (2.978), willingly receive Satan's flattering promises that his mission will yield rich booty and restore their rightful power and sovereignty over the realms lately possessed by the divine Emperor. "[I] shall soon return," Satan assures his daughter and lover, Sin, "And bring ye to the place where Thou and Death . . . shall be fed and fill'd / Immeasurably, all things shall be your prey" (2.839–40, 843–44). Further on, Satan implores the personified Chaos to "direct my course," for, he promises,

> Directed, no mean recompense it brings
> To your behoof, if I that Region lost,
> All usurpation thence expelled, reduce
> To her original darkness and your sway
>   (2.980–84)

So Chaos blesses the venture and shows the way, and Satan wastes no time in launching out on the last leg of his journey to "this frail World" (2.1030).

After Satan's voyage and earthly landfall, Milton's reimagining of earth and Eden as an idealized western planting permeates the poem. Though he explicitly compares the "gentle gales" that "dispense / Native perfumes" to the exotic east of "Mozambic" and "Araby the blest" (4.156–63 passim), aromatic breezes also announce the American shore: from Columbus's first scent of San Salvador and Hispaniola, to Michael Drayton's Edenic Virginia and Andrew Marvell's imagined Bermudas, the west is also the land of spices.[20]

Yet Milton evokes not only pre-Columbian America's fragrant garden delights but also its golden and urban splendors. The conquistadors came west for treasure, and Satan has an eye for it as well—the "golden Chain" that Satan sees linking Earth to Heaven (2.1051), the "potable gold" of Earth's rivers (3.608), and especially the "vegetable gold" hanging from the Trees of Life and Knowledge (4.218–20; 9.575–78). Similarly, Cortés wonders at the Mexicans' "simplicitie" in undervaluing their abundant gold and touts it as a literally consumable elixir, telling Montezuma's emissary that "he and his fellowes had a disease of the heart, whereunto Gold was the best remedie" (Purchas 15.507–8). Similarly Satan, by claiming to have consumed the golden fruit, persuades innocent Eve in book 9 of its transformative powers (9.568–612).

---

20. For America's sweets and Columbus, see Lunenfeld, ed., *1492: Discovery, Invasion, Encounter,* 44–45; for Virginia, see Michael Drayton, "Ode. To the Virginian Voyage," in *Poems,* 1: 124, ll. 43–48; for Bermuda, see Andrew Marvell, "Bermudas," in *Andrew Marvell: The Complete Poems,* 116–17.

However, when Satan first sees the Earth, Milton compares the view to a city, not to a garden, and the view is strikingly similar to the Spanish scout's first sight of the Mexican capital from the barren volcanic pass of Mount Popocatepetl, looking down on the cities glittering on Lake Texcoco. In *Paradise Lost*, the epic simile unfolds as Satan

> Looks down with wonder at the sudden view
> Of all the World at once. As when a Scout
> Through dark and desert ways with peril gone
> . . . .
> Obtains the brow of some high-climbing Hill,
> Which to his eye discovers unaware
> The goodly prospect of some foreign land
> First seen, or some renown'd Metropolis
> With glistering Spires and Pinnacles adorn'd,
> Which now the Rising Sun gilds with his beams.
> (3.542–44, 546–51)

Likewise, in Gómara's words, Tenochtitlán and its sister cities were "an exceeding goodly sight. But when Cortés saw that beautiful thing, his joy was without comparison. . . . Whoever hath good eyesight might discern the gates of [Tenochtitlán]. . . . These Towres [of the cities Coyoacan and Vizilopuchtli] are planted in the Lake, and are adorned with many Temples, which have many faire Towres, that doe beautifie exceedingly the Lake. . . . [and] many drawne Bridges built upon faire arches" (Purchas 15.520–21, 522, 523). Even the roadways into Tenochtitlán and Eden are similarly convenient. Gómara writes that the Mexican capital was entered over "a faire calsey [causeway], upon which eight horsemenne may passe on ranke, and so directly straight as though it had been made by line" (Purchas 15.523). Likewise, Satan sees "A passage down to th' Earth, a passage wide" (3.528).

The plumed serpent in the Garden: Satan, Cortés, and the natives

Beyond these details of setting and plot, Milton's parallels to Mexico's overthrow affect character, as well. In book 4 of *Paradise Lost*, the poet famously complicates Satan's psyche as the fiend soliloquizes his self-doubts after first entering Eden. Likewise, Gómara tells of how Cortés, having penetrated to the heart of the Aztec empire, began to be "disquieted with those thoughts which commonly attend Ambition (discontent in the present, hopes and feares of the future)." But soon Cortés, like Satan, hardens himself for the work of destruction, indeed burning his own ships and vanquishing Spanish troops sent from Cuba by the governor to stop him (Purchas 15.514; *Paradise Lost* 4.109–13).

Milton's handling of Satan's chief victims, Adam and Eve, partakes of the conquest narratives as well, although in their case Milton's most influential sources seem not to be those of Cortés's postconquest chaplain, Gómara, but of the missionary priests Las Casas and Acosta. J. Martin Evans argues plausibly that Adam and Eve resemble Las Casas's native Americans, "obedient children eager for instruction" and needing special protection.[21] And indeed, the first inhabitants of Eden's "steep savage Hill" (4.172) are noble, naïve "primitives," and very biblically naked (4.288–99). However, in keeping with Eden's urban aspect, Adam and Eve are also imperial, "in native honor clad," mastering all that they survey. Theirs is a promised dynastic rule over all creation, and the top of Paradise's mountain "to our general Sire gave prospect large / Into his nether Empire neighboring round" (4.144–45). Eve in particular, golden and nubile, calls to mind the eroticized American landscape itself, personified in Renaissance engravings as a classically proportioned queen, crowned and unclad.[22]

However, the most arresting resemblance between Milton's Satan and Purchas's Cortés is in their means of attack. Vastly outnumbered in terms of force, each triumphs by insinuating himself into religious premonitions and imaginings at the cultic center of native life, thus capturing hearts and minds. Gómara reports the overwhelming odds: "400 Spaniards, fifteene horses, and six peeces of Artillery, and 1300 Indians" from insurgent Cempoala, against hundreds of thousands of Aztec soldiers (Purchas 15.510, 511). Even considering the technological advantage of Cortés's few cannon, Mexico's sudden "fall" has often beggared explanation.[23] But the priest Acosta explains this fall with certainty as a spiritual coup: Cortés brilliantly exploited native metaphysics. Upon landing, he soon discovered that he was being taken as a kind of Aztec Second Coming. The news of bearded white men in ships, says Acosta, "much troubled Moteçuma, and conferring with his Counsell, they all said that without doubt, their great and aunciet Lord Queztalcoalt [Quetzalcóatl, or "plumed serpent"] was come, who had said, that he would returne from the East. . . . Cortés finding

---

21. Evans, *Milton's Imperial Epic*, 95–98.
22. Lunenfeld, ed., *1492: Discovery, Invasion, Encounter*, 119–24, figs. A-3, A-4, A-5, and A-6.
23. Inga Clendennin, "'Fierce and Unnatural Cruelty': Cortés and the Conquest of Mexico," 12–17.

this a good occasion for this entry, commanded to decke his Chamber richly, and being set in great state and pompe, caused the [Aztec] Ambassadors to enter . . . to worship him as their god" (Purchas 15.288–89). There is certainly an important difference between the human Cortés embracing godhood himself and the immortal Satan promising it to others. Yet by the time he reaches Eden, Satan has in book 2 already accepted divine worship from his fellow demons in Hell. It is in this shared blasphemous pride and actor's skill that the link between conquistador and devil would probably be strongest in Milton's imagination. Indeed, Cortés's careful staging of his scene with the worshipful ambassadors resonates with Milton's actorly Tempter, who, in book 9, a "new part puts on" to seduce Eve (9.667).

Furthermore, Eve's biblically based role as Satan's mediatrix of deception and overthrow has intriguing analogues in Mexico's destruction. Significantly, Cortés was aided throughout the conquest by the Aztec-Mayan noblewoman "Doña Marina," who served as his translator and go-between. Indeed, it is possible, though not demonstrable, that Milton knew Bernal Díaz del Castillo's *Historia verdadera de la conquista de la Nueva España* (*The True History of the Conquest of New Spain*), which was not published until 1632 and therefore not translated or included by Purchas. If so, Milton may have found in Doña Marina an especially powerful Edenic resonance. According to Bernal Díaz, it was Doña Marina (alias Malinali, Malintze, or "La Malinche") who helped persuade Montezuma to yield himself and his empire to Cortés's fatal protection. She was not only the *caudillo*'s translator but his concubine, a medium of both linguistic and sexual intercourse.[24] Milton's Eve, whose intercourse with the attracted and attractive serpent is not physically sexual, uses her verbal appeal and sexually "sweet attractive grace" to bring Adam into uxorious idolatry of herself and service to Satan.

"Death's ministers, not men": devastating triumphs

The aftermath of Eden's loss also seems colored by Mexico's. In 1521, over a rebuilt causeway, on August 13—the Aztec day "1-Serpent"—the self-declared servants of the pontiff streamed into ruined Tenochtitlán. In Milton's epic, over a

---

24. See Hugh Thomas, *Conquest: Montezuma, Cortés, and the Fall of Old Mexico*, 224, 242, 325, 580, 622. See also Stephen Greenblatt's discussion of Doña Marina as a representative "Go-Between"—"half divinity, half whore, the savior and the betrayer" in *Marvelous Possessions*, 143–45.

causeway built "by wondrous art / Pontifical," the infernal occupiers crowd onto the Earth, bringing chaos, disease, and death with devastating force (10.312–51). In destroying old Mexico, says Gómara, Cortés "now did the utmost that Rage and Revenge could effect, helped no lesse within with Famine and Pestilence, then with Sword and Fire without. At last Mexico is razed, the Earth and Water sharing betwixt them what the Fire had left, and all which had sometime challenged a lofty inheritance in the Ayre" (Purchas 15.517). The conquest seems to shake not only the foundations of a culture but of the cosmos; it enlists the Four Elements themselves. After suffering this desolation—"of the Mexicans, a hundred thousand [slain]"—the former Aztec capital becomes the staging ground for the further subjugation of all New Spain.

In book 11 of *Paradise Lost*, Adam stands grief-stricken while Michael displays in a panorama the coming waves of human warfare and massacre spreading outward from surrendered Eden: "O what are these," Adam cries,

> Death's ministers, not men, who thus deal death
> Inhumanly to men, and multiply
> Ten-thousandfold the sin of him who slew
> His brother; for of whom such massacre
> Make they but of their brethren, men of men?
> (11.675–80)

So from each conqueror's voyage and first landfall, through his brilliantly insidious tactics, to his devastating triumph, Milton appears to associate Satan with Cortés pervasively. Yet he makes this connection less explicit than he does with Satan's classical or oriental analogues.

This hide-in-plain-sight pattern is itself suggestive about his rhetorical purposes. Perhaps Milton insinuates—rather than proclaims—Satan's Hispanic "lineage" in order to augment his well-known device of glamorizing the Adversary at first in order to undo him more tellingly at last. Much like Satan's attractive early rhetoric of heroic self-determination—which is finally reduced to self-deceived idiocy—his initially dogged and resourceful pursuit of empire turns out to be an adventure in mass extermination, worthy of Spain's *leyenda negra*. The marks of weakness and woe were of course there all along, indicated by the narrator's warning voice, but it is the incremental outworking of Satan's soul-numbing atrocity that makes us finally feel his evil in our pulses.

I have already noted that these strands of historical allusion do not make *Paradise Lost* a full-fledged historical allegory like Spenser's *Faerie Queene*. Still, these allusions do not merely serve Milton's portrayal of eternal versus infernal empires, but they inevitably reflect upon specific temporal empires as well.

Satan may be Milton's great universal figure of soul-killing pride, but Satan's resemblances to Hispanic—and at other times Islamic—conquerors suggest that for Milton, some particular cultures and religions predispose the soul to imperial arrogance more than do others. Thus Satan's frequent Spanish inflections and his "pontifical art" suggest that Milton's deeply felt anti-imperialism was nevertheless conditional—that anti-imperialism might indeed require some answering imperialism of one's own, some empire of liberty.

This conditionality has lately become the subject of debate. As I have noted, David Quint, Andrew Barnaby, and Diane Kelsey McColley have argued for a late Milton who is straightforwardly anti-imperial. Barnaby notes, I think correctly, that at some time between the writing of *The Second Defense of the English People* in 1654 and *The Readie and Easie Way To Establish a Free Commonwealth* in 1660, Milton soured on the "Imperial Republic" because late Commonwealth colonial policy had abandoned its transatlantic spiritual mission for mere expansion and trade.[25] Yet Milton's very disillusionment still contained his enduring ideal of an English Protestant empire, one able to redeem lost paradises beyond the seas. Evans shows that, while an English colony like Virginia in the hands of royalists and prelates might seem to Milton little better than its Iberian adversaries, a puritan colony like New England was for him "a shining example to the rest of Europe," a light to the heathen, and a hedge against the Spaniard (146–47).

Though Milton grew disenchanted with Cromwellian compromises, we should not confuse his forced post-Restoration retreat with acquiescence or surrender. In terms of England's domestic affairs, Milton's return to poetry after 1660 was no mere quietism or withdrawal from politics, but rather, as Laura Lunger Knoppers has suggested, "a complex internalization of Puritan discipline that can carry on the Good Old Cause in the very theater of the Stuart monarchy."[26] Thus in *Paradise Lost,* as well as in *Paradise Regain'd* and *Samson Agonistes,* Milton seeks to restore right reason with an eventual view to restoring right rule at home. In other words, his retreat is strategic. Similarly, beyond the domestic sphere, when *Paradise Lost* exploits colonial imagery so extensively so soon after the failure of Cromwell's "imperial republic," Milton is not merely spiritualizing a language of defeated earthly hopes. Instead, he is practicing another kind of strategic retreat, engaging in what Blake aptly called "mental fight"—stiffening the heart's sinews against all temporally and temporarily ascendant tyrannies,

---

25. Barnaby, "'Another Rome,'" 67–84.
26. Laura Lunger Knoppers, *Historicizing Milton: Spectacle, Power, and Poetry in Restoration England,* 12.

whether in the heart or at home or abroad. He is biding his time, the reader's time, the nation's time, serving by standing and waiting for Providence to show his hand. Like Cortés the conquistador, like the conquistadorial Satan, Milton knows that conquest, and reconquest, start with the soul's invisible empire. And Milton never fully abandons his belief that war against flesh and blood has its place in the wars of the spirit.

Atrocious Comparisons: John Sparke on the Slave Coast

I have argued that early English Protestant imperialism could shine in relative beneficence—even for an imagination as morally acute as Milton's—because it enjoyed the dire backdrop of the dark Iberian Other. Yet it is instructive to remember that the Spaniards had a looming adversarial Other as well, and their own corresponding "White Legend": the medieval *Reconquista* of their peninsula from the Moors, and their wars against the Turks. Anthony Pagden has written that Spain's empire began in the early sixteenth century as "the self-assured champion (and exporter) of Christian cultural values, the secular arm of the papacy, and the sole guardian of political stability within Europe," and ended as "the paradigm of an archaic tyranny, a political analogue of that oriental despotate whose expansionist ambitions it had once fought so hard to keep in check."[27] Joseph Conrad's Marlow warns that "the conquest of the earth... is not a pretty thing when you look into it too much."[28] And the conquerors had best avoid looking into the mirror; it is not uncommon among persons, as among nations, to be changed through enmity into the image of one's enemy. How susceptible the English were to this ironic transformation can perhaps be guessed at in the account of John Sparke.

Again, it was Hakluyt who published Sparke's narrative, which includes his 1564 encounter with the people he calls "Sabies" on the island of Sambula, off the West African "Slave Coast" (*PN* 10.17–21). He first meets the Sabies as slaves of their neighboring enemies, the "Samboses," and of the Portuguese; then he and his fellow English voyagers penetrate to unconquered Sabie country and observe them at home. Sparke's copious praise for the Sabies is especially

---

27. Pagden, *Spanish Imperialism*, 2. Indeed, the English epithet "Spanish cruelty" had its earlier Spanish equivalent in the phrase "Moorish barbarism"—a phrase that Las Casas applies to the Spanish conquistadors themselves. See Pagden's introduction to Las Casas's *Short Account*, xxxix.

28. Conrad, *Heart of Darkness*, 32.

striking because it focuses not on prodigious native physiques or doglike loyalty (typically backhanded European compliments for "savages") but rather on their harmonious and provident social order. He has not learned (or does not use) the language of colonial condescension; instead, he describes their communities in terms that could apply to Englishmen. Indeed, in their village of Sambula, the streets are straight, the counselors are wise, the fruit is plentiful, and the "Palmito wine" is free. Sparke is no larking humanist supposing a utopia; rather, he describes a particular West African island kingdom that, with some effort, an Englishman might visit, and in visiting might greatly admire—Sparke seems, in a degree remarkable for his time, to have ventured not only beyond his nation but beyond his nationalism. He renders a society that is beautiful with the beauty of a real thing, like some well-observed tropical fruit radiating in delicious symmetry from its firm core. It is like a fruit that an admirer might grasp, pluck, and consume.

As indeed the admiring John Sparke did; his description of the Sabies is remarkable not only for its admiration but also because his captain was John Hawkins, their ship the *Jesus of Lubeck,* and their enterprise the inauguration of the English slave trade. We are reminded in mid-paragraph that this cross-cultural litany of praise is also a bill of lading; he had begun by saying that "[i]n this Island we stayed certaine daies, going every day on shore to take the Inhabitants, with burning and spoiling their townes." Now, unblinking, Sparke returns from his encomium to business: "In this Island aforesayde wee sojourned unto the one and twentieth of December, where having taken certaine Negros, and as much of their fruites, rise, and mill, as we could well cary away, (whereof there was such store, that we might have laden one of our Barkes therewith) we departed." One thinks again of Milton's Satan, struck momentarily good by the sight of unfallen Eve in book 9, standing still in a kind of ethical fermata—and then resuming his mission (ll. 444–66).

Yet the real frisson that one feels at this passage comes not from any overt Satanism in Sparke but from his very lack of it. One longs strangely for Luciferian malice, for the comfort of Las Casas's glamorously grotesque conquistadors, their souls burning with hellfire, relishing their victims' anguish like strong wine. One at least wishes that, like Hannah Arendt's Eichmann, Sparke had had the decency to be soulless and banal. But for him to look in the face of a good thing, to feel its goodness and its smile, and to smile in return and say to us "Look!"—and then, tearless and dutiful, to clap it in irons and burn it to ashes. What, one wonders, could have possessed him?

If asked, perhaps he would say that it was simply a matter of victors' spoils and trade—that the "Samboses" enslave conquered Sabies and that the Sabies sell their own convicted thieves to the Portuguese. Very likely he would add that, for the people of the Slave Coast, the choice was between chains Iberian or English, and that some of the English profit at least would go to fight the Roman Antichrist. And probably he would remind us that, in this transaction with the Sabies, there was, at least, no worship given or asked, and no *Spanish* cruelty.

Thus did early English imperialism—replete as it was to be with piracy, kidnapping, slaving, and the more than occasional massacre—imagine possession. Such transactions are the true price of defining oneself by oppositions, and in them we scent the true odiousness of comparisons. What possessed a man like John Sparke? An adversarial spirit, one might say; weighing lesser cruelties against greater ones—trading in the coin of the atrocious, indispensable enemy.

Three

Stooping to Conquer

Heathen Idolatry, Protestant Humility, and the "White Legend" of Drake

Humble yourselves therefore under the mighty hand of God, that in due time he may exalt you. —*1 Peter 5:6*

[W]hen lenity and cruelty play for a kingdom, the gentler gamester is the soonest winner. —Henry V *3.6.111–13*

Thou concludest like the sanctimonious pirate, that went to sea with the Ten Commandments, but scraped one out of the table. —*Lucio in* Measure for Measure *1.2.7–8*

I have been examining the religious origins of the British imperial imagination. Thus far I have considered how Tudor-Stuart Protestants reformed the Arthurian chronicles and claimed the *translatio imperii* from the Caesars; I also have described how they proposed to free the subject peoples of the rival Spanish Empire from spiritual and political bondage. Both of these unifying religious elements—a sense of divine imperial destiny and a sense of reforming righteousness—served to bind reviving "Britain" together in imagining an empire. But actually making an empire required more than antiquarian claims and the Black Legend of a common religious enemy; it required action, emboldened by a robust moral exceptionalism, the certainty that one's virtuous conduct validated one's cause. No Elizabethan personified this kind of active, expansive, pious, and at times ruthless confidence better than did Sir Francis Drake.

Yet the Muses seem to have neglected Drake. "It is curious," writes W. T. Jewkes, "that Drake's voyages and exploits have made such a small impact on major English literature, particularly in his own age."[1] On one level, Jewkes is right; as Michael J. B. Allen has noted, there is nothing about Drake in English to compare with Luis de Camoëns's brilliantly realized *Os Lusiadas,* his national epic about the Portuguese mariner Vasco da Gama. So, says Allen, Drake's influence on English literature is only felt "gradually, obliquely, inconspicuously almost," in the imagery of *The Tempest,* in Donne's hymn on his sickness, in Marvell's ode on the Bermudas. "Drake's finest interpreter might have been Conrad," Allen suggests; but he laments that Conrad "left Drake unillumined by his intricate, musical prose."[2]

However, while Jewkes and Allen guard admirably against overstatement, they succumb to its less culpable but still unsatisfying opposite; for in his way, Drake has prospered in the English imagination. Indeed, it is to Drake's encounter with the adoring natives of northern California—at a place that he called "Nova Albion"—that we can most probably trace one of the great sustaining legends of the British Empire, the counter to Spain's *leyenda negra:* the "White Legend" that pious English self-restraint merits possession. In Nova Albion—a name evoking Brutus's ancient conquest of Britain—Drake would get the better of Spain both geographically and morally. Thus Drake's legend comprises the third crucial unifying element in Britain's imperial religion, the exceptionalist conviction that by "re-forming" their ancient empire, reformed British Christians were "reforming" (that is, improving) the conduct of empire itself. As I will show, this legend lived not only in the early exploration narratives but in the fictions of England's most important writers—from Spenser and Shakespeare to Kipling and Conrad—who were to illumine, in lights both splendid and ironic, Drake's colonialist credo: that one can indeed stoop to conquer.

Elementing the Myth: Humble Possession and the Great Taboo

The legend began on the beach. On about June 17, 1579, Drake sailed his lone, treasure-laden ship, the *Golden Hind,* into a protected lagoon a little to the north of present-day San Francisco, probably the bay that now bears his name.

---

1. W. T. Jewkes, "Sir Francis Drake Revived: From Letters to Legend," 112.
2. Michael J. B. Allen, "Fitzgeffrey's Lamentation on the Death of Drake," 109–10.

Having plundered the undefended ports of Spanish America's western coast, he needed a place beyond the viceroy's reach to put ashore for repairs. This he did; and after three days the Miwok people came. What followed was fearsome, farcical, wonderful, and portentous.

At first, the natives stood looking from the nearby hills, in the words of the fullest account, "as men rauished in their mindes . . . their errand being rather with submission and feare to worship vs as Gods, then to haue any warre with vs as with mortall men."³ As they laid down their weapons and approached, Drake and his men handed them English linen loincloths, "withall signifying vnto them we were no Gods, but men, and had neede of such things to couer our own shame." However, the Englishmen's carefully modest protestations had little effect; two days later the Miwok returned. The men came down to the fort with gifts, prostrating themselves, as "the women . . . vsed vnnatural violence against themselues, crying and shrieking piteously, tearing their flesh with their nailes from their cheeks in a monstrous manner, the blood streaming downe along their brests," throwing themselves onto the rocky ground. As they gathered around Drake and his greeting party, their cries grew louder and their prostrations more frequent. In response, Drake called all hands to himself and issued orders: the chaplain, Francis Fletcher, was to read from the Bible, and all the crew were then to join Drake in prayers and the singing of psalms, with their eyes lifted toward heaven. During these devotions, Drake pointed repeatedly away from himself to the sky and motioned often for the prostrate natives to rise.⁴ Then Drake suggested again that they cover their genitals, and the Miwok departed quietly, still mystified.

After three more days they returned, this time with an important chief surrounded by one hundred skin-clad men carrying weapons. Following a ceremonial dance and then a speech by the chief, Drake allowed the male and female dancers into the fort. Again, they surrounded him, singing and shouting; they

---

3. Sir Francis Drake, Bart., *The World Encompassed by Sir Francis Drake*, ed. W. S. W. Vaux (1628, reprint; London: Hakluyt Society, 1854), 120. Vaux's edition is a reprint of Nicholas Bourne's 1628 edition compiled by Drake's namesake nephew and heir, based on the notes of Drake's chaplain, Francis Fletcher. For a full account of the origins of this narrative and its relation to the condensed account in Richard Hakluyt's *Principal Navigations, Voyages, Traffiques and Discoveries*, see David B. Quinn, "Early Accounts of the Famous Voyage"; and below. In Hakluyt's 1589 first edition, the circumnavigation narrative appears as a last-minute insert: leaves Mmm 4–10, a six-leaf gathering between pages 649 and 650; reprinted Glasgow, 1903–1905, 11.101–33. Except where otherwise noted, all citations of the *Principal Navigations* are to the reprint of 1903–1905, and all citations of *The World Encompassed* will be to the reprint of 1854.

4. Drake, *World Encompassed*, 122, 123–24.

motioned for him to sit, placed a shell-and-bone necklace around his neck and a feather headdress on his head. Then joyfully they cried "Hioh! Hioh!" and motioned toward the hills behind. Without pause, Drake formally accepted the free gift of all their lands on behalf of their new sovereign Elizabeth, by the grace of God the first of that name, queen of England, Ireland, and France, and Defender of the Faith. To prove her claim, Drake displayed her picture and her arms in the form of a sixpence fixed into a plate and nailed to a post.[5]

For three weeks, Drake surveyed the coast; it was probably the Dover-like cliffs of the Marin headlands that suggested to him the name "Nova Albion," with its promise of a regeneration of ancient British imperial glory. He remarked on the Edenic qualities of the uplands—"a goodly country, and fruitfull soyle, stored with many blessings fit for the vse of man"—and the Adamic qualities of the people, who, though seduced by "the power of Sathan," were nevertheless "of a tractable, free, and louing nature, without guile or treachery"; and their weapons "more fit for children then for men."[6] Indeed, one early narrative of the landing adds, both wishfully and prophetically, that "there is no part of earth here to be taken up, wherein there is not a reasonable quantity of gold or silver."[7]

Having surveyed the land, where "the Spaniards neuer had any dealing, or so much as set a foote," Drake put out to sea, heading straight west to the Moluccas, beyond the reach of King Philip's galleons.[8] The Reverend Mr. Fletcher, whose careful and at times unsparing journal would provide the basis for all accounts of the voyage, observed that as the crew sang psalms over the ship's rails, the queen's new subjects stood weeping, sacrificing, and tearing their flesh on the receding California shore. Within six years, on Nichola Van Sype's 1585 map of Drake's voyages, the title of "Nova Albio" [sic] designated most of what is now the United States.[9]

Despite the grandiosity of Van Sype's map, Drake's California landfall did not amount to anything in directly geopolitical terms. In fact, many other incidents

---

5. Ibid., 132.
6. Ibid., 132, 129, 131.
7. Hakluyt, *Principal Navigations* (1589), leaf Mmm 8r; in the second edition (1598–1600), Hakluyt amends this circumspectly to "some probable shew of gold or silver," 3.738; in the 1903–1905 edition, see 11.123.
8. Drake, *World Encompassed*, 132.
9. Sugden, *Sir Francis Drake*, illustration 11, between pages 164 and 165. For the journal of Francis Fletcher, see the surviving fragmentary manuscript in the British Library; extensive excerpts in Vaux's 1854 reprint of *The World Encompassed;* and a full printing in N. M. Penzer, ed., *The World Encompassed and Analogous Contemporary Documents.*

on the circumnavigation had more immediate results: his drumhead trial and execution of the mutinous gentleman Thomas Doughty began the leveling of social distinctions onboard English ships; his storm-blown passage southwest of the Strait of Magellan cast doubt on the supposed vastness of "Terra Australis Incognita"; his Spanish treasure raided up the "Backside of America" became the nest egg for future British foreign investment; and his dealings with the Sultan of Ternate began England's East Indies trade.[10]

Indeed, even Drake was aware that the English claim to Nova Albion would be difficult to realize. That major geographic obstacle known as South America in the end ensured that the cities of the California coast would be called San Diego, not Charleston; Monterey, not Plymouth; and San Francisco, not Boston— although the possibility of Puritan settlements in Marin County is delicious to contemplate. And actually, it is likely that the Miwok were offering the English neither their worship nor their land but rather were greeting them as returning spirits of departed ancestors.[11]

Yet none of these cross-purposes diminishes the importance of this event as something imaginatively rich and strange. For, as first reported by Richard Hakluyt in his 1589 *Principal Navigations* and then revived, retold, and redacted over the next four centuries, the tale brings together in unique combination many elements crucial to England's developing imperial imagination: the exotic, paradisal setting reached after tremendous and purifying struggle; the promise of great wealth in the rich, golden land; the handsome, friendly, apparently harmless native people who are nevertheless in bondage to dark spiritual forces and threatened by sinister European powers; the brave, kind, and pious Englishman to whom the benighted natives instinctively and gladly offer worship and sovereignty; and the Englishman's modest refusal of that worship, which further confirms his moral right to rule, and thus redeem, a gratefully subject people. "Humble yourselves therefore under the mighty hand of God," writes Saint Peter, "that in due time he may exalt you."[12] In Drake's case, the "due time" seemed wondrously brief, the exaltation marvelously complete.

As we will see, this legend of heathen idolatry encountering Protestant humility has had a rich and influential life in the literature of exploration and

---

10. See Sugden, *Sir Francis Drake*, for each of these incidents, respectively: Doughty, 113–14; Terra Australis, 118; the "Backside of America," 120–31; and Ternate, 139–41.

11. Sugden, *Sir Francis Drake*, 136. See also Robert F. Heizer, *Elizabethan California*. For Drake's wish that Nova Albion "had layen so fitly for her maiestie to enioy," see Drake, *World Encompassed*, 129.

12. 1 Peter 5:6.

travel, particularly in the many accounts devoted to Drake's "Famous Voyage" of 1577–1580—the provenance and efflorescence of which I will treat in some detail below. However, as I discuss the discovery narratives, I also will look beyond them to consider the place of this legend in the works of important English poets and authors. For Drake's drama of refused deity and embraced sovereignty on the Marin shore is recognizably present in major works by England's literary masters from Drake's time on: in Una's encounter with the "salvage nation" in book 1 of Spenser's *Faerie Queene;* in the themes of awe and possession so central to Shakespeare's *Tempest;* and in the meeting of Defoe's Crusoe with the adoring Friday. Like Hakluyt's *Principal Navigations, The Faerie Queene* displays Britain's imperial imagination in its fast-growing youth, while *Robinson Crusoe* is an expression of that ideology in its robust young adulthood.[13]

Yet I also am interested in imperialism's guilt-ridden late middle age; for implicit in Drake's transaction with the Miwok is a great taboo: that the man who would be God is not worthy to be king. This taboo was at first associated in English minds with the Black Legend of Spain's demonized conquistadors, and I will show in chapters five and six how often it was invoked against Britain's own imperial over-reaching—even during the empire's early growth and heyday. But in this chapter I will narrow my focus to certain works that in one way or another invert the terms of Drake's encounter in order to question or subvert the empire's certainties: Swift's once-superior Gulliver, reduced to shame-faced Yahoo prostration on the beach before his "Houyhnhnm Master"; Kipling's Peachey Carnehan and Danny Dravot, who accept godhood as well as kingship and learn that their subjects reserve their fiercest savagery for fallen idols; and Conrad's Marlow, who discovers the horror at the heart of imperial relations—that the light in them was darkness after all. None of these three writers, not even Kipling, could hold to the orthodox imperial faith—born in Elizabeth's reign—that territorial expansion and fabulous wealth dovetailed neatly with chivalric virtue and apostolic zeal. Thus each of them ironized Drake's legend of righteous possession in order to imagine the empire's moral, or actual, dissolution.

---

13. Thus my argument both complements and modifies Martin Green's, "that the adventure tales that formed the light reading of Englishmen for two hundred years and more after *Robinson Crusoe* were, in fact, the energizing myth of English imperialism." This is true insofar as prose fiction is concerned, but it is prose nonfiction—the writings of Hakluyt and Purchas, and their fellow clerical colonialists—that first captured the English imagination for the expansionist cause. They provided, in the words of the late Victorian and Edwardian literary critic Walter Raleigh, "the great prose epic of the modern English nation." For Green, see *Dreams of Adventure, Deeds of Empire*, 3, 5. For Raleigh, see Hakluyt, *Principal Navigations*, 12.1.

Gentler Gamesters: Besting Spain

Significantly, this sense of empowering righteousness is central to the first surviving literary notice of "Syr Frauncis Drake," in 1585; a doggerel poet named Henry Roberts portrays Drake as "litle David" setting off to beat down the abominable Iberian "Goliah" in the West Indies.[14] As I discussed in chapter two, England's sense of imperial identity was first formed in the giant shadow of Catholic Spain, and Drake—small in stature and great of heart—was the giant-killer.

Like Drake individually, the English nationally were relative latecomers and presumed weaklings in the great games of Renaissance exploration and conquest; but it was their dubious achievement to triumph finally by transforming their almost fatal miscalculation into an opportunity and a virtue. For Spain in the New World had grasped not only tremendous power and incalculable riches; it also had acquired an international reputation for colonial cruelty on a dumbfounding scale. We saw in chapter 2 that through graphic accounts by Bartolomé de Las Casas, the English of Elizabeth and Drake's generation had learned to imagine Spanish America as the ne plus ultra of pharaonic cruelty, confirming recent English experience under "Bloody Mary" Tudor and her Spanish coregent, Philip II.[15] John Foxe's *Acts and Monuments*—first published in 1563, five years after Mary's death and Elizabeth's accession—had documented these domestic martyrdoms in moving detail and had so virtually guaranteed that the nation's emerging imperial imagination would be ardently Protestant.[16]

However, what probably horrified this Protestant imagination as much as the cruelties of Spain's colonial overlords were the repeated accounts of Spain's explorers and conquistadors allowing and even forcing the native peoples to worship them as gods. As William S. Maltby writes, Protestant polemicists typically assumed the Iberians to be "pagans at heart," their inner heathenism being

---

14. Henry Roberts, *A most friendly farewell.* . . . , A3r.

15. See Anthony Pagden's introduction to his translation of Las Casas, *A Short Account of the Destruction of the Indies*, xvii–xxx, for a full biographical sketch. *Brevíssima relación de la destrucción de las Indias*, first published in Seville in 1552, was eventually translated into English in 1583 as *The Spanish Colonie, or, Briefe Chronicle of the Acts and gestes of the Spaniardes in the West Indies, called the newe World*, with the more famous running title, which as we have seen became a kind of epithet, *The Spanish Cruelties*.

16. John N. King notes that in 1571, the English bishops ordered copies of *Actes and Monuments* chained in all cathedrals, giving it "the location that Erasmus's *Paraphrases* had occupied alongside the English Bible under Edward VI"—the canonical position that it also would occupy in countless English and New England homes for the next two centuries. See King, *English Reformation Literature*, 435. Significantly, Drake carried Foxe's "Book of Martyrs" with him around the world. See Sugden, *Sir Francis Drake*, 100.

"restrained only by fear"—not of God, but of the king and the Inquisition.[17] And the distance between America and Seville did seem to cast out fear and cast off restraint. When Ferdinand Magellan, on his voyage of circumnavigation, made his first American landfall at what is now Rio de Janeiro on Christmas of 1519, he accepted the adoration of the native Guaraní who, seeing the mariners as rain-bringing deities, fell about them with upraised hands.[18] In November 1519, while Magellan was approaching Brazil, Hernando Cortés, with a small band of about six hundred troops, was marching virtually unopposed into Tenochtitlán, the heart of Montezuma's Aztec empire, because Cortés had been taken by the Aztec to be the white god Quetzalcóatl.[19] In 1541, Hernando de Soto arrived on the banks of the Mississippi in Arkansas and proclaimed to the inhabitants that he was the child of the sun god, demanding and receiving their worship.[20]

In contrast, the ideal English voyager behaved with becoming modesty when met by worshipful landsmen. Indeed, while Drake is probably the most famous Englishman to attract and refuse adoration on foreign shores, he was not the first. When Richard Chancellor arrived on the Arctic coast of Russia in 1553, he encountered obsequious Slavs who, "being amazed with the strange greatnesse of his shippe . . . prostrated themselves before him, offering to kisse his feete: but hee (according to his great and singular courtesie), looked pleasantly upon them, comforting them by signes and gestures, refusing those dueties and reverences of theirs, and taking them up in all loving sort from the ground" (*PN* 2.248–49). His humility with these and other "barbarians" is rewarded as he travels to Moscow, meets the czar, and opens all the Russias to English wool. Where a Spaniard would crave gold and godhood, this Englishman is satisfied with trade and a handshake.

These contexts put us in a better position to understand Drake's imaginative transaction at Nova Albion. As with many Tudor sea captains, Drake's religious scruples played a remarkably large part in shaping his actions on sea and land. One did not need to be, like Drake, a proto-Puritan enthusiast to fear God's wrath against divine impersonation or to wish the gospel's increase among the natives on shore. As Louis B. Wright notes, most English ship's commanders deliberately and personally mixed devotion with prudence: "prayers and piety brought upon a voyage the favor of the Almighty; and the conversion of the

---

17. Maltby, *Black Legend*, 93–94.
18. Ian Cameron, *Magellan*, 94–95.
19. Jon Manchip White, *Cortés and the Downfall of the Aztec Empire*, 89–91, 112–13. See also Thomas, *Conquest: Montezuma, Cortés, and the Fall of Old Mexico*, 184–85.
20. Lawrence A. Clayton et al., eds., *The DeSoto Chronicles: The Expedition of Hernando DeSoto to North America in 1539–1543*, 1:137–38, 415.

heathen tended to the glory of God and the benefit of the English nation."[21] If in his privateering Drake sought the high moral ground of seagoing knight taking vengeance on the perfidious viceroy of New Spain, in his first encounter with the Miwok he played the role of the Protestant evangelist.

Drake almost certainly knew of how Magellan, Cortés, and de Soto had accepted worship; his conceivable sources for these stories include published accounts, intelligence gleaned at court before sailing, and, most likely, the international network of mariners who traded (and often coerced) tales, news, and navigational details.[22] Indeed, it is likely that Drake's fierce Protestantism assured that he would see an evil appropriateness in popish idolaters becoming willing idols themselves. Certainly he also knew that in the New Testament Acts of the Apostles, when Paul and Barnabas were surrounded by an adoring heathen crowd, they tore their garments in mourning and preached an emergency sermon about the oneness of the true God.[23] So on the Marin beach, Drake likewise seized the moral high ground. In a response both visceral and calculated, he acted, to borrow Conrad's phrase, "[s]omething like an emissary of light, something like a lower sort of apostle."[24]

Of course, as we have noted, the meaning of the Englishmen's pious words and gestures was probably lost on the Miwok. But it was not lost on the English. By deploying this strategic counterworship, Drake was, not unconsciously, working to construct what we might call a "reformed imperialism," both in the sense that the English were to see it as morally better than earlier "cruel and bloody" Iberian imperialisms, and in the sense that they saw it as spiritually better because it was specifically Protestant—in other words, Reformed.[25] In

---

21. Wright, *Religion and Empire*, 6.
22. In addition to Las Casas's 1552 *Brevissima relación*, relevant books that Drake might have seen by 1577 include, about Magellan, Antonio Pigafeta's *Primo viaggio intorno al globo;* about Cortés, the anonymous *Newe Zeitung von dem Lande das de Spanier funden haben*, and Francisco Lopez de Gómara's *Historia de la Conquista de México* (1553); about both Cortés and Magellan, the second edition of Giovanni Battista Ramusio's *Navigationi e viaggi*, and Richard Eden's English translation of Pietro Martire d'Anghiera's *Decades of the New World;* and about de Soto, the so-called Gentleman of Elvas's *Relaçam Verdadeira.* Drake, who retraced much of Magellan's route and bested him by returning alive, clearly knew much about Magellan's voyage, particularly through the Strait—see Sugden, *Sir Francis Drake*, 106, 113–17; and while it is unlikely that Drake was fluent in the European languages, he probably would have developed enough facility to make out the essentials of these travelers' tales.
23. Acts 14:8–18.
24. Conrad, *Heart of Darkness*, 39.
25. Discussing Drake's dealings both with Spanish prisoners and with "peoples of another culture and color," John Sugden writes instructively of Drake's "relative humanitarianism"—

86 *Reforming Empire*

keeping with his religionational certainties, Drake believed in the univocal, unambiguous power of words, gestures, and symbols, and in the moral rectitude of his mission and his deeds. Generations of English imperial warrior evangelists were to believe so as well; this was to be a vital source of their power—and often the cause of their undoing.

Early Tellings: Patriotic Doggerel, Spenserian Allegory, and a Calvinist Epic

For an event that was to have such lasting influence in shaping Britain's Protestant imperial imagination, Drake's Nova Albion encounter took what now seems a surprisingly long time—nine years—to see print, not appearing until 1589 in Richard Hakluyt's *Principal Navigations*. What makes this delay even more striking is that, from early in his career, Drake had shown a knack for capturing the popular fancy. When he had dropped anchor at Plymouth on a summer Sunday morning in 1573 after his first West Indian raids, "the newes of our Captaines returne . . . did so speedily passe ouer all the Church, and surpass their mindes, with desire and delight to see him, that very fewe or none remained with the Preacher, all hastening to see the evidence of Gods loue and blessing towards our Gracious Queene and Countrey." Even here, the beginnings of an imperial religion are discernible—a religion parallel to, derivative of, but already competing with Protestant Christianity. Thus the narrator's concluding tag carries an unintended, almost corrective irony: "Soli Deo gloria."[26] It would not be the last time that Drake's particularly muscular piety pushed the preacher aside.[27]

His status as national and proto-imperial hero was sealed when he returned from the circumnavigation in 1580. Having staked claims for his queen around

---

relative to the harshness of other Englishmen like his cousin John Hawkins and of Richard Grenville, and of course relative to the famous cruelty of the conquistadors. Sugden sees this quality as an expression of Drake's personality and piety but also of his policy: "beneath his kindness lay thoughts of eventual profit." See Sugden, *Sir Francis Drake*, 106–7.

26. Philip Nichols, *Sir Francis Drake Reuiued. . . .* , 94.

27. One important instance showing Drake's impatience with clerical authority took place after the execution of Thomas Doughty for treason. Drake called a worship service for group repentance and confession, but when Chaplain Fletcher stood up to deliver the sermon, Drake stepped in, saying "Nay, soft, Master Fletcher, I must preach this day myself." His homily was a precedent-setting call for equal work from seaman and gentleman alike—and for firm obedience to God and the "General," Drake himself. Sugden, *Sir Francis Drake*, 113–14.

the globe while bearding the Spanish Goliath in single combat and plundering him to boot, Drake drew tremendous national adulation, becoming one of the first commoner "celebrities" in English history. Queen Elizabeth, with her unerring eye for symbolic gesture, appropriated to herself not only much of Drake's treasure but also his glamor: she knighted him aboard the *Golden Hind* in Deptford Harbor in the presence of a crowd so large that a bridge holding hundreds of spectators collapsed—though in miraculous keeping with the festive occasion, none was injured.[28]

Yet at first Drake's tremendous reputation spread without the help, or for that matter the hindrance, of published accounts about his voyages. For to many on the queen's Council, particularly Burghley and Walsingham, the idolized mariner was an object of suspicion, and his successful thievery a diplomatic embarrassment. This courtly cloud helps to explain why no account of the "Famous Voyage" was published until Hakluyt's in 1589, and why even that account was much shortened from its sources and nearly suppressed, as we now might say, for "security reasons."[29]

But the pious and patriotic masses of merchants, sailors, laborers, and stall-keepers loved Drake, so it is not surprising that his first surviving published notices in 1585 and 1587 were doggerel ballads worthy of Peter Quince. Henry Roberts, as I have noted, compares Drake to David in his "Most Friendly Farewell," a poem otherwise notable for its tone of aggrieved advocacy for Drake as a sufferer of poetic neglect and of calumny in high places. He apologetically and rather endearingly likens his poem to a compensatory "sweatie hat" full of water offered by a poor shepherd to a Persian king and proceeds then to compare Drake with the archetypal imperial conqueror, Alexander the Great.[30] So were the "middling sort" already quick to class the thrusting commoner with the highest and most ancient royalty.

Yet bourgeois praise did not translate to the trust of the queen's Council. By the time that Hakluyt's *Principal Navigations* introduced general readers to Nova Albion, Drake's star—while even higher with the populace for his role in defeating the Spanish Armada of 1588—was in complete eclipse at court after his disastrously failed invasion of Portugal in the summer of 1589. David B. Quinn

---

28. John Stow, *The Annales of England . . . from the first inhabitation vntill this present yeere 1592*, 1177–78.

29. Quinn, "Early Accounts of the Famous Voyage," 35–36.

30. Roberts, *A most friendly farewell*, A2v., A2r. See also Henry Haslop, *Newes out of the Coast of Spaine*, celebrating Drake's Cadiz exploits of 1587.

gives a thorough and persuasive account of Hakluyt's remarkable achievement in finally getting his excellent short version of the circumnavigation into print at this awkward time. Not only did he have to reduce his probable source—some redaction of Francis Fletcher's voluminous journal—to twelve pages of type, but he had to do so at great speed and under the probing eye of his employer, Francis Walsingham, who was by this time no friend to Drake. His success can be measured by the proportion, tightness, and elegance of the prose; the eyewitness immediacy and relative objectivity of the tone; and, most impressively, the demonstrable match between Hakluyt's version and the independently surviving half of the Fletcher journal on which it is probably based.[31] Significantly, Hakluyt gives strong emphasis to the Nova Albion landing, particularly to Drake's rejection of worship as an authorizing prelude to his claiming the land in the queen's name.[32]

In 1590, a year after this first printing of Hakluyt's *Principal Navigations*, Drake was still in temporary self-exile at his Buckland Abbey estate near Plymouth. Yet it was then that Edmund Spenser made, under the veil of allegory, what is arguably the first extended allusion to the California encounter in all of English literature—in book 1 of *The Faerie Queene*. Spenser was, as we have observed, fascinated by the "salvage man" as a type of fundamental human nature, "*salvagesse sans finesse*" yet untouched by civilization or divine grace. Thus "salvages" appear in a variety of forms, both positive and negative, throughout the epic—in book 3 as amatory consorts to Hellenore; in book 4 as Lust, as Artegall, and as would-be ravishers and consumers of Serena; and in book 6 as the Salvage Man himself, whose natural force is finally directed into his service of Arthur. But it is Una's encounter with the satyrs in book 1 that gives us the first of Spenser's many reimaginings of savagery.

My discussion of Artegall in chapter one described Spenser as schooled in the Neoplatonic and Pauline notions of the "carnal" and the "natural" man. Clearly, he applied these categories to interpreting published descriptions of European encounters with real "savages," particularly such works as Hakluyt's 1582 *Divers Voyages* and Hariot's 1588 quarto edition of his *New Found Land of Virginia*. Although Hakluyt's 1589 *Principal Navigations* was by 1590 probably familiar to Spenser, he need not have relied on it directly for his knowledge of something as sensational as Drake's circumnavigation; he would likely have

---

31. Quinn, "Early Accounts of the Famous Voyage," 33–36.
32. However Hakluyt, with his special concern for marketing English textiles, seems to suggest that it is the offered loincloths that provoke the Miwok to worship Drake and his crew; clothes make the god, as it were. See Linton, *The Romance of the New World*, 77–80.

had the details of the voyage years earlier through many sources, especially his contacts with Ralegh and his circle.[33]

While Willy Maley has written plausibly about the "savages" of book 1 in an Irish colonial context, the resemblances between Spenser's poetic "salvage nation" and Drake's worshipful California Miwok seem more than coincidental—both respond adoringly when they encounter Protestant humility.[34] In canto 6 of book 1, Una—having just escaped rape at the hands of the infidel Sansloy—meets with the pagan people of the wood and wins their love and allegiance through her metaphysical modesty:

> The doubtful Damzell dare not yet commit
>   Her single person to their barbarous truth
>   . . . .
>   They in compassion of her tender youth,
>   And wonder of her beautie soueraine,
>   Are wonne with pitty and vnwonted ruth,
>   And all prostrate vpon the lowly plaine,
> Do kisse her feete, and fawne on her with count'nance faine.
>
> Their harts she ghesseth by their humble guise,
>   And yieldes her to extremitie of time;
>   So from the ground she fearlesse doth arise,
>   And walketh forth without suspect of crime:
>   They all as glad, as birdes of ioyous Prime,
>   Thence lead her forth, about her dauncing round,
>   Shouting, and singing all a shepheards ryme,
>   And with greene braunches strowing all the ground,
> Do worship her, as Queene, with oliue girlond cround
>   . . . .
> Glad of such lucke, the luckelesse lucky maid,
>   Did her content to please their feeble eyes,
>   And long time with that saluage people staid,
>   To gather breath in many miseries.
>   During which time her gentle wit she plyes,
>   To teach them truth, which worshipt her in vaine,
>   And made her th'Image of Idolatryes;
>   But when their bootlesse zeale she did restraine
> From her own worship, they her Asse would worship fayn.
>   (1.6.12–13, 19)

---

33. For Spenser's likely reading list of exploration narratives, see Roy Harvey Pearce, "Primitivistic Ideas in the *Faerie Queene*."

34. Willy Maley, *Salvaging Spenser: Colonialism, Culture and Identity*, 78.

While Drake repairing his ship on the beach no doubt lacks Una's "tender youth" and venereal attractions, the two share in common a vital significance: each represents a virgin queen who combines true religion and godly rule. Indeed, Una's "beautie," which excites the benighted satyrs to idolatry, is "soueraine" (1.6.12.6), a sign of her true right to reign. Thus, like Drake's guileless Miwok, Una's savages possess the instinct to know majesty when they see it, but in their spiritual blindness they worship the creature rather than the Creator.

Besides this adoration and subjection offered by ingenuous natives in an exotic, peaceful setting, one other crucial element of the Protestant possession myth is present here as well—the adamant rejection of the offered worship, confirmed by zealous attempts at catechizing the idolaters. Again, the worthy ruler's worth is demonstrated by modest piety. Yet interestingly, as at Nova Albion, these protestations and efforts are amusingly "bootlesse": the Miwok keep up their wailing and lacerations; the satyrs deify a donkey. In the end, the poor literal-minded souls are more interested in their god's person and effects than in his or her religious opinions.

So the emerging myth seems already to be developing a useful loophole—possession depends not on the actual conversion of the natives (that may take some centuries) but rather on our pious efforts and on their willing submission, all taken in good faith. Perhaps one finally can't help being taken for divinity; submission is submission, after all. It is through this loophole, eventually, that Mr. Kurtz hears the darkness call his name. In any case, the likely connection of this passage to Drake's real act of possession—the first for England on the North American mainland—rings true to Spenser's central concern in the epic with the spiritual foundations of a destined British Empire.

While Spenser and Hakluyt were engaged in literary empire building, Drake —seeking to rebuild his reputation at court—was busy about a publishing project of his own, one which was to have colonialist reverberations throughout the next century. In the early 1590s, Drake apparently commissioned the Reverend Philip Nichols to write thorough accounts of his voyages in order to demonstrate the extent of his service to the queen. It is probably to this effort that we owe our most complete published version of the circumnavigation, and especially of the encounter with the natives at Nova Albion. Nichols probably worked from Drake's personal recollections and the circumnavigation journals confiscated from Francis Fletcher and others. By 1593, Nichols had very likely completed two narratives, one about the 1572–1573 West Indian raids, the other about "the world encompassed" from 1577 to 1580. However, by 1593, with further Spanish trouble stirring, Drake had been restored to royal favor without such documentary assistance. Thus Nichols's works remained unpublished until the later 1620s, after which, as we will see, they took on a print life of their own as incitements to imperial expansion.[35]

But Drake himself was headed toward his tragic anticlimax. In 1595, in favor again with the government, he sailed with his cousin Sir John Hawkins for another raid on the West Indies, hoping to prosecute the renewed war with Spain and repeat their successes of the last three decades. They were again urged on by the now rather proprietary Henry Roberts, whose latest leave-taking compared the "Noble Generall" to Moses, who "[l]earned hath, that God is our Chieftaine, / [Who] brings him forth and safely back again."[36] The comparison was perversely apt; like Moses on Pisgah, Drake and Hawkins would never return and never know a grave among their fathers. Having died aboard ship, Drake quite miserably of the "bloody flux," they were buried at sea, leaving the treasure house of Nombre de Dios unachieved.

The news of Drake's ignominious failure and death off Panama's north coast brought mainly silence from the English court; celebration in Seville, Havana, and Carthagena; and heartfelt grief in the Protestant homelands of London and the West Country.[37] It also inspired the Reverend Charles Fitzgeffrey to write and publish in 1596 the single most ambitious literary celebration of the hero, an elegiac epic of 285 rhyme royal stanzas entitled *Sir Francis Drake, His Honorable lifes commendation, and his Tragicall Deathes lamentation.* This effort has been admirably described and discussed by Michael J. B. Allen, who speculates appealingly about what this work might have been had the twenty-year-old Fitzgeffrey's not inconsiderable poetic abilities been matched by a more mature sense of theme; he might have created a new *Odyssey* about the circumnavigator, a Reformed mariner who by courage and self-restraint escapes "both Atlantic Polyphemuses and Pacific Circes."[38]

Instead, Fitzgeffrey's admiring fervor compels him to perform an ornate classical lamentation and then apotheosis of Drake—laying special emphasis on the perfidy of Drake's detractors and the ingratitude of England's still-negligent poets. He refers repeatedly to the circumnavigation, but only in general terms, and only once in passing to Nova Albion. Having fled deification by pagans on the Marin shore, Drake cannot escape it at the hands of a Calvinist parson.

---

35. Quinn, "Early Accounts of the Famous Voyage," 36–40.
36. Henry Roberts, *The Trumpet of Fame*, 2.
37. There is another piece to be written by a hispanicist on Drake and the *Spanish* imperial imagination, where he serves as one of their most enduring bogies, *El Draque* (the Dragon). See Sugden, *Sir Francis Drake*, 315.
38. Allen, "Fitzgeffrey's Lamentation on the Death of Drake," 106–7.

Jacobean Shadows: Drake and *The Tempest*

During the first two decades of the seventeenth century, Drake's official semieclipse continued. Hakluyt's 1598–1600 edition of the *Principal Navigations* did print the Nova Albion episode as a separate piece (in keeping with Hakluyt's desire to establish English rights in North America); however, despite his voluminous expansion of the overall collection, the summary account of the whole circumnavigation remained virtually unchanged from the 1589 version—a fact also true of Samuel Purchas's reprintings in 1615 and 1625.[39]

After Elizabeth's death in 1603 and James's accession in 1604, silence about Drake deepened. James, although interested in American colonization, inaugurated his reign by proclaiming a policy of peace with Spain and hostility to Puritanism, and he sought to obscure and even obliterate the achievements of the dead queen (who had, after all, executed his mother, Mary Stuart). The most famous object of his jealous retribution was Ralegh, whom he sent to the Tower and, after fourteen years' delay, to the block. Drake's active antihispanicism, his Puritanism, and his close association with Elizabeth's glory and Ralegh's enterprise all made him rather dangerous to remember.

Still, one could hardly have called Drake a forgotten man. His exploits were warmly recalled by the Puritan and anti-Spanish parties in court and city. During these Jacobean decades, his legend began to burgeon in the intertextual space into fanciful tales of a superhero who could hurl a cannonball through the earth, transform wood chips into ships, and, Arthur-like, return from the dead when his old drum beat to signal a threat of invasion by sea.[40] In particular, Drake's refusal of godhood in the far Eden of Nova Albion seems already to have become a fixed facet in the national imagination and to have piqued the interest of the aging William Shakespeare. One finds this theme—that only pious self-restraint merits possession—prominently displayed in *The Tempest*.

The play presents this quasi-colonial choice between authorizing humility and over-reaching arrogance at varied levels, from the farcical antics of Stephano and Trinculo to the tragicomic devices of Prospero. The link between these levels is Caliban, who, significantly, combines elements of the native buffoon,

---

39. In Hakluyt's 1598–1600 second edition, the Nova Albion excerpt appears independently in 3.440–42; the full account is in 3.730–42. In the 1903–1905 reprint, these selections appear, respectively, in 9.319–26 and in 11.101–33. The 1905–1907 Purchas reprints the circumnavigation in 2.119–49. See also Quinn, "Early Accounts of the Famous Voyage," 42–43.

40. Sugden, *Sir Francis Drake*, 317; Jewkes, "Sir Francis Drake Revived: From Letters to Legend," 118–20.

the vengeful monster, and the noble savage. Shakespeare portrays Caliban's idolatrous heathenism most patently at the level of farce. As a burlesque of the credulous and obsequious native, Caliban tastes from Stephano's bottle and immediately offers him both worship and service, which to him are identical things:

> That's a brave god and bears celestial liquor.
> I will kneel to him.
> . . . .
> And I will kiss thy foot. I prithee be my god.
> . . . .
> I'll swear myself thy subject.
> (2.2.115–16, 145, 148)

As an answering burlesque of the over-reaching, outlandish conqueror, Stephano haughtily accepts Caliban's prostration, the blasphemy made laughable by their shared drunkenness: "Come on then. Down and swear! . . . Come, kiss" (2.2.149, 152).

But Caliban desires more from his god than the inspirations of his bibulous "book"; like Drake's Miwok threatened by Spanish encroachment, Caliban needs protection from another, crueler overlord:

> A plague upon the tyrant that I serve!
> I'll bear him no more sticks, but follow thee,
> Thou wondrous man.
> . . . .
> 'Ban, 'Ban, Ca-Caliban
> Has a new master: get a new man.
> Freedom, high-day! high-day, freedom! freedom, high-day, freedom!
> (2.2.158–59, 179–81)

As if to confirm that he is a natural underling even in his rebellion, Caliban can conceive of liberty only in terms of shifting service, and he expects a kind of regeneration from the change; he can "get a new man"—become a new person—while his old "tyrant" must "get a new man," another slave.

The old tyrant is, of course, Prospero—now cast by the vengeful Caliban as an oppressor worthy of the *leyenda negra*.[41] Typically for Shakespeare, the low comedy is no mere relief from, but a complement to, the play's central

---

41. Anne Barton has rightly corrected Stephen Greenblatt's oversimplified reading of the play: "[Caliban's] claim that 'This island's mine, by Sycorax my mother' sounds less like

themes: Caliban and Stephano provide an antimasquers' parody of the protagonist's struggle with possession. For Prospero has taken hold of the island, of Ariel, and especially of Caliban by filling the metaphysical vacuum left by the banishment of the witch Sycorax and of her (and Caliban's) god, Setebos (a deity of Brazil's Guaraní, a people whom Magellan encountered). At first he comes as deliverer, freeing Ariel from the "cloven pine" in which Sycorax—herself a colonial oppressor—had imprisoned him and treating Caliban with well-remembered kindness and encouraging his nobler bent:

> Thou strok'st me and made much of me; wouldst give me
> Water with berries in't; and teach me how
> To name the bigger light, and how the less,
> That burn by day and night; and then I loved thee
> And showed thee all the qualities o' th' isle
> (1.2.277, 333–37)

But Shakespeare is alive to the fragility of such relations; whereas the explorer Drake could simply leave California while the inhabitants were still awestruck and obliging, the exiled Prospero is perforce a colonist; he must stay, and the welcome wears. In the wake of Caliban's sexual advances to Miranda, Prospero discovers that the soft superior hand is not enough; if he is to rule at all, he must rule by fear and coercion.

Having stepped reluctantly into the place of a savage deity, Prospero warms to the office. He dismisses as ingratitude the indentured Ariel's just request for "liberty," and, through the metaphysical technology of his magic, he shackles and torments the erring Caliban. In so doing, the magus reverses Drake's transaction, expediently violating what I have called the "great taboo": he would, for a time, be king, so he must, for a while, be a god. Hence the wide variations in our emotional response to Prospero. Even from a Eurocentric viewpoint, he is a troubled and troubling ruler—alternately beneficent and vindictive, serene and capricious, the good man in a devil's bargain who is rapidly being possessed by his possession.

So, even in the infancy of England's colonial enterprise, *The Tempest* is already interrogating the kind of sunny, eager native subjection associated with Nova Albion—what Conrad was to call "an exotic Immensity ruled by an august Benevolence."[42] Yet the play ends in a hopeful reaffirmation of the possession

---

a cry of the oppressed than the frustration of a second-generation colonialist displaced by later arrivals.... If the island belongs to anyone by right, it would seem to be Ariel." See Barton, "Perils of Historicism," 54.

42. Conrad, *Heart of Darkness*, 87.

myth: Prospero, unlike Kurtz, is finally able to break his own spell and renounce his transgressive power. The old duke has perhaps glimpsed "the horror," but he has discovered the deeper magic of forgiveness. By grasping a sorcerer's rod as a scepter and compelling abject service, he had shown himself less than worthy, and morally less than able, to rule the island; but by drowning his book and breaking his staff—as well as by embracing his humble mortality and showing mercy to the usurping Antonio—he shows worthiness to rule again in Milan.

Of course, one hesitates to invoke this swan-song romance yet again in connection with colonialist issues, for it has become the *locus classicus* (and at times the *ignis fatuus*) of new historicist and cultural materialist discussions of the playwright and empire. It is too easily overlooked that the play is not really about "imperialism"; rather, these echoes of colonial possession—at Bermuda, Jamestown, Roanoke, and before them all, at Nova Albion—are present as metaphors for something else, for the dramatist's powers over us, the audience, and for the costs of these powers to the artist and his eventual renunciation of them.[43] Yet the prominence of colonialism as a figure for artistic possession demonstrates how well established, even by 1611, were these imaginative tropes of discovery and conquest.

"Sir Francis Drake Reviv'd": Drake in the Century of Revolution

After these decades in the Jacobean shadows, Drake's sun reemerges at the king's death and shines, one might say, with a vengeance. Indeed, retellings of Drake's life and deeds constitute a minor publishing phenomenon throughout the rest of the century and well into the next, appearing at crucial junctures in national and imperial history. Drake, while not precisely a Once-and-Future King, kept returning in print as a kind of tutelary spirit for Protestant colonialism. Significantly, King James was less than a year in his grave when, in 1626, there appeared the first of three different seventeenth-century books entitled—in this case, almost crowingly—*Sir Francis Drake Reuiued*. With young King Charles on the throne eager to renew hostilities with Spain over the failed match with the Infanta, the time seemed ripe for the spirit of the old Elizabethan dragon to rise, censorious, "Calling vpon this Dull or Effeminate Age, to folowe his Noble Steps for Golde & Siluer."[44]

---

43. For a fine stylistic assessment of the play along with a critique of "colonialist" over-readings, see Russ McDonald, "Reading *The Tempest*."
44. Nichols, *Sir Francis Drake Reuiued*, title page.

For thirty-four years, Drake's namesake nephew and heir had stewarded the earlier-noted manuscript authored by the (now late) Reverend Philip Nichols; at this point he published it, dedicated to the new king and prefaced with old Drake's 1592 epistle to his queen, in which he promised a thorough accounting of "service done to your Ma^{ti} by your poore vassall against your great enemy." These dedications are followed by a third, "To the Courteous Reader," calling on us "to obserue with me the power and Iustice of the Lord of Hostes, who could enable so meane a person, to right himselfe vpon so mighty Prince"; here the Protestant David and the knightly challenger are combined.[45] The subject of this book is not the circumnavigation, but the West Indian raids of 1572–1573; yet even here we see Drake celebrated not only for his anti-Spanish boldness and fierceness but also for his friendly alliance with the Panamanian Indians and the "Symerons"—*cimarrones,* or escaped African slaves—and his magnanimous restraint in handling captured Spaniards themselves.

Far more important for our discussion is the publication by Drake's nephew, two years later in 1628, of *The World Encompassed by Sir Francis Drake.* This book, along with its surviving manuscript sources, remains our most complete account of the famous voyage, and it portrays Drake as an imperial pioneer of a biblically inspired global vision. As I have noted, it is "carefully collected out of the notes of Master Francis Fletcher," again by Philip Nichols and the older Drake, and dedicated by the younger to the Earl of Warwick.[46] Thus, while it is filled with often gripping eyewitness testimony in far more detail than Hakluyt's brief version, it is hardly an unbiased account. Drake is portrayed throughout in the best possible light; all of Fletcher's hostile commentary has been removed, most of which centers around the murky proceedings leading to the execution of Thomas Doughty for treason at Port St. Julian near the Strait of Magellan.[47]

At the beginning of the narrative, Drake is introduced as a kind of seafaring Adam—fulfilling the Almighty's creation mandate "to subdue the earth"—and as a surveyor of the "maine Ocean"; this great watery estate "by right is the Lords alone [not the pope's or the Spaniard's], and by nature left free, for all men to deale withall."[48] In keeping with this biblicist frame, the narrative lays even more emphasis than does Hakluyt's on the metaphysics of the New Albion transaction. The natives' frenzied idolatry and the Englishmen's heartfelt Protestant horror

---

45. Ibid., A3v, A4r.
46. Drake, *World Encompassed,* 1628 title page of 1628 edition; A2r.
47. Drake, *World Encompassed,* 61–63 n. 1. For a thorough and balanced weighing of this still controversial incident, see Sugden, *Sir Francis Drake,* 102–14.
48. Ibid., 5–6.

at being its objects are portrayed in literally gory detail: the worshiping women approach,

> their bodies bruised, their faces torne, their dugges, breasts and other parts bespotted with bloud, trickling downe from the wounds, which with their nailes they had made before their comming . . . crying out with lamentable shreekes and moanes, weeping and scratching and tearing their very flesh off their faces . . . euen old men, roaring and crying out, were as violent as the women were.
> We groaned in spirit to see the power of Sathan so farre preuaile in seducing these so harmlesse soules, and laboured by all meanes, both by showing our great dislike, and when that serued not, by violent withholding of their hands from that madnesse, directing them (by our eyes and hands lift vp towards heauen) to the liuing god whom they ought to serue; but so mad were they vpon their Idolatry, that forcible withholding them would not preuaile. . . .
> Their griefes we could not but take pitty on them, and to our power desire to helpe them: but that (if it pleased God to open their eyes) they might vnderstand we were but men and no gods.

With similar emphasis, the Miwok ceremony of submission to Drake is joyously voluntary: having crowned him, they perform "a song and dance of triumph; because they were not onely visited of the gods (for so they still iudged vs to be), but the great and chiefe God was become their God, their king and patron, and themselues were to become the onely happie and blessed people in the world."[49] It is, then, in these terms that the next four generations of English readers would conceive of their "colony" on the far shore of California and, by imaginative association, of their presently expanding colonial holdings elsewhere.

I have mentioned that Drake's legend became attached to the Arthurian myth of a returning King, come to redeem the imperiled nation. The power of this attachment is immediately evident in Drake's later-seventeenth-century publishing history; not only do three different Drake titles announce herewith his "revival," but all of these, and most others, appear at moments of national and international anxiety or crisis. I have discussed the 1626 *Sir Francis Drake Reuiued*, from the first year of Charles I's disastrous reign, and the 1628 *World Encompassed*, printed soon after Buckingham's assassination (it saw other editions in 1636 and 1652). After these come Thomas Fuller's brief "Life of Drake" in 1642, as the kingdom collapsed at the outbreak of civil war; an anonymous *Voyages and Travels* in 1652; and Nicholas Bourne's *Sir Francis Drake Revived* in 1653, as Oliver Cromwell began to establish his Protectorate, reassert English sea power, and challenge Spain in the Caribbean; William Davenant's opera, *The*

---

49. Ibid., 128–30.

History of Sir Francis Drake in 1659, during the last tottering months of Richard Cromwell's regime; Samuel Clarke's *Life and Death of the Valiant and Renowned Sir Francis Drake* in 1671; and Nathaniel Crouch's *The English Hero: or, Sir Francis Drake Reviv'd* in 1687, on the eve of the Glorious Revolution.[50] Most of these books repeat the story of Nova Albion as told in the *World Encompassed*, while all of them derive in some way from Hakluyt or from the works published by Drake's nephew in 1626 and 1628. Even those that do not mention the California landfall emphasize the virtues on display there—Drake's courage, his magnanimity, and above all his pious restraint. Fuller, for example, extracts maxims for the "Good Sea-Captain" from Drake's life: the first is that "the more power he hath, the more careful he is not to abuse it"; and the second is that "in taking a prize he most prizeth the mens lives whom he takes." The latter is especially illustrative of the "reformed imperialist" mind; privateering is a given, but the godly privateer will observe humane protocols.[51]

Indeed, such humane plunder provides the central spectacle of Davenant's *History of Sir Francis Drake*. As I observed in chapter two about Davenant's *Cruelty of the Spaniards in Peru*, it suited the Cromwellian regime—having presided over the theatrical famine begun in 1642—to ease that hunger with a few carefully "reformed" entertainments complementary to the Protectorate's expansionist West Indian intiatives, particularly its conquest of Jamaica. So this confluence of Drake's legend with a campaign of propaganda and with the considerable talents of Davenant helped to popularize opera in England.[52]

Loosely based on Nichols's account of Drake's Panamanian raids of 1572–1573, the action is set in an exotically imagined "Peru," represented by "Coco-Trees, Pines, and Palmitos. And on the boughs of other Trees are seen Munkies, Apes, and Parrots."[53] It is a landscape that stirs rapacious desire. The English

---

50. Thomas Fuller, "The Good Sea-Captain" and "The Life of Sir Francis Drake," in *The Holy State and the Profane State*, 2:128–41; *The Voyages & Travels of that Renowned Captain, Sir Francis Drake;* Nicholas Bourne, *Sir Francis Drake Revived;* William Davenant, *The History of Sir Francis Drake;* Samuel Clarke, *The Life and Death of the Valiant and Renowned Sir Francis Drake;* and Nathaniel Crouch, *The English Hero: or, Sir Francis Drake Revived.*

51. Fuller, *Holy State*, 2:128–29.

52. See Susan J. Wiseman, "Opera and Colonialism in the 1650s," esp. 194–98. See also her *Drama and Politics in the English Civil War*. Significantly, preceding the Drake opera at the Cockpit, Davenant wrote and produced *The Cruelty of the Spaniards in Peru*, a sensational reworking of passages from Las Casas's *Brevíssima relación*, newly retranslated and printed as *The Teares of the Indians* with a dedication to Cromwell.

53. Davenant, *History*, 2–3.

mariners who appear sing lustily (in both senses) that soon "The bowels of Peru / Shall be ript up and be our own," and even "Drake Junior" (a fictional composite of Drake's brothers and cousins) seems eager for brutal pursuits.[54]

Worst of all, as "Drake Senior" prepares for his assault on golden "Venta Cruz," he receives word that some of his overzealous "Symeron" allies have captured a Spanish bride and bridegroom and are plotting unspecified and unspeakable cruelties against them. It is at this point that the opera's most sensational special effect unfolds: "The Scene is suddenly chang'd into the former prospect of . . . Venta Cruz; but, about the Middle, it is vary'd with the discov'ry of a Beautiful Lady ty'd to a Tree, adorn'd with the Ornaments of a Bride, with her hair dishevel'd, and complaining with her hands towards Heaven: near her are likewise discern'd the Symerons who took her prisoner." Drake Senior responds to this spectacle with virtuous anger—"Arm! Arm! the honour of my Nation turns / To shame, when an afflicted Beauty mourns." He calls off his planned raid and vows instead to attack the "cruel Symerons," who outnumber him; but he is forestalled when Pedro, a virtuous Symeron leader, rushes in to assure him that Beauty has been freed. After the scene "is suddenly chang'd again, where the Lady is vanisht," Drake relents and shows mercy to the captors, on the grounds of "the cruelties which they have often felt beneath the Spaniards sway."[55] Thus he shows his own restraint even in the act of restraining others.

The opera ends with moral exempla all around: Drake Senior has upbraided Drake Junior for his cruelty to a wounded boar and exhorted the soldiers and mariners that their mission of ambushing a treasure convoy "is not for Gold, but Fame." When the attack is joined, the Spaniards cravenly abandon their piles of bullion, and Drake praises the glory of the victory, not the prize itself. A multicultural "Grand Dance" precedes the curtain: "two Land-souldiers, two Sea-men, two Symerons, and a Peruvian; intimating, by their severall interchange of salutations, their mutuall desires of amity."[56]

Again, the elements of the possession myth are present: the exotic setting, the fabulous wealth, the abominable European rival, the valiant but misguided savages in need of proper nurture. Above all, the action quite literally centers on the hero's self-mastery as prerequisite for command. And the wages of humility are rich and impressively automatic. As Drake Senior tells his friend the Symeron king, subjection to virtue is far more than its own reward:

54. Ibid., 19.
55. Ibid., 26–29.
56. Ibid., 32–37.

> Slave to my Queen! to whom thy vertue showes
> How low thou canst to vertue be;
> And, since declar'd a Foe to all her Foes,
> Thou mak'st them lower bow to thee.[57]

Extending the old Prayer Book paradox into the realm of colonial relations, the black ally's service to England is indeed perfect freedom. "Slavery" to a righteous ruler promises liberation.

It is revealing of Drake's increasingly exalted status that as the seventeenth century progressed, printed accounts about him grew more unified and more complete—indeed, more like biographies. On the one hand, Fuller's *Life,* though brief, attempts to sum up the man, not merely his travels. On the other hand, Bourne's 1653 *Sir Francis Drake Revived* brings together both the 1626 West Indies and 1628 circumnavigation narratives with recountings of his later Caribbean cruises in 1585 and 1595.[58]

Then, in 1671, Samuel Clarke's *Life and Death* does both, recounting all these travels with relative thoroughness while drawing out lessons in character and divine providence. What is probably most significant about this quarto volume is that its author's name uniquely signaled Drake's canonization into the pantheon: between 1665 and 1683, the prolific Clarke published a highly successful series of popular "Lives," each devoted to one of "those eminent persons who obtained the sirnames of Magni, or the Great." His subjects include Nebuchadnezzar, Cyrus, Artaxerxes, Alexander, Hannibal, Pompey, Julius and Augustus Caesar, Herod, Charlemagne, Tamburlaine, William the Conqueror, Edward the Black Prince, and Queen Elizabeth. Among these ancients, monarchs, and emperors, the only commoner so honored is Drake.[59]

Furthermore, the favored themes of Clarke—an ejected nonconforming minister and a close friend of Richard Baxter—are the destructive hubris of kingship and the exalting power of humility. Especially noteworthy among the overreaching heathen "Great" are Nebuchadnezzar, whose demand for worship drives him to madness as a grass-eating beast; Alexander, whose pretenses to deity wreck all of his tremendous virtues and condemn his corpse to lie stinking and unburied for two years; and Julius Caesar, whose acceptance of godhood is

---

57. Ibid., 12.
58. Ironically, in 1653, four years after the execution of Charles I, the held-over phrase about "so mean a person right[ing] himself upon so mighty a prince" seems almost to enlist Drake posthumously in the cause of regicide. Bourne, *Sir Francis Drake Revived,* A3v.–A4r.
59. While many of these Lives were, like Drake's, published separately, most also were printed together in Samuel Clarke's *Marrow of Ecclesiastical History,* vol. 4.

swiftly followed by his assassination.[60] Christian kings are not immune, either: Clarke gives rather gloating attention to the demise of William the Conqueror, who, having raised the wrath of God by abrogating the English common law, is abandoned and stripped at death, left rather too long awaiting interment, and then is forced into much too small a tomb, with nauseating results.[61]

On the other hand, down is the way up; piety, even pre-Christian piety, attracts blessing. Cyrus, the restorer of Jerusalem, is unbeatable; Augustus refuses deification and reigns in peace; and "Tamerlane"—here the utter opposite of Christopher Marlowe's implacable scourge—equably refuses the offered Greek empire because his has grown large enough.[62] Best of all is Elizabeth, whose early experiences of persecution and humiliation at popish hands develop the devotion and inner command necessary to prosper so splendidly in her eventual exaltation.[63] Yet, with the exception of the Virgin Queen, Drake equals or excels them all. In his world-girding skill and courage, in his fairness and kindness to Christian and heathen alike, in his love of Scripture and his heartfelt recourse to prayer, he is, in all but blood and title, greater than "the Great."

The seventeenth-century popular exaltation of Drake is crowned, in 1687 and thereafter, with the third "revival": *The English Hero: or, Sir Francis Drake Reviv'd*. Even the title's definite article suggests Drake's stature. Nathaniel Crouch, writing under his more sonorous pseudonym of Richard Burton, provides a reasonably complete popular "life" in 206 duodecimo pages, with woodcuts. He works a thorough stylistic revision on the materials found in the first and second "revivals" of 1626 and 1653, modernizing the language and changing first person to third person throughout; but in substance and in emphases, the book is identical to its sources.

Furthermore, especially after Clarke's death in 1683, Crouch/Burton came to occupy what we might call Clarke's market niche—books of Nonconformist devotion, geographical surveys, English history, and lives of "the Great"—but on an even larger scale. *The Dictionary of National Biography* attributes forty-four separate titles to Crouch, in hundreds of editions; indeed, *The English Hero* ran through at least twelve editions before his death in 1725 and was still in

---

60. For Nebuchadnezzar, Alexander, and Caesar, see respectively Clarke, *Marrow*, 4:11–12; 4:60–61, 71–72; and 4:216–19.

61. *The Life and Death of William, Surnamed The Conqueror: King of England and Duke of Normandy. Who dyed Anno Christi, 1087*, 33–34, 39–40.

62. For Cyrus, Augustus, and "Tamerlane," see respectively Clarke, *Marrow*, 4:24; 4:242; and 4:269–70.

63. Samuel Clarke, *The Historie of the Glorious Life, Reign, and Death of the Illustrious Queen Elizabeth*, "To the Reader," A2–A4.

print in 1769.⁶⁴ Drake had, as the saying went, humbled himself in the sight of the Lord; now his name was lifted high.

Clarke's *Life and Death of Pompey the Great* crystallizes this paradox of authorizing humility. After a victory over some pirates early in his career, the dutiful Roman general forewent a ceremonial triumph and

> hoisting sail, passed to Athens, where he landed and sacrificed to the Gods, and so returned to his ships. As he was going out of the city there were two writings in his praise affixed to the gate. That within was this,
> The humbler that thou dost thy self as Man behave,
> The more thou dost deserve the name of God to have.
> That on the outside of the gate was this,
> We wisht for thee, we wait for thee,
> We worship thee, we wait on thee.⁶⁵

So the epic apotheosis that Charles Fitzgeffrey had attempted in verse was finally accomplished in prose; it now remained for the prose masters of the next centuries to turn his legend to their varying ends.

The Myth Exalted and Exploded: Drake, Crusoe, and Gulliver

There can then be no doubt that most early-eighteenth-century readers were familiar with Drake's California encounter as an ideal of Protestant colonial possession. So we would expect to find his experiences—and not merely those of more recent models like William Dampier and Alexander Selkirk—behind the archetypal work of fictional colonization, *Robinson Crusoe*.⁶⁶

Although Crusoe's fruitful island is, unlike New Albion, at first conveniently uninhabited, nevertheless he discovers that alarming footprint in the sand, and he eventually witnesses a cannibal feast carried out by interlopers from another island. Revolted and incensed, he resolves to massacre the whole lot with his guns and save their victims, when he begins to have second thoughts along a line that would now be called multicultural: "what authority or call [had I], to

---

64. *The Dictionary of National Biography*, ed. Leslie Stephen and Sidney Lee, vol. 8, "Burton." See also the twelfth edition of Crouch's *The English Hero* (172[?]).

65. Clarke, *Marrow*, 4:174.

66. Indeed, at about the time that Defoe wrote *Crusoe*, he was proposing that England follow through on Drake's New Albion landing and actually lay claim to California—still not in Spanish hands. See Green, *Dreams of Adventure*, 73.

pretend to be judge and executioner upon these men as criminals, whom Heaven had thought fit for so many ages to suffer unpunished, . . . how far [were these] people . . . offenders against me, and what right [had I] to engage in the quarrel of that blood which they shed promiscuously upon one another[?]"[67] Defoe gives a good deal of space to this moral struggle; Crusoe wrestles with his revulsion for many pages covering five full years, foregoing other opportunities to intervene against cannibalism, painfully maintaining this policy of toleration. Then comes the day when he sees a savage fleeing two fellow cannibals: "It came now very warmly upon my thoughts . . . that now was my time to get me a servant . . . and that I was called plainly by Providence to save this poor creature's life." It is important to note which thought comes first to mind.

His crisis of conscience resolved by this "divine motion," Crusoe dispatches the pursuers with his guns, and the rescued man obligingly resolves any question of authority as do Drake's California natives: "[H]e came nearer and nearer, kneeling down every ten or twelve steps . . . at length he came close to me, and then kneeled down again, kissed the ground, and then laid his head upon the ground, and taking me by the foot, set my foot upon his head." Crusoe's immediate response is that of "God's Englishman": "I took him up, and made much of him, and encouraged him all I could." As with Drake, this refusal of worship confirms worthiness to rule; having renamed "my savage" for the Friday of his deliverance, the first word Crusoe teaches him, without a hint of self-contradiction, is "Master."[68]

Following this rescue, the fictional Crusoe is able to fulfill the possession myth in a way obviously impossible for the historical Drake; Crusoe's apostolic work bears fruit in Friday's wholehearted conversion to the Protestant gospel, and in Friday's zeal (rather in excess of his master's) to evangelize the cannibal mainland. Their two-man, two-tier commonwealth thrives, and Crusoe's position as its lord exalts him even in European eyes; when mutineers strand their captain on the island, and Crusoe appears suddenly to offer help, the captain, "looking like one astonished, returned, 'Am I talking to god or man! Is it a real man, or an angel!'" Apotheosis beckons, but again the godly deliverer demurs: "'Be in

---

67. Daniel Defoe, *Robinson Crusoe*, 177, 172–207, passim. J. Paul Hunter sees Crusoe's inner struggle as one against his own bad motives. Crusoe's righteous indignation in wanting to exterminate the brutes is fueled mainly by an impulse for self-preservation; and his outrage "bears a tinge of pharisaism: Crusoe reports that he 'gave God Thanks that . . . I was distinguished from such dreadful creatures.'" However, Hunter does not note Crusoe's obviously mixed motives in saving a "savage" to make him a servant. Hunter, *The Reluctant Pilgrim*, 183 n. 21.

68. Daniel Defoe, *Robinson Crusoe*, 206–7, 209.

no fear about that, sir,' said I, 'if God had sent an angel to relieve you, he would have come better cloathed . . . I am a man, an Englishman.' "[69]

If Crusoe's foray into self-doubt seems designed to relieve the reader's doubts about the colonial enterprise after all, Jonathan Swift gives no such quarter. As I will discuss more fully in chapter five, *Gulliver's Travels*, like *Utopia* and *Don Quixote*, belongs to the Christian humanist tradition of anti-imperial satire; and it is a critical commonplace that Gulliver personifies an optimistic, expansionist Whiggery, and that he is driven mad by confrontation with the Augustinian (if not Calvinist) reality of his own innate depravity.[70] And Swift's satire of Whiggish hubris would strike with special ferocity for any reader schooled in the Elizabethan possession myth, because its climactic episode in book 4— on the beach in Houyhnhnmland—explodes the iconography of Drake's New Albion encounter.

In book 2, Swift already begins inverting the terms of intercultural engagement. The gigantic King of Brobdingnag, far from worshiping his tiny English castaway, listens carefully to Gulliver's boastful account of England's institutions and concludes "the bulk of your natives, to be the most pernicious race of little odious vermin that Nature ever suffered to crawl upon the face of the earth"— a judgment that Gulliver confidently dismisses as resulting from the isolated king's "*prejudices,* and a certain *narrowness of thinking.*"[71] But it is not until book 4 that Gulliver's Anglocentricity begins to give way, and when it does, the collapse is total; for Swift brings him into collision with human corruption in the form of the Yahoos, the most outrageously ignoble savages in fiction. Whether defecating on him from the trees or making fulsome sexual advances to him during his bath, these utterly carnal, scatological Others produce a visceral revulsion in Gulliver that only increases as his resemblance to them becomes

---

69. Ibid., 252–53.
70. Jonathan Swift, *Gulliver's Travels*, 25–26.
71. Ibid., 173–74. Intriguingly, there is a river in Kentucky named Lulbegrud, after Lorbrulgrud, the capital of Brobdingnag. It was so named by Daniel Boone, who had brought along what he called "the History of Samuel Gulliver's Travels" while exploring the Blue Lick region in the winter of 1770. His companion Alexander Neeley, also taken with the tale, returned to camp from a hunting foray to brag the "he had been that Day to Lulbegrud and had killed two Brobdernags [he meant buffalo] in their Capital," and the tag stuck. So on the edge of the Anglo-American frontier, on the eve of the American Revolution, the archetypal leatherstocking was reading antiexpansionist satire "for amusement" as he named and claimed the land for white settlement. As John Mack Faragher shows, Boone was a courageous, equitable, and relatively broadminded frontiersman, and indeed later a blood brother to the Shawnee; but he was not an ironist. See Faragher, *Daniel Boone: The Life and Legend of an American Pioneer*, 83.

more apparent—both to himself and to the equine Houyhnhnm master whom he serves and, increasingly, venerates. Eventually these supremely rational horses vote to banish him, being unable to abide his savagery and his smell; "for now I could no longer deny, that I was a real Yahoo in every limb and feature, since the females had a natural propensity to me as one of their own species."[72]

Crushed by this verdict, Gulliver constructs a canoe of Yahoo skins (the children's making the best sailcloth) and bids his master farewell on the beach. In so doing Gulliver recapitulates in reverse the part of all submissive barbarians, from the Russian coast to Crusoe's Island: "I took a second leave of my [Houyhnhnm] master; but as I was going to prostrate myself to kiss his hoof, he did me the honor of raising it gently to my mouth." Like Chancellor's and Drake's adoring greeters and Crusoe's man Friday, Gulliver revels in his self-abasement; like Chancellor, Drake, and Crusoe themselves, the Houyhnhnm master, by raising his abject worshiper, exalts himself yet more in the worshiper's eyes. "Detractors are pleased to think it improbable that so illustrious a person should descend to give so great a mark of distinction to a creature so inferior as I."[73]

It is instructive that the last chapters of book 4 have been cited from Swift's time until our own as proving the author's actual insanity.[74] Certainly this recurring confusion of a fictional character's psyche with his creator's—without corroborating evidence outside the text itself—has much to do with Gulliver's final disgust at his family and his misanthropic preference for the company of horses. But perhaps it has much to do with Swift's direct attack on England's increasingly central self-image as modest possessor of the world. The "benign eccentric" deviates from the cultural center but still responds to its orienting gravity; the "dangerous madman" navigates by a different gravity altogether. Swift's anti-imperialist madness would not come to occupy the gravitational center of English consciousness for more than two centuries; it would take Britain that long to lose its mind—and find another.

It took a different sort of Tory, Samuel Johnson, to recast Drake's story for the late Augustan sensibility. His 1740 *Life of Sir Francis Drake* preserves the narrative line of the 1653 *Sir Francis Drake Revived,* the 1628 *World Encompassed,* and of Hakluyt, but with an important change in emphasis: Drake is no longer praised for his flamboyant daring or his imperial vision but rather for his diligence and industry in raising himself from low to high station. Yet he remains a hero of piety; Johnson gives special attention to the Nova Albion landing (about

---

72. Swift, *Gulliver's Travels,* 315.
73. Ibid., 331.
74. Ibid., 19–21.

10 percent of the entire *Life*), particularly stressing Drake's refusal to accept worship from the "Indians."[75] Johnson also uses the California episode as an opportunity to pronounce, in his characteristically sententious and symmetrical style, for the benefits of Christian civilization and against the rising European cult of romantic primitivism: "The question is not, whether a good Indian or a bad Englishman be most happy; but, which state is most desirable, supposing virtue and reason the same in both."[76] As I will discuss in chapter five, Johnson had no use for colonial possession or expansion in the name of "improving the savages"; yet he clearly considers the Miwok better off for even their brief encounter with a good Englishman like Drake.

Though literary revivals of Drake grew less frequent as the eighteenth century passed, these decades saw the fulfillment of Drake's vision for British sea power on a scale that would have delighted him; indeed, by the century's end he seemed to have been reincarnated in the equally diminutive and indomitable Lord Nelson—and it was claimed that both Nelson and Napoleon had heard "Drake's Drum" beating out judgment on England's enemies.[77] But Drake's paradigm of pious restraint could bring judgment on England's heroes as well, as in the case of Captain James Cook.

The Taboo Broken: From Cook to Kipling and Conrad

The circumnavigator Cook, so much like Drake in colonial vision as well as in courage, endurance, kindness to his crew, and relative humaneness with native peoples, was strikingly lacking in Drake's Protestant religious zeal. As Bernard Smith writes, "Cook did not depend much upon God; he kept his powder dry, mentioned Providence rarely, and performed the Sunday naval service intermittently; but he was perfectly willing to play God himself, as he did at Hawaii, if the cultivation of peaceful relations depended upon it."[78] Thus Cook ran afoul of the "great taboo" against divine impersonation, and, like later fictitious adventurers in Kipling and Conrad, he paid dearly for it. After Cook's murder at Hawaii's Kealakekua Bay in 1779, it eventually became known that he had previously accepted some form of adoration as the white deity Lono; this revelation dealt his

---

75. Samuel Johnson, *The Works of Samuel Johnson*, 14:207–95; the California episode takes up from page 277 to page 284.
76. Samuel Johnson, *Life of Drake*, 284.
77. Jewkes, "Sir Francis Drake Revived: From Letters to Legend," 118–19.
78. Bernard Smith, "Cook's Posthumous Reputation," 168.

reputation a severe posthumous blow. In particular, Cook's name was execrated in the "Sandwich Islands" and the United States, especially after the publication of a diatribe by the American missionary Sheldon Dibble, who wrote:

> Captain Cook allowed himself to be worshipped as a god.... The priests [at Kealakekua] approached him in a crouching attitude, uttering prayers, and exhibiting all the formalities of worship.... He was conducted to the house of the gods, and into the sacred enclosure, and received there the highest homage. In view of this fact, and of the death of Captain Cook which speedily ensued, who can fail being admonished to give to God at all times, and even among barbarous tribes, the glory which is his due? Captain Cook might have directed the rude and ignorant natives to the great Jehovah, instead of receiving divine homage himself. If he had done so, it would have been less painful to contemplate his death.[79]

"If only Cook had read *The World Encompassed*," Dibble seems to be saying, "he would not be in hell!" Indeed, Cook had read it; but, pragmatic apostle of Enlightenment that he was, he felt insufficient awe at monotheistic thunder.[80] So the spectacle of his hubris and of the damning divine retribution served warning that Jehovah, despite his fondness for Protestant England, would tolerate no trifling with his prerogatives. Pious Englishmen agreed; as the poet William Cowper wrote when he learned how Cook had died, "God is a jealous god."[81]

Drake's pious restraint might be called to witness against Captain Cook. But as the nineteenth century began, Drake himself was to be seen again, revived, singing, and dancing—at the New Royal Circus in "the entirely new and splendid national spectacle," *Sir Francis Drake and Iron-Arm* (1800). This patriotic wartime pastiche, which rather impertinently claims a basis in Johnson's *Life of Drake*, conflates the Caribbean raids of 1573 and 1585 with the treachery of Thomas Doughty during the circumnavigation. The prologue to the entertainment extols Drake for his "fortitude, perseverance, and magnanimity"; and, to display Drake's manly self-control to maximum effect, the librettist J. C. Cross sets him against the prodigiously rapacious Spanish giant of the title.[82] Iron-Arm is the Iberian Goliath incarnate, the Black Legend on two legs; with the help of the turncoat Doughty, he multiplies atrocities against Englishmen, Indians, Negroes, and Spaniards alike (as in Davenant's opera, one victim is a young

---

79. Sheldon Dibble, *History and General Views of the Sandwich Islands' Mission*, 27–28.
80. For Cook's knowledge of *The World Encompassed*, see Richard Hough, *Captain James Cook*, 246.
81. Marshall Sahlins, *Islands of History*, 134.
82. J. C. Cross, *Sir Francis Drake and Iron-Arm. As Represented at the New Royal Circus, on Monday, August 4, 1800*, 3.

virgin), until the long-suffering Drake, in the rousing finale, incinerates the beast along with the entire city of Carthagena. Drake is becoming here what we would today call an "action hero," accompanied by an implicit warning: beware the fury of a patient man.

It is as a swashbuckling figure of the popular imperial imagination that Drake appears most often in nineteenth-century books—indeed, usually "boys' books." After the period of increasingly inward-looking domesticity between the Napoleonic and Crimean Wars, England again grew more aggressively interested in imperial expansion, and by the High Victorian age Drake titles were rolling off the presses: *Under Drake's Flag; With Hawkins and Drake; At Sea with Drake; Drake on the Spanish Main; For Drake and Merry England; Sea Dogs All; The Fighting Lads of Devon; The Boy's Drake*, and so on.[83] In the meantime, the Hakluyt Society edition of *The World Encompassed* (1854) had made the fullest account of the circumnavigation and the exemplary encounter at New Albion widely available to a rising generation of empire builders.

But in 1888, with the imperial sun near its apogee, Rudyard Kipling transmutes the elements of the action-packed adventure tale—the golden ambition, the far-flung setting, the adoring and deadly natives—into an elegy for empire's end in "The Man Who Would Be King." The Central Asian setting of "Kafiristan" is, of course, exceedingly distant in time and geography from Drake's California landing; the story's most obvious historical models, to which it explicitly alludes, are the regime of Sir James ("White Rajah") Brooke in East Indian Sarawak during the 1840s, 1850s, and 1860s, and the Indian Mutiny of 1857.[84] But this is a tale of the "great taboo"—that the man who would be God is not worthy to be king—and Kipling could not have been ignorant of Drake's precedent three centuries before.

The story's principals, the soldiers of fortune Danny Dravot and Peachey Carnehan, take breezy blasphemy as their starting point. They have outgrown the Raj and cross the Hindu Kush with a load of rifles to create an army of conquest and to become "Kings of Kafiristan with crowns upon our heads.... The Kafiris have two-and-thirty heathen idols," the two say to the narrator before departing, "and we'll be the thirty-third."[85] Their strategy of exploiting native superstition proves a quick and stunning success, and soon Danny has unified a vast and rich mountain empire, which he rules as the divine reincarnation of Alexander the Great, with Peachey as his godlike advisor.

83. Sugden, *Sir Francis Drake*, 318.
84. Rudyard Kipling, *The Man Who Would Be King and Other Stories*, 252, 275.
85. Ibid., 252.

However, there is soon a falling out among the gods, and the "great taboo" against impersonating the Almighty begins to take effect. The practical Peachey wants the two of them to load the vast Kafiri treasure on their mules and run back to India before their game is discovered, while Danny has come to believe in his own deity and in the goodness of his imperial rule. In dispensing his laws, Danny decrees that he will marry to produce an heir. But on the wedding day Danny's bride, a tool of the local priests, bites Danny's cheek, which bleeds, displaying his mortality in the sight of all. His fall is memorably literal: marched to the middle of a rope bridge shouting, "Cut, you beggers!" he plummets "turning round and round and round twenty thousand miles" into the ravine below. Peachey carries even more iconic weight; "crucified between two pine trees," he survives and then is sent to limp over the mountains back to India, all the way clutching Danny's crowned, severed head.[86]

"You behold now," says the returned Peachey to the revolted and fascinated narrator, "the Emperor in his habit as he lived—the King of Kafiristan with his crown upon his head. Poor old Daniel that was a monarch once!"[87] Danny and Peachey violate the great taboo, and they learn at a cost its terrible lesson: that the man who would be a god-king must, willingly or unwillingly, walk the *via dolorosa*. He must pay for his grab at deity by receiving the stigmata; he will end by wearing a crown of pain or by losing his crowned head altogether.

Yet Kipling's story goes beyond merely reaffirming the great taboo; it interrogates the imperial myth more deeply. For over against Drake's sunny confidence in the clarity of signs, in the beneficence of his intentions, and in the compatibility of the cross with the sword, Kipling's tale, as fantastic as it is, is built around the clash of mutually uncomprehending cultures; the disastrous unintended consequences of that clash; and, above all, the inevitable claim to divine favor, if not to actual deity, undergirding the imperial faith. Certainly, the ill-fated action is displaced across the Hindu Kush, away from the real business of empire in India, and is performed by a pair of rogues; but these rogues display all of the virtues for which the Englishman congratulates himself: magnanimity, good humor, shrewdness, and, at the hour of death, solidarity, high bravery, and defiance. They are such unintentionally beneficent conquerors that, despite their devil's bargain, it is difficult not to admire them—just as, in the context of brutal Renaissance discoverers, it is difficult not to admire Drake's restraint and humanity. Indeed, as Kipling's story progresses, we come to feel that the devil's bargain is inseparable from the sovereignty itself. Thus, while the denouement

---

86. Ibid., 277–78.
87. Ibid., 278.

apotheosizes Danny and Peachey in memory, it also dramatizes how inherently unstable are regimes built by the sword in the name of the conqueror's spiritual superiority. Their tale ends in a kind of glory, but it is the glory of funeral music.

The few years between Kipling's story and Joseph Conrad's *Heart of Darkness* were pivotal for the British Empire. The official pursuit and celebration of imperialism were still emphatic—this period saw the "Scramble for Africa" completed, the apotheosis of the martyrs Livingstone and Gordon, and the exaltation of living heroes like Kitchener, "General Bobs," Stanley, and the young Churchill (to his own delight, a distant relative of Drake). It also saw the painstaking and voluminous republication of Hakluyt—whose works the atavistically named literary critic Walter Raleigh called "the prose epic of the English nation."[88] But by the end of 1902, England had also seen the Boer War fought to a shockingly bloody draw; the death of Victoria herself; and the continued Darwinian erosion of old metaphysical certainties—William James reconsidering religion, and J. A. Hobson imperialism itself.[89]

The grand loss portrayed elegiacally by Kipling may prophesy the empire's doom, but Conrad writes its grisly and sardonic epitaph: "The horror! The horror!"[90] Yet *Heart of Darkness* begins by evoking Drake, a "great knight-errant of the sea," and "the Golden Hind returning with her round flanks full of treasure, to be visited by the Queen's Highness and thus pass out of the gigantic tale." Significantly, Conrad mentions Drake's glittering feat along with the disastrous polar expedition of Sir John Franklin, thus placing the Elizabethan possession myth in an ironic setting of foreboding and defeat. The "venerable

---

88. For Churchill's relation to Drake, see William Manchester, *The Last Lion: Winston Spencer Churchill: Visions of Glory, 1874–1932*, 93. For Raleigh on Hakluyt, see Hakluyt, *Principal Navigations*, 12.1.

89. William James, *The Varieties of Religious Experience*; J. A. Hobson, *Imperialism: A Study*. Conrad first published the story serially as "The Heart of Darkness" in *Blackwood's Magazine* in 1899; he dropped the definite article when he republished it as part of *Youth* in 1902.

90. Conrad, *Heart of Darkness*, 111. It is surprising that for all of their striking similarities, "The Man Who Would Be King" and *Heart of Darkness* seldom have been compared. The only two critics who seem to have done so in any detail make contrasting political judgments of the stories but agree that the difference in concluding tone between the stories relates to the crucial difference in the framing narrators' moral stances. Tim Bascom concludes that Kipling's unnamed journalist alter ego, having tried to maintain an objective voice, nevertheless eventually succumbs to the powerful emotional pull of imperial "Brotherhood" with Dan and Peachey and finally tries to induct us as well; David H. Stewart praises this attraction and decries Conrad's Marlow for his "atomistic" isolating despair. See Bascom, "Secret Imperialism: The Reader's Response to the Narrator in 'The Man Who Would Be King,' " 170–71; and Stewart, "Kipling, Conrad, and the Dark Heart," 203–4.

stream" of the Thames is observed in the "august light of abiding memories," but there is only "gloom to the west" brooding over the "monstrous town" of London.[91] Literally and figuratively, the light of August presages a fall.

Of course it is Kurtz who inflicts the story's most wrenching inversion on Drake's imperial legend. Kurtz is far from rejecting worship, or even from accepting it for mainly pragmatic reasons, like Cook or Kipling's Dan and Peachey. Rather, this former "emissary of light" counts godhood a thing to be grasped, shaken out, throttled, and devoured with a relish—rather like the victim at a cannibal feast. Once relocated to the jungle, Christian Europe's great justifying idea of empire—"an exotic Immensity ruled by an august Benevolence"—turns out to be merely another blood-soaked local idol. In the jungle, this idea-as-idol becomes "something you can set up, and bow down before, and offer a sacrifice to."[92] Kurtz is this imperial god made flesh, the logic of conquest without restraint. So we will revisit him more fully in chapter 6, as an imperial Death's Head.

Drake and Imperial *Kenosis*

As I will discuss more fully in my final chapter, the heart of Britain's Protestant imperial myth essentially stopped with Conrad. Yet we have seen that for more than three centuries the British Empire sustained itself on this White Legend of modest possession, derived in part from Drake's calculated humility on the Marin shore. England's imperial religion closely mimicked the Protestantism that attended its birth and growth, and Drake provided the imperialist faithful with a simulacrum of *kenosis,* Christ's incarnational emptying of himself: "He did not count equality with God a thing to be grasped . . . ," writes Paul to the Philippians, "therefore God has highly exalted him."[93] In the English imagination, Drake, as a kind of second Adam in a new Eden, had redeemed by his self-effacing piety the imperial scepter from the old Adam of over-reaching Spain; so England would not merely grasp but actually merit the supremacy.

Drake's transaction is of course a shoddy parody of Christian humiliation—he hardly suffers, in Paul's further words, "death on a cross"—but his sanctimonious piracy and Anglo-Saxon condescension could pass for self-abasement in the context of his more vaunting and rapacious rivals. For Drake zealously

---

91. Conrad, *Heart of Darkness,* 28–29.
92. Ibid., 87, 32.
93. Philippians 2:5–11.

observed all divine law—consistent with personal and national interests; he was absolutist—in a relative sort of way. Thus he made an appropriate patron for the truncated creed of Anglican empire: Christ calls all men to a life of service; you serve him and us, while we serve him. This kind of religion could bind together not only pious privateers but a nation; and the peoples of Britain's expanding imperial coastlands it could begin to bind under.

Four

The Nubile Savage and the Soulless Slave

Imagining Race from Pocahontas to the Colonial Color Line

They have married with the Indians, and make 'em bring forth as beautiful faces as any we have in England: and therefore the Indians are so in love with 'em that all the treasure they have they lay at their feet. —*Seagull to Spendall in George Chapman, Ben Jonson, and John Marston,* Eastward Hoe *(1605), 3.3.18–21*

[T]he tawney Moore, black Negro, duskie Libyan, ash-coloured Indian, olive-coloured American, should with the whiter European become one *sheep-fold,* under *one great Shepheard* . . . without any more distinction of Colour, Nation, Language, Sexe, Condition, all may be *One* in him that is One. —*Samuel Purchas,* Purchas his Pilgrimage *(1613)*

[A]s to make negroes Christians, their savage brutishness renders them wholly incapable. —*Sir Richard Dutton, governor of Barbados (1681)*

[A] sprightly Lover is the most prevailing Missionary that can be sent amongst these, or any other Infidels. . . . for if a Moor may be washt white in 3 Generations, Surely an Indian might have been blancht in two. —*William Byrd,* Histories of the Dividing Line *(1738)*

I have called Francis Drake's contribution to British imperial mythology a "White Legend" by analogy with the *leyenda blanca* of the Spanish *Reconquista*, and in opposition to Spain's *leyenda negra* of American conquest. Together with the complementary myth of Bruto-Arthurian recovery discussed in chapter one, these three elements—imperial revival, relative righteousness, and metaphysical modesty—formed for the English a kind of imperial religion. This tribal creed was derivative of but distinct from Protestant Christianity, and it could be invoked to unite a newly expanded (but still fractious) "Great Britain" for a greater expansion overseas. I turn now from these nation-building powers of binding *together*, to the empire-building powers of binding *under*—that is, to religious powers of subjection. And immediately one must recognize that there is a fearful symmetry at work between these legends and the intercultural collisions that they provoked. For the metaphysically fraught terms of "white" and "black," initially innocent of racial meaning, eventually came to be read as literal signs of spiritual light or darkness; the texts read would be human faces.

As the seventeenth century began in England, there was, strictly speaking, no such thing as "race." There was instead a volatile mixture of xenophobia and openness, as the insular kingdom struggled to assimilate its bewildering new encounters with human diversity. So there were both economic suspicion of "blackamoors" in the city and a poetic cult of "black beauty" at court; there was a noble but jealous Moor on stage; there were hopes for and warnings against intermarriage with the "tawney" natives of America; and soon there came the redeemed savage princess Pocahontas to London, lionized as the morning star of the Gospel in Virginia—and accompanied by a son, the first fruit of her marriage to John Rolfe. Britain, in the midst of this ambivalence, seemed at times on the verge of betrothing darkness. But within a few decades, such mixed unions—at least literal ones—became illegal if not unthinkable. In this chapter, I will explore how seventeenth-century Britons suddenly, haphazardly, and incompletely articulated the metaphysics of race—that is, how the invisible boundary between whiteness and blackness, good and evil, became flesh and came to dwell among us as the color line.

The Nubile Savage: Pocahontas as Heathen Convert and Virgilian Bride

In her recent study, *Things of Darkness: Economies of Race and Gender in Early Modern England*, Kim F. Hall seeks to complement Winthrop D. Jordon's groundbreaking work on the developing colonial color line "by refining his contention that the language of dark and light is racialized [in the seventeenth century] and by examining the ways in which gender concerns are crucially embedded in discourses of race."[1] So, given her linkage of race and gender, it is surprising that Hall's otherwise perspicacious book overlooks the case of Pocahontas and the crucial question that it raises: Why would a Jacobean Englishman marry an American "savage"?

More specifically, why did John Rolfe marry Matoaka, alias Pocahontas, alias Rebecca, daughter of the "Emperor of Virginia"? The crucial word is "marry"— Rolfe neither raped nor seduced Pocahontas, nor took her as a concubine; rather, on April 5, 1614, in the church within the walls of James Fort and according to the rites of the English church, he took her to wife. Some reasons for the marriage are provided or suggested by Rolfe himself and by Ralph Hamor in the latter's 1615 *True Discourse of the Present State of Virginia*, and by Captain John Smith's 1624 *Historie of Virginia:* the bride's beauty, her diplomatic worth, and her Christian conversion.[2] Intriguingly, however, these writers overlook the (to us) obvious element of race. Where is the expected Anglo-Saxon shudder at the idea of mixed blood?

A modern reader might reasonably expect to find racists thick on the ground in early colonial Virginia—after all, by the 1620s planters were importing Africans for the tobacco fields, and by 1662 miscegenation was a crime. Yet during Jamestown's first decades, biblicist and classicist elements in the developing British imperial imagination fused to make it temporarily possible for a white man to wed a woman of color, bring her home to England, and, rather than being ostracized for his miscegenation, to find himself celebrated for it. Indeed, for King James I, Pocahontas's social rank trumped her race. Although the king eventually welcomed the Powhatan bride to his palaces twice, he was at first perturbed when he learned of the marriage—not because of the bride's color, but rather because Rolfe, a commoner, had without his sovereign's permission wed the daughter of a foreign prince.[3] "Savage" though she might be, Pocahontas had renounced, in Governer Sir Thomas Dale's significant phrasing, "her countrey

---

1. Kim F. Hall, *Things of Darkness: Economies of Race and Gender in Early Modern England*, 2. See also Winthrop D. Jordan, *White over Black: American Attitudes towards the Negro, 1550–1812*, and *The White Man's Burden: Historical Origins of Racism in the United States*.
2. Ralph Hamor, *A True Discourse of the Present State of Virginia;* John Smith, *The Complete Works of Captain John Smith*.
3. Philip L. Barbour, *Pocahontas and Her World*, 162.

idolatry" and was now christened "Rebecca" after that original biblical wife fetched from a far place.[4] Even more significant, this reborn Rebecca was to James above all royal, like the classical woodland princess Lavinia, sought out and wed by Virgil's Aeneas in the West.

Thus Pocahontas's rusticity, now baptized and civilly dressed, only increased her nobility and hence what we might call her "nubility"—that is, her eligibility to marry and to carry British blood. In fact, as I observed in chapter one, the writings of some Elizabethan moralists seem to suggest that intermarriage might improve not only the spiritual and cultural state of the "savages" but also the deracinated bloodlines of the husbanding English. Whether such contemporary reactions to intermarriage are based on scriptural or Virgilian models, they are evidence of a time in English history when "preracist" and "protoracist" paradigms were still in flux, a time when color and blood were far less determinative than religion, rank, and "civility."

The Mutability of Color

This fluidity of attitude can be illustrated in a number of ways. Literal illustration abounds in Theodore DeBry's many engravings of Africans and Amerindians: the otherwise meticulous DeBry renders his subjects' bodies as classically European in proportion and feature, and their skin color as indeterminate, indeed usually the same as that of the "whites" in the pictures.[5] As further evidence of this indeterminacy, witness a pair of late Elizabethan proclamations, from 1596 and 1601, calling for the expulsion of "blackamoors" from the realm. This term indicates both skin color and place of origin ("Moor," from Latin *Maurus*, for Mauritanian Africa), so the decree does anticipate future ideologies of ethnic and racial purification.[6] However, the actual rationale of these decrees is not racial but economic and religious: these foreigners must go because they work

---

4. Hamor, *A True Discourse*, 55, 60; Genesis 24. Peter Hulme detects a "subtle intertextual strategy" in the renaming of Pocahontas: in Genesis 26, the biblical Rebecca is told by the Lord that "two nations are in thy wombe"; Hulme suggests that Rolfe and the English Christians anticipate their Rebecca giving birth to two nations, "a red and a white, and the red will [like the biblical Esau] despise his birthright and sell it for a mess of pottage." Hulme, *Colonial Encounters: Europe and the Native Caribbean, 1492–1797*, 145–46.

5. See, for example, Michael Alexander, ed., *Discovering the New World based on the Works of Theodore DeBry*, 46–55, 64–65, 138–41.

6. Indeed, as Winthrop D. Jordan indicates, "blackamoor" was used sometimes to distinguish darker West Africans from the Berber Arab Moors of North Africa. See Jordan, *White Man's Burden*, 5.

as servants while "the subjects of the land and Christian people . . . perish for want of service." Put simply, the "infidel" foreigners were taking English jobs, and their masters will "do charitably and like Christians" to eject these "strangers" in favor of "their own countrymen"—and coreligionists.[7]

If these xenophobic decrees from Elizabeth's last years treat blackness as incidental yet potentially damning, a countervailing Jacobean poetic fashion celebrated "black beauty" as spiritually superior. James's ambassador to France, Sir Edward Herbert, wrote two sonnets on the subject sometime before 1621, praising blackness as not merely equal to but better than whiteness, and on metaphysical grounds: it is immune to change, it contains all other colors, and it is the color of night—when the stars yield their clearest revelations.[8] John Collop takes much the same line in praising "an Ethiopian beauty," inverting the conventional moral color scheme by insisting that "Surely in black Divinity doth dwell; / . . . Devils ne'er take this shape, but shapes of light."[9] As Kim Hall writes, these poets "revel in the mystery of blackness," both spiritualizing and subtly eroticizing it.[10]

Yet sometimes this celebration was more ambivalent, as in Ben Jonson's *Masque of Blackness* (1605). This production, which launched the poet's long collaboration with Inigo Jones on lavish royal entertainments, both reflects and inflects the vogue for blackness at James's court. Commissioned by Queen Anne herself, this masque indulged the histrionic queen's fascination with negritude, presenting her and her ladies in blackface and exotic dress as the "Daughters of Niger." As the masque opens, these "Ethiops" make their entrance in a "vast concave shell" floating in an artificial ocean, and the opening song, sung by admiring tritons and sea-maids, both praises and excuses their black beauty:

> Fair Niger, son to great Oceanus,
> Now honoured thus
> With all his beauteous race,
> Who though but black in face,
> Yet are they bright,
> And full of life and light,

---

7. Russ McDonald, *The Bedford Companion to Shakespeare: An Introduction with Documents*, 296.
8. "Sonnet of Black Beauty" and "Another Sonnet to Black it self," in Edward Herbert, *Occasional Verses of Edward Lord Herbert of Cherbery and Castle-Island*, 38–39. For dating of these sonnets, see Edward Herbert, *The Poems of Lord Herbert of Cherbury*, xxxi. Perhaps not incidentally, the dark-complected Herbert went by the sobriquet "Black Ned."
9. John Collop, *The Poems of John Collop*, 116.
10. Hall, *Things of Darkness*, 120.

> To prove that beauty best
> Which not the colour, but the feature
> Assures unto the creature.
>
> (ll. 80–89)[11]

In language that both denies and anticipates the importance of color, the singers treat these blackened faces as paradoxically "fair" and "bright," while significantly locating their true beauty somehow under the blackness, in the masquers' European "feature."

It is this implicit denigration—the assumption, as even the word "denigration" implies, that whiteness is more intrinsic and natural than blackness—that the Daughters' father, Niger, at first eloquently resists. Attacking what we might call Eurocentrism, he describes how the envious fictions of "Poor brain-sick men, styled poets here with you" (l. 132) have afflicted his black beauties with self-loathing. His daughters, says Niger, have been humiliated by the poets' tale that Phaëton steered the sun's chariot too close to earth and scorched the "Ethiops" black, who before were "as fair / As other Dames" (ll. 139–40). Niger will have none of this, insisting on the contrary that "in their black the perfect'st beauty grows," since their color is "fixed" and constant. Thus, he proclaims, "Their beauties conquer in great beauty's war; / And more, how near divinity they be, / That stand from passion and decay so free" (ll. 120–30).

Yet, despite his warm defense of black beauty, "Father Niger" in the end reverses himself, admitting that blackness is after all not "fixed," but only temporary. His recantation is compelled, he concedes, "By miracle": he has seen the vision of "a face all circumfused with light" telling him to seek a milder land where his daughters can indeed be fully beautified (ll. 160–72). Significantly, Jonson's art here imitates Tudor-Stuart natural philosophy, which, like the Greek Phaëton myth, explained skin color in terms of exposure to the sun.[12] Thus, much as Jonson's blackface court ladies will restore their natural whiteness after the performance, so their alter egos, the "Daughters of Niger," are on their way to "Albion" to be whitened in more temperate climes. In Britannia, a land of further miracles, the rays of the mild "sun"—allegorically identified with King James—"are of a force / To blanch an Ethiop and revive a corse" (ll. 222–26). In fact, in Jonson's significantly named sequel, *The Masque*

---

11. David Lindley, ed., *Court Masques: Jacobean and Caroline Entertainments, 1605–1640*, 1–9.
12. Jordan, *White Man's Burden*, 7.

of Beauty (1608), these dark nymphs are "restored" to their rightful "red and white": "Yield, night, to the light, / As blackness hath to beauty."[13]

But if Niger's attempt at instilling black pride is exposed as unnecessary and even wrongheaded, it is at least still portrayed as psychologically plausible and well-meaning. Indeed, Niger acts out of innocent ignorance and is portrayed—like a true noble savage—as magnanimously yielding to a superior revelation. A cultural critic like Kim Hall can reasonably perceive such a portrait as pro-toracist, noting how male members of the masque's original audience reacted negatively (albeit privately) to Queen Anne in blackface.[14] Yet we should also note that the main import of Jonson's masque is to discredit notions of racial fixity and to subordinate matters of pigment to matters of spirit. Thus the mutability of color implicitly prefigures the religious conversions that, many Jacobeans hoped, would soon whiten dark souls in Africa and America, fitting them for civil—and perhaps marital—intercourse.

Biblicism: Abrahamic or Apostolic Jamestown?

Returning to Pocahontas, I should note that the first crucial factor in framing this cross-cultural window of marital opportunity was English Protestant biblicism. Historians and critics still commonly contrast the secularity of what Jamestown's Governor Dale called "this business" with the holy "errand into the wilderness" of Puritan Massachusetts.[15] However, we should keep in mind that Dale and other of Virginia's apologists were as likely to refer to their western enterprise as "this *holy* business" and "this religious warfare," and it is only in comparison to the superbiblicists of Boston that the southern colony's founding rhetoric can be thought even relatively "secular." By about any other measure than that of the New England Puritans, it seems theocentric, if not theocratic. Indeed, to read Rolfe's letter to Dale is to encounter a sensibility as profoundly Calvinist in its way as John Winthrop's, shot through with self-scrutiny, resorting for help to Calvin's own *Institutes of the Christian Religion,* and saturated in Scripture.[16]

---

13. Ben Jonson, *Ben Jonson: The Complete Masques,* ll. 240–41.
14. Hall, *Things of Darkness,* 129–30.
15. Hamor, *A True Discourse,* 51.
16. Indeed, Perry Miller—one of the most influential interpreters of Puritan New England—writes elsewhere of Virginia that the "intellectual affinities of the writers [Smith, Dale,

But for colonists like Rolfe, Hamor, and Dale to take up the biblical model of sacred travelers is really to invoke more models than one; for in the biblicist apologetics and self-exhortations of early Virginia, three paradigms are in regular juxtaposition, and frequently in conflict. I will call them, without any particular originality, the Abrahamic, or sojourner model; the Davidic, or holy warrior model; and the apostolic, or evangelistic model. I will deal first with the Abrahamic and the apostolic models, for these seemed most strongly to influence Jacobeans negatively or positively toward intermarriage.

The Abrahamic model is seen powerfully at work in the preaching of William Symonds in his farewell sermon to the second wave of Virginian voyagers in April 1609, John Rolfe probably among them. Symonds imagined the Jamestown colonists as Abrahamic sojourners, "strangers in a strange land." Taking Genesis 12:1–3 as his text—"Get thee out of thy Countrey . . . And I will make of thee a great nation"—Symonds warns them to guard ceaselessly against intermarriage with pagan nations. His words are all the more intriguing because they are spoken years before Pocahontas and Rolfe met, indeed probably well before she was heard of in England; and yet Symonds in 1609 sees intermarriage as a clear and present danger:

> Then must Abrams posteritie keepe them to themselues. They may not marry nor giue in marriage to the heathen, that are vncircumcised. And this is so plaine, that out of this foundation arose the law of marriage among themselues. The breaking of this rule, may breake the neck of all good successe of this voyage [to Virginia], whereas by keeping the feare of God, the Planters in shorte time, by the blessing of God, may grow into a nation formidable to all the enemies of Christ, and bee the praise of that part of the world, for so strong a hand to bee ioyned with the people here [in England] that feare God.[17]

Commenting on the exclusivism of this passage in his *Pocahontas: The Evolution of an American Narrative,* historian Robert Tilton is quick to note that "Symonds here makes one of the earliest cases for the power of racial purity." This "fear of miscegenation," observes Tilton, becomes "a constant feature of colonial and

---

Rolfe, et al.] . . . are not with Thomas Jefferson or with . . . Franklin . . . but with Calvin and Loyola. . . . In their own conception of themselves, they are first and foremost Christians, and above all militant Protestants." See Miller, "The Religious Impulse in the Founding of Virginia: Religion and Society in the Early Literature," 493.

17. William Symonds, *Virginea [Virginea Brittania]. A Sermon Preached at White-Chappel, in the presence of many, Honourable and Worshipfull, the Adventurers and Planters for Virginia, 25. April. 1609,* 35.

early American thought."[18] Tilton is of course right that on display in Symonds's sermon are the powerful idea of purity and the common colonial fear of mixing; and he is right about the racial fixation that would eventually become central to American frontier thinking. But in terms of British thinking on the very early Stuart frontier, some careful distinctions must be drawn.

For strictly speaking, Symonds's exhortation is not to racial but to religious purity—"marriage to the heathen, that are *vncircumcised*"—and his great fear is not of miscegenation but of spiritual syncretism—Jamestown's not keeping the fear of the jealous Jehovah, but combining with what he calls "the enemies of Christ." Though Symonds elsewhere speaks plentifully about the American savages' demonic darkness, it is to his mind a darkness generally spiritual rather than epidermal. Indeed, even the "uncircumcision" against which he warns is spiritual; he is not after all a Hebrew like Abraham concerned literally with foreskins, but a Christian concerned typologically with baptism.

Certainly Symonds sounds to us like an ancestor of colonial and American racism, and in a way he is; but he is not himself a racist in any meaningful sense of the word, for race does not much matter to him. He is what we today might call a zealot, even a bigot, but his bigotry is metaphysical, not physical. Lest this seem like a distinction without a difference, the difference is this: even the strictest construction of what I am terming the "Abrahamic model" of sojourning community allows for a permeability that real racism does not, for circumcision is the sign of the covenant, and if one accepts the community's covenant, one can be circumcised and join the community. In other words, religion allows for legitimate conversion, while racism does not, indeed cannot. For under racism all conversion is, in every sense, illegitimate. Thus even the Abrahamic model, with its strong stress on exclusion, contains a principle of inclusion; that is, it contains in principle the apostolic model.

What these Abrahamic and apostolic models have to do with Pocahontas is made even clearer by the example of another sermon preached in London ten months after Symonds's. In February 1610, William Crashaw—best known to literary historians as the father of the baroque poet and Catholic convert Richard Crashaw—presented his "Newyeeres Gift to Virginea" in the form of an extended exhortation on Christ's words to Peter in Luke 22:32: "But I have praied for thee, that thy faith faile not: therefore when thou art conuerted strengthen thy brethren." The text, overtly evangelical both in its Gospel source and in its substance, leads Crashaw to emphasize—as if responding directly to

---

18. Robert Tilton, *Pocahontas: The Evolution of an American Narrative*, 13.

Symonds's earlier sermon—the apostolic model over the Abrahamic for the holy community of Jamestown. Crashaw proclaims that the English, now themselves converted to Christ, have crossed the Atlantic not primarily to keep separate, but to bring the gospel to their savage "brethren," with whom they can and should join equally in all sorts of alliances.

And indeed Crashaw takes remarkable pains to emphasize the essential equality of the English and the Indians as humans. After an extended introduction warning against "Popish devices" for capturing souls in the Old World and the New (a warning apparently ignored by his son), Crashaw directly raises the question of whether or not the savages are "our brethren." Yes, he answers; we Britons, Angles, and Saxons were once heathen savages too—there but for the grace of God go we. "[W]e by the blessing of God are conuerted lately from Popery, and formerly from paganisme: Nor can it be denied that they (in this case) are *our brethren:* for the same God made them as well as vs, of as good matter as he made vs, gaue them as perfect and good soules and bodies as to vs, and the same Messiah & Saviour is sent to them as to vs. . . . for the time was when wee were sauage and vnciuill, and worshipped the diuell, as now they do, then God sent some to make us ciuill, others to make vs christians." Crashaw is so intent on portraying the native Virginians as flesh of his flesh that he dismisses their different skin color with a diverting scenario, as "little more blacke or tawnie, then one of ours would be if he should goe naked in the South of England."[19]

In fact, Crashaw believes that the English nation, grown soft with excessive luxury and civility, could do with some rejuvenating time in the American woods. Echoing moralists from Tacitus to Spenser, he says that comparison with the savages "discouers the pusillanimitie, the basenesse, the tendernesse and effeminatenesse of our English people: into which our nation is now *degenerate*, from a strong, valiant, hardie, patient and induring people, as our forefathers were," and, by implication, as their Indian "brethren" still are.[20] Here, intriguingly, the tables turn, and it is the English "apostles" who will find a physical rather than a metaphysical regeneration in Virginia. They convert America, and America converts them; the savages need Christian civility, and the Christians need savage virility.

Significantly, this counterconversion of degenerate Britons into revitalized Americans informs the earliest descriptions of Pocahontas's conversion to Christianity; these accounts actually gesture toward the same civilized/savage divide.

---

19. William Crashaw, *[A Newyeeres Gift to Virginea] A Sermon Preached in London before . . . the Lord Warre . . . Febr. 21, 1609* (1610), C3r, C4v, E2r.
20. Ibid., F4v.

Both Governor Dale and the colony's parson, Alexander Whitaker, mention how Pocahontas, as a necessary prelude to her baptism and marriage, publicly renounced what they call "her countrey idolatry."[21] This repeated phrase refers not only to the cultic practices of her particular country or nation (that is, the Powhatan Confederacy of the southeastern Algonquian) but also to cultic practices thought to be generally typical of the country*side*, the heath, the wood, the Latin *pagus*, or rural village; practices hence "heathen," "savage," "pagan." It is in this sense that Pocahontas gives up her "countrey idolatry" and afterward "liues ciuilly and louingly" with Rolfe; she needed urban manners and Christian charity. As Rolfe himself was to write after his marriage, the Indians also "beare the *Image* of our heavenly Creator," and it is humbling for the now-civilized English to ask themselves, "what were we before the Gospell of Christ shined amongst vs?"[22]

Although neither William Symonds nor William Crashaw was in 1609 and 1610 yet aware of Pocahontas personally, it is not hard to see how their muted debate over brotherhood with the savages, as well as Crashaw's call for an apostolic Jamestown, helped to prepare the ground in which Rolfe's desire for the Powhatan princess could mature into matrimony. By 1615, Dale, Whitaker, and Rolfe can argue that a converted "Rebecca"—having undergone the Christian "circumcision" of baptism—has been adopted into the "Israel of God," the church. Baptism has washed the princess white in the sense that matters most to these apologists—their claim is that the "heathen" suffer from the common human darkness of sin, not a particular racial darkness of skin.

But why, in 1609, would Symonds have seen the prospect of colonial intermarriage as so imminently dangerous? One reason that I already have mentioned was the vogue for celebrating "black beauty" at court. Another probable reason for Symonds's anxiety is that in 1596 Sir Walter Ralegh had written—after his 1595 expedition to Guiana—encouraging eventual intermarriage with the native Arawaks there. Ralegh stresses the ease with which the Indians had turned to Catholic Christianity in Brazil and Mexico, proposing that selected native men be sent into Protestant England, "which being ciuilled and conuerted heere, vpon there returne and receiving of others in their romes thei may be matched in marriage with English women."[23] And indeed, intermarriage was a live issue being debated in other colonial settings. In 1612, only two years before the

---

21. Hamor, *A True Discourse*, 55, 60.
22. John Rolfe, *A True Relation of the state of Virginia lefte by Sir Thomas Dale Knight in May last 1616*, 40.
23. Ralegh, *The Discoverie of . . . Guiana*, 146–48.

Rolfe-Rebecca union, Sir John Davies, the English poet and attorney-general for Ireland, writes arguing that English intermarriage with native Irishwomen (still forbidden by the old Anglo-Irish aristocracy) would prove a pacifying gesture of good faith to the Irish, demonstrating to these "savage and barbarous people" that the English colonists do not intend "in the end to root out the Irish."[24]

Classicism: Virgilian Virginia

It may seem strange to find purveyors of English civility like Ralegh and Davies so eager to encourage intermarriage with peoples whom they term "savages." Yet this strangeness is reduced when we consider the second crucial factor, after Protestant biblicism, that was to enable Virginia's short-lived Anglo-Powhatan marriage alliance: that is, the revived British classicism that cast the colonists as New Trojans descended from the marriage of Aeneas to the woodland princess Lavinia, spreading a destined empire abroad and raising the American "savages" to civility. In chapter one, I observed how, at first fitfully under the early Tudors and then emphatically after the Reformation, English writers had recovered and reinvented the "British" identity inherited from medieval legends in Geoffrey of Monmouth's *History of the Kings of Britain*. Though as yet their nation possessed little beyond the pale of Dublin, Edmund Spenser in books 2 and 3 of *The Faerie Queene* and Michael Drayton early in his *Poly-Olbion* idealized "Albion" as the nurse of a once-and-future empire.[25] They imagined ancient Britain as the place inhabited by noble savages of Trojan descent—in this legend Britain was named for Aeneas's grandson Brutus, and London was called "Troynovant" or "New Troy"—who had been seasoned and trained by the civilization of conquering Rome. Then, in turn, both British savagery and Roman civilization had been redeemed and transformed by a Christianity that, under the British-born Roman Emperor Constantine, was both prepapal and imperial.

Significantly, the Virgilian legend provided striking parallels, and thus a potent paradigm, for the fledgling Jamestown enterprise: in book 7 of the *Aeneid*, Virgil imagines Latium as a place of sylvan rusticity inhabited by a warrior race

---

24. Sir John Davies, *A Discovery of the True Causes Why Ireland Was Never Entirely Subdued....* (1612), 133.
25. Michael Drayton, *Poly-Olbion. Being the Fourth Volume of his Works;* Spenser, *Poetical Works.*

under a noble chieftain looking to give his daughter in dynastic marriage to a prophesied foreign prince with whom he will share equal rule.[26] Add to this Virgilian connection a further Trojo-Britannic legend: the belief held by some early Stuart Englishmen that the American "natives" were actually descended from old Troy themselves. In *New English Canaan* (1635), Thomas Morton speculates that after "Brutus, who was the fo[u]rth from A[e]neas, left Latium upon the conflict had with the Latines, . . . this people were dispersed"—some to conquer "Albion" and found Britain, the others driven by a storm across the great ocean. So, Morton concludes, "the originall of the Natives of New England may be well conjectured to be from the scattered Trojans."[27] The fantasy of finding an exotic but identifiable alter ego in a far country has always had strong imperial implications, from medieval legends of Prester John in Africa to Rudyard Kipling's fictional "Kafiristan." "I'll make an Empire!" says Kipling's Danny Dravot of his plans for the light-skinned "Kafiris" north of the Hindu Kush in "The Man Who Would Be King." "These men aren't niggers, they're English!"[28] Significantly, Danny—like Aeneas, Brutus, and Rolfe—seeks to consolidate his empire through intermarriage.

---

26. Virgil, *Aeneid*. Peter Hulme has discovered another classical reference in Rolfe's letter to Dale. Rolfe writes uneasily of his conscientious agonies regarding his "Carnall affection" for Pocahontas, "to whome my hart and best thoughtes are and have byn a longe tyme soe intangled & inthralled in soe lintricate a Laborinth, that I was even aweariad to vnwynde my selfe therout." Here, says Hulme, "the classical reference needs a Puritan rewriting. Rolfe is Theseus; but Pocahontas as Ariadne, rather than helping, has Rolfe so intangled in her erotic threads that he has to unwind *himself* out of the labyrinth in order to escape the unmentioned Minotaur, that monstrous result of unholy unions." Hulme, *Colonial Encounters*, 144.

27. Thomas Morton, *New English Canaan of Thomas Morton*, 126, 128–29.

28. Kipling, *The Man Who Would Be King*, 269. Significantly, like Rolfe, Danny also makes a marriage and, as an indirect result, ends up dead. Hope for discovery of a hidden English or British remnant just beyond the colonial frontier expressed itself in varied ways, even after there was no longer a frontier. North Carolina's "Lost Colony" legend has generated tales of blue-eyed Indians from the 1590s until the present; some of these tales have wishfully linked the disappeared Virginia Dare with Pocahontas herself. See Robert D. Arner, "The Romance of Roanoke: Virginia Dare and the Lost Colony in American Literature," 6. Even after the American Revolution, theories of old British survival persisted: in 1799, English poet Robert Southey composed the epic *Madoc* based on old chronicles about an exiled Welsh prince who, in 1170, was supposed to have sailed to America. See Robert Southey, *The Poetical Works of Robert Southey*, 3:199–393. Besides providing John Dee with one of his claims to "British" possession of America, Madoc was supposed to have left a tribe of descendents after him. It was perhaps this remnant whom Thomas Jefferson had in mind in 1804 when he instructed Meriwether Lewis—at the suggestion of Benjamin Rush—to enquire after blue-eyed, Welsh-speaking Indians in the upper reaches of the Missouri River Valley. James P. Ronda, *Lewis and Clark among the Indians*, 3, 156.

Thus a Virgilian Virginia could recapitulate the master epic, promising another cycle of imperial regeneration, with Rolfe an Aeneas of sorts, Chief Powhatan a transatlantic Latinus, Pocahontas the new Lavinia, and Jamestown yet another Troy. Furthermore, as I have noted, Tudor moralists well before William Crashaw had deplored the decline of British hereditary stock from ancient noble savagery to contemporary effete urbanity. Such laments suggest that some influential Elizabethans might have viewed colonial intermarriage as benefiting the bloodlines not only of the "savages" but also of the "civilized"—especially if the Indians were distant Trojan cousins.

For particularly graphic evidence of a strong and positive connection in the late Tudor imagination between the noble savages of old Britain and the New World, we must turn to Thomas Hariot's remarkable 1590 account of Roanoke Island, *The Brief and True Report of the New Found Land of Virginia*, and particularly to Theodore DeBry's accompanying engravings. Here we find not only plentiful images of naked Roanoke warriors; we also find an appendix of pictures worth many thousands of words on my subject—pictures, as Hariot writes, "of the Pictes which in olde tyme dyd habite one part of the great Bretainne,... for to showe how that the Inhabitants of the great Bretannie haue bin in times past as sauuage as those of Virginia."[29]

What follow are five engravings of ancient British warriors, male and female, resplendent with body paint (and nothing else), bristling with weaponry, and one sporting a severed enemy head.[30] Like Crashaw after him, Hariot notes the equivalence of American and British savages in his commentary on the engravings. It is especially suggestive that DeBry's classicizing hand pictures the noble, nubile maidens of Roanoke Island coyly covering their otherwise bare bosoms. An eye like Ralegh's, already full of admiration for savage virtue, might see in these virgins—and not only in the land that they emblematize—a rich new ground for the regeneration of Britain's warrior might.

Such a suggestion also seems present as one makes the transition from the late Tudor to the early Stuart in Michael Drayton's 1606 "Ode. To the Virginian Voyage," which shows that the poets as well as the preachers claimed a part in exhorting the colonists. But where Symonds and Crashaw deploy the biblical models that I have discussed, Drayton's vision, as even his chosen form would indicate, is bracingly classical. Having called the "brave heroic minds" of the adventuring "Britons"—not "Englishmen"—to brave the absolute deep

---

29. Thomas Hariot, *A Brief and True Report of the New Found Land of Virginia*, 75. This book originally was published in 1588 in Latin and without engravings.

30. Ibid., 76–85.

to arrive at "Virginia, / Earth's only paradise" and view its "golden age," Drayton raises the remarkable hope that these men will

> in regions far
> Such heroes bring ye forth
> As those from whom we came,
> And plant our name
> Under that star
> Not known unto our north.[31]

What is so extraordinary about this call for a new race of heroes conceived on the American shore is that it lacks any apparent reference to English wives. Indeed, there were no English wives, nor even any English women, in that band that sailed in 1606, and in fact only two white women had arrived by 1610, one a colonist's wife, the other her servant. English men continued to outnumber English women at Jamestown by a rate of twenty to one until the years 1619–1620.[32] In Philip Young's groundbreaking essay on Pocahontas, he writes of her legendary status as a redeeming American Eve: "we [Americans], by our descent from her, become a new race, innocent of both European and all human origins."[33] Similarly, could not Drayton have had it in mind that his new heroic race, like Virgil's Romans, might actually blend the old blood of Troy with the rejuvenating strains of the noble natives?

Such a between-the-lines possibility might seem far-fetched, except for two facts: first, that a contemporary preacher like William Symonds feared that it would happen, and second, that, very famously, it did. Indeed, it happened more than once: consider the little-known parallel case of another converted Indian princess wed to another early Stuart colonist: Mary Brent, née Kitomagund, in Maryland. The daughter of the "Pascataway Emperor," Kitomagund was educated by the Jesuits at St. Mary's City, became a convert christened Mary, and in the early 1630s wed Giles Brent, a planter.[34] But these striking similarities to the marriage of Pocahontas point to an equally striking difference in the way the marriages were received: unlike Governor Dale in 1614 Virginia, Lord Baltimore in 1630s Maryland condemned the union.

---

31. Michael Drayton, *Poems*, 1:123–24, ll. 1, 7, 23–24, 37, 55–60.
32. Alf J. Mapp Jr., *The Virginia Experiment: The Old Dominion's Role in the Making of America, 1607–1781*, 55.
33. Philip Young, "The Mother of Us All: Pocahontas Reconsidered," 408–9.
34. Maryland State Hall of Records, the Carmelite Monastery Papers, Mary E. W. Ramey, "Chronicles of Mistress Margaret Brent," 7.

Significantly, though, his reasons for withholding his gubernatorial blessing were apparently not racial but jurisdictional. Lord Baltimore feared, with some cause, that Giles Brent made this marriage to circumvent the English Crown's territorial distribution rights by securing a personal claim to the Pascataway chief's lands.[35] In other words, while Rolfe, like the pious Aeneas, made his savage match for the professed good of the colony and the nation, Brent may have been putting his own patrimony before patriotism. Unfortunately, nothing further is known about the Brent-Kitomagund marriage, but it is suggestive that the incident seems to show English colonial authority by the 1630s turning away from the kind of dynastic union portrayed by Virgil, suggested by Crashaw and Drayton, and proposed by Ralegh and Davies. Having gained a firm foothold in America and elsewhere in their growing empire, the English were beginning to discover a purity in their own blood that previously had not been thought to exist.

"Yelps for Liberty among the Drivers of Negroes": English Freedom and the Color Line

I have presented these accounts and their imaginative contexts as evidence for a "preracist" moment in early Stuart colonization. Still, as I have shown, these "preracist" themes coexisted with "protoracism," sometimes in the same texts. For all of the Dark Lady's attractions, she was usually the loser in love, quite famously in Shakespeare's sonnets but also in other "Poems of Blackness" addressed to what we would call women of color. Kim Hall itemizes such Tudor-Stuart verse and finds that in lyrics by many hands, the "Ethiop," though often lovely and sympathetic, is generally used and then rejected by the white man of her desires.[36] However much black beauty seemed on the verge of becoming white beauty's "successive heir," these poetic jiltings did not bode well for marriage alliances like John Rolfe's. Yet far more portentous were the protoracist elements in the classical and Judeo-Christian models themselves: Aeneas must fight Turnus and the savages for Lavinia and Italy; Brutus must displace a race of woodland monsters led by "Gogmagog" to possess his island and rename it

---

35. I am indebted for this analysis of the Brent-Kitomagund marriage to Professor Debra Meyers of Long Island University.
36. These include well-known poets like George Herbert, John Cleveland, Henry King, and Richard Lovelace, and less-known ones like Edward Guilpin, Henry Rainolds, and Eldred Revett. Hall, *Things of Darkness*, 270–90.

"Britain"; and both the biblical patriarchs and the apostles were often succeeded by holy warriors intent on eliminating the irredeemable enemies of the Lord.

Ironically, it was John Rolfe who inadvertently precipitated this fateful paradigm shift and became, in many ways, the unwitting grandfather of the colonial color line. After "Rebecca's" death of smallpox in March 1617—she is buried at Gravesend in England—Rolfe gave their two-year-old son, Thomas, into the care of his English family and returned to Virginia. There he pursued the cultivation of tobacco with Calvinistic dedication and success, a success that brought demand for more and more land and so aroused the hostility of the surrounding Algonquian. After the death of Powhatan and the accession of his half-brother Opechancanough, their rage against English encroachment exploded in the massacre of March 22, 1622, in which, by one account, 347 unarmed colonists were taken by surprise, murdered, and hideously mangled.[37] Accounts disagree, but Rolfe himself may have been killed in the attack, or he may have died of illness soon before, in the last days of what came to be called, in retrospect, "the Peace of Pocahontas."[38]

After that peace was broken and the news reached London and Westminster, the English authorities, as well as popular sentiment, assimilated the disaster by means of a sudden imaginative conversion to the venerable model of holy war. In the next chapter, I will discuss how the imperial disenchantment of one colonial official, Nicholas Ferrar, grew from his blighted hopes for an apostolic Jamestown; indeed, it was in the Jamestown massacre that those hopes died. The Virginia Company's stated aim of "brotherhood with the savages" was now repudiated—both in England and in America—as the source of the trouble: Virginia, the Company declared, was a new Canaan, and with idolatrous, treacherous Canaanites the sword of a Joshua or a David was the best argument. When the colony's governor, Sir Francis Wyatt, had first arrived in 1620, he was most concerned with the possibility of Spanish attacks; now he found his devils closer at hand. In an August 1622 letter from the Company's Council for Virginia in London, Wyatt was given carte blanche for revenge: "we must advise you to root out from being any longer a people, so cursed a nation, ungrateful to all benefits, and uncapable of all goodness: at least, to the removal of them so far from you as you may not only be out of danger, but out of fear of them."[39] To this document can be traced the Anglo-American policies of retributive extermination and removal that run from the Pequot War through the Trail of Tears to Wounded

---

37. Barbour, *Pocahontas and Her World*, 206.
38. Young, "Mother of Us All," 394; Barbour, *Pocahontas and Her World*, 213.
39. Barbour, *Pocahontas and Her World*, 200–201, 207–12.

Knee. It is also one of the first official statements—and the most deadly earnest up to its time—of what soon came to be called the "incapacity" in people of color for spiritual enlightenment; as Prospero says of Caliban in *The Tempest*, "a born devil, on whose nature / Nurture can never stick" (4.1.188–89).

Compounding the irony of this revenge and removal policy was that, as the colony spread up the James Peninsula and south across the James River, the exponential growth in tobacco production, combined with a lack of willing colonial workers, brought the first influx of African labor to Virginia. However, though these workers were sometimes called slaves, they had not yet become mere chattel; that is, they were not yet subject to the complete, perpetual, hereditary loss of freedom. Indeed, the kind of Calvinist theology that still dominated in Jacobean England presented serious obstacles to the establishment of chattel slavery in the new colonies. Although their Old Testament emphasis made such Protestants tolerant of bond service and penal servitude, they generally hewed close to the Mosaic line in their strong opposition to "man-stealing," one of the foundations of the slave trade.[40]

Even more problematic was their emphasis on the fundamental equality of all human souls before God. William Perkins, the arch-Calvinist of the late Tudor and early Jacobean era, is entirely typical. Commenting on Galatians 3:28—"There is neither Iew nor Grecian: there is neither bond nor free: there is neither male nor female: for ye are all one in Christ Iesus"—Perkins concedes that under "the lawe of corrupt nature" slavery may be allowed "if it be vsed with mercie and moderation." However, he concludes his commentary by telling pomp to take physic: "[T]hey which are of great byrth and of heigh condicion, must be put in mind not to be heigh minded, nor to despise them that are of lowe degree, for . . . the obscure and base person hath as good part in Christ, and the greatest men that be. Therefore we may not swell in pride for outward things."[41] Furthermore, nowhere in this passage—published in 1604—does Perkins mention race or color, but if he did, it would probably be as another thing "merely outward." There was as yet no metaphysics of race to make dark skin darken the soul.

That this "moderate" policy toward slavery persisted in Virginia at least into the 1640s can be inferred from the official silence on the subject of miscegenation until 1662, when racial essentialism begins to take statutory form. In that year, Virginia doubled the usual fine for fornication if the act was between

---

40. Jordan, *White Man's Burden*, 31–32, 94–95; Exodus 21:16.
41. William Perkins, *A Commentarie or Exposition, vpon the fiue first Chapters of the Epistle to the Galatians: penned by the godly, learned, and Judiciall Diuine, Mr. W. Perkins*, 269–70.

"any christian . . . with a negro man or woman"; in 1664, Maryland officially condemned "freeborne English women" who "intermarry with Negro Slaves"; and in 1691, Virginia officially forebade all interracial unions, whether with blacks or with Indians, denouncing them for their "abominable mixture and spurious issue."[42] What alchemy had transformed the Jacobean attraction to blackness into loathing by the century's end?

One place to seek answers is in the decades of official silence on race between the 1630s and the 1660s—and the answers are, again, laden with irony. For during these midcentury years, England's civil wars for liberty seem to have hastened the tightening of American bondage. During the very years—1640 to 1660—when colonial tobacco production was metastasizing and the demand for African labor soaring, the English motherland was fighting itself over the meaning of liberty and social equality. Puritan radicalism attempted to kill not merely the king—which it did in 1649—but kingship itself, and with it the entire system of hierarchies that supported the monarchy: church episcopacy and the House of Lords were abolished, and universal manhood suffrage loudly proposed. Though the return of the monarchy in 1660 came to be called the Restoration, officially reestablishing bishops and lords, much "leveling" of the war and Interregnum years was irreversible: the center of cultural authority had shifted from the court, with its inherited ethos of warrior aristocracy, to the city, with its thrusting new ideology of individual achievement and social mobility.

What this leveling at home meant for race relations in the colonies was, ironically, that one vital bond of sympathy linking English to native American and to African cultures was fatally weakened. To the pragmatic Restoration political imagination—especially after the Glorious Revolution in 1688—monarchy and nobility were no longer divine absolutes but contingent social contracts for the purpose of securing civility. To such an imagination it seemed increasingly laughable to speak of Indian kings and princesses, of noble savages and African royalty. Where were their cities? Where were their trades and industries, their coinage and their arts, their centers of learning and science? Where, after all, were their clothes? While "primitive" had still been a term of praise to the Jacobeans, indicating a kind of prelapsarian purity, it was becoming a pejorative word in the newly "progressive" culture of their grandchildren. By the end of the century, "savage" blood promised not renewed vitality but retrograde vice; to bear it brought an unwashable mark, like a hereditary curse.

Thus the impulse to social gradation, far from disappearing, instead accommodated itself to the newly reigning language of liberty. Robin Blackburn has

---

42. Jordan, *White Man's Burden*, 44.

noted that in "the period 1630–1750 the British Empire witnessed an increasingly clamorous, and even obsessive, 'egotistical' revulsion against 'slavery' side by side with an almost uncontested exploitation of African bondage."[43] This accommodation is strikingly evident in *The Fundamental Constitutions of Carolina*, composed in 1669 by the fledgling political philosopher John Locke. In over one hundred separate legal headings, Locke repeatedly lays the burden on colonial authorities to guard the native liberties of Englishmen, particularly liberties of speech, press, and religion. Yet under one of the last of these headings, he makes it clear that a crucial mark of free men will be their ownership of others: "Every freeman of Carolina shall have absolute power and authority of his negro slaves, of what opinion or religion soever." Locke is still enough of a social Calvinist to have stated, a few headings earlier, that slaves may belong to any church they wish, "as fully members as any freeman."[44] But for him now the emphasis is on the absolute monarchical power that makes the freeman free, and on the blackness of the "negro" that marks him inexpungibly as a bondslave. Locke is rightly numbered among those fathering the liberties of the American Revolution and Constitution; yet for that very reason he also is implicated in Samuel Johnson's antirevolutionary indictment of 1775, "how is it that we hear the loudest yelps for liberty among the drivers of negroes?"[45]

Furthermore, soon even Locke's allowance for a slave's freedom of religion came to be seen as an infringement on his master's liberty. By the later seventeenth century, a debate over the darker brother's spiritual "capacity" was well under way; English Protestant planters from Jamaica to Virginia were claiming that their slaves either could or should not be converted to Christianity at all. So said Sir Richard Dutton, governor of Barbados, in 1681, that "as to make negroes Christians, their savage brutishness renders them wholly incapable"; and in the colonies the changing language was already drawing the color line, with the words "Christian," "free," "English," and "white" all being used indiscriminately as synonyms.[46] Yet as Peter Kalm, a contemporary Swedish observer, noted, questions about spiritual capacity were driven largely by issues of economic and social necessity: the planters' opposition to slave evangelism arose "partly by thinking that they would not be able to keep their negroes so subjected afterwards; and partly through fear of the negroes growing too proud

---

43. Robin Blackburn, *The Overthrow of Colonial Slavery, 1776–1848*, 42.
44. John Locke, *The Works of John Locke*, 10:196, headings CX, CVII.
45. Samuel Johnson, *The Yale Edition of the Works of Samuel Johnson*, 10:454.
46. Lawrence James, *Rise and Fall of the British Empire*, 22; Jordan, *White Man's Burden*, 53.

on seeing themselves upon a level with their masters in religious matters."[47] It was as if the "Ethiop" might, alarmingly, change his skin after all by changing his religion: first a white soul, then a white wife, and he would be blanched to full brotherhood in a few generations. And then how would they own him?

In this context Aphra Behn's *Oroonoko, or The Royal Slave* (1688) stands both in bold contrast to and as indirect confirmation of the emergent ideology of libertarian slaveowning.[48] On the one hand, as even the subtitle suggests, the eponymous hero of this "history" is just the sort of "noble savage" with whom the Elizabethans and Jacobeans had been able to identify. Oroonoko is an African prince possessing the warrior virtues of fidelity, fierceness, courage, and magnanimity, and he is the heir to the Gold Coast throne of Coramantien, having received a European education and military training. Also, as Peter Hulme notes, Oroonoko is "far from being a representative African"; rather, he is "distinguished in every possible way from his fellow-countrymen, even in his physical characteristics": though his skin is "of perfect ebony, or polished jet," his nose is Roman, his lips thin, his hair long, and his form classical.[49] Behn, a Stuart royalist writing in that year of Lockean triumph over Stuart royalism, makes her sable hero naturally royal. This native nobility is so evident that even after his betrayal and capture by white slave traders, his new colonial owner, Telfrey, treats him as an honored guest while, significantly, renaming him "Caesar." He has that about him which even his master would fain call master.

Yet, on the other hand, it is Oroonoko's tragedy to be undone by his kingly dignity and by the fecklessness of his fellow Africans. Allowed to marry the enslaved African princess Imoinda, he becomes alarmed that their child will be born a slave, so he leads a slave rebellion that fails when his cowardly and inept black countrymen abandon him. Recaptured by the black-hating Deputy-Governor Byam, Oroonoko is viciously flogged and, after an unsuccessful suicide attempt, is tortured and killed in a horrendous public execution. Although he stands to his death with stoic strength and even Christ-like forgiveness, never recanting his African pride, his moral and physical prowess exalt him so far above his fellow blacks as to make him seem the exception that proves the racist rule.

Still, *Oroonoko* is remarkable in its time for its contrarian courage, and it remained a favorite text of the antislavery movement through the next century. Thus it stands well within the Christian humanist countertradition that I will

---

47. Jordan, *White Man's Burden*, 89.
48. Aphra Behn, *Oroonoko, or The Royal Slave*.
49. Hulme, *Colonial Encounters*, 240–41.

explore in the next two chapters—with works like *Utopia, Gulliver's Travels,* and *Rasselas,* all of which portray encounters with non-European cultures that force Europeans to critique themselves. Significantly, as I will show, it is often these writers' Toryism—with its hierarchical loyalties, its royalist nostalgia, and its reaction against Whiggish "progress"—that shapes their opposition to "empires of liberty"—white democratic vistas cleared by dark people in chains.

It is this same atavistic respect for "nobility of birth" that, a few years after Behn's *Oroonoko,* informs Charles Gildon's 1694 defense of *Othello.* The year before, in his *Short View of Tragedy,* Thomas Rymer had mocked Shakespeare's portrayal of a noble—and marriageable—Moor as ridiculously improbable: "With us a *Black-amoor* might rise to be a Trumpeter: but *Shakespeare* would not have him less than a Lieutenant-General. With us a *Moor* might marry some little drab, or Small-coal Wench: *Shakespeare* would provide him the Daughter and Heir of some great Lord or Privy-Counsellor, and all the Town should reckon it a very suitable match."[50] Although Rymer concedes that colonial antimiscegenation law does not technically apply "with us" in England—indeed intermarriage was never outlawed in the home country—Rymer's visceral contempt for such matches resonates with the harsher colonial position.[51]

Significantly, although Rymer's attack on Shakespeare was immediately answered by both John Dennis and John Dryden, it is Gildon's response, with its praise of black dignity, that yields the most striking defense of Shakespearean decorum:

> 'Tis granted, a *Negro* here does seldom rise above a Trumpeter, nor often perhaps higher at *Venice*. But then that proceeds from the Vice of Mankind.... Now 'tis certain, there is no reason in the nature of things why a *Negro* of equal Birth and Merit should not be on an equal bottom with a *German, Hollander, Frenchman,* &c.... The Poet [Shakespeare] has therefore ... cast off this customary Barbarity of confining Nations, without regard to their Virtue and Merits, to slavery and contempt for the meer Accident of their Complexion....
>
> After all this, *Othello* being of *Royal Blood,* and a Christian, where is the disparity of the Match? If either side is advanc'd, 'tis *Desdemona*.[52]

If Gildon's antiracist rhetoric seems to us ahead of its time, that is largely for being also behind it: his emphasis on noble birth and royal blood; his dismissal

---

50. Brian Vickers, ed., *Shakespeare: The Critical Heritage, 1693–1733,* 2:29.
51. Edward Scobie, *Black Britannia: A History of Blacks in Britain,* 37–42.
52. Vickers, ed., *Critical Heritage,* 73–74. Gildon reads Iago's words—"And then for her / To Win the Moor, were't to renounce his Baptism" (2.3.331–32)—as confirming "that Othello is suppos'd to be a Christian."

of the "meer Accident" of color; his stress on the equalizing power of Christian conversion; his ironic twist about the *white* partner marrying "up"—all of these ideas, the freshest things reigning in the days of Princess Pocahontas, were outmoded in the Whiggish world of 1694.

Indeed, the social and political meanings of religious conversion were undergoing a profound conversion of their own. By 1701, official English Protestantism had made an uneasy but long-lasting peace with chattel slavery in the colonies: in return for permission to evangelize Africans in America and the Caribbean, the newly founded Society for the Propagation of the Gospel in Foreign Parts (the S.P.G.) chose not to oppose perpetual Negro servitude and promised the planters that their gospel of submission would make these new believers better slaves.[53] In fact, on the S.P.G.'s own plantation in Barbados, each slave was branded on the chest with the word "Society"; though as Lawrence James writes, on that plantation "the rate of conversion was disappointing."[54]

Back in Virginia, Thomas Rolfe—the only child of John and "Rebecca"—had returned and settled south of the James River by 1635, where he went on to establish the main line of slaveholding colonial aristocrats, "of Jeffersons and Lees, of Randolphs, Marshalls, and an estimated two million other people."[55] Indeed, their seed was scattered so widely that in 1924 the Virginia Assembly amended its antimiscegenation laws—dating originally from 1691—to state that "persons who have one-sixteenth or less of the blood of the American Indian and have no other non-Caucasian blood shall be deemed as white persons."[56] This fraction matched the degrees of separation between the line of Pocahontas and some of the legislators; they were, in effect, unbastardizing themselves and their children, 233 years after the fact. They also were whitening their sepulchre: by conceding the relativity of race in this special case, while reasserting an absolute color line in all others, they were displaying racial hypocrisy in startlingly bold relief and building law on insupportably obvious contradictions. By 1969, three hundred years after Locke's *Fundamental Constitutions of Carolina* explicitly made American freedom depend on American slavery, the whole institutional edifice had collapsed, and the antimiscegenation laws were repealed.[57]

But regretful hindsight came much sooner than 1969. When William Byrd wrote in 1738 that "a Moor may be washt white in 3 Generations, [and] an

---

53. Jordan, *White Man's Burden*, 91, 94.
54. James, *Rise and Fall of the British Empire*, 22–23.
55. Young, "The Mother of Us All," 394; Barbour, *Pocahontas and Her World*, 214–15.
56. Tilton, *Pocahontas*, 29.
57. Ibid., 14; see also Edmund S. Morgan, *American Slavery, American Freedom: The Ordeal of Colonial Virginia*.

Indian . . . blancht in two," he was imagining what might have been if the English had chosen the ancient Roman, or contemporary French, policy of colonial intermarriage. There is certainly whimsy in his praise of amorous interracial evangelism—he suggests that "a sprightly Lover is the most prevailing Missionary that can be sent amongst these, or any other Infidels"—and there is Eurocentrism in his assumption that it is the "Moor" and the "Indian" who will be cleansed by the transaction. Yet there is sad earnestness too: "The [Virginia] Natives cou[l]d," he writes, "by no means, perswade themselves that the English were heartily their Friends, so long as they disdained to intermarry with them. . . . Had such Affinities been contracted in the Beginning, how much Bloodshed had been prevented."[58]

In the beginning, in 1613, it had seemed possible to Pocahontas's clerical admirer Samuel Purchas that "the tawney Moore, black Negro, duskie Libyan, ash-coloured Indian, olive-coloured American, should with the whiter European become one *sheep-fold*, under *one great Shepheard*"; that they might live together "without any more distinction of Colour, Nation, Language, Sexe, Condition, [and] all may be *One* in him that is One"; and that their blood might blend in shared offspring.[59] Yet even by the time that Purchas died in 1625, this millennial hope had been deferred, as the natives showed little interest in the "lonely God" of the Christians and as English and Algonquian blood ran red in the field.

Soon the colonials had invented British racial purity, so that the marriage of Pocahontas came to be remembered as purely emblematic—of her father's kingdom, cleared of its human undergrowth and transferred to new husbandry. Yet deferral was not defeat; as I will show in the last two chapters, the English Protestant conscience was never fully colonized. Its oppositional voice could and did cry out, not only for liberty, but also for justice.

---

58. William Byrd, *Histories of the Dividing Line betwixt Virginia and North Carolina*, 4.
59. Jordan, *White Man's Burden*, 8.

Five

Prophets against Empire

Countertraditions, 1516–1815

My kingdom is not of this world. —*John 18:36*

Justice removed, then, what are kingdoms but great bands of robbers? What are bands of robbers themselves but little kingdoms? —*Augustine of Hippo*, The City of God 4.4

Or what rich Treasorous state, hath not vndone
The Conquerer, and wonne those, who hath wonne[?] —*Samuel Daniel*, "Epistle to Prince Henry" (1609–1610), ll. 35–36

Are such things done on Albion's shore? —*William Blake*, "A Little Boy Lost," l. 24

"The strength of empire is in religion," said Ben Jonson, and I have been exploring how English Protestantism served as a cohesive force binding together a reimagined Britain as it projected itself across the oceans. I have discussed how elements of Protestant belief bolstered old myths of British imperial recovery; how Reformation accounts of Spanish Catholic atrocities established England's abiding sense of relative righteousness and redeeming mission; and how the metaphysical modesty of Drake at Nova Albion modeled the authorizing humility that would for centuries justify English acts of colonial possession. I also have detailed how the Protestant imagination gradually and uneasily articulated the metaphysics of racial hierarchy, providing the apologia for binding some peoples over to landlessness and of binding others under in slavery.

What, in effect, I have been describing is the development of a parallel faith, a religion of Protestant imperialism, derivative of but distinct from Protestant Christianity itself. I turn now to those distinctions. For Christianity, like Judaism before it, has posed a cumbrous problem to every empire, indeed every government, since Rome's: the believer's ultimate allegiances lie beyond this world and can be set against it. The creed that seems to promise nation-binding unity and harmonious hierarchy can turn perversely oppositional, binding back the national conscience and its imperial arm.

So, in these last two chapters, I take up what might be called Britain's own Black Legend by exploring two persistent English strains of binding religious conscience that dogged the British Empire from its Renaissance beginnings to its modern end. The first of these countertraditions was the more clearly anti-imperial: the Christian humanist critique of empire building as not only oppressing the colonized but as disastrously weakening the colonizer. The second—which I call the tradition of Protestant imperial "trusteeship"—was not flatly opposed to empire yet sought, often effectively, to ameliorate its worst evils.

These countertraditions feature some of the best and most robust voices in English literary history: this chapter traces the anti-imperial conscience from Thomas More's *Utopia,* Samuel Daniel's advice to Prince Henry Stuart, George Herbert's "Church Militant," and Nicholas Ferrar's Little Gidding, to John Milton's *Paradise Regain'd,* Jonathan Swift's Houyhnhnmland, and Jane Austen's *Mansfield Park.* Towering over the rest, and crossing the political spectrum, are three figures: the radical William Blake—though less radical than he at first appears; the Whig Edmund Burke—imperialist against empire; and above all the Tory Samuel Johnson—perhaps the most consistent and courageous opponent of empire that the island ever produced. The final chapter surveys the ironic destinies of these countertraditions through the end of the empire in the mid-twentieth century—from the early Victorians in India, to Alfred Tennyson's presciently mournful *Idylls of the King,* to the post-Protestant fictions of Joseph Conrad and E. M. Forster and the anti-Protestant satire of Evelyn Waugh. All of these writers show, in varied ways and degrees, why Christian ideas of spiritual universality, so often attractive to kings and emperors, can make Christianity an uneasy, even dangerous partner to kingdoms and empires.

Significantly, when Ben Jonson wrote about religion strengthening empire, he was referring not only to cohesiveness and subordination but also to this power of divine restraint: "For [the prince] that is religious, must be merciful and just necessarily. And they are two strong ties upon mankind." Religion not only binds together, but it also binds back, restraining hubristic over-reach. Yet despite this positive affirmation of religious conscience, Jonson's examples are negative—and pre-Christian: the Greeks finally sack Troy in spite of its revered Palladium; the irreligious Emperor Tiberius is ultimately overthrown by his even more profane and bloody henchman, Sejanus.[1] It is as if pagan religion, because it is virtually indistinguishable from each nation's own patriotic mythos, can do little or nothing to correct it. The salt has no savor; the ties do not bind.

And indeed, any history of classical, and particularly Roman, anti-imperialism is likely to be short. Even an exponent of Stoic and republican virtues like Cicero, easily offended by the corrupting excesses brought about by colonial wealth, sees in book 6 of *De Republica* the expansion of Roman power as a beneficent, divinely ordained inevitability.[2] Like many later advocates of colonial "trusteeship," he prefers to euphemize: he writes in *De Officiis* that "[a]s long as the empire of the Roman people was maintained through acts of kind service and not through injustices, we could more truly have been titled a protectorate (*patrocinium*) than an empire of the world."[3] But clearly the Roman Republic, well before the Caesars, had already conquered or colonized much of the Mediterranean world, thus building the greater *ecumene* that created the occasion for an emperor.

So, ironically, the closest thing to an ancient Roman anti-imperial conscience that one is likely to find besides Cicero's is probably Virgil's—if, that is, one reads Aeneas's final descent into remorseless violence as an indirect comment on the dehumanizing process of conquest. And yet even Virgil's possible qualms are not inspired by Roman religion. On the contrary, in the epic's most famous prophetic speech, a pre-Capitoline Jove seems to endorse all of these bloody means to the indisputably good end of *Pax Romana*.[4]

The triune Creator of Christianity is, on the other hand, not so locally patriotic. The Ark of the Covenant will not cohabit long with Dagon; nor does *Christos Pantocrator* fit any state's pantheon. There were of course from early times Christians who—like the Catholic and Protestant imperialists of the Renaissance—enthusiastically endorsed Constantine's own authorizing humility in submitting to the conquering cross. Paulus Orosius, Augustine's fifth-century contemporary from Roman Spain, composed his *History against the Pagans* to demonstrate that the conversion of the empire to Christianity was not Rome's end as a great

---

1. Ben Jonson, *Ben Jonson: The Complete Poems*, 410, 411.
2. Marcus Tullius Cicero, *Laelius, On Friendship & The Dream of Scipio*, 137.
3. Marcus Tullius Cicero, *On Duties*, 72.
4. Virgil, *Aeneid*, 36, ll. 276 ff.

power but the culmination of Daniel's prophecy that a sanctified Rome would conquer the ever-wider world, to everyone's benefit.[5]

Yet, however often Christian imperialists like Orosius have managed to read "Our kingdom come" for "Thy kingdom come," strict attention to the possessive pronoun is against them, and many other believers have discerned the difference. Early and highly influential among them was Augustine himself, who, although Orosius's friend and mentor, throughout *The City of God* refutes such a jovial (and Jovian) view of Rome's expansion. Decrying the "waging of constant and unremitting war," Augustine laments the unhealthy, unsustainable bulk of empire. "Why must an empire be unquiet in order to be great?" he asks. "Consider the human body. Is it not enough to have moderate stature with good health? Or is it better to attain gigantic size yet, having attained it, to find no rest, but to be plagued with ills which are greater in proportion to the size of the body's members? . . . By contrast, the man of moderate means is self-sufficient on his small and circumscribed estate. He is beloved of his own family, and rejoices in the most sweet peace with kindred, neighbors, and friends."[6] Imperial conquest, in other words, is disastrously bad for the conqueror.

But conquest is of course far worse for the conquered. Under a regime governed by greed and blood lust, subjects know no justice, and rulers become indistinguishable from robbers. "It was a pertinent and true answer which was made to Alexander the Great by a pirate whom he had seized. When the king asked him what he meant by infesting the sea, the pirate defiantly replied: 'The same as you do when you infest the whole world; but because I do it with a little ship I am called a robber, and because you do it with a great fleet, you are an emperor.'"[7] And where Orosius argues for a progressive *translatio imperii* from wicked Babylon to virtuous Rome, Augustine—in language that would haunt the Renaissance papacy—regards Rome as no better than "the Western Babylon" of John's Apocalypse, all its evils rooted in the same sort of blasphemous pride that brought God's wrath on Nebuchadnezzar.[8]

With such an authority as Augustine writing so trenchantly against empire, we should not be surprised to find similar ideas revived and voiced in Tudor-Stuart England by religious reformers, for whom the African bishop was a pervasive influence. We already have seen abundantly how the humanist dictum *ad fontes*

---

5. Paulus Orosius, *Seven Books of History against the Pagans*, 318–25, bk. 1, chaps. 1–3. Significantly, Orosius augments the Christianized *translatio imperii* theme by naturalizing Jesus Christ as a Roman citizen. See also Daniel 7:1–12.

6. Augustine, *The City of God against the Pagans*, 103.

7. Ibid., 146–47, 148.

8. Orosius, *Seven Books of History*, 320–21; Augustine, *City of God*, 856.

([return] to the sources) could fire restorationist hopes of British imperial glory; now we will see how that dictum conjured empire's nemesis.

Nolandia's Ruin: The Hollow Imperial Center in More's *Utopia*

In the summer of 1516, two events occurred—one in Burgundy, the other at Louvain in the Spanish Netherlands—that illustrate the difference between religiously sanctioned imperialism and its Christian humanist critics. One event was the unveiling of a royal seal; the other, the publication of a satirical book. The seal was the official impresa of Carlos I, newly crowned king of Spain, duke of Burgundy, and heir apparent to the Holy Roman Empire. The seal depicted two pillars rising from the sea, connected by a banner with the motto "Plus Ultra." The pillars were those of Hercules, representing the Strait of Gibraltar, so that the total signification of the device was "further beyond the Pillars of Hercules." The seal proclaimed Carlos's ambition—encoded even in his name—for a revival of Charlemagne's greatness, expanding a single neo-Carolingian empire beyond Europe to America and then uniting Christendom for the reconquest of the Holy Land.[9] When, three years later, the king received the imperial crown as Charles V, and the conquest of Mexico soon after from Cortés, his ambition seemed well on its way to fulfillment.

The newly published book was *Utopia* by Sir Thomas More. Conceived and largely written while More was on a diplomatic mission to Spanish authorities in the Low Countries, it is, among its many dazzlingly ironic layers and facets, bitingly prescient about the costs of empire, both to the conquered and to the conquerors. Raphael Hythloday, the world-traveling "talker of inspired nonsense" who is the book's chief Socratic speaker, presents in the guise of a parable what, in retrospect, reads like an account of Spain's future catastrophic imperial success. When Raphael is urged by More's fictional self to overcome his aversion to courtly life and deliver his invaluable philosophical advice to kings, he responds with a hypothetical anti-imperial scenario that demonstrates the impossibility of his ever catching the royal conscience.

Imagining himself at a meeting of the French king's council at which various designs are debated for subjugating Italy, "up gets little Raphael, and proposes a complete reversal of policy. I advise the King to forget about Italy and stay at home." Raphael then elaborates from his own store of traveler's wisdom "with an incident in the history of Nolandia, a country just south-east of Utopia":

---

9. John Pitcher, *Samuel Daniel, the Brotherton Manuscript: A Study in Authorship*, 32.

[T]he King of Nolandia thought he had a hereditary claim to another kingdom, so his people started a war to get it for him. Eventually they won, only to find that the kingdom in question was quite as much trouble to keep as it had been to acquire. . . . They never got a chance to demobilize, and in the meantime they were being ruined. All their money was going out of the country, and men were losing their lives to pay for someone else's petty ambition. Conditions at home were no safer than they'd been during the war, which had lowered moral standards, by encouraging people to kill and steal. There was no respect whatever for the law, because the king's attention was divided between the two kingdoms. . . . [T]he Nolandians finally decided . . . to ask the king, quite politely, which kingdom he wanted to keep.

"You can't keep them both," they explained. . . .

So that exemplary monarch was forced to hand over the new kingdom to a friend of his—who was very soon thrown out—and make do with the old one.[10]

More's Raphael gives us all the elements of the Augustinian critique: the initial imperial megalomania; the constant military mobilization and drain on men, money, and resources; the brutalization of the conquered abroad; and the eventual lowering of domestic moral and legal standards at home.

We cannot of course overlook certain uniquely Utopian ironies. Other characters in the book's initial dialogue dismiss Raphael's anti-imperial and anti-courtly discourse as retreatist and impractical, and the most notable of these naysayers is More's own fictional self (59, 63). (And yet, in another twist, this undercutting seems itself to be undercut by the author More's constantly implicit Greco-Latin pun on his own name, "More-moron-fool.") In addition (and more troubling), even Utopia's anti-imperial polity is, by Raphael's own account, the direct result of an ancient conqueror's radical social engineering, by which the founder "Utopus . . . transform[ed] a pack of ignorant savages into what is now, perhaps, the most civilized nation in the world" (69–70). Most troubling of all, the Utopians practice a kind of colonialism themselves—relieving their island's overpopulation by starting settlements "at the nearest point on the mainland where there's a large area that hasn't been cultivated by the local inhabitants," and even declaring wars of annexation when the unproductive "natives" resist Utopian cultivation (79–80).

Yet even with such ironic framing, Raphael's Nolandian parable expresses what became commonplaces for a reemerging Christian anti-imperialism, both Catholic and Protestant. In "Sacred Theology" lectures delivered at the University of Salamanca in the 1530s, Dominican scholar Francisco de Vitoria rejects

---

10. Thomas More, *Utopia*, trans. Paul Turner (Harmondsworth: Penguin, 1965), 58–59. All further citations of this edition will be made parenthetically. More's Greek word behind "Nolandia" is "Achora," from *a-* (not) and *chora* (country). See More, *Utopia*, 154.

as immoral and absurd the temporal claims made by both the pope and Charles V: American aborigines do not forfeit their lands, says Vitoria, on the grounds of their paganism; instead they possess the same natural land rights as all native peoples, however "ignorant or heathen."[11] Echoing Augustine on the Protestant side, John Calvin in 1536 exhorts the French King Francis I that an unjust monarch "exercises not kingly rule but brigandage"; he also roundly condemns expansionism, writing in the *Institutes* that "a king or the lowest of the common folk who invades a foreign country . . . must, equally, be considered as robbers and punished accordingly."[12] It is a scholarly commonplace that Erasmus's and More's warily jocular calls for reform inadvertently incited the earnest Protestant revolt. However, in 1516, the year of *Utopia*'s publication and a year before Luther's remonstrance at Wittenberg, More and Erasmus themselves stood on the leading edge of protest. It is only in retrospect that their final—and in More's case fatal—loyalty to Rome seems inevitable. In this sense English Protestant anti-imperialism—exposing the dystopian moral and material bankruptcy at the heart of empire—begins with English Catholicism's greatest martyr.[13]

"Chased from . . . this paradise of the world": The Genesis of Protestant Imperial Guilt

Raphael Hythloday was probably right about his lack of influence on royal policy; though Henry VIII was certainly amused and diverted by *Utopia*, it seems unlikely that his mercurial conscience was ever caught by Nolandian parables. Nevertheless, there was no real empire building during his long reign nor during the brief reigns of his next two children, Mary and Edward, as the domestic religious struggles of mid-century prevented much outward thrust. Furthermore, we already have observed that the first English Protestants looked dimly on dubious and semipagan Arthurian warrants for empire, and indeed on the entire business of fleshly conquest, being instead urgently concerned with the spiritual warfare of purifying their church. So initially English Protestant rhetoric tended toward the anti-imperial: I have shown how earlier Elizabethan accounts of the Spanish conquests decry not only the godless butchery of American natives

---

11. Lunenfeld, ed., *1492: Discovery, Invasion, Encounter*, 193, 194.
12. Calvin, *Institutes of the Christian Religion*, "Prefatory Address," par. 2; 4.20.11.
13. More did not attack Protestantism in print until 1523, in *Responsio ad Lutherum;* Erasmus waited until 1524, in *De Libero Arbitrio*. See, respectively, Richard Marius, *Thomas More: A Biography*, 280–90; and Léon-E. Halkin, *Erasmus: A Critical Biography*, 155–57.

but also the over-reaching arrogance of pope and emperor who would, on the thinnest of pretexts, lay claim to peoples and lands on the far side of the world.

However, I observed in chapter one that as Elizabeth's reign lengthened, Protestant consolidation combined with the reviving myth of British imperial recovery and with the common hatred of Catholic Spain, strengthening the English will to empire. So long as little England had no actual American colonies, anti-imperialist language combined easily with expansionist ambition in attacks on Spain and its "cruel and bloody" oppressions beyond the Atlantic. Indeed, we have seen that anti-imperial rhetoric was integral to Elizabethan England's enabling moral exceptionalism, as it began to dream of rescuing golden realms from Spanish tyranny and pagan night and of receiving treasure and grateful native submission as reward. In George Chapman's words—written in 1595 to encourage Ralegh in Guiana—this was a dream of "Riches with honour, Conquest, without blood / Enough to seat the Monarchie of earth, / Like to Joves Eagle on Elizas hand."[14]

Yet as Protestant England actually began to acquire its first overseas footholds, the sword of the Black Legend proved hard to control. Having made their first exploratory thrusts in the name of a reformed and reforming moral order, the English felt the weapon bite and found some blood on their hands. Early contacts in Africa and America quickly degenerated into slave taking and landgrabbing, and the English claim to an utterly different kind of conquest—nonviolent because spiritually humble and benevolently liberating—was wounded too. I noted in chapter two how an early English slaver like John Sparke might exculpate his trade by comparison with the sensational blasphemy and atrocity of demonized Dons; but this is already a tacit acknowledgment that there is no real difference in kind, only in degree. When absolute exceptionalism failed, such relativism often sufficed.

But scattered among these early accounts in Hakluyt are clear indications of the bad conscience that would haunt the enterprise from its beginning to its twentieth-century end. This strain of conscience must be distinguished from the Augustinian anti-imperialism advanced by the Christian humanists, for unlike More's Nolandian parable, or Vitoria's or Calvin's strictures, these guilty voices generally admit their investment in the colonial project, yet they still express a certain degree of remorse and foreboding—sometimes a very high degree. In a sense, even the scathing anticonquistadorial denunciations by Las Casas belong to this latter category because, despite his famously horrific detail, he never

---

14. George Chapman, "De Guiana carmen Epicum," in Hakluyt, *Principal Navigations*, 10.446–47.

challenges Charles V's fundamental claims of possession but rather the bloody means, and he appeals to the emperor as the true protector of his slaughtered "lambs."

On the British colonial frontier, a striking early example of imperial guilt appears in Hakluyt's accounts of the voyages to "Virginia," that is, to the Roanoke Island colony in present-day North Carolina. Remarkably, this example involves many of the greatest colonial players in the first English attempt at American settlement. Financed by Walter Ralegh under a special patent from Queen Elizabeth and established in 1584, the Roanoke colony was relieved and reinforced in 1585 by Ralegh's violently confrontational cousin Sir Richard Grenville. The narrator of this second voyage—certainly not Hakluyt and apparently a member of the expedition—matter-of-factly describes Grenville's brand of draconian justice. This writer, having just reminded the reader of Spanish treachery in an ambush at San Juan de Ullua two decades before, tells of Grenville's punitive response when native hospitality turns sour. "The 11 [–15 July 1585] . . . we first discovered the townes of Pomejok, Aquascogok and Secotan . . . and were well entertained there of the Savages. The 16. wee returned . . . to Aquascogok, to demaund a silver cup which one of the Savages had stollen from us, and not receiving it according to his promise, wee burnt, and spoyled their corne, and Towne, all the people being fled" (*PN* 8.315, 316). The calculus of a torched town for a stolen cup does not seem to trouble the conscience of this narrator.

However, as the account of the third and following voyage of 1586 unfolds under the hand of a different writer, such acts of scorched-earth diplomacy are portrayed as raising the ire of the Almighty. The restless colonists, now awaiting Grenville's return from England with more supplies, received an unexpected visit from Sir Francis Drake's fleet "in his prosperous returne from the sacking of Sant Domingo, Cartagena, and Saint Augustine." Drake agreed to leave them three ships should they choose an emergency return to England, and when many of the colonists had gone aboard Drake's flagship to trade tales and to write letters home, "a great storme arose, and drove the most of their fleet from their ankers to Sea . . . : the rest on land perceiving this, hasted to those three sailes which were appointed to be left there; and for feare they should be left behind they left all things confusedly, as if they had been chased from thence by a mighty army: and no doubt they were; for the hand of God came upon them for the cruelty and outrages committed by some of them against the native inhabitants of that countrey" (*PN* 8.346–47). Since the writer here is probably Richard Hakluyt himself, his language is especially significant: this empire-building preacher is arraying the heavenly hosts against a nascent English colony because it is no longer on the side of the angels.

The tone of divine judgment is only increased by the incident's crowning irony, presented as an expulsion from Eden: "Immediately after the departing of our English Colony out of this paradise of the world, [the advance relief ship] arrived . . . and not finding them, returned with all the aforesayd provision into England" (*PN* 8.347). Two weeks later, Grenville himself arrived at the empty settlement with supplies and reinforcements, searched fruitlessly for the bolted colonists, and also returned to England. Then, in 1587, Ralegh sent a fourth expedition of one hundred men and women to secure his foothold in "this paradise of the world"; by the time that Governor John White returned for them in 1590, they had disappeared quite famously from the face of the earth (*PN* 8.386ff; 8.416–19).

A modern reader might question whether all of this terrible confusion demonstrates God's law or Murphy's; but Hakluyt recognizes the Lord's angry hand driving out the colonists, as he did in the biblical Garden and at Babel, and his recognition casts doubt on England as the new Israel. Here the "cruelty and outrages" are English, not Spanish, and Jehovah is siding with the Canaanites. Hakluyt seems to suggest that Roanoke was lost spiritually well before it became the "Lost Colony." If the English are to be God's new chosen, then they, like the Israelites under Moses in the wilderness, are under a strict covenant. So we see the genesis of the empire's uneasy conscience, involved in the act of gaining the New World and yet painfully aware that it might cost one's soul. Put negatively, we can call this mindset "imperial guilt." Put more positively, as a spur to ameliorating empire's evils, we can call it "imperial trusteeship": the belief that colonial possession is probational, conditioned on colonial beneficence and self-restraint, and that God is to be feared as vigilant judge and avenger of abused properties and peoples.

Of course, not all critiques of early English colonialism were offered from the troubled conscience of the empire builder or from the high moral ground of Christian humanist antiexpansionism. Imperialism, with its tendency to grandiosity, avarice, and credulity, can be, in C. S. Lewis's words, "roaring farce," presenting a wide target for satire.[15] Such mockery may still be informed by a strongly held moral and spiritual antipathy, as we can see in cases from More to Swift to Waugh; but one need not necessarily be opposed in principle to laugh at the fact. We have elsewhere observed Shakespeare's characteristically complex treatment of colonial relations in *Cymbeline* and *The Tempest*—an attitude that we might call ironic rather than oppositional.

---

15. C. S. Lewis, *The Four Loves*, 46.

Still, when Falstaff in *The Merry Wives of Windsor* (1597) tells Pistol and Nym of his ill-fated designs on Mistresses Page and Ford, the playwright foreshadows the fat knight's comeuppance by making him speak like an avaricious and lustful gull infatuated by Ralegh's glowing reports of El Dorado: "She [Mistress Page] bears [her husband's] purse, too. She is a region in Guiana, all gold and bounty. I will be cheaters to them both, and they will be exchequers to me. They will be my East and West Indies, and I will trade to them both. . . . Sail like my pinnace to these golden shores" (1.3.58–62). Similarly, George Chapman, Ben Jonson, and John Marston, though they elsewhere celebrate Britain's renewed overseas ambitions, give would-be colonists no quarter in *Eastward Hoe* (1605). Seagull deals in bawdy absurdity as he assures Spendall and Scapethrift that "Virginia longs till we share the rest of her maidenhead," and he credulously transposes to Virginia Thomas More's famous passage on Utopian gold, while missing its ironic point: "Why man, all their dripping pans and their chamber pots are pure gold; . . . all the prisoners they take are fettered in gold: and for rubies and diamonds, they . . . hang [them] on their children's coats, and stick [them] in their caps" (3.3.14–15, 25–30).[16] Derision of such greedy and obtuse hopes was still echoing in 1606 as the first Jamestown colonists boarded the *Susan Constant* for Virginia.

"The Conquerer Undone": Samuel Daniel's "Epistle to Prince Henry" and George Herbert's "Church Militant"

If Chapman and Jonson (and cowriter John Marston) invoke the Christian humanist critique only obliquely, this tradition finds bold and full-blooded restatement soon after in Samuel Daniel's "Epistle to Prince Henry" (1609–1610). Writing nearly a century after the time of More and Charles V to another young Christian prince on the cusp of transatlantic colonization, Daniel repeats and amplifies Raphael Hythloday's Augustinian warnings against expansionism, though without the ironic framing. He decries the damage done to conquered and conquerors alike and uses Spain's current decrepitude as crucial evidence against imperialist ethical and economic decline. Written on the occasion of Henry Stuart's installation as Prince of Wales at the age of sixteen, Daniel's verse letter responds to Sir Robert Cotton's procolonial prose treatise of 1609, commissioned by the prince himself. As a favored poet in King James's court,

---

16. George Chapman, Ben Jonson, and John Marston, *Eastward Hoe*, in *The Complete Plays of Ben Jonson*, 2:392. See More, *Utopia*, 86–89.

Daniel takes it upon himself to exhort the future Henry IX about the adventurist mistakes of earlier monarchs.

Daniel quickly establishes his opposition not only to Cotton but also to the claims of Dee and Hakluyt:

> Theare be great Prince, such as will tell you howe
> Renown'd a thing it is, for States t'inlardge
> Their gouerments abrode . . . and howe we [British] were made
> To haue that glorie onlie, to transpass
> Those bounds of th'ocean, hercules forbad;
> Besides the inrichment, and the benefitt
> That new detected world, hath brought wth it.
> (ll. 1–3, 10–14)[17]

Yet Daniel is unstintingly contrarian: against such expansionist claims of manifest British destiny, against rediscovered titles "To other mightie Provinces" (l. 132), and against promises of treasure, Daniel counsels skeptical "inquisition." The wise prince will

> Consider whither all the good that came
> From that new world to this, acquits the some [sum]
> Of th'ill events, wch since hath by the same
> Accrewd to theis our parts of Christendome . . .
> (19–22)

The first of these ills masquerading as goods is the promise of "that excessiue vayne / Of gould" (ll. 24–25), a promise that is worse if true than if false:

> Examin whither ever any state
> Hath not miscarried, when dilisiousnes
> The child of wealth was borne
> . . . .
> Or what rich Treasorous state, hath not vndone
> The Conquerer, and wonne those, who hath wonne;
> (ll. 31–33, 35–36)

To heighten Henry's fear of effeminate decadence and economic ruin—the fear that America may be to Europe and England "As Fatall . . . as Asia was to Rome" (l. 38)—Daniel points to the disastrous imperial logistics and finances

---

17. Pitcher, *Samuel Daniel*, 21, 131. The complete transcribed text of "To Prince Henry" appears on pages 131–37, and all further citations of the poem will be given parenthetically by line number.

of Spain's Charles V. In Charles's eagerness to conquer and hold the mines of Mexico and Peru, "his powers [he] disperc'd, his state constrain'ed / To vnman Spaine to furnish him with gould, / Who yet was still a borrower" (ll. 41–43). Daniel notes that Charles's outlay of manpower and borrowed capital left Spain a debtor nation despite its mother lodes, vulnerable to the nearly successful invasions of French King Francis I in the 1520s. Because his power was spread abroad, Charles came close to losing his homeland to his nearest European rival, which "stood girt with home force" because Francis had not squandered his military on colonial over-reaching (ll. 45–48).

Moving on to England's Virginian venture and its promise of a foothold against Spain in the Americas, Daniel makes a barely veiled jab at Jamestown's viability. The settlement's recent decimation by disease and famine in 1608–1609 and its continued anxiety about Spanish attack raise the question of whether colonization is a suicide mission, and whether "States doe not, wheare fitt meanes shall want, / Expose their people, rather than transplant" (ll. 53–54). And even if such distant colonists endure, Daniel wonders (with extraordinary foresight) how long they can "be kept ours, come once to be their owne" (l. 52)—that is, once they come to feel and perhaps declare their independence and make alliance with England's enemies. The prospect of a rebel America turning against its English maker thus begins to haunt the national imagination.

But beyond these economic and political concerns, Daniel reserves much of his condemnation for empire's false spiritual promises. From Columbus to Ralegh, European explorers had described an earthly paradise across the sea, a paradise to be gained, or regained, by bold striving rather than by repentance and faith. Daniel challenges such "presumption," fusing classical and biblical allusion: were not "the Pillors of Alsides . . . sett / As bounds of heaven, to keepe vs in our state / Least getting further, wee . . . taste / The goulden Apples of Hisperides / (Preserv'd for Dragons)"—an act that may "cast / Vs out of what we did possess with ease" and worse, "Depriue men of the Paradice of rest"? Did not nature herself "sett the barrs of those huge fearfull seas / Betwixt vs as the cherubines about the bounds of Edonn" (ll. 56–58, 59–61, 62, 68, 100–102)? Such transgression threatens to cast the English not only out of their transatlantic garden but out of their domestic garden—and perhaps out of all spiritual rest—as well.

Furthermore, Daniel looks askance at the very concept of "Christian conquest," wondering archly how

>   [S]poile and ruyn of your neighbors, may
>   Square with the line of christianitie
>   . . . .

> Since time shewes how, by former deedes
> Th'inheritannce of violence succeedes
> . . . .
> And war must nurse those, whome yᵉ war hath bred . . .
> (ll. 152–53, 155–56, 164)

Echoing Augustine, he envisions a cure that is itself worse than any illness—perpetual imperial bloodletting. Continuing the medical metaphor, he suggests understatedly that "open vaynes, perhaps will not agree / With the complection of the comon wealth" (ll. 167–68). Notably, Daniel takes for granted that nations, and not just private individuals, are responsible to Christian standards of justice and equity, and that God will bring blood back on the aggressors' heads, whether they be Roman, Spanish, or English. Daniel thus presents Prince Henry with a stark choice between initiating a tragic cycle of violence abroad and seeking peace by staying at home.

The redefinition of heroism involved in Daniel's argument is itself remarkable. Although he concedes that Henry's "noble inclinacion [is] bent to martiall glorie," Daniel concedes nothing to the aggressive martial ethic. Even when he seems to do so by encouraging the Prince to "Colonise neere home, wᶜʰ we may do without adventuring vnto parts vnknowne" (ll. 115–16), he is actually referring not to further advances in Ireland or on the continent but only to those usually inglorious arts of peace, England's perennial home industries: woolens and fish. These he recasts in heroic terms: if properly managed, English hillsides will produce "a richer fleece of gould / Then ever Colchos bred"; without setting foot on "any other Forraine continent," a victorious host of English fishermen "may take / Huge wealth, with netts" (ll. 121–23).

Finally, it is intriguing that Daniel, who would hold England to an international Christian standard of justice, nevertheless takes a dim view of evangelism as a rationale for colonization. One reason for his attitude is colonial hypocrisy—he says that saving Indian souls is really "not our end" (l. 74) or main purpose but is only incidental to the chief geopolitical and economic business. But his more notable objection is that the spread of Christian civilization "to Infidels" is in any case an inevitable, and a decidedly mixed, blessing:

> I grannt that time, their turne must bring about
> When the vniversall wheele of things shall move
> Vnto that point, and those rude lands throughout
> Th' Europian arts and Customes shall approue;
> And they [indigenous Americans] shall curious grow, and delicate
> (Wᶜʰ we call Civill) and enioy their part

> Of our vaine glories, putting of[f] the state
> Of nature to be suted vnto art . . .
>
> (ll. 75–82)

Daniel seems to assume that the trouble with Christian civilization is that it is in effect more civil than Christian and more epicurean than civil. With Christendom come order and abundance; with abundance comes decadence; with decadence comes collapse, a process already well under way in Europe, where soon

> . . . we perhaps, arriv'd vnto a more
> Then Asiatique weaknes
> . . . .
> . . . may be made
> A prey vnto some Gothicq barbarous hand
>
> (ll. 83–84, 86–87)

Daniel imagines history as a continuous movement of empire and religion from East to West, with tyranny and corruption dogging their steps. Though the cycle cannot be stopped, he says, surely it should not be accelerated by death-dealing bands of imperial crusaders, particularly if they are from England. The truly Christian nation, he assumes, will negate Charles V's vaunting motto, writing "ne plus ultra" on its banners. It will respect the bounds of ocean, the bounds of Eden, the bounds of heaven; it will stay home, mind its own business, and let God manage the mysteries of global justice and mercy.

Daniel's appeal to domesticity may resonate in our own largely postheroic age, and we may admire the poet's courage in reading his future king such a stiff lesson, but his arguments hardly seem designed to appeal to the rather dashing young Prince Henry, who already was of an aggressive and expansionist mind. One still can see, in the Tower of London, Henry's boyishly small but gorgeously rich suit of full armor: this artifact is perhaps emblematic of the fact that by his mid-teens the prince was speaking contemptuously of his father's pacifistic effeminacy and envisioning a renewal of Philip Sidney's proposed Protestant crusade in Europe.[18]

In any case, however much or little Daniel's epistle may have persuaded the young prince (there is no record of his reaction), it was labor lost; in 1612, Henry died of typhoid fever at the age of eighteen, one of the more intriguing

---

18. Roger Lockyer, *The Early Stuarts: A Political History of England, 1603–1642*, 156.

might-have-beens in the Crown's history. Jamestown continued by fits and starts, erratically managed by its governors, alternately a curiosity and joke butt in the city and Westminster, and neither promoted nor disowned by the king.

But Daniel's "Epistle to Prince Henry" was not alone in portraying the "vniversall wheele of things." In George Herbert's better-known poem "The Church Militant," this lyricist of the inner spiritual life shifts to the prophetic mode and presents a similar vision of events to come. Written in 1618–1619, though published posthumously in 1633, Herbert's prognosis is even more dire than Daniel's: "Religion stands on tip-toe in our land, / Readie to passe to the *American* strand" (ll. 235–36).[19] Having established a pattern whereby westward-moving "Empire," "Arts," and "Religion" establish order only to be overthrown in turn by "Sinne," Herbert predicts that England's doom is near:

> When height of malice, and prodigious lusts,
> Impudent sinnings, witchcrafts, and distrusts
> (The marks of future bane) shall fill our cup
> Unto the brimme, and make our measure up
> . . . .
> Then shall Religion to *America* flee:
> They have their times of Gospel, ev'n as we.
> (ll. 237–40, 247–48)

As Sacvan Bercovitch has shown, these words were taken in early New England to prophesy success for godly Boston.[20] However, Herbert's "they" almost certainly refers not to England's Massachusetts or even Virginian settlers, but to America's native inhabitants, as shown a few lines later when he condemns Europe's theft of American gold:

> We think we rob them, but we think amisse:
> We are more poore, and they more rich by this.

---

19. George Herbert, *The Works of George Herbert*, ed. F. E. Hutchinson (Oxford: Clarendon Press, 1964), 196. All further citations of this edition will be made parenthetically to line numbers for poetry and to page numbers for prose.

20. Sacvan Bercovitch, *The Puritan Origins of the American Self*, 145–46. Herbert's *The Temple*, of which "The Church Militant" forms the concluding part, was among the first books purchased for the Harvard College Library in 1636. Raymond A. Anselment and Kenneth Alan Hovey have written with helpful clarity of Herbert's cyclical vision, but neither of them notes the *native* identity of the Americans who will inherit Christendom's blessings and banes. See Anselment, " 'The Church Militant': George Herbert and the Metamorphoses of Christian History," and Hovey, " 'Wheel'd about . . . into *Amen*': 'The Church Militant' on Its Own Terms."

> Thou wilt revenge their quarrell, making grace
> To pay our debts, and leave her ancient place
> To go to them, while that which now their nation
> But lends to us, shall be our desolation.
> (ll. 253–54, 257–58)

Like Daniel, and in keeping with the humanist critique of expansion, Herbert sees the American treasure stolen by Europe as Europe's undoing and America's salvation. As if it were a desecrated and abandoned temple, the Old World will stand empty of departed glory, and God will shed his grace on the New.

It is significant, then, that for Herbert, as for Daniel, Christendom's spread will not remove the natives *from* the land but rather bless—and curse—them *in* the land. This cyclical vision is not one of displacement but of inheritance of the *translatio imperii*. Even more significant, while Herbert attacks European greed, he does not idealize its victims. He portrays them as no worse and no better than any other heathens previously converted on the gospel's way from Palestine to England—in other words, as converts who also will eventually squander God's grace: "They have their period also and set times / Both for their vertuous actions and their crimes" (ll. 261–62).

Still, there is a difference in emphasis between Herbert and Daniel that amounts to a crucial divergence between their attitudes toward empire. Although the "militance" announced by Herbert's title is primarily spiritual in meaning, and despite his strong condemnation of aggressive, decadent Christendom, he nevertheless assumes that from "of old the Empire and the Arts / Usher'd the Gospel ever in mens hearts" (ll.263–64). It is swords that, after all, break up the heathen ground before grace can, for a time, convert the swords to plowshares. Where Daniel wants England to delay the inevitable evils of empire as long as possible, Herbert would instead manage those evils and, by grace, convert them to at least limited good. This concession to empire puts Herbert more in the meliorist line of the "trusteeship" tradition; as he writes elsewhere, colonization can be "a noble," and even "a religious imployment" if pursued with evangelistic and compassionate motives (278).[21] Ironically, as we will see, few pursued this work with more sincerely religious zeal than Herbert's friend Nicholas Ferrar of the Virginia Company—and few were more deeply disappointed.

---

21. Significantly, Herbert makes these concessions in his pastoral manual, *A Priest to the Temple, Or, The Country Parson*, written in the early 1630s; he is discussing useful callings for "younger sons" of the rural gentry and nobility, to keep them from unwholesome "idleness." See also my discussion in Christopher Hodgkins, *Authority, Church, and Society in George Herbert: Return to the Middle Way*, 190–93.

Gold and Smoke: Imperial Conceit and Disenchantment in the Ferrar-Collett Little Gidding *Conversations* of 1631

Nicholas Ferrar's disappointment derived most crucially from expectations raised about Jamestown's guiding religious purposes. The Virginia Company had been founded in 1606 and had revived the colonizing mission of Sir Walter Ralegh. In 1592, Ralegh had sold his rights of Virginian settlement to Sir Thomas Smith—the man who became the colony's nonresident governor and, eventually, the nemesis of Deputy Treasurer Ferrar. These two would face off in an ideological clash between profit and gospel that contributed to the Company's 1624 demise.[22] It was Ferrar's colonial defeat that, as much as anything, moved him out of worldly affairs to found the unique religious community at Little Gidding; there, in the summer of 1631, his followers expressed their imperial disenchantment in a "conversation," or Socratic dialogue, "On the Retirement of Charles V."[23]

This dialogue is notable for at least three reasons: first, it takes as its subject that exemplar of imperial over-reach, Charles V of Spain, and examines his repentance; second, it is led by Mary Collett, Ferrar's remarkable teenaged niece; and third, the "conversation" seems to have as its subtext Ralegh's 1596 account of Guiana, discussed in chapter two. Collett responds directly, and adversarially, to Ralegh's chief claims and themes: his quest for empire in an earthly paradise, his promise of American gold, his hispanophobia, and his Protestant moral exceptionalism. The ex-colonialist, Ferrar's young disciple, speaks as one thoroughly disenchanted with what she calls empire's "strong and rauishing conceit" and its dream of edenic possession (Williams 70).

Ferrar had had a bellyfull of colonial possession by the summer of 1631, when he set this spiritual exercise for his Little Gidding followers. Most modern readers have heard of Little Gidding—and Ferrar—only through the fourth of T. S. Eliot's *Four Quartets,* where it figures as a representative site of spiritual death and rebirth, of "Midwinter spring," a place to which "broken kings" retreat and where, if you came, "you would have to put off / Sense and notion." Yet Eliot, with all his concern for spiritual transcendence and "timeless moments," recognizes this place of "valid" prayer as embedded in history, "in place and

---

22. Fuller, *Voyages in Print,* chap. 2, 83.
23. A. M. Williams, ed., *Conversations at Little Gidding: "On the Retirement of Charles V" and "On the Austere Life"* (Cambridge: Cambridge University Press, 1970). All further citations of this edition will be made parenthetically.

time, / Now and in England."²⁴ So, even if we are to understand Little Gidding as a retreat, we still must ask, retreat from what?

Ferrar had retreated from public life to found the community in 1625 at the age of thirty-three, with his widowed mother and the families of his sister and brother; and the career from which he retreated had been rich and varied. He had been both Cambridge scholar and don, as well as physician, courtier, continental traveler, and—like his friend George Herbert—member of Parliament; and he had just refused an ambassadorial appointment on the Continent. Most significantly, he had also recently endured, in 1624, King James's dissolution of the Virginia Company, of which his father, Nicholas Senior, had been an early member and in which he himself had served as deputy treasurer (Williams xiii–xvii).

This dissolution resulted from a clash over many practical issues of supply and management, but, as I have noted, it mainly concerned the colony's guiding purposes. The Company's original 1606 charter had stated that the English settlers should both pay dividends to its stockholders and "tende to the glorie of [God's] Divine Majestie in propagating of Christian religion" among the native inhabitants, a goal reiterated in the charters of 1609 and 1612.²⁵ This evangelistic fervor remained high in the minds of the Ferrars and their allies on the Company board.²⁶ However, with the very important exception of the Christianized Pocahontas—who died in England in 1617—evangelism in Virginia was by 1619 a miserable failure. And not surprisingly: as Ferrar notes in his scathing written attack on Sir Thomas Smith's mismanagement of the colony, Smith and his allies, although paying lip service to the charter, were really of the opinion that "as for the convertinge of the Infidells it was a thinge impossible they being the Cursed race of Cham."²⁷

After Ferrar and his faction gained the upper hand in the Company in 1619, they sought to revive the colony's gospeling emphasis, while at the same time taking the portentous step of strengthening the colony's financial returns by greatly encouraging the production of tobacco.²⁸ But their window of opportunity was to be small: as I have described, in 1622 the Powhatans, enraged

---

24. T. S. Eliot, *The Complete Plays and Poems, 1909–1950*, 138–39.
25. Samuel Bemiss, ed., *The Three Charters of the Virginia Company of London. With Seven Related Documents; 1606–1621*, 2, 54.
26. Jeffrey Powers-Beck calls this group "the Sandys faction," after Sir Edwin Sandys, the Company's treasurer and, after 1619, its governor. See Powers-Beck, *Writing the Flesh: The Herbert Family Dialogue*, 196.
27. Nicholas Ferrar, *Sir Thomas Smith's Misgovernment of the Virginia Company*, 12.
28. For the renewed emphasis on evangelism, see Powers-Beck, *Writing the Flesh*, 196. It was at this time (November 1622) that John Donne preached his oft-quoted "Sermon

by continuing encroachments on their land, arose and massacred hundreds of Englishmen; this disaster aggravated English prejudices against irredeemable savages. Blame came to rest, however unfairly, on the present government of the colony; and in 1624, King James withdrew the Company's charter and took direct control for the Crown.[29]

Ironies abounded: though James had in 1618 sent Ralegh to the block, he handed the colony's practical matters back to Ralegh's successor, Sir Thomas Smith, whose policies had created most of the intercultural problems; Smith brought an end to evangelistic efforts, instead empowering the governor to "root out" the Indians and redouble tobacco farming; and James, who passionately hated tobacco and aspired to a Christian empire, became the namesake of a colony indifferent to the spread of religion and synonymous with smoke. Most ironic of all, the tobacco plantations of Jamestown produced what Ralegh's Edenic Guiana could not; for in King James's new Garden in the West, smoke was converted to gold.

Ralegh's paradisal conceit, so ironically realized in Virginia, provides a suggestive context for reading "On the Retirement of Charles V." One of two surviving dialogues enacted at Little Gidding in 1631, this "conversation" was conducted that summer for spiritual edification within the so-called "Little Academy" of the Ferrar family's extended circle. Although Nicholas Ferrar stage-managed by assigning general roles, topic, and themes in the dialogue, he neither scripted nor directed the conversation; indeed, he withdrew early on from actual involvement, allowing discussion to play out improvisationally; later he recorded and edited that discussion for use by the community (Williams xxxiii–xxxv).

Playing Socrates to Ferrar's Plato was his sister's adolescent daughter, Mary Collett, who in the dialogue is called the "Chief" and who firmly assumes the mistress-of-ceremonies role from the outset. Thus she introduces the topic of Charles V—king of Spain, Holy Roman Emperor, and lord of the Indies, Mexico, and Peru—who in 1555, at the height of his power and wealth, had chosen freely to give up his throne and his treasure for a monastic cell. The dialogue progresses as the Chief goes back and forth with the other conversationalists in numerous rounds of discussion: What is "the world"? Isn't Charles over-reacting? Isn't

---

to the Virginia Company," exhorting the colonists to preach to the native inhabitants both "Doctrinally" and "Practically," treating them with kindness and fairness, to the end that they should "reverence" the name of King James but "adore" the name of King Jesus. Donne, *Sermons*, 4:280. For tobacco production, see Ferrar, *Misgovernment*, xix.

29. Mapp, *Virginia Experiment*, 79–80.

there some good to be done through empire building? Then, in true Socratic form, she interrupts the give-and-take about halfway through to present an extended monologue arguing her point in full.

It is this monologue that, while not an explicit response to Ralegh's Guianan narrative, nevertheless seems to take it as a subtext and refutes Ralegh's general vision of Edenic and golden empire: "The Remembrance of Eden," says the Chief, "wherein our First Parents were sett . . . hath in all Ages brought forth a strong and rauishing conceit; That there was yet remaining in the world a place of Perfect Happines. . . . The Maineteners of this Fancie haue alwaies cunningly described it to ly hid in farre remoued Coasts & . . . [to be inhabited by] certain people liuing alwaies in an vninterrupted Course of Felicitie" (Williams 70). The Chief speaks as one well acquainted with the cunning fabulations of explorers, as in fact she was: at meals the Little Gidding families often read aloud from "Journeys by land, Sea Voyages, & the like," probably including Ralegh's Guianan account found in Richard Hakluyt's famous *Principal Navigations*.[30] She recognizes the "rauishing" power in the quest for an earthly paradise, which requires of the seeker not the spiritual means of faith, hope, and charity but merely the human means of persistent navigation, dogged marching, and adequate supplies—and arms. She also recognizes that integral to this earthly Eden is "Abundance of Gold & siluer" for the supposed "improuement of Europes Felicitie" (Williams 72).

However, far from celebrating these "delightful Surmises," the Chief turns a cold eye on them and returns to Emperor Charles for their most damning refutation. Like a latter-day Solomon, Charles is God's chosen agent for "the Confutation of all those idle dreames." Before his conversion, his imaginative "ravishment" by fabulous wealth had led him to active rapaciousness, as he "compassed the whole Circumference of this Earthly Globe, & ransacked euery obscure & hidden corner" and found only *vanitas vanitatis*. Amplifying the humanist attack on conquered treasure, the Chief says that the sum of Charles's discoveries is that "those Fortunate Ilands . . . are but a few petty barren rocks yeelding a scanty maintenance to their short-liued inhabitants. . . . the Pacifique Sea . . . is a furious Gulf euer combated by Stormes and Tempests. . . . There's no man, I suppose, wilbe so mad as to value that Abundance of Gold & siluer, which hath been imported from the Indians into Spaine any improuement of Europes Felicitie. . . . [Rather, he] will execrate the very Name of it & almost

---

30. B. Blackstone, *The Ferrar Papers*, 46. See also Reid Barbour, "The Caroline Church Heroic: The Reconstruction of Epic Religion in Three Seventeenth-Century Communities," 771.

the place itself, whence it came, as a new Pandoras box" (Williams 71, 72). So much, says the Chief, for the earthly Eden and the golden returns of empire.

Yet, significantly, her concluding critique of imperial vanity comes under the summary figure of that other American gold in the bright leaf. Of all "the ioynt Commodities or rather Calamities" brought from the New World, all are fitly represented by "that prime & vniversally accepted Commoditie there of Tobacco. A true & Liuely Embleme of this world's Happinesse, Though most loathsomly noysome in the Tast, vnbeseeming in the vse, & preiudicial in the operation, yet bewitching all that meddle there with, & violently retaining them . . . I cannot think the invention of man can streigne higher to represent the dreadfull visages of infernal spirits in their invasions on mens souls then by Coppying out the Postures & Countenances of a Gallant Tobacconist" (Williams 72). The ghosts of Walter Ralegh, and of the abolished Virginia Company, haunt these lines, lending them some of that "Rellish of Loathsome Bitternes" that the Chief ascribes both to tobacco and to Charles V's disenchantment. Significantly, the Chief notes that tobacco is "of much later importation than Charles his time" (73); and there was no tobacconist more crucial to that importation, or more "Gallant," than Ralegh. Nor, in Nicholas Ferrar's view, was there any commodity more responsible for the financial success, and the spiritual failure, of Virginia, than the "sotweed." Although Ferrar is not directly present here as speaker, he is here as Mary Collett's teacher and as her editor—and as a disenchanted colonialist. We hear his mediated voice in this condemnation of imperial folly for being as ephemeral and infernal as smoke.

Yet Mary Collett's subversion of Ralegh's Edenic imperial dream goes beyond insisting that Adam's curse fell not only on the Old World but also on the New. She also effectively rejects the hispanophobia and Protestant moral exceptionalism that helped Ralegh and other Tudor-Stuart empire builders to imagine possession. By her unstinting praise of the greatest Spanish Catholic king, she profoundly undermines the prevailing exceptionalist assumption that Spanish depravity is nationally specific and English virtue culturally unique. Indeed, her prime figure for colonial depravity—tobacco production—does not derive from Spain's empire at all but fits England's upstart Virginian enterprise only too well.

There is, then, a kind of implicit *a fortiori* at work in this Little Gidding "conversation": if Charles V, the "popish" Spaniard who presided over most of *la leyenda negra*, can provide a model for spiritual reformation by abandoning his grandiose imperial dreams, how much more should already Reformed English Christians turn from a blasphemous quest for an earthly Eden? Should it not be the Protestants who put away works of conquest for works of the gospel? And if poisonous tobacco is the representative imperial outcome, isn't empire building the epitome of human vanity?

Like Mary Collett's monologue, a pair of 1993 essays by Mary C. Fuller and Louis Montrose also warn us to turn a doubtful eye on Ralegh's Guianan dream (if we still needed warning).[31] Fuller and Montrose differ in focus: she stresses Ralegh's desperate narrative strategy of golden promise and deferral, while he is concerned chiefly with how Ralegh genders the Guianan landscape and its inhabitants as virginally feminine. Yet Fuller and Montrose share a common skepticism about the goodness of Ralegh's intentions in reporting his adventures—in other words, they share a hermeneutic of suspicion.

Fuller and Montrose participate in a larger new historicist project that can be faulted for assuming something of a postmodern monopoly on such suspicion about the rhetoric of empire. The practitioners of cultural poetics have taught us a great deal about how dominant ideologies like English Protestant imperialism, in Stephen Greenblatt's phrase, "imagine possession" of cultural Others by deploying the totalizing languages of religion and law. However, they have little—and often nothing—to say about real dissent that comes from within such dominant ideologies and is roughly contemporary with them. In other words, many new historicists apparently find it hard to imagine an articulate anti-imperialism—like Ferrar's and Collett's—arising from the same material and metaphysical grounds that produced the early British Empire.

But can the palpable disenchantment with empire at Little Gidding really be called anti-imperialist? After all, Charles V abdicated his empire; he did not abolish it. Yet, like Samuel Daniel, what Mary Collett demands is the abdication of empire building itself. If we define anti-imperialism pragmatically—as the power to imagine an alternative to any present system of territorial expansion, exploitation, or coercion—then we can reasonably call this Little Gidding "conversation" anti-imperialist. The fact that Mary Collett and Nicholas Ferrar opposed colonial conquest on the grounds of the Christian *contemptus mundi* tradition does not make their opposition fundamentally quietist. No doubt their attack upon fables of an earthly paradise presupposes a heavenly one, and they prayed daily for that Kingdom to come from heaven to earth. But Ferrar sought to put his prayers into action. Significantly, he was absent from much of the summer 1631 "conversation" because he was in London opposing a further military mission to Virginia, advocating nonmercantile and noncoercive evangelism instead.[32]

In the end, the most striking difference between Ferrar and Ralegh is what each learned from colonial disaster, and why. To read Ralegh's *Discoverie of*

---

31. Montrose, "The Work of Gender in the Discourse of Discovery"; Fuller, "Ralegh's Fugitive Gold"; Fuller, *Voyages in Print*, 55–84.

32. A. L. Maycock, *Nicholas Ferrar of Little Gidding*, 157; Powers-Beck, *Writing the Flesh*, 210.

Guiana is to see the desperate optimism of a fallen man with nowhere else to turn, trying by all means to make his necessity seem like virtue. His earlier failures had taught him only that he must succeed now at all costs or lose his world. Ferrar, on the other hand, found in his colonial failure a desire to lose the world. Then, beyond his failure, he found other worlds: the world of Little Gidding where he could retreat from the imperatives of profit and conquest in order to advance his vision of a more peaceable kingdom; and beyond Little Gidding and this world, the promise of golden Paradise restored.

Tempting Virtue: Empire Rejected in *Paradise Regain'd*

No English writer dealt more directly with Eden lost and redeemed than John Milton, and I have already had much to say in chapter two about his uses of Paradise to express his ambivalence about empire. We have seen that after the establishment of Puritan Massachusetts in 1630, British colonial energies (and Milton's) were absorbed by internal conflicts through the civil wars of the 1640s and into the Interregnum of the 1650s—an introversion brought to an end by Oliver Cromwell in 1654–1656 with his unilateral Western Design against Spanish America. However much *Paradise Lost* (1667) reveals Milton's double-mindedness about such designs, there can be little doubt that the high-water mark of Miltonic anti-imperialism is found in *Paradise Regain'd* (1671). It is in this brief epic that heroism is most fully reimagined along Augustinian and humanist lines. Here Jesus, Christendom's moral model, rejects first the temptations of patriotic conquest and, beyond these, the temptations of universal virtue.

In book 3 (ll. 251–385), Satan brings Jesus to the mount of vision and shows him all the world's successive empires. Satan offers strategic help that will suborn Rome's rival Parthia and "reinstall thee / In David's royal seat" and bring "Deliverance of thy brethren" the Jews—and the conquest of Rome as well (3.372–74). Yet the irony implicit in this epic catalogue is that all the empires, with the exceptions of Rome's and Parthia's, are extinct, their vanity exposed by mere time. So says Jesus, renouncing "fleshly arm, / And fragile arms . . . soon to nothing brought" (3.387–89) and condemning all "that cumbersome / Luggage of war there shown me" as "argument / Of human weakness rather than of strength" (3.400–402). Furthermore, Jesus tells Satan, Jewish political freedom will do them no good as long as Israel—"Unhumbled, unrepentant, unreformed"—remains spiritually enslaved; the dog unchained will simply return to its vomit (3.429). Instead, Jesus foretells and awaits the time when Israel's sincere repentance will bring them to repossess their "Promised Land" through "providence" rather than through armed struggle (3.433–40).

Satan responds to this rejection by continuing to play, as Balachandra Rajan aptly puts it, on Messiah's "liberationist dreams," but at a higher, indeed a worldwide level.[33] Offering the temptations of virtue, he proposes that Jesus move from the imperial margins and claim the center by overthrowing the sensationally odious Tiberius:

> With what ease,
> Endued with regal virtues as thou art,
> Appearing, and beginning noble deeds,
> Might'st thou expel this monster from his throne,
> Now made a sty, and in his place ascending
> A victor people free from servile yoke?
> (4.97–102)

However, this proposal merely serves Jesus as an opportunity to enlarge upon the vanity of earthly empire, and in terms that reveal him as a thoroughgoing Augustinian humanist. If he will not make himself King of the Jews, how much less will he make himself Imperator of the far more decadent Romans? They were, he says, "once just, / Frugal, mild, and temperate," and so they "conquered well"; but now, after conquest, they

> . . . govern ill the nations under yoke,
> Peeling their provinces, exhausting all
> By lust and rapine; first ambitious grown
> Of triumph, that insulting vanity;
> Then cruel, by their sports to blood inured
> Of fighting beasts, and men to beasts exposed;
> Luxurious by their wealth, and greedier still,
> And from the daily scene effeminate.
> (4.133–42)

Repeating humanist attacks on the social and spiritual disaster of conquest, Jesus pictures a people increasingly unmanned in proportion to their imperial success.

Yet, as ringingly anti-imperial as this speech is, it could nevertheless contain a loophole. No doubt, when Jesus says that the Romans once "conquered well,"

---

33. Balachandra Rajan and Elizabeth Sauer, eds., *Milton and the Imperial Vision*, 7.

Milton may mean him to mean no more than that originally, a disciplined Rome conquered effectively. However, the slight suggestion here of an initially "good conquest" may remind us of the more double-minded attitude to empire that I have noted in *Paradise Lost* and that Willy Maley and Linda Gregerson have found amply illustrated in Milton's prose works, particularly *Eikonoklastes* and the *History of Britain*. In the former, Milton argues that continued English sway over Ireland will protect the reformation at home, while in the latter he praises (as well as blames) the Roman conquerors' influence in ancient Britain.[34]

Indeed, as Nicholas von Maltzahn has shown, Milton's multivocality about empire helped maintain and indeed raise his already ascendant poetic and political reputation over the next hundred years. Eighteenth-century Whig poets such as James Thomson and Thomas Gray found in Milton's tracts and his epics a patriotic celebration of England's unique mission: to spread the gospel of Christian, and republican, virtue around the world. Despite Jesus's strongly Augustinian words to the contrary in *Paradise Regain'd*, these Augustan admirers of "that grand Whig Milton" found the temptations of virtue impossible to resist.[35]

Remembering Our Ends: Scatology, Eschatology, and Colonial Disgust in Swift's Houyhnhnmland

One Augustan who overcame the attractions of Whiggish virtue—and of the expansionism that helped to make the age "Augustan"—was the ex-Whig and downright Tory Jonathan Swift. As a case in point, so adamant and eloquent was Swift's opposition to the successful Whig War of the Spanish Succession (1702–1713) that his polemics turned both popular opinion and the government against the duke of Marlborough's bloody victories and forced a relatively lenient peace with defeated France.[36] In addition, two colonial catastrophes of the new century—the Darien disaster of 1698–1700 and the South Sea Bubble of 1711–1720—provided Swift with rich material for his famous satire of the "modern colony."[37] The Darien scheme, an attempt by Scots to colonize that region on

---

34. Willy Maley, "Milton and the 'Complication of Interests' in Early Modern Ireland," and Linda Gregerson, "Colonials Write the Nation: Spenser, Milton, and England on the Margins."
35. Nicholas von Maltzahn, "Acts of Kind Service: Milton and the Patriotic Literature of Empire."
36. Greene, "Great War," 38.
37. Jonathan Swift, *Gulliver's Travels*, ed. Peter Dixon and John Chalker (London: Penguin, 1985), 343–44. All further citations of this edition will be made parenthetically.

the Isthmus of Panama, bankrupted the Scots' national treasury and brought them penniless into the new Union of 1707; the Bubble, an attempt to establish a South Sea Company for trade with Spanish America, generated wild stock speculation before bursting in 1720.[38] Both of these undertakings involved Tory as well as Whig politics; yet significantly neither enterprise made much virtuous pretense of spreading the gospel or improving the natives. Rather, they promised easy, quick, exploitative wealth and geopolitical prestige. Above all, both undertakings were the work of the "projectors" whom Swift so abominated, and both involved gullible investors in what one contemporary called "a gross, palpable illusion."[39]

In any case, regardless of his party affiliation, the corrosive Swift fits rather uneasily into the line of Christian humanist anti-imperialism—even though that line includes master ironists from Erasmus, More, and Rabelais to Montaigne, Cervantes, and Burton. For these writers, irony is generally like a double-edged sword, while for Swift, it is more like shrapnel, exploding and cutting in seemingly all directions. Can a writer so apparently misanthropic—and potentially nihilistic—ultimately be classed with the humanists at all, or even with the anti-imperialists? One might almost imagine that Swift opposed adventurism and colonization on the unnervingly general grounds that they are human activities.

Still, despite Swift's incongruity, he belongs with the Christian humanists because for him human beings, for all of their present grotesquery, are fallen from a higher origin and are at least hypothetically capable of restoration. For Swift's King of Brobdingnag in book 2 of *Gulliver's Travels* (probably the closest thing to an authorial spokesman in the book), Gulliver's race may be, at present, "little odious vermin"; yet they, like the king's own race, have greatly declined from a better original (172–73, 177–79). Mankind, in Swift's view, is not necessarily rational but is at least capable of reason—and the more to be blamed for wasting that capacity and descending to beastliness. Our humanity lies, for Swift, in our beginning and in our end, our eschatological purpose. Yet for Swift eschatology often takes a distinctly scatological twist—this focus on origins and ends and the ever-present menace of bestiality is especially prominent in book 4, where Gulliver finds himself in Houyhnhnmland, surrounded by aloof, sentient horses

---

38. See John Prebble, *The Darien Disaster: A Scots Colony in the New World, 1698–1700*, and Glyndwr Williams, *The Great South Sea: English Voyages and Encounters, 1570–1750*.

39. Abel Boyer, *The History of the Life and Reign of Queen Anne*, 495. See Williams, *Great South Sea*, 161–62, and Prebble, *Darien Disaster*, 283–86, for accounts of varied anti-Whig influences on these projects.

and feral, feculent Yahoos. How might Swift's own lived colonial experience as an Anglo-Irishman have informed his disgust with imperial ends?[40]

That Gulliver changes radically in book 4 is clear. From his earlier status as a patriotic, Whiggishly optimistic and morally obtuse English Everyman, he crosses over into a misanthropic madness so impenetrable that it often has been cited as evidence that Swift was actually insane (19–21). It is equally clear that book 4 contains Swift's most overt satire of colonial practice, for example in the oft-quoted passage about "a crew of pirates" whose "acts of inhumanity and lust" establish "a *modern colony* sent to convert and civilize an idolatrous and barbarous people" (343–44).[41] But if in Houyhnhnmland Swift ferociously skewers colonial oppressors, he shows little positive sympathy with the oppressed nor even identifies them with any certainty. The Yahoos, far from being childlike native victims à lá Las Casas, are among the most revoltingly ignoble savages in print. Gulliver's beginning Yahoo encounter is literally with their ends, as they void their bladders and bowels on him from the trees (269–70), to which Gulliver responds with a visceral revulsion that intensifies to an exterminating hatred as the story progresses.

But how specifically should we read the Yahoos and their Houyhnhnm masters? The Yahoos—many of them red-haired, all of them hostile, melancholy, and starving—certainly seem in some way to implicate Ireland. C. H. Firth and D. T. Torchiana have wanted to read them as types of the "old Irish," and the Houyhnhnms as the English, with readers' sympathies distributed according to our views on the "Irish question": that is, either as enacting Irish irredeemability versus English order (Firth), or Irish debasement by English tyranny (Torchiana).[42] Ann Cline Kelly rightly complicates such binary readings with her claim that "the Yahoos represent the potential nadir of any oppressed group," including, for Swift, his own *Anglo*-Irish stock; she notes that in the first edition of the book, Swift even suggested—in a passage later excised—that the Yahoos were once *English* colonists who have degenerated in the wild country. Yet even in these expanded terms, as Kelly herself observes, Swift's satire is multidirectional: bitter toward the English for centuries of cruelty and bitter toward the Irish and the Anglo-Irish for their animalistic degeneracy.[43]

---

40. See also on this point John Middleton Murry's chapter on "The Excremental Vision" in *Jonathan Swift: A Critical Biography*, 432–48.

41. For example, this passage is quoted by Stephen J. Greenblatt as a *locus classicus* on imperial brutality in the introduction to the volume he edited, *New World Encounters*, vii–viii.

42. C. H. Firth, "The Political Significance of *Gulliver's Travels*"; D. T. Torchiana, "Jonathan Swift, the Irish, and the Yahoos: The Case Reconsidered."

43. Ann Cline Kelly, "Swift's Explorations of Slavery in Houyhnhnmland and Ireland," 848, 849. In the passage in question, Gulliver observes that "these [Yahoos], for any thing

Is Yahoo beastliness then an expression of some inborn national character, or the environmental result of long-time brutalization by oppressors, or both? And to complicate these readings yet further, what might such local targets have to do with Swift's universal satire of human nature? Significantly, when Gulliver is finally compelled by the sexual advances of a female Yahoo to admit "that I was a real Yahoo in every limb and feature" (315), he is appalled not by his connection to Irishness (the would-be seductress was not a redhead, he assures us) but by what this says about his relation to humanity in general. After all, we are told, an ancient Houyhnhnm tradition has it "that many ages ago, two of these brutes appeared together upon a mountain"—like Adam and Eve in Milton's Eden—"and their brood in a short time grew so numerous as to overrun and infest the whole nation" (319).

Furthermore, in a tour de force on Yahoo behavior in "society" and at "court," Swift parades humanity's Seven Deadly Sins writ small: he describes Yahoo "avarice"; envy and wrathful fights over "shining stones"; the "gluttony" and drunkenness of their "undistinguished appetite"; their filthy sloth and lechery; and the absurd pride of their pack leader and his favorite, whose task is to *"lick his master's feet and posterior, and to drive the female Yahoos to his kennel"* (308–12). Although the Houyhnhnm master admits the obvious technological superiority of Gulliver's nation to the Yahoos, he observes that these "convenient instruments of death" merely magnify their shared nature (307, 310).

Indeed, the colonial setting of Swift's narrative seems to have a similar magnifying function. Swift begins with the Augustinian premise that human nature is naturally perverse, and this perversion is only intensified and further deformed in the bizarre mirror of Houyhnhnmland. Like Prospero in his earlier dealings with Caliban, the Houyhnhnms had initially made the optimistic assumption that their rationality and discipline could improve the Yahoo "herds," though like Prospero they discover that on such natures nurture can never stick. Houyhnhnm virtue remains incommunicable through colonial discipline.

Furthermore, for Swift it is the Houyhnhnms' aloof virtue that is their vice: if the Yahoos display the bestiality that results when humans forget their divine origins, the Houyhnhnms display the answering arrogance when human reason forgets its humbling link to the body and to the beasts. The resulting split between hideous brutalism and proud angelism is made darkly ludicrous by

---

I know, may have been *English,* which indeed I was apt to suspect from the Lineaments of their Posterity's Countenances, although very much defaced. But how far that will go to make out a Title, I leave to the Learned in Colony-law." From Jonathon Swift, *The Prose Works of Jonathan Swift,* 11.322, textual notes.

Swift's multiple inversions: "Houyhnhnm" puns on "Human," but when the horses dispassionately debate a genocidal Final Solution to the Yahoo Problem, we are brought up short by remembering that human—or humane—is just what the Houyhnhnms are not (318–20).

Yet ironically, it is not the Houyhnhnms who in the end actively exterminate Yahoos but rather the assimilated "Yahoo," Gulliver. As the Houyhnhnms (again like Prospero) display increasing symptoms of imperial anxiety—fear of insurrection, contempt for their inferiors' shiftlessness and ingratitude, revulsion at their filth—Gulliver feels compelled to prove his assimilation in more extreme ways. It is from Gulliver that his "master" Houyhnhnm gets his idea for castrating young Yahoo males, a more gradualist Final Solution that suits well with the loveless Platonic eugenics practiced by Houyhnhnms among themselves (320, 316). Eventually Gulliver grows so "Houyhnhnm-identified" that, "when I happened to behold my own form in a lake or a fountain, I turned away in horror and detestation of myself" and "fell to imitat[ing] their gait and gesture" so that "my friends often tell me . . . *I trot like a horse;* which, however, I take for a great compliment" (327).

Such self-loathing comes to a grisly head after the horses banish him as a potential leader of Yahoo rebellion (328). Shattered by grief and humiliation, he is given two months to finish a boat, "a sort of Indian canoe" that he fashions into an unspeakably literal emblem of the shame that he feels for his Yahoo nature. The boat's materials look forward to the fatted infants of "A Modest Proposal" (1729) and eerily anticipate Nazi lampshades: covered with "the skins of Yahoos well stitched together" and caulked with "Yahoos' tallow," the vessel hoists a sail "composed of the skins of the same animal; but I made use of the youngest I could get, the older being too tough and thick" (330). We are reminded that mass killing is in fact uniquely human behavior.

Would Swift have us weep or laugh, convulse with rage or with nausea, for the Yahoo dead? Are we to mourn or to mock their already distorted human images, now stretched like faces in a carnival mirror, carrying their madly earnest killer home to exile? It is hard, very hard, to know where our sympathies should lie. Sympathy depends upon identification, yet with whom in Houyhnhnmland can we identify—the spartan masters? the groveling slaves? the murderous colonial subaltern? *Gulliver's Travels* may not be a book primarily about imperial relations, but surely for Swift imperial relations are about the arrogance, degradation, and deadly folly that result when slaves forget their divine beginnings and masters forget their mortal ends. So the only known cure for the "Yahoo's-evil" is a graphic scatological reminder: "a mixture of *their own dung* and *urine* forcibly put down the Yahoo's throat" (309), an emetic taste of vile truth.

"A Den of Tyrants and a Dungeon of Slaves": The Tory Radicalism of Samuel Johnson

If Jonathan Swift were to have named a war, it might well have been the War of Jenkins' Ear. Precipitated by the arrant sword-stroke of a Spanish customs officer—some say pirate—at Havana in 1731, the war was declared in 1739 after the offended Captain Jenkins presented his severed member to the House of Commons.[44] The incident inflamed dormant English antihispanicism in defense of free trade in the Caribbean and set in motion nearly three decades of imperial warfare from which Britain emerged the master of North America and South Asia.

On the eve of this long bloody season, in the June 1738 issue of *The Gentleman's Magazine*, the young Samuel Johnson, styling himself with the Swiftian name of "Gulliver junior," began a series of reports on British parliamentary deliberations, thinly veiled as debates in the "senate of Lilliput." He writes that the Lilliputians

> have made conquests and settled colonies in very distant regions, the inhabitants of which they look upon as barbarous, though in simplicity of manners, probity, and temperance superior to themselves; and seem to think that they have the right to treat them as passion, interest, or caprice shall direct, without much regard to the rules of justice or humanity; they have carried this imaginary sovereignty so far that they have sometimes proceeded to rapine, bloodshed, and desolation. If you endeavor to examine the foundation of this authority, they . . . either threaten you with punishment for abridging the Emperor's sovereignty, or pity your stupidity, or tell you in positive terms, that "Power is right."[45]

There are a number of things notable about Johnson's commentary: that it trades on Swift's continuing currency and popularity twelve years after the publication of *Gulliver;* that it gives the lie to Britain's "imaginary sovereignty" with radical terseness; and that what it lacks in Swiftian madcap it makes up in trenchant clarity.[46]

Johnson once said that Sir Thomas More was "the person of greatest virtue these islands ever produced," and in Johnson's writings More's anticolonial tradition reaches its climax—and without More's ironic ambiguity.[47] During

---

44. James, *The Rise and Fall of the British Empire*, 59.
45. *The Gentleman's Magazine* 8: 283–87. Reprinted in Benjamin B. Hoover, *Samuel Johnson's Parliamentary Reporting*, 172–81.
46. For Johnson's authorship, see Greene, "Great War," 45, n. 9.
47. Arthur Kenny, *Thomas More*, 2. Johnson was as admiring of More the writer as of More the man. James Boswell quotes his comparison of More with other sixteenth-century

Johnson's lifetime Great Britain grew vastly greater, but it was a greatness that he despised, because he loved Little England. His trenchant and unflagging opposition to colonial adventurism—and, in fact, to colonial possession itself—is remarkable because Johnson's arch-conservative and chauvinistic views on English politics and culture are so well known. He retained a certain sympathy for the Jacobite cause well into the 1750s, and throughout his life he remained ardently devoted to the principle of class and gender subordination. He always maintained the natural superiority of civilized over what he called "savage" life—and in his mind, savagery began at the Scots and Welsh borders. He also was famously critical of the American colonists' claims to independence, writing in 1774 and 1775 at the government's request the notorious tracts *The Patriot* and *Taxation No Tyranny*. And Johnson's anti-imperialism appears all the more striking because he expressed it in the midst of England's most popular and successful imperial war, the "Great War for Empire" of 1756–1763—which added the Canadian and Indian jewels to the Crown.

Though as an attacker of empire Johnson was less ingenious than More and less acidly ironic than Swift, in terms of explicit anti-imperialism he equals and overgoes not only them but also the twentieth-century Left. Indeed, Johnson's Tory radicalism confounds our categories of Left and Right altogether: because he was an arch-conservative nationalist, he held that other peoples, however "savage," had a right to their own nationalisms as well. Thus he could toast "the next insurrection of the Negroes in the West Indies," commend racial intermarriage, condemn British claims to the Falkland Islands, deny the authority of the English Crown in Ireland, and sympathetically predict the varied nativist liberation movements that would eventually undo the empire.[48] With the exception of the Moravian Brethren—the Hussite sect that in the 1730s abandoned any national or political affiliation in order to minister among American and Caribbean Indians and slaves—no one in the eighteenth century distinguished so clearly

---

humanists: "'From the Muses, Sir Thomas More bore away the first crown, Erasmus the second, Mychallus the third.'" Boswell, *Boswell's Life of Johnson*, 5:430. Donald J. Greene's otherwise excellent essay "Samuel Johnson and the Great War for Empire" does not connect Johnson with this Christian humanist anti-imperial tradition, noting only the influence of Swift.

48. Greene, "Great War," 42, 45; James Boswell, *Boswell's Life of Johnson*, 2:134, 255; Johnson, *The Yale Edition of the Works of Samuel Johnson*, 10:435. Boswell's recollection of Johnson's remarks of May 7, 1773, on the Crown's illegitimate Irish claims are particularly trenchant: "'The Irish are in a most unnatural state; for we see there the minority prevailing over the majority. . . . King William was not their lawful sovereign: he had not been acknowledged by the Parliament of Ireland, when they appeared in arms against him'" (*Boswell's Life of Johnson*, 2:225).

between the cross and the sword nor predicted so clearly the consequences of confusing the two.[49]

The source of these strikingly prescient convictions, as Donald J. Greene has written, was Johnson's religion, which taught him that "all human beings, whatever the color of their skin or the nature of their culture, are of equal worth before God and have equal rights."[50] So Johnson unfailingly targeted not only the conduct of empire and its corrupting effects on the imperialist nation but also and especially the central imperialist claim: the right of any one nation to conquer or control any other. He believed that a man's land and labor belong to himself, not to the man or nation strong or white or even Christian enough to take them.

Significantly, Johnson's remarkable foresight about the revolutions that would end the British Empire derive from his awareness of its beginnings. Unlike many writers since, he understood England's colonial project as rooted in the attitudes and ideas of the Elizabethans.[51] So he begins his critique of the empire by attempting to discredit the late Tudor myths discussed in my first three chapters: Britain's divine imperial destiny, her rivals' abominable "popery," and English Protestant moral exceptionalism. In the inaugural issue of the *Literary Magazine* (May 1756), Johnson begins his "Introduction to the Political State of Great-Britain" with characteristic plain speaking:

> The present system of English politics may properly be said to have taken rise in the reign of Queen Elizabeth. At this time the Protestant religion was established, which naturally allied us to the reformed states, and made all the popish powers our enemies.
>
> We began in the same reign to extend our trade, by which we made it necessary to ourselves to watch the commercial progress of our neighbors; and, if not to incommode and obstruct their traffick, to hinder them from impairing ours.
>
> We then likewise settled colonies in America, which was become the great scene of European ambition; for, seeing with what treasures the Spaniards were annually inriched from Mexico and Peru, every nation imagined, that an American conquest or plantation would certainly fill the mother country with gold and silver. This produced a large extent of very distant dominions, of which we, at this time, neither knew nor foresaw the advantage or incumbrance: We seem to have

---

49. J. Taylor Hamilton and Kenneth G. Hamilton, *History of the Moravian Church: The Renewed Unitas Fratrum, 1722–1957*, 34–59.

50. Greene, "Great War," 60.

51. Martin Green and Donald J. Greene, in contrast, see the empire as an eighteenth-century creation; Patrick Brantlinger, Lawrence Wurgaft, and Edward Said treat it as beginning, for all practical purposes, in the nineteenth century. See note 13 in the introduction to this volume.

170   *Reforming Empire*

> snatched them into our hands, upon no very just principles of policy, only because every state, according to a prejudice of long continuance, concludes itself more powerful as its territories become larger.⁵²

Writing just as Britain is entering its decisive war for empire, Johnson begins his demythologization directly: British destiny becomes "no very just principles of policy" based on "a prejudice of long continuance"; "popish" Spain becomes simply a practical rival in a trans-Atlantic treasure hunt; and Protestant moral exceptionalism evaporates in the heat of England's desire to imitate its thieving enemies.

Johnson is especially hostile to imperialist arguments based on Protestant exceptionalism. In blistering denigration of English imperial conduct, he mocks the old Protestant dream of "liberating" Spanish America from popery. Noting Cromwell's unprovoked Caribbean war, Johnson comments on the successful invasion of Jamaica, "which was afterwards consigned to us, being probably of little value to the Spaniards, and continues to this day a place of great wealth and dreadful wickedness, a den of tyrants, and a dungeon of slaves." Decrying the treatment of the Irish, he "bursts forth" that " '[t]here is no instance, even in the ten persecutions [by Roman Emperors from Nero to Diocletian], of such severity as that which the Protestants of Ireland have excercised against the Catholics.'" And as for England's current enemy, papist France, despite their faults they eclipse Protestant England in their relative righteousness: they at least "admit the Indians, by intermarriage, to an equality with themselves, and those nations with which they have no such near intercourse, they gain over to their interest by honesty in their dealings." In marked contrast, says Johnson, "[o]ur traders hourly alienate the Indians by their tricks and oppressions."⁵³

In addition to this remarkable dissent from English injustice abroad, Johnson rearticulates for his own day Sir Thomas More's "Nolandian" critique of colonial damage at home. Writing in the same year, 1756, for Christopher Smart's *Universal Visitor*, Johnson foretells that dependence on empire eventually will bring down England's domestic economy. As Greene notes, Johnson foresees that "when the rest of the world has caught up with and surpassed British superiority in technology and navigation, the basis for that prosperity will vanish"—a startlingly accurate prediction of England's mid-twentieth-century productivity crisis. Domestic morality is also increasingly debased by empire, in Johnson's view, as when the "transient shew" of fireworks celebrate the short-lived 1748

---

52. *Yale Johnson*, 10:130.
53. *Yale Johnson*, 10:137; Boswell, *Boswell's Life of Johnson*, 2:255; *Yale Johnson*, 10:150.

peace of Aix-la-Chapelle, or worse, when the church celebrates with great *Te Deums* paltry war victories like the 1758 capture of Louisbourg in Canada. In words reminiscent of Augustine's story about Alexander and the pirate, Johnson dismisses the epochal struggle with France over Canada and India as "only the quarrel of two robbers for the spoils of a passenger."[54] Scorning the expansionist fervor of the moment, he ends his *Literary Magazine* essay with a parting jab at Britain's self-congratulatory "greatness": "we continue every day to shew by new proofs, that no people can be great who have ceased to be virtuous."[55]

In the watershed year of 1759, which brought Wolfe death and victory at Quebec, Johnson supplemented such straightforward polemics with the more imaginative mode of Utopian fiction in *The History of Rasselas, Prince of Abyssinia*. Though primarily concerned with the "choice of life," *Rasselas* also works as anti-imperial satire, exposing the moral vanity of the title character's optimistic, progressive expansionism. Like More in *Utopia*, Johnson's first strategy is to displace English debates overseas, thus (more than two centuries before Edward Said) de-exoticizing his Oriental setting by showing his Orientals struggling with the same issues as Europeans.[56]

His second strategy is to give to his own Tory philosophy a weary, wise, Solomonic voice in the person of Imlac, long-suffering advisor to the Whiggish prince. Rasselas is possessed by an exceptionalist imperial imagination; that is, he supposes that he can hold and expand his father's kingdom as the agent of good without being lured by the corruptions of power. Imlac attempts to dampen this dangerously well-meaning enthusiasm: "No form of government has yet been discovered, by which cruelty can be wholly prevented.... [I]f power be in the hands of men, it will sometimes be abused. The vigilance of the supreme magistrate may do much, but much will still remain undone. He can never know all the crimes that are committed, and can seldom punish all that he knows." Rasselas initially takes his teacher's point, reluctantly renouncing his expansionist impulses and his "innumerable schemes of reformation," and desiring instead "a little kingdom, in which he might administer justice in his own person, and see all the parts of government with his own eyes."[57] Yet, as Steven Scherwatzky observes, in the end nothing is really settled; Rasselas, like William Pitt and the giddy British public of 1759, "continues to indulge

---

54. Greene, "Great War," 54, 48, 56, 53.
55. *Yale Johnson*, 10:150.
56. See Edward Said, *Orientalism*. See also on this point Steven Scherwatzky, "Johnson, *Rasselas*, and the Politics of Empire," 107.
57. *Yale Johnson*, 16:32, 153, 175.

political designs" and is "unable to remain content with the 'little kingdom' he hopes to govern."[58] Johnson's own anticolonialism is immovably anchored, but he knows that he is standing in a rising tide.

Indeed, Johnson's outspokenness was not without cost—Greene observes that the journals for which he wrote his anti-imperial essays terminated his various series repeatedly, making his journalistic career during the Seven Years' War a leap-frog affair. But he persisted to fight another day, and with remarkable constancy. Even his famous opposition to the American Revolution is, by his own uncompromising lights, consistent with his sympathy for the oppressed. Johnson viewed the rebellious Anglo-American colonists not as native freedom fighters but rather as natural English subjects betraying their lawful king—and as imperialist "drivers of negroes" to boot, whose "yelps for liberty" masked their expansionist ambitions in Kentucky and Ohio.[59]

Instead, Johnson reserved his sympathy for the indigenous Americans who were, in his view, the true losers of both the "French and Indian" and Revolutionary Wars. In his last published comment on the "Great War for Empire"—in the *Idler* of November 1759 (no. 81)—a Canadian chieftain watches as the disciplined ranks of the British army advance on Quebec. This Indian leader contemplates a grim future, a kind of British *leyenda negra*, in which his vanquished people will be worked to death in mines, only to be replaced by black slaves who also will "perish here under toil and torture." Significantly, the moral standard to which he holds the English invaders is their own Bible: they "have a written law among them, of which they boast as derived from Him who made the earth and sea.... Why is not this law communicated to us? It is concealed because it is violated. For how can they preach it to an Indian nation, when I am told that one of its first precepts forbids them to do to others what they would not that others should do to them?" Imperial armies, even Christian ones, have not generally fought under the banner of the Golden Rule.

Yet, as Greene notes, Johnson's Indian alter ego ends his meditation not on a note of resignation but on one of defiant hope. He looks forward to a day when the European invaders will fall again to letting each others' blood and their conquest will undo itself. Then, says the chieftain, "let us look unconcerned upon the slaughter, and remember that the death of every European delivers the country from a tyrant and a robber.... Let us endeavor, in the mean time, to learn their discipline, and to forge their weapons; and, when they shall be weakened with mutual slaughter, let us rush down upon them, force their remains

---

58. Scherwatzky, "Johnson, *Rasselas*, and the Politics of Empire," 111.
59. Greene, "Great War," 56–57, 59–60.

to take shelter in their ships, and reign once more in our native country."[60] For Johnson, the Golden Rule means, among other things, that Cree patriotism is no less honorable than the English variety. Like the fictional Aziz at the end of *A Passage to India*, or like Jomo Kenyatta in 1950s Kenya, Johnson's chieftain speaks in the assurance that the conqueror's injustice is self-consuming, that he will be held to his own standard, and that the day of wrath, expulsion, and liberty is coming.

Samuel Johnson was a good and true prophet; perhaps, to borrow his own words about More, the truest that his island ever produced. What he saw, he told, and what he told, came to pass—if not precisely in Canada, certainly in India and Africa, as well as in Ireland and in nearly every land that once had flown the Union Jack. It would be nearly two centuries before English intellectuals would match Johnson's sustained anti-imperial fire, but by then foresight was largely unnecessary, because the edifice was collapsing around them. What makes Johnson's opposition to empire most remarkable is that, like an English Isaiah, he was called to speak doom in the day of fatness, and that his vision came not from revolutionary futurism but from Christian humanist hindsight.

Empire against Imperialism: Edmund Burke and the Ironies of "Colonial Trusteeship"

Samuel Johnson generally could not abide a Whig; yet he had this to say about his younger contemporary Edmund Burke: "You could not stand five minutes with that man beneath a shed while it rained, but you must be convinced you had been standing with the greatest man you had ever seen."[61] The admiration of the arch-Tory for the great Whig hints at Burke's paradox. Throughout his parliamentary career (1765–1794) he sought, in the name and by means of the British Empire, to eradicate what seem to modern minds the essential facets of British imperialism: autocratic administrative and economic control from the imperial center (he sought free trade for Ireland and the American colonies, and home rule for America before 1776); "anti-popery" (he sought Catholic emancipation in Ireland); on-site colonial corruption and despotism (he indicted the East India Company and impeached Indian Governor-General Warren Hastings for venality and brutality); and the slave trade (he sought total abolition). In advocating this far-reaching program—mostly unrealized in his lifetime—he maintained that

60. Ibid., 58–60.
61. Samuel Johnson, *Johnsonian Miscellanies*, 1:290.

the empire was itself not sovereign but rather a "trusteeship" subject to "the chartered rights of men"; that is, to a divinely sanctioned natural law higher than mere commercial self-interest or even national legislation.[62] It is in Burke that the troubled Protestant imperial conscience, observed at earlier stages in Hakluyt, Donne, Herbert, and Milton, comes of age and begins its brilliant but conflicted public career.

Two keys to the Burkean imperial paradox are, as with Swift, his religious nurture and his Irish origins, and the two are closely connected. The son of an Anglo-Irish Protestant father and an Irish Roman Catholic mother, he was raised as a firm Anglican Protestant, yet with a keen sympathy for the condition of his mother's (and sisters') coreligionists. This sympathy was sharpened by the tutelage of his Quaker schoolmaster, who seems also to have contributed to his larger views on social justice, including his abolitionism.[63] Burke insisted that true Protestantism should always be more than a mere negative creed of "anti-Popery" (Burke 482–85); it also should be a positive creed providing spiritual solace, social cohesion, and a love of liberty—one's own liberty *and* others' (313). "Liberty," he wrote, with a universalism unfashionable in his day and again in ours, "is the birthright of our species" (278).

So, as Jeff D. Bass has written, it is a mistake to class Burke with later imperialists who converted his doctrine of imperial "trusteeship" into a metaphysical justification before the fact for further expansion.[64] For all of Burke's concern about human liberty, nowhere does he propose a "mission" of further beneficent colonization in order to rescue native peoples from a rival evil empire (like Hakluyt or Cromwell); nor does he seek to deliver indigenes by force from their own savagery, superstition, and chaos (like British empire builders from Hakluyt to Disraeli).

Instead, the only imperial oppressors whom Burke attacks are British Protestant ones, like Clive, Hastings, and the "boy despots" who "in India drink the intoxicating draught of authority and dominion before their heads are able to bear

---

62. Edmund Burke, *Burke's Politics: Selected Writings and Speeches of Edmund Burke on Reform, Revolution, and War,* 255. All further citations of this edition will be made parenthetically.

63. J. C. Beckett, "Burke, Ireland, and the Empire," 4–5.

64. Jeff D. Bass, "The Perversion of Empire: Edmund Burke and the Nature of Imperial Responsibility," 209. Bass points to Patrick Brantlinger's *Rule of Darkness* and Edward Said's *Culture and Imperialism* as offering blanket condemnations of "imperial responsibility" as, in George Lichtheim's words, "'mere subterfuge, artfully contrived to blind democratic electorates to what was being done behind their backs.'" He also faults these writers for treating the British Empire as a mainly nineteenth-century phenomenon, thus overlooking its earlier origins.

it" (Burke 264). Burke does advocate the improvement of human conditions, but only in Britain's existing empire, for which, furthermore, he envisions eventual autonomy, if not independence. In his speeches first against the Company and later against Hastings, he seeks to shame the nation for allowing such profiteering in the name of paternalism, which he sarcastically calls the "protection that destroys India." In fact, Burke compares English government unfavorably with the earlier Tartar invasion.

> The Tartars, as bloody as their conquest was, at least returned most of their wealth to the Indian economy through spending and public works; but [e]very rupee of profit made by an Englishman is lost forever to India. . . . England has erected no churches, no hospitals, no palaces, no schools; England has built no bridges, made no highroads, cut no navigations, dug no reservoirs. . . . Were we to be driven out of India this day, nothing would remain to tell that it had been possessed, during the inglorious period of our dominion, by anything better than the orangoutang or the tiger. (263)

And while previous invaders assimilated into Indian life, says Burke, the British remain arrogantly aloof, forgetting that they rule "a people for ages civilized and cultivated—cultivated by all the arts of polished life, whilst we were yet in the woods" (260). Like Thomas Hariot and William Crashaw two hundred years before, and Conrad a century later, Burke reminds his countrymen of their own humbling descent from the "savages."

Informing all of these exhortations to colonial justice and good works is Burke's belief in "chartered rights," a natural law theory that derives authority from divine law but that is not confined to the adherents of any particular religion or nation. Thus for Burke "chartered rights" do not mean the extension of local British law or the imposition of Christianity in foreign dominions; rather, they are rights grounded in humanity's divine image but worked out differently in varied cultural settings. Arguing that the East India Company operates in violation of both English and natural law, Burke sought, in the East India Bill of 1783, to strip Company officials of all the political and military powers that they had acquired during the imperial wars with France and to vest these powers in a government board of commissioners, who would be responsible directly to the Crown.

So the empire becomes for Burke not the disseminator of Englishness overseas but rather the guarantor of a universal standard of justice, holding out the implicit promise of eventual self-rule. "This bill, and those connected with it, are intended to form the *Magna Charta* of Hindostan. Of this benefit I am certain [the Indians'] condition is capable: and when I know that they are capable of more, my vote shall most assuredly be for our giving to the full extent of their capacity of receiving" (258). But Burke's imperial meliorist doctrine—like his crusade against the East India Company and Hastings—enmeshed him in ironies. First, it put him on the record as looking for eventual Indian home rule at the same time that he was opposing home rule for his native Ireland. This inconsistency made excellent political sense—Burke feared (as it turned out, rightly) that a semiautonomous Irish parliament dominated by Protestants would scuttle his more cherished goal of Catholic emancipation. More significantly, he considered Ireland an irreducible part of "Britain," not a "Colony" like India, Canada, or the (by then lost) Virginia or Massachusetts.[65]

A second irony is that, by Burke's own later admission, it was in the affairs of India that "I showed the most industry and had the least success" (275). After nearly seven years of impeachment proceedings, Hastings was acquitted in 1794. And though the East India Bill of 1783 passed the Commons by a two-to-one margin, it was defeated by the Lords, leading to William Pitt's 1784 compromise that created the system of "double government" that lasted until after the Indian "Mutiny" of 1857. Yet in a third irony, the Mutiny brought in 1858 the vindication of Hastings's impeachment and the enactment, in essence, of Burke's 1783 plan: India became, like Virginia in 1624, a Crown colony, and the monopolistic Company was abolished. This crucial reform accelerated the implementation of those Indian public works first adumbrated by Burke—hospitals, schools, highroads, canals, bridges, and most famously, railways. Thus the passionate defender of the British Empire against Jacobin attack did more to liberalize imperial practice than anyone for another half-century.

But, in another ironic layering, the eventual and unintended consequence of Burke's applied imperial virtue was a revival of the imperial expansion that he opposed. As we will see, this reinfusion of the empire with a sense of higher political morality contributed greatly to the rhetoric of imperial "mission" under the mid- and late Victorians. Once again militant English Protestantism would rally to save the heathen from themselves and from rival, evil empires—thus drawing a glittering curtain over their conquests in the dark places of the earth.

Perhaps the greatest irony is that Burke, as much as Johnson, saw the practically insuperable difficulties of any empire ruling well for long. Arguing for the 1783 East India Bill, he acknowledges the cultural chasm dividing India and England, admits the obstacles to real English understanding or sympathy, yet offers this conclusion: "All these circumstances are not, I confess, very favorable to the idea of our attempting to govern India at all. But there we are; there we

---

65. Beckett, "Burke, Ireland, and the Empire," 2–3.

are placed by the Sovereign Disposer; and we must do the best we can in our situation. The situation of man is the preceptor of his duty" (265). "But there we are." Conflating realpolitik with providentialism, Burke echoes the Elizabethan Hakluyt, dismayed by England's moral and material inadequacy abroad but still certain that God is working his will through his Englishmen. Significantly, Burke never considers that it might be the will of the Sovereign Disposer for the British to withdraw, that the apparent intractability of the situation might make it their duty to leave India to the Indians. Of course, a dozen practicalities would crowd in on Burke to argue against such an unprecedented victors' withdrawal, most notably the continuing protection of English trade and the ongoing geopolitical enmity of France.

But such arguments regard England's well-being, not India's, and they smack slightly of what Milton called "necessity, / The tyrant's plea" (*Paradise Lost* 4.393–94). It is hard to fault the empire's most virtuous advocate for wanting to restore good order to India while preserving British prosperity. Similarly, it is hard to fault a man when pressing danger compels him to ride a tiger. But such extenuating circumstances will not in the end alter the tiger's appetite. So there is in Burke's angel voice a devil's bargain. It is usually the best people who feel the temptations of virtue, and often they fail to anticipate the coming catastrophe of their success.

"The Terrors of His Harp": William Blake, Bard against Empire

In contrast to Edmund Burke's complicated and ironic anti-imperialism, William Blake's would seem to have been straightforwardly fierce. He sided with the British Empire's enemies in revolutionary America and France, abhorred the institution of slavery, mocked the hypocrisies of English royal and church authority, and cried out against British militarism and the "dark Satanic mills" that supported it. Indeed, David V. Erdman, one of Blake's most influential modern interpreters, calls him a "Prophet against Empire," a title that I have adopted—and adapted—for this present chapter.[66]

Still, as Erdman himself concedes, on closer examination both Blake and his relation to imperialism appear more complex. T. S. Eliot warned against the tendency to regard Blake "as a naif, a wild man, a wild pet for the supercultivated"; aside from George Herbert, probably no other English poet has

---

66. David V. Erdman, *Blake: Prophet against Empire: A Poet's Interpretation of the History of His Own Times.*

been so commonly misunderstood as "simple."[67] This is as true of his politics as of his poetry. First of all, like his younger Romantic contemporaries Wordsworth and Coleridge, Blake's attitudes toward practical imperialism depended on the imperialist: Blake was susceptible to a kind of "alienism" that was quick to lionize Britain's French revolutionary enemies. Indeed, as Erdman notes, during the Great Terror of 1794 Blake could write of how he saw Jesus "himself put on the robes of blood" to direct the antiaristocratic violence that Blake believed was necessary to protect French liberty and fraternity from extinction.[68]

But Blake was much slower than either Wordsworth or Coleridge to be disillusioned as France's "empire of liberty" degenerated further into domestic terror and autocratic conquest. More than two decades later, Blake had not fully lost his sympathy for Napoleonic France. In the person of his allegorical figure Luvah, Blake portrays the defeated Napoleon as a Christlike sufferer cruelly nailed by English executioners "to Albion's Tree."[69] For all of Blake's eventual disappointment with the French Revolution, he continued to see Bonaparte as a kindred soul, a fellow transgressor of orthodoxies and proprieties.

It is his transgressive vision that makes Blake less a prophet than a bard against empire: despite the density of his biblical imagery, he threatens tyrants with "the terrors of his harp," not with the wrath of a righteous Jehovah.[70] This anti-orthodox bardic identity also makes him an especially odd fit in a discussion of the Christian humanist anti-imperial tradition. Raised as a radical dissenter and by temperament a visionary, Blake's utterly idiosyncratic spiritual system rejected all traditional Christian creeds.[71] He transvalued the language of the Bible so thoroughly that he worshipped "Poetic Genius" in the place of a transcendent Godhead and judged all acts and institutions not by divine commandments but by whether they bound or liberated "the divinity of the creative individual," which he measured by his own "joys and desires."[72] He thus approaches the ironic ideal of Burke's "most perfect Protestant": the man "who protests against the whole of the Christian religion" (*Burke's Politics*, 485). Furthermore, of all the imperial critics whom I have discussed so far, he had the least contemporary influence or effect on affairs: Augustine was a powerful bishop; More, a privy counsellor and eventual lord chancellor; Daniel, a court

---

67. T. S. Eliot, *The Sacred Wood*, 151.
68. Erdman, *Blake: Prophet against Empire*, 378.
69. Ibid., 467, 468.
70. Ibid., 48.
71. Peter Ackroyd, *William Blake*, 18.
72. Erdman, *Blake: Prophet against Empire*, 143.

poet; Ferrar, a former colonial official; Milton, a Cromwellian spokesman; Swift and Johnson, leading intellectuals and occasional government pamphleteers—while Blake was an obscure engraver.

And yet, to exclude Blake from this discussion of English Protestant opposition to empire would be absurd. As the American bard Walt Whitman wrote, "No true bard will ever contravene the Bible." However much Blake translated the Scripture into his own idiom, his "Protestant" imagination was saturated in the same Word that moved the Reformers, and his poetry depended (and depends) for much of its power on what Whitman called the Bible's "accrued and incorporated . . . passions, [the] many joys and sorrows, it has itself aroused."[73] Despite Blake's thoroughgoing and enthusiastic heresy, his invaluable long-term achievement against British imperialism depended upon the Dissenting spirit; and although he was devoted to rambling prose polemics, that achievement is primarily lyric. In his *Songs of Innocence* (1789) and *Songs of Experience* (1793), he imagines a spiritual alternative to the empire's social and racial metaphysics that is, to appropriate Eliot's words, "peculiarly terrifying."[74] Blake is, like Swift, capable of acid irony, and, like Johnson, of sustained earnest outrage. But like neither of these others, Blake is a visionary given glimpses of the Peaceable Kingdom. Swift may scald, Johnson may convince and shame, but Blake enraptures. In these brief lyrics—none of which uses the word "empire"—he lays his axe to the spiritual roots of Albion's imperial tree, and plants the seeds of its replacement.

In particular, Blake's *Songs* dissolve the binding ties of religious nationalism by presenting a spirituality of connection that transcends inherited boundaries. In "The Divine Image," universal prayer prefigures universal brotherhood:

> To Mercy, Pity, Peace and Love
> All pray in their distress;
> And to those virtues of delight
> Return their thankfulness.
>
> For Mercy, Pity, Peace, and Love
> Is God, our father dear,
> And Mercy, Pity, Peace and Love
> Is Man, his child and care.
>
> For Mercy has a human heart,
> Pity a human face,

73. Walt Whitman, *The Poetry and Prose of Walt Whitman*, 894, 893.
74. Eliot, *The Sacred Wood*, 155.

> And Love the human form divine
> And Peace the human dress.
>
> Then every man, of every clime
> That prays in his distress,
> Prays to the human form divine
> Love, Mercy, Pity, Peace.
>
> And all must love the human form,
> In heathen, Turk, or Jew:
> Where Mercy, Love & Pity dwell
> There God is dwelling too.[75]

What Erdman calls Blake's "Humanitarian Christianity," with its emphasis on the divine image *in* the human, is of course potentially subversive of orthodox beliefs about God's omniscience and omnipresence; God's dwelling "in heathen, Turk, or Jew" can be read as diminishingly local.[76] Yet mere localism cannot speak against tribal, cultic, and national arrogance, let alone arrive at this poem's moral imperative—"all *must* love the human form." Rather, this imperative depends for its emotional and intellectual resonance on an idea of divine transcendence that recalls orthodox affirmations, even if it does not explictly reimport them.

For as I have been describing, it is not "humanitarian Christianity" but Christian humanism—as a species of Augustinian orthodoxy—that has for sixteen centuries most consistently affirmed the inalienable worth of the individual. For these humanists, the human form is "divine," not because of tribal, creedal, or national identity, but because each person bears the image of the transcendent Creator and Father. And in this poem it is to a divine father—however variously represented by the "human form"—that "all pray in their distress." Intentionally or not, Blake's universal love evokes a universal Lover.

The racial implications of this divine love are enacted in "The Little Black Boy." The poem begins with apparent acquiescence to English racist metaphysics:

> My mother bore me in the southern wild,
> And I am black, but O! my soul is white;

---

75. William Blake, *The Songs of Innocence and Experience* (Harmondsworth: Penguin, 1995), 17–18. All further citations of this edition will be made parenthetically by page and line number.
76. Erdman, *Blake: Prophet against Empire*, 128.

> White as an angel is the English child,
> But I am black as if bereav'd of light.
> (p. 8, ll. 1–4)

The speaker seems to acknowledge the inferiority of his racial blackness. He protests that he is spiritually "white" despite his outer darkness, as if the English child's white complexion were the truest manifestation of inner purity.

These lessons seem initially to be borne out by the black boy's mother, who "took me on her lap, and kissed me," teaching him that

> . . . we are put on earth a little space,
> That we may learn to bear the beams of love:
> And these black bodies and this sunburnt face
> Is but a cloud, and like a shady grove:
>
> For when our souls have learn'd the heat to bear
> The cloud will vanish; we will hear [God's] voice,
> Saying: Come out from the grove, my love & care,
> And round my golden tent like lambs rejoice.
> (ll. 7, 13–20)

Though speaking with moving tenderness, the mother seems complicit with the racist system, apparently promising her son eventual liberation from the spiritually obscuring "cloud" or "grove" of his skin color into a "golden" Caucasian heaven; his salvation, it appears, will be from his negritude.

However, these racial markers become confused and indeed neutralized as the black boy applies this maternal teaching to his relations with the white child:

> Thus did my mother say, and kissed me:
> And thus I say to little English boy;
> When I from black and he from white cloud free,
> And round the tent of God like lambs we joy,
>
> I'll shade him from the heat, till he can bear
> To lean in joy upon our father's knee:
> And then I'll stand and stroke his silver hair,
> And be like him and he will then love me.
> (ll. 21–28)

Here in the end we learn that we have been misreading whiteness and blackness all along. The immediate parallelism of "Thus" and "thus" in lines 21–22 indicates an identity between the mother's lesson to her son and the son's words to the "little English boy." English outer whiteness turns out to be a kind of darkness as well, in fact a deeper darkness because it induces pride and incapacitates the English boy spiritually. He may be "white as an angel" (l. 3), but there is a suggestion by the end of a fallen angel. The whole fleshly realm, whether dark-skinned "southern" or light-skinned northern, is "cloudy" and obscure, but it is the loveless white boy whose racism makes him unable to bear the beatific vision; he will need the black boy's forbearing love to shade him until he can face God, "our father," and acknowledge his brother.

The poem's most moving effect, however, comes from the total absence of rancor in the speaker's voice. Is this meekness the complicity of the oppressed, longing for the approval of his oppressors, whom he would emulate—in all senses—slavishly? The final stanzas suggest rather the meekness that inherits the earth—the Mercy and especially the Pity that knowing humility feels for ignorant pride.

So, much as "The Divine Image" presents an alternative to the binding ties of Protestant imperial nationalism, "The Little Black Boy" undermines notions of racial superiority founded on English spiritual exceptionalism. And even when Blake leaves the tender and hopeful visions of innocence for the hard ironies of experience, English exceptionalism remains one of his main targets. "A Little Boy Lost" plays subversively on Protestant England's assumed superiority over her "popish" enemies. The poem attacks evil priestcraft by portraying the innocent frankness of a child menaced and eventually destroyed by inquisitorial zeal. The lyric begins in the midst of a catechetical lesson, as the boy ingenuously but scandalously observes that the Golden Rule and indeed any dogmatic certainty are unachieved and unachievable:

> Nought loves another as itself
> Nor venerates another so,
> Nor is it possible to Thought
> A greater than itself to know:
>
> And Father, how can I love you,
> Or any of my brothers more?
> I love you like the little bird
> That picks up crumbs around the door.
> (p. 48, ll. 1–8)

With troubling honesty, the boy confesses what either his innocence or his experience has taught him: that no one in fact lives for others or loves them as himself, nor can anyone be entirely certain of a truth greater than his own mind. The expression of this heterodoxy is paradoxically both sweeping and modest; the boy compares himself with unconscious pathos to a tiny creature more concerned with eking out its survival than with theological imponderables.

We have, perhaps, met this boy before in *Songs of Experience*—in "The Little Vagabond" (pp. 40–41), where an impoverished child asks his mother why the "cold" Protestant English church cannot be as friendly, welcoming, and warm as the alehouse. In that poem, the child could at least imagine an alternative world where "the Parson might preach & drink & sing, / And we'd be as happy as birds in the spring" (9–10); but in "A Little Boy Lost" the child's honesty merely outrages his inquisitorial questioner and precipitates an auto-da-fé:

> The Priest sat by and heard the child,
> In trembling zeal he seiz'd his hair:
> He led him by his little coat;
> And all admir'd the Priestly care.
>
> And standing on the altar high,
> Lo, what a fiend is here! said he:
> One who sets reason up for judge
> Of our most holy Mystery.
>
> The weeping child could not be heard,
> The weeping parents wept in vain:
> They strip'd him to his little shirt,
> And bound him in an iron chain,
>
> And burn'd him in a holy place,
> Where many had been burn'd before:
> The weeping parents wept in vain.
> (ll. 9–23)

Significantly, the poem's inquisitor is described in terms that seem to identify him and his actions with the Church of Rome. The outraged cleric is called both "Father" and "Priest"; he officiates at an "altar high" as a zealous defender of an irrational "holy Mystery"; and the boy is stripped to his shirt and chained to be offered up as a burnt offering, like a heretic in Seville or Lisbon. Blake's Protestant contemporaries are invited to imagine the Iberian *leyenda negra* and perhaps to imagine themselves as free from "Spanish cruelty."

But the poem's last line is designed to backfire: "Are such things done on Albion's shore?" (24). Might not this burning boy be a more domestic victim, like one of Foxe's Smithfield martyrs? Yet now is he done to death not by dark foreigners but by a national church-state as cruel and corrupt as imperial Spain's?

Indeed yes, for as the poem "London" ironically affirms, England's "charter'd" liberties mask profound rot:

> In every cry of every Man,
> In every Infant's cry of fear,
> In every voice, in every ban,
> The mind-forg'd manacles I hear.
>
> How the chimney sweeper's cry
> Every black'ning Church appalls,
> And the hapless Soldier's sigh
> Runs in blood down palace walls
> (p. 52, ll. 5–12)

However much the empire may be on the march abroad, it is dead or dying at its heart.

Are the beatific *Songs of Innocence* vitiated by such grim irony? Does the voice of experience repudiate the hopes that preceded it? But if that were so, then why does experience speak with such passionate anger? Indignation implies a continuing belief in dignity; however disillusioned the speaker is in *Songs of Experience*, his satiric bite actually depends on his earlier affirmations of innocence. Indeed, Robert F. Gleckner has written of "Blake's insistence on the higher innocence inherent in experience," a hard-won vision of the "Lamb" behind the "Tyger."[77]

What Whitman said of the Bible also describes Blake: "No really great song can ever attain full purport till long after the death of its singer."[78] Despite Blake's relative obscurity in his own times, and despite his reverse exceptionalism where French conquest was concerned, these lyric mustard seeds of alternative faith took root and grew. If Samuel Johnson was the most consistent and convincing anti-imperialist of England's imperial age, Blake remains the most moving through his sheer psalmic power. One cannot, of course, ignore what Morris Eaves has called "the problem of the Romantic audience"—that is, the potentially complete solipsism that can result "when art becomes expression" and the artist creates asocially, for and about himself alone.[79] Yet however idiosyncratic Blake was, and however often he wrote against the killing confines of religious dogma and moral stricture, poems like "The Divine Image" and "The

---

77. Robert F. Gleckner, *The Piper and the Bard: A Study of William Blake*, 284, 286
78. Whitman, *The Poetry and Prose of Walt Whitman*, 893.
79. Morris Eaves, *William Blake's Theory of Art*, 171.

Little Black Boy" express themselves in ways that resonate remarkably with the Tory Johnson's highly public Augustinian morality.

Indeed a few such poems—and their engravings—were worth reams of anti-imperial argument. British imperialism depended on a sanctioning religious imagination to bind Britain together and its colonies under; so opening or shattering those "mind-forg'd manacles" required not a materialist negation but rather a religious vision both higher and deeper; one that fights fire with fire, and spirit with spirit.

"Something . . . wanting *within*": Colonialism and Domestic Damage in Jane Austen's *Mansfield Park*

Though Blake's bardic voice often has been remembered as the sharpest of his age against empire, I have shown Samuel Johnson's anti-imperialism to be at least as radical and indeed more consistently trenchant. What then becomes of the humanist countertradition after his death? Who, if anyone, inherits his mantle? Commenting on Johnson's literary legacy, C. S. Lewis has written that Johnson's "daughter" was Jane Austen. She "inherits his common sense, his morality, even much of his style." All of her novels, Lewis says, embody strict moral values that are "those of all the heroines, when they are most rational, and of Jane Austen herself. This is the hard core of her mind, the Johnsonian element, the iron in the tonic."[80]

One naturally asks whether Austen's Johnsonian morality extended to colonial relations. There are indeed indications that she disapproved of the slave system that supported England's Caribbean plantations. Claire Tomalin notes that Austen was an admirer not only of Johnson but of the fervent abolitionist (and evangelical Calvinist) William Cowper, and that all of her novels were published after the abolition of the slave trade throughout the empire in 1807. Thus in *Emma* (1816), Jane Fairfax's intolerable situation as a despised governess is compared to the morally indefensible condition of chattel slavery; and in *Mansfield Park* (1814), when Fanny Price finally questions Sir Thomas Bertram on his West Indian affairs, Tomalin states that she "bravely makes her own abolitionist sympathies clear."[81]

---

80. C. S. Lewis, "A Note on Jane Austen," 23–24.
81. Claire Tomalin, *Jane Austen: A Life*, 289, 232. For a useful discussion of the links between *Mansfield Park* and contemporary evangelicalism, and of the resulting problem of readers unsympathetic to Fanny Price, see Marilyn Butler, *Jane Austen and the War of Ideas*, 242–49.

However, these sympathies are not so clear to other modern readers. In particular, Edward Said devotes an extensive section in *Culture and Imperialism* to arguing that Austen, however admirable as a literary artist, displays in *Mansfield Park* her deep complicity with and support of colonial possession.

> More clearly than anywhere else in her fiction, Austen here synchronizes domestic with international authority, making it plain that the values associated with such higher things as ordination, law, and propriety must be grounded firmly in actual rule over and possession of territory. She sees clearly that to hold and rule Mansfield Park is to hold and rule an imperial state in close, not to say inevitable association with it. What assures the domestic tranquility and attractive harmony of one is the productivity and regulated discipline of the other.[82]

Put simply, Sir Thomas Bertram's West Indian slaves build the base on which the charming superstructure of his English country house rests, and when Fanny Price rescues that estate at the novel's climax, her newfound domestic joy is purchased with unseen Caribbean toil.

Said is, I think, wrong here, but brilliantly wrong. He is the first interpreter of Austen's most ambitious novel to recognize the centrality of colonialism to the book's action and meaning.[83] Yet, any real understanding of Austen's attitude toward empire must recognize her relationship to Johnson and to the Protestant humanist countertradition. For Sir Thomas's Antiguan plantations prove to be not the sustenance but rather the near-ruin of his house. It is his extended (indeed overextended) voyage to what Said calls his "colonial garden," pursuing far-flung power and wealth, that brings domestic disaster. As an "imperial estate," Mansfield Park strikingly resembles More's Nolandia, and it fulfills Johnson's warnings that dependence on empire eventually will undermine England's domestic life.

Yet in her approach to the weighty topic of empire, Austen's touch is characteristically light. Said rightly notes that by a "very odd combination of casualness and stress, Austen reveals herself to be *assuming* . . . the importance of an empire to the situation at home."[84] Antigua is seldom mentioned explicitly, and then only as a source of anxiety or, more important, as the cause of Sir Thomas's crucial year-long absence.[85] His absence reenacts the Christian humanist critique of emptiness at the imperial center, both revealing the hollowness of the

---

82. Said, *Culture and Imperialism*, 87.
83. See also on this point Judith Terry, "Sir Thomas Bertram's 'Business in Antigua.'"
84. Said, *Culture and Imperialism*, 89.
85. Jane Austen, *Mansfield Park*, 64, 65.

Bertram family circle and giving occasion for further damage: the attractive and amoral opportunists, Henry and Mary Crawford—and the thoroughly nasty Aunt Norris—fill the void.

As to the origin of this domestic void, Said is again right in seeing the colonial-domestic connection here, since Sir Thomas's aloof magisterial manner—practiced on his plantations—has long ago cooled family affection. When, early in the novel, he finds that the Caribbean estate is making "such poor returns" that he must "go to Antigua himself, for the better arrangement of his affairs," his wife reacts with indifference and his children with relief. The vain and slothful Lady Bertram "was not disturbed by any alarm for his safety, or solicitude for his comfort, being one of those persons who think nothing can be dangerous or difficult, or fatiguing to any body but themselves." To Sir Thomas's pretty and frivolous daughters, Maria and Julia, "his absence was unhappily most welcome. They were relieved by it from all restraint, and to have every indulgence within their reach."[86]

In the case of his consistently slighted poor relation and ward, Fanny Price, Sir Thomas has alienated her feelings as well, though not her loyalty. His regularly "cold address" to her reflects his utilitarian concern for performance and profit: on taking his leave, he wounds her deeply by suggesting that her many years at Mansfield have been spent almost "entirely without improvement." So when Sir Thomas departs, Fanny grieves, but only "because she could not grieve . . . that she should see him go without a tear!—it was a shameful insensibility." And yet the memory of his insult does soon bring bitter tears, so that her cousins, "on seeing her with red eyes, set her down as a hypocrite."[87]

Into this domestic vacuum come the witty and appealing Crawfords, worldly in-laws of the local parson. Henry Crawford flirts with the Misses Bertram, and Mary Crawford with the usually upright Edmund, whom she attempts to turn away from his clerical vocation—though her cap actually is set, we are told, for his older brother, the wastrel heir Tom. Their rounds of "indulgence" come to a climax in their production of the "loose" romantic play, *Lovers' Vows,* to be performed on a stage erected in their absent father's private rooms. Only Fanny, loyal to Sir Thomas despite her marginal status and his chilly treatment, refuses to participate, invoking his unwelcome name.

At this crucial point, halfway into the novel, Sir Thomas suddenly and unexpectedly returns. It is important that although he has succeeded in restoring financial prosperity abroad, his appearance tells another story: he wears the

---

86. Ibid., 65–66.
87. Ibid., 66–67.

"burnt, fagged, worn look of fatigue and a hot climate." As Johnson had warned, money and exhaustion are the only rewards of empire; Sir Thomas arrives ungreeted and unwanted to find himself "bewildered in his own house," his *sanctum sanctorum* violated, his affairs and estate out of order, and his children compromised and dissipated—all but the neglected yet loyal Fanny.[88]

There is worse to come. Though Sir Thomas superficially restores order by marrying Maria to the ostentatious and fatuous Mr. Rushworth, the alien influences allowed by his colonial absence and domestic neglect have taken root— just as the humanist critics of empire would have predicted. Julia elopes with the foppish Mr. Yates, her acting partner; Maria adulterously absconds with Henry Crawford; and the debauched heir Tom falls ill, nearly dying in disgrace. It is left to the plain and principled Fanny to act the true child, restoring and healing the domestic sphere that has been so badly deranged by the poisonous prosperity of empire. Significantly, by marrying Edmund and reaffirming the pastoral calling from which Mary Crawford nearly seduced him, Fanny also restores religion to its proper role as guardian of home and hearth.

So Said miscasts the question when he asks, in reference to *Mansfield Park*, why "Britain's great humanistic ideas, institutions, and monuments . . . coexisted so comfortably with imperialism" and why "there was little significant opposition or deterrence to empire at home."[89] Before discussing the many ways in which "humanism" certainly failed, Said should have begun by asking how it actually *did* oppose empire. Though he glancingly acknowledges the anti-imperialism of Swift and Johnson, he does not note their strong connection to each other or to Jane Austen in the English humanist continuum back to More.

This misunderstanding is most conspicuous in Said's discussion of Sir Thomas Bertram's crucial moment of recognition near the book's end, as he takes account of his domestic disaster. Sir Thomas has come bitterly to deplore his own "grievous mismanagement" of his home: his forbidding demeanor to his daughters and his reliance on the indulgent and flattering Mrs. Norris to guide them during his long vacancy. But, as bad as this error was, "he gradually grew to feel that it had not been the most direful mistake in his plan of education. . . . Something must have been wanting *within*, or time would have worn away much of its ill effect. He feared that principle, active principle, had been wanting, that they had never been properly taught to govern their inclinations and tempers, by that sense of duty which can alone suffice. They had been instructed theoretically in their religion, but never required to bring it into daily practice. . . . He

---

88. Ibid., 194–95, 199.
89. Said, *Culture and Imperialism*, 82.

had meant them to be good, but his cares had been directed to the understanding and manners, not the disposition."[90] In short, what Sir Thomas sees is spiritual failure, a dereliction of his own religious duty to nurture in his children an inner life of "self-denial and humility." They have simply been gaining the world at the expense of their souls.

However, Said reads this passage as illustrating the Marxian claim that base precedes and determines superstructure, that financial principal underwrites moral principle. He writes that "[w]hat was wanting *within* was in fact supplied by the wealth derived from a West Indian plantation and a poor provincial relative, both brought in to Mansfield Park and set to work." What he seems to mean is that Sir Thomas's Antiguan money is necessary to finance the luxury of Fanny's Christian discipline, and that Austen is teaching us how externals make the inner life possible. But it is highly unlikely that Austen shared this belief in the material origins of morality. For her to show material and emotional "comfort" flowing from Fanny's spiritual reforms at Mansfield is not, as Said suggests, her confirmation that "morality is in fact not separable from its social basis"; it is instead her confirmation that social and material happiness are not separable from their spiritual and moral basis.[91] Jane Austen was a parson's daughter; she believed that spirit underwrites matter.

This metaphysical distinction has strong implications for anti-imperial morality. Since Augustine, the Christian critique of empire has been founded on Jesus's words to Caesar's representative, Pilate: "my kingdom is not of this world" (John 18:36). Though both church and state often have read this as a safely quietist statement, Augustinians have usually read it instead as a statement of omnipotence. Their countertradition presupposes a place to stand above and outside of Caesar's realm—indeed, beyond the world itself—in order to judge it.

Jane Austen would surely disclaim any world-altering ambitions; yet we have seen how her novel enacts humanism's anti-imperial critique, how she does judge her little world. This is not to claim that Austen imitates Dr. Johnson's trenchant anti-imperialism but rather that she assumes it. I in no way reduce the value of *Mansfield Park*—as comedy of manners, as contemporary social commentary, as cultural document, or novelistic milestone—when I recognize that the book also functions as a kind of anti-expansionist allegory. Sir Thomas Bertram is finally forced to agree with Raphael Hythloday that "There was no respect whatever for the law, [when] the king's attention was divided between

---

90. Austen, *Mansfield Park*, 448.
91. Said, *Culture and Imperialism*, 92.

the two kingdoms"; he must learn, like Augustine's "man of moderate means," to be "self-sufficient on his small and circumscribed estate. He is beloved of his own family, and rejoices in the most sweet peace with kindred, neighbors, and friends." Daniel, Ferrar, Milton, Swift, Johnson—all warn against the hollow delights of empire. Whomever we invoke for the particulars, Jane Austen's tightly drawn little world maps their macrocosm.

Six

"Hollow All Delight!"

Countertraditions, 1815–1945

And they cast dust on their heads, and cried, weeping and wailing, saying, Alas, alas that great city, wherein were made rich all that had ships in the sea by reason of their costliness! for in one hour is she made desolate. —*Revelation 18:19*

There came on Arthur sleeping, Gawain kill'd
In Lancelot's war, the ghost of Gawain blown
Along a wandering wind, and past his ear
Went shrilling: "Hollow, hollow all delight!
Hail, King! to-morrow thou shalt pass away."
—*Alfred Lord Tennyson,* Idylls of the King

We English are a nation of brutes, and ought to be exterminated to the last man. —*John Bright, 1888 speech*

In my beginning is my end. —*T. S. Eliot,* Four Quartets, *"East Coker"*

The British Empire began in hope and in fear. My earlier chapters have dealt with Britain's Elizabethan hopes of imperial recovery, her sense of relative righteousness and redeeming mission, the sacred complex of her authorizing humility, and her rationale for colonial subjection and enslavement. All of these aspirations and attitudes found their binding power in a religion of Protestant imperialism, both derived and distinct from Protestant Christianity itself. But born along with these hopes were holy fears: forebodings of the divine judgments to be visited on the means of empire building or on the very ends themselves.

So in these latter chapters I illustrate the reverse of the medal—how religious conscience sought to bind Britain's imperial joys and desires, to frustrate her colonial romance. In particular we have seen two countertraditions at work: one, the Christian humanist condemnation of imperialism as hollow folly, and the other a Protestant meliorist belief in colonial "trusteeship" that expressed determination to make the best of a necessary evil. In this final chapter, I survey the strange fates of these countertraditions in the age of Britain's imperial ascendency and decline—as the evangelical burden of the early Victorians in India and the haunted expansionism of Alfred Tennyson gave way to the post-Protestant, Darwinian disenchantment of Joseph Conrad and E. M. Forster, and eventually to the savage laughter of the Roman Catholic convert Evelyn Waugh. In other words, I will consider how Protestant "trusteeship" made its peace with the empire just as Britain and the empire began to cast off the ties of Protestantism. What would bind the empire in the secular age to come?

The complex relationship of post-Protestant secularity to imperialism is well illustrated by the famously secular libertarian John Stuart Mill. As noted in the previous chapter, Edward Said asks why "Britain's great humanistic ideas, institutions, and monuments . . . coexisted so comfortably with imperialism" (82). Significantly, Said exemplifies this lack of a British humanist resistance to empire by referring to Mill; Said rightly observes how ironic it was for Mill to decry colonial injustice while comfortably employed for decades by the East India Company: "Liberal though he was, . . . [Mill] could still say, 'The sacred duties which civilized nations owe to the independence and nationality of each other, are not binding towards those to whom nationality and independence are certain evil, or at best a questionable good.' Ideas like these were not original with Mill. . . . Almost all colonial schemes begin with an assumption of native backwardness and general inadequacy to be independent, 'equal,' and fit."[1] Yet Said might have noted a further irony: that Mill's denial of a universally binding divine principle of human rights—his secularity would admit none—makes it atavistic of him to assert the "binding" power of "sacred duties" owed to "independence and nationality." In Mill's view these duties are merely local

---

1. Said, *Culture and Imperialism*, 80; quoting John Stuart Mill, *Disquisitions and Discussions*, 3:167–68.

and relative, applying only among the "civilized." In striking contrast to Samuel Johnson's religiously sanctioned multicultural Golden Rule—the God-given right even of the "savages" to self-determination—Mill assumes a Eurocentric monopoly of such "human" rights, and implicitly of full humanity itself. Indeed, Mill could be even more frank on this point, writing in *On Liberty* (1859) that "[d]espotism is a legitimate mode of government in dealing with barbarians, provided the end be their improvement, and the means be justified by actually effecting that end."[2]

In fairness to Mill, we should note that he made this latter concession to despotic rule in the immediate shadow of the alarming 1857 Indian "Mutiny"; we also should note that in *Culture and Imperialism,* Said's own anti-imperialism appears selective, since he scarcely acknowledges Soviet despotism except as a necessary—and now worrisomely absent—counterbalance to American hegemony.[3] Indeed, Said's entire critique of English humanist imperialism is somewhat misleading, as I have noted, because he largely overlooks the Christian humanist countertradition stretching back from Johnson through Swift and More to Augustine.

Yet Said's neglect of this countertradition is understandable, since his book's primary focus is on the nineteenth and twentieth centuries. For as Britain approached her Victorian imperial zenith, outspoken anti-imperialism—whether religious or secular—waned. Indeed, standing with the secular humanist Mill in 1859, one must look nearly a century back, to the Christian humanist Johnson, in order to discover a full-throated English rejection of Mill's view that "native backwardness" and "barbarism" justify colonialist coercion. In the intervening generations—and especially between the Napoleonic and Crimean Wars—the anti-imperial Tories had receded from view. But their expansionist foes had fallen on hard times as well; both positions were supplanted by a mediating belief in Burkean imperial "trusteeship." So from Mill's mid-Victorian viewpoint, the empire seemed in some sense regrettable but also inevitable and strangely invisible. In fact, well before the beginning of Victoria's reign in 1837, secular utilitarianism and Protestant evangelical religion had met in an uneasy alliance. Somewhat ashamed of each other's company, they were more than a little embarrassed at their attempts to follow Burke's paradoxical advice: build the empire without growing it.

---

2. John Stuart Mill, *On Liberty, Annotated Text Sources and Background Criticism,* 11.
3. Said, *Culture and Imperialism,* 242.

The Hated Name of Empire: Evangelical Revival and Colonial Embarrassment

The decades between 1815 and 1860 saw a sharp and pervasive revival of evangelical religion in England; yet during the same era, imperial prestige was in decline. Indeed, even Patrick Brantlinger, who has argued in *Rule of Darkness* for a broadly imperialist culture in England throughout these decades, admits that the expansionist impulse was then at a low ebb.[4] Imperial historian A. P. Thornton has written that as late as 1860, the word "empire" was to the British "a foreign joss, whose worshippers, where they were not simply benighted, were assumed to be the sinister agents of the forces of wrong"—forces like Nicholas I of Russia or Napoleon III of France. In short, as in our own day, "'Empire' was a word that had a history to live down." In contrast, the English of 1860 generally understood their own colonial possessions as did their Liberal prime minister, Lord Palmerston—in terms of devotion to progress, free trade, and the *Pax Britannica*.[5] Like the Milton of *The History of Britain* and *Paradise Lost*, they heard in "empire" the echo of Romish, satanic arrogance, but they looked upon an English sphere of influence with modest pride. Looking back from the 1880s, John Robert Seeley was to write of this attitude as "a fit of absence of mind."[6] The late Regency and early Victorian mind was embarrassed, if not by the fact of empire, at least by the guilty associations of its name.

The relationship between these two trends—religious revival and colonial embarrassment—is double-edged. On the one side, the embarrassment implies continued possession—these parallel developments suggest how hard it is fully to embrace, or to reject, ill-gotten gains once they are gotten. The only thing more corrosive to virtue than poverty is wealth, and it is difficult to argue with one's own success. And yet, on the other side, if the old Christian humanist prophets had failed to eradicate or even reduce colonial possession, they had managed to curtail colonial pleasure. Despite Victoria's namesake goddess, there were no Roman triumphs in the early decades of her reign—rather there was to be strenuous improvement of what Britain now possessed, in an uneasy collaboration of self-interest and self-sacrifice.

Indeed, well before Victoria's accession, the emerging wave of evangelical revival was reshaping colonial practice, asserting religious sanctions in regions that had come under English rule and yet that had been until then beyond the

---

4. Brantlinger, *Rule of Darkness*, 4.
5. A. P. Thornton, *The Imperial Idea and Its Enemies: A Study in British Power*, 1.
6. John Robert Seeley, *The Expansion of England: Two Courses of Lectures*, 8.

pale of English law and Christian morality. Burke's impeachment of Hastings, though technically unsuccessful, had stung the imperialists in general and the India Company in particular. So it is suggestive that as the nineteenth century began, William Carey, an obscure Baptist cobbler and self-taught linguist, was able to win from the India Company a concession for evangelism in Bengal, previously closed to the gospel by Company policy.[7] As in early Virginia, Anglo-Indian colonists and planters had frequently objected to native evangelism on the grounds that it disrupted the colonial order by encouraging intervention from home, by upsetting the local religious balance, and by giving the indigenes egalitarian ideas.

What this concession suggests is that the Anglo-Indian authorities were becoming at least dimly aware of their need to sacralize their enterprise—or rather resacralize it in the name of the older Protestant imperial mission. In 1809 and 1814, their policy change was further extended into print, as Carey was permitted to publish his Bengali Bible and India Company chaplain Henry Martyn posthumously to publish his Urdu New Testament.[8] Martyn, a model for *Jane Eyre*'s St. John Rivers, also pioneered the role of the English missionary martyr, dying en route to England in 1812.[9]

Significantly, while both Carey and Martyn necessarily cooperated with India Company authorities in order to inaugurate the era of British foreign missions, their main loyalty was clearly not to Caesar. As Mary Ellis Gibson writes, in the first half of the nineteenth century, English missionaries had not yet developed "an explicitly nationalist tone; evangelical attitudes rather propounded a more generalized Christian version of honor and self-sacrifice."[10] So the evangelicals and imperialists lived in an uneasy symbiosis—gospellers needing official sanction but loathing the Company's allegiance to Mars and Mammon; the Company needing religion's reviving prestige but despising "enthusiasm" and fearing interference.

Forestalling such interference, colonial administrators took it upon themselves to step into the forefront of reform. Significantly, in India their most notable efforts were directed not at English abuses but at the native customs of *sati* and *thugi*—the self-immolation of Hindu widows and the hereditary

---

7. William A. Smalley, *Translation as Mission: Bible Translation in the Modern Missionary Movement*, 40.
8. Ibid., 40–43.
9. Mary Ellis Gibson, "Henry Martyn and England's Christian Empire: Rereading *Jane Eyre* through Missionary Biography," 419–20.
10. Ibid., 420.

religious practice of ritual murder. Between 1828 and 1835, the Indian administration, led by Governor General Lord William Bentinck, initiated a program of criminalizing and then suppressing these customs—virtually eradicating *thugi* by 1841 and drastically curtailing *sati* by 1860. Bentinck, in his youth a disciple of Burke and in later years an evangelical, employed—through his anti-*thugi* Superintendent Captain William Sleeman—the kind of despotism praised by the utilitarian Mill: the program depended heavily on a system of informers and bypassed the ordinary processes of law, trying suspected "Thugs" under a special commissioner. Yet this despotism was plausibly liberal: Bentinck also opposed any policy of coercive Christianization and was the first to advance Indians in the administration and to allow a virtually free native press. Bentinck was beginning to revive, at least for the British popular imagination, the strong arm of liberalism in the name of *Pax Britannica*. For Bentinck's modern biographer, John Rosselli, this pragmatism calls to mind Machiavelli's sardonic dictum, "it is better to act, and be sorry, than not to act, and be sorry."[11] The sorrow was left mainly to Bentinck's successors.

At the same time that these exotic cruelties were being eradicated abroad, the English home government was uprooting its own most savage custom. Between 1791 and 1833, the charming but flinty evangelical William Wilberforce spurred a reluctant Parliament to abolish first the slave trade—in 1807—and finally slavery itself throughout the colonies and possessions. Like Burke before him, Wilberforce maintained that Britain abroad was subject to a divinely sanctioned natural law higher than mere commercial self-interest or even national legislation. And, like Burke, he sought to make British colonial power the guarantor of this universal standard of justice. It was the conscious intent of neither reformer to extend Britain's sway to new territory. However, the zeal for reform has its own internal logic: in February 1807, after the passage of the Abolition Act, "Mr. Wilberforce," according to one eyewitness, "turned playfully to [Parliamentary ally] Henry Thornton and said exultingly, 'What shall we abolish next?' "[12]

After 1807, Britain moved incrementally to the side of the abolitionist angels. Leading the diplomatic initiative, she imposed—at Wilberforce's urging—an anti-slave-trade pledge on the European powers at the Congress of Vienna in 1814, and after Waterloo began to assert her naval power enforcing it, redoubling

---

11. John Rosselli, *Lord William Bentinck: The Making of a Liberal Imperialist, 1774–1839*, 31, 39–43, 208–14, 230–31 (informers and due process); 210–11, 20 (plausibly liberal); 9 (Machiavelli).

12. Ford K. Brown, *Fathers of the Victorians: The Age of Wilberforce*, 107.

these efforts into many foreign waters after full abolition in 1833.[13] The sight of a Royal Navy ship was coming to mean something other than trade or invasion—in more and more places, it was coming to mean freedom. In India, Bentinck was pushing British justice beyond his official frontiers, allowing his forces to enlarge their areas of de facto control in pursuit of suspected "Thugs."[14] In the absence of legal sovereignty, actual British suzerainty was expanding. The unintended consequence of giving colonialism a new mission was, eventually, to give expansionism a new vitality. *Imperium et libertas* were coming to be seen as mutually linked, though at home few as yet were willing to translate "imperium" into the hated name of empire.

Calibanism in the Island: Browning and the Implied Colonial Subject

Besides the evangelical revival, another reason for lowered imperial prestige after Waterloo was the largely opposite legacy of the later Romantics—who were to influence, among many others, the youthful Robert Browning. Unlike the radicalism of the earlier Romantics Blake, Wordsworth, Coleridge, and Southey, that of Byron and Shelley was formed well after the heady hopes for French liberty had passed. Thus their anti-imperialism did not look to France for redress (though Byron, for one, mourned Napoleon's defeat) and was inclined neither to the millenarianism of Blake nor to the counterrevolutionary disillusionment of the Lake Poets.[15] In any case, these later Romantics, along with Keats, were spared the reactionary potential of long, disenchanting lives. Dying, respectively, in 1822 and 1824, Shelley and Byron met their ends in self-exile abroad, championing the cause of secular liberty in Italy and in Ottoman Greece. Their atheist anticreed traced the line of hierarchical oppression up to the imperial Deity himself, whom they found inseparable from the earthly machinery of church, crown, and empire, and thus unworthy of allegiance or belief.

And yet a penumbra of spirituality remained. Neither of these protesting poets was above adopting Protestant-like biblicist language or personae on political topics, invoking a kind of egalitarian nontheological Christianity: Byron's imperial Sennacherib is destroyed by the invisible hand of a liberationist Jehovah,

---

13. Philip Curtin, *The Atlantic Slave Trade*, 231–33, 266–69.
14. Rosselli, *Bentinck*, 230–31.
15. Byron's poem "Napoleon's Farewell" makes clear how strongly Byron regarded the defeated emperor as a surrogate. See Byron, *Lord Byron: The Complete Poetical Works*, 3:312–13, 473.

and Shelley enlists the teachings of Jesus in his advocacy of national and international leveling.[16] It is this kind of Romantic radicalism, with a touch of the visionary about it, that first attracted the young Robert Browning.

A reader of both Byron and Shelley from his early teens, Browning in his long life (1812–1889) personifies the mutation—and the muting—of Victorian anti-imperialism. Raised by a devout evangelical mother and a liberal, indulgent father, Browning was by his adolescence an avowed Shelley disciple, espousing atheist radicalism.[17] But by the time that he published his hymn to Shelley in *Pauline* (1833), he was a believer again "in God and truth / And love"; he celebrates Shelley the "Sun-treader" not for his radical politics but for his passionate aesthetic immediacy, which the twenty-one-year-old Browning credits with fathering his own sense of poetic vocation.[18]

The immersion of politics in aesthetics was a common nineteenth-century phenomenon; however, in Browning's case it was not so much a dissolution of those politics as a transforming baptism. Browning's atheist radicalism may have mellowed soon into Christian liberalism, but he never disavowed the value of that radical stage in his development. Nor could he comfortably assimilate himself to the reviving ethnocentric expansionism that characterized England's mid- and later Victorian life—a nonconformity suggested by his own quasi-Romantic self-exile in Italy at the heart of the century and by his enduring allegiance to "emancipated" ideals. These tensions between personal and political are still evident near the end of his life, in an 1885 sonnet explaining "Why I Am a Liberal":

> . . . If fetters, not a few,
> Of prejudice, convention, fall from me,
>   These shall I bid men—each in his degree
> Also God-guided—bear, and gayly too?
>
> But little do or can the best of us:
>   That little is achieved through Liberty.
> Who, then, dare hold, emancipated thus,

---

16. Lord George Gordon Byron, "Destruction of Sennacherib," in *Complete Poetical Works*, 3:309–10; Percy Bysshe Shelley, *The Defense of Poetry*, in *Shelley's Poetry and Prose*, 496. See also Shelley's unfinished "Essay on Christianity" and "The Moral Teachings of Jesus Christ" in Shelley, *Shelley: Political Writings*, 89–96. It is perhaps significant that Byron's poem belongs to a series of "Hebrew Melodies," written to be set to music by a Jewish friend named Isaac Nathan; Byron is most comfortable with sacred subjects as an exercise in appreciating a foreign, exotic culture. See Byron, *Complete Poetical Works*, 3:465.

17. Sarah Wood, *Robert Browning: A Literary Life*, 138.

18. Robert Browning, *Robert Browning's Poetry*, 3–4; Wood, *Robert Browning*, 18, 19, 115–16.

> His fellow shall continue bound? Not I,
> Who live, love, labor freely, nor discuss
> A brother's right to freedom. That is "Why."[19]

Paradoxically, the poem combines its urgent, plainspoken tone ("Not I . . . That is 'Why' ") with a convoluted syntax and substance. One clue to this urgency of tone is the 1885 date. The poem probably voices something of a riposte to the national outrage at Gladstone's Liberal government after the January 1885 death of General Charles Gordon at Khartoum. Though Gordon had insubordinately transformed Gladstone's mission of strategic retreat into a bloody last stand, it was the "Grand Old Man" Gladstone who was execrated by many as the "M.O.G." (Murderer of Gordon) for his perceived anti-interventionist nicety.[20] Read in this context, Browning seems to say that he is not to be stampeded from his emancipationism by man-on-the-spot expansionism. His vision is inimical to armed coercion in the name of liberty and justice; rather it is a vision of free individuals, indeed "brothers," unbowed, unchained, enfranchised.

And yet the poem's terse declarations are circuitously couched—an indirection fitting Browning's actually passive stance. There is nothing here about how these "brothers" can become free. Browning will not "hold" others "bound," but his anti-interventionism will not remove any chains, either. Instead there is a sober qualification reminiscent of Burke, and even more of Johnson: "But little do or can the best of us"; the implication is that drastic or coercive means to liberation are likely to do more harm than good. So the poem, despite its ending declaration, is rhetorically inert: for one does not make a rousing political program out of circumspect noncoercion in the name of liberty. *Primum non nocere* (first, do no harm) is a sensible dictum both in medicine and in politics, but if not followed by positive action, it is generally indistinguishable from mere indifference.

It is not surprising, then, that Browning—with his skepticism about liberalizing despotisms from above and liberationist revolutions from below—seldom addresses the colonial subject. He is the preeminent poet of the idiosyncratic personal voice, Donnean in his use of material occasions as windows into psychological or metaphysical reality rather than as incitements to transform political or physical reality. So when, in "Caliban upon Setebos" (1864), he revives

---

19. Robert Browning, *Poems of Robert Browning*, ed. Donald Smalley (Boston: Houghton Mifflin, 1956), 473, ll. 5–14. All further citations of this edition will be made parenthetically by line numbers, unless otherwise specified. "Caliban upon Setebos" appears on pp. 288–95.

20. James, *The Rise and Fall of the British Empire*, 275–79; Lytton Strachey, *Eminent Victorians*, 192.

Shakespeare's wild man plotting against God and Master, the primary theme is neither oppression nor insurrection—crucial concerns for Shakespeare—but instead, as the subtitle says, "Natural Theology in the Island."

A "colonialist" reading of the poem—of the kind worked by Stephen Greenblatt on *The Tempest*—might blame Browning for making his Caliban an especially unsympathetic caricature of the pagan savage: cowardly, vindictive, and above all benighted about Christian theological rudiments, foolishly building his image of God from his own cruel behavior and his predatory jungle world. As Caliban sprawls "in the pit's much mire, . . . letting the rank tongue blossom into speech," he imagines that he is unheard by Setebos, "whom his dam [Sycorax] called God" (1–2, 23, 15–16). Thus the first striking attribute of Caliban's God is his limitation. Setebos is not only nonomniscient in Caliban's conception, this deity is not omnipotent, either, having made only the moon, "with the sun to match, / But not the stars" (26–27)—a clear negation of biblical monotheism as portrayed in the first chapter of Genesis.

Setebos's second striking attribute is derived from his first and leads to his third: because he is limited in knowledge and power, he is anxious, "ill at ease" (31) about maintaining his own lordship. And indeed Caliban does think him subordinate to "something over Setebos," "the Quiet," a kind of affectless Unmoved Mover (129–31, 137). This insecurity makes Setebos utterly arbitrary to those under him—as is Caliban when he has the chance: "[I] Am strong myself compared to yonder crabs . . . [I] Let twenty pass, and stone the twenty-first, / Loving not, hating not, just choosing so. . . . such shows no right and wrong in Him, / Nor kind, nor cruel: He is strong and Lord" (100, 102–3, 98–99). Browning develops Caliban's theological extrapolations extensively, as in section after section the savage speaker ruminates on the meaning of his own wanton acts—"making and marring" clay birds (75–97), alternately nurturing and mutilating crabs and lizards (104–8, 181–87), building structures only to destroy them (192–99). In each case Caliban concludes by inferring that as he himself does, "so He," so does Setebos (43, 97, 108, 126, 169, 199, 240). The poem's picture of heathen ignorance would seem to be crowned by its psalmic epigraph, "Thou thoughtest that I was altogether such a one as thyself" (Psalm 50:21).

But that psalm verse is really an early clue that Browning's satire here is multidirectional. In context, the verse's slap at anthropomorphic "natural theology" is aimed not at the benighted heathen but at the psalmist's willfully ignorant coreligionists: "the wicked" whom the Lord asks, "What hast thou to do to declare my statutes, or that thou shouldest take my covenant in thy mouth?" (Psalm 50:16). Along these lines, Donald Smalley has noted strong resemblances between Caliban's natural theology and one influential form of

Christian doctrine, the Westminster Confession Calvinism that, at least in its bluntest formulations, Browning had come to reject. In Caliban's obsession with potter-clay relations, capricious divine lessoning, and arbitrary making and marring (232–40), Smalley sees an ironic reflection on the Confession's presentation of a God who "extendeth or withholdeth mercy as he pleaseth, for the glory of His sovereign power over His creatures" (521). Browning implies that, in worshiping the absolute divine decree, the Calvinist is indistinguishable from the "Calibanist" in supposing a God in his own stunted image.

Yet Browning's ironic Calibanism cuts more ways still. There are two other possible targets: contemporary Bible critics, with their emerging doctrine of God as a human projection, and the emerging evolutionism of Charles Darwin, with his theory of human origins by natural rather than supernatural means. The poem's 1864 publication date comes five years after *The Origin of Species,* and indeed the poem may have been written in the more immediate aftermath of the 1860 debate between Bishop Samuel Wilberforce (the abolitionist's son) and Darwinian apostle Thomas Huxley. These ironic confluences suggest that Browning's Caliban might also speak for Darwin and for those attempting to reinterpret the Christian God in Darwinian terms—as an indifferent Life Force whose chosen means of "salvation" is natural selection, the mutually improving warfare of all living things for their next meal and a place in the sun, the devil take the hindmost.

So theologically the poem turns out to be a kind of extended triple entendre, mocking least of all the island savage, who merely turns out to be practicing the same sort of metaphysics as the home island's most influential and even advanced thinkers. Browning insinuates a mutually disagreeable agreement between the seemingly antithetical positions of animism, Calvinism, and Darwinism: the shaman, the predestinarian, and the natural selectionist all worship gods of power. To Browning's mind none of these cults is capable of recognizing or embracing a God of unconditioned love, as revealed in Jesus Christ. In a satirical move at least as old as Montaigne's essay "Of Cannibals," Browning finds that the most dangerous savages live in cities and wear breeches.[21]

Yet once one has recognized these central theological and anthropological concerns of the poem, one can return to the question of its possible colonialist contexts. In so doing, one will recognize that the implied social setting of this dramatic monologue is, as in Shakespeare's play, an island held in powerful subjection by outside forces. It is, after all, crucially important for the poem's

---

21. See Michel de Montaigne, *The Complete Essays of Montaigne,* 150–59.

ultimate purposes that at the beginning Caliban is hiding not only from a supposedly inattentive Setebos but also from a sleeping "Prosper and Miranda" (20); and it is also crucial that his most vivid images of arbitrary lordship are drawn from his experience of Prospero's literally enthralling magic (150–69). Indeed, when Caliban, as it were, plays God, he "Plays thus at being Prosper in a way" (168).

The most crucial evidence that the poem conflates Caliban's God with his human overlord comes at the poem's end. As a sudden tempest rises to whip the waves and snap the trees, the terrified Caliban grovels to Setebos, abject and contrite, convinced that Setebos somehow has overheard his mutinous thoughts (284–95). But if we (quite reasonably) infer from Shakespeare's *Tempest* that Browning's poem ends where the play begins, then the poem's final storm can be read as Prospero's doing—that is, as the very "tempest" that Prospero raises to mimic divine vengeance by stranding his sinning brother Antonio on the island. The strong implication is that if Caliban's God is grim, it is not only because the island savage has divinized nature's cruel ways; it is also because Prospero, the enlightened possessor of the primitive island, has modeled these ways as well.

"Caliban upon Setebos" is pregnant with meaning for Britain's high imperial future. Browning seems to reject in advance the emerging alchemy of Protestant triumphalism and Darwinian survivalism that would justify the next wave of colonial expansion. If Britain's first empire was undergirded by a quasi-Calvinist sense of divine election, her second empire eventually arrived at a creed of natural selection. Either creed made England a chosen nation, endorsing her expansion not only as a means but as an end in itself.

Losing "the Faith that Made Us Rulers": Religious Doubt and Imperial Foreboding in Tennyson's *Idylls of the King*

Browning's apprehensions about "Calibanism"—about an emergent syncretism involving worshiping old and new gods of power—were soon to some degree confirmed in the writings of John Robert Seeley. In 1865, Seeley's *Ecce Homo* anglicized the German secularism of Strauss's *Leben Jesu* by producing an English life of Jesus that emphasized the human limitations of its subject while turning a doubtful eye on biblical supernaturalism. Like many other mid- and late Victorians, Seeley sought to save the appearances of Christian ethics by explaining them as a necessary stage in the maturation of civilized life, a stage now being fulfilled (and superseded) in those nations—especially

England—that were emerging into a kind of spiritual adulthood, respectfully independent of the divine Father. In practical terms this meant that traditional creedal Christianity, like John the Baptist, must decrease, giving place to the coming kingdom of Anglo-Saxon rationality and scientific progress.[22]

Similarly, in *The Expansion of England* (1883), Seeley argues that the inadequacies of the old colonialism require not the abandonment of empire but rather its expansion on a new, more deliberately rational basis. "We seem, as it were, to have conquered and peopled half the world in a fit of absence of mind," he writes.[23] But in the emerging era the nation must put these half-hearted restraints—including outmoded religious ones—behind itself and embrace its unifying, civilizing mission. Faced with thrusting Russian and American competition, Seeley argues, England can only afford to retain and grow its dominions, with the eventual goal of a global federation—"Greater Britain"—centered in Westminster and Whitehall. The stark alternative is the loss of empire entirely and a grim future as a third-rate power (*Expansion* 293–309).

It is in these decades of trepidation over divine and human kingdoms that Alfred Tennyson produced, fitfully and laboriously, *Idylls of the King*. If Samuel Johnson and William Blake served, in their very different ways, as voices of cultural conscience, then Tennyson is something like their opposite, the voice of cultural consciousness. T. S. Eliot puts it negatively: "Tennyson . . . is a poet almost wholly encrusted with parasitic opinion, almost wholly merged into his environment."[24] To put it more positively, Tennyson was officially and really the national poet. As laureate from 1850 until his death in 1892, his substance and style were profoundly representative of Victorian aspirations and anxieties; and nowhere was this truer than in his treatment of empire in *Idylls of the King*.

Ian McGuire notes that recent interpreters using Freudian or nineteenth-century idealist frameworks have neglected the poem's important imperial concerns; and even Patrick Brantlinger's influential study of Victorian literature and empire, *Rule of Darkness,* virtually ignores the *Idylls*.[25] Perhaps this is because the poem's treatment of empire seems incoherent, juxtaposing as it does elements of newly expansionist imperial "trusteeship," Christian humanist anti-imperial critique, Darwinian doubt, and apocalyptic dread. McGuire writes that the poem is ideologically at war with itself because it is written to serve

---

22. Deborah Wormell, *Sir John Robert Seeley and the Uses of History*, 22–23.
23. John Robert Seeley, *The Expansion of England* (Boston, Little, Brown, 1912), 8. All further citations of this edition will be made parenthetically.
24. T. S. Eliot, *The Sacred Wood*, 154.
25. Ian McGuire, "Epistemology and Empire in *Idylls of the King*," 388; Brantlinger, *Rule of Darkness*, 36.

both as a "metonym"—a founding mythology—and as a metaphor, presenting a costumed version of the contemporary Victorian empire with all of its flaws and weaknesses. Thus Arthur's fall, which metonymically points to the Victorian *rex futurus,* metaphorically has the opposite effect, foreshadowing the modern empire's collapse.[26]

But this very contradiction is itself significant. Although such an amalgam is indeed intellectually incoherent, it nevertheless presents a pretty fair reflection of England's complex imperial emotions and attitudes during the five decades—from the 1830s until the 1880s—in which Tennyson worked and reworked his materials into a neo-Arthurian epic. Tennyson's own mind was seriously divided: though a lifelong British chauvinist, he was a friend of Gladstone's and sometimes voted Liberal; Peter Levi writes that "[o]ne day he hated the English withdrawal from Afghanistan, on another (October 1886) he thought England should leave India."[27] That the final version of the *Idylls* is a rather lugubrious blend of national pride, anxiety, ideological penetration, and self-pity says as much about the divided Victorian psyche as it does about Tennyson's own melancholy idealism. It was, after all, during these decades that Liberal humanitarianism began to grow sick of empire, while the Tories—formerly the redoubt of nativist anti-expansionism—were transformed by Disraeli and Salisbury into the party of the imperial interests.[28]

The element most obviously on display is that of Tennyson's apparently optimistic expansionist "trusteeship." As finalized in 1885, the poem both begins and ends with imperial affirmations in the opening "Dedication" and the epilogue, "To the Queen." The former, written in 1862, soon after the death of the prince consort, memorializes Albert as the pattern of Arthurian virtue itself, the "Voice in the rich dawn of an ampler day" whose unparalleled example will inspire the conduct of "Kings to be"—his sons—to higher and wider good.[29] The 1873 epilogue, "To the Queen," is more overtly expansionist, celebrating "[o]ur ocean-empire with her boundless homes / For ever-broadening England, and her throne / In our vast Orient" (254). In fact, throughout Tennyson's long career he believed in Britain's unique civilizing greatness; by the early 1840s he was a convinced imperialist, and eventually he became a proponent of a federal or

---

26. McGuire, "Epistemology and Empire," 391.
27. Peter Levi, *Tennyson,* 299.
28. Kenneth O. Morgan, ed., *The Oxford History of Britain,* 552.
29. Alfred Lord Tennyson, *Idylls of the King and a Selection of Poems,* ed. George Barker (New York: Signet, 1961), 13–14. All further citations of this edition will be indicated parenthetically by *Idylls* followed by page number.

commonwealth successor to the empire.[30] So in this epilogue Tennyson scorns the Liberal suggestion that the imperial "burden" of Canada (which achieved dominion status in 1867) should be fully given up: "Is this the tone of empire? here the faith / That made us rulers?" (254). For added emphasis he again summons the memory of suffering Albert's last days, "pale as yet and fever-worn," who persevered in his beneficent duties to the end. For Tennyson here, empire is a covenant to be kept, a "faith" to be confirmed in strenuous good works.

But this invocation of the dying Albert actually sends importantly mixed signals. For despite this fore-and-aft overlay of colonial confidence, *Idylls of the King* is fundamentally a meditation on loss, particularly on the relationship between the loss of faith and the loss of empire. Indeed, the first sketches that the young Tennyson made for the poem in the 1830s already focus on Arthur's fatal battle against Modred; the epic grew to its final form as the poet crafted the many preceding episodes leading to Arthur's fall.[31] Like Spenser in *The Faerie Queene*, Tennyson purges Arthur of Geoffrean and Malorian vices, treating him as "ideal manhood closed in real man" (254); but unlike Spenser, Tennyson shows this ideal manhood overwhelmed by forces set in motion by his very idealism.

Furthermore, the episodes leading up to Arthur's undoing strongly echo the Christian humanist critique of imperial over-reach. In particular, Tennyson displays in the Grail Quest a favorite Augustinian theme, the folly of trying to achieve divine perfection through fallible human agents. In fact, Tennyson puts his first indictment in the traditionally humanist mouth of a licensed fool, the jester Dagonet, who mocks Arthur:

> "Ay, ay, my brother fool, the king of fools!
> Conceits himself as God that he can make
> Figs out of thistles, silk from bristles, milk
> From burning spurge, honey from hornet-combs,
> And men from beasts—Long live the king of fools!"
> (215)

And indeed, Arthur himself opposes the Quest on similarly Christian humanist grounds: first, because it is a task fit only for the purity of a Galahad and not for his more corruptible knights; second, because the wandering Quest will take the knights away from their more mundane domestic task of righting wrongs within the kingdom. Arthur nevertheless waves them fatalistically on their way, while foretelling their doom:

30. Levi, *Tennyson*, 167.
31. F. B. Pinion, *A Tennyson Chronology*, 22, 23.

> "Go, since your vows are sacred, being made.
> Yet—for ye know the cries of all my realm
> Pass through this hall—how often, O my knights,
> Your places being vacant at my side,
> This chance of noble deeds will come and go
> Unchallenged, while ye follow wandering fires
> Lost in the quagmire! Many of you, yea most,
> Return no more. Ye think I show myself
> Too dark a prophet . . ."
>
> (178)

In effect both blessing and cursing the knights' mission, Tennyson's Arthur demonstrates a double-edged political awareness that is, as McGuire puts it, "as analytically acute as it is ideologically doomed."[32]

For of course Arthur is not too dark a prophet; the Grail Quest does, as in Malory, decimate the Round Table. Worse yet—and, significantly, it is Tennyson's invention—this decimation leads to the recruitment of Pelleas, the green young knight whose naïveté at first appears to be virtue (192). But when Pelleas discovers the adultery of Lancelot and Guinevere and confronts the sin and hollowness at the heart of Arthur's court, his disillusionment transforms him into an anti-Galahad (204–5). Withdrawing from Camelot, he becomes the mad and murderous Red Knight, "a scourge . . . to lash the treasons of the Table Round" (205); committing horrific atrocities, he exposes the vulnerability of Arthur's throne and opens the way to Modred's rebellion.

Moreover, Britain's hollowness is shown not only in the hypocrisy at Camelot but also in Arthur's own loss of religious certainty—"the faith that made us rulers." Tennyson had Arthur begin his reign, as in Geoffrey of Monmouth, as a confident Christian challenging the spiritually exhausted paganism of Rome. Refusing to pay Roman tribute, Arthur had proclaimed, "The old order changeth, yielding place to new, / And we that fight for our fair father Christ . . . / No tribute will we pay" (26). But on the eve of the Last Battle with Modred, Tennyson's Arthur is himself spiritually bewildered and exhausted. As if himself overwhelmed by "Calibanism," Arthur cries out:

> O me! for why is all around us here
> As if some lesser god had made the world,
> But had not force to shape it as he would,
> Till the High God behold it from beyond,

---

32. McGuire, "Epistemology and Empire," 390.

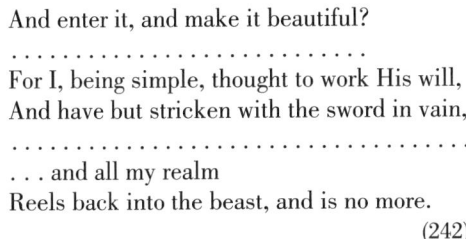
> And enter it, and make it beautiful?
> ....
> For I, being simple, thought to work His will,
> And have but stricken with the sword in vain,
> ....
> ... and all my realm
> Reels back into the beast, and is no more.
> (242)

The Darwinian impact here is unmistakable. Tennyson had early evolutionist sympathies, and he had been assured personally by Charles Darwin that evolutionary theory did not fundamentally threaten Christian faith; nevertheless, he was deeply affected by the evolutionist challenge to traditional theistic design.[33] On an 1879 visit to Gladstone's home, Tennyson was overheard by Gladstone's daughter Mary lamenting that "[w]e shall all turn into pigs if we lose Christianity and God."[34] Significantly, the poet's Circean nightmare echoes the adulterous carnality that brings about the collapse of his poem's Camelot. This carnality undercuts Arthur's aspirations toward a greater imperial order by confronting him with mankind's once-and-future beastliness. Arthur is unable to face, let alone defeat, the "beast" because he has lost his confidence in the original created goodness of the world and thus in the possibility of its restoration to that goodness. In short, in the face of unyielding human evil, he has lost his assurance of divine omnipotence.

So doubt, ambiguity, and beastliness reign on the foggy field at Lyonesse at the "last weird battle in the west." Beforehand, his spirit is clouded by a night visit from

> ... the ghost of Gawain blown
> Along a wandering wind, and past his ear
> Went shrilling: "Hollow, hollow all delight!
> Hail, King! to-morrow thou shalt pass away."
> (242)

Ironically, like Shakespeare's arch-villain Richard III (see act 5, scenes 3–4), Arthur is unnerved by this ghostly visitation for the coming battle: for "even on Arthur fell / Confusion, since he saw not whom he fought, / For friend and foe were shadows in the mist"; prayers are replaced by "shrieks / After the Christ,

---

33. Levi, *Tennyson*, 54; F. B. Pinion, *A Tennyson Companion*, 48.
34. Alfred Lord Tennyson, *A Collection of Poems by Alfred Tennyson*, 62.

of those who falling down / Look'd up for heaven, and only saw the mist" (244). Then, in this dire setting, bleeding from his deadly wound, Arthur experiences a moment of clarity even more terrible than his earlier confusion: a "bitter wind" blows the mist away to expose a ghastly deathscape, bodies awash in the bloody surf "Tumbling the hollow helmets of the fallen, / And shiver'd brands that once had fought with Rome" (245).

It is here, in the dispirited transition from the "ancient" epic to the modern epilogue, that the poem undergoes its weirdest tonal shift. Having portrayed the futility of Christian empire, having implicitly indicted British moral hypocrisy and cast doubt on divine omnipotence, Tennyson ends by attempting reinspiration. As in Malory, Arthur tells Bedivere to cast Excalibur into the "mere," a command that must be repeated three times because Bedivere is nearly ravished by the weapon's glory and conquering power (246–49). In Tennyson's treatment, this action is allegorically double-edged: it seems designed, on the one hand, to emphasize the seductions of power and the uselessness of the sword in divine matters; yet on the other hand, once Bedivere casts the sword away, the emergence of the mystic, receiving hand from the lake seems to reconfirm a divine presence that reconfers divine blessing on some future British holy warrior. Here again is the old myth of authorizing humility; an ancestral act of surrender empowers the heirs to rule. The mystic hand points to Victorian Britain and the kind of renewed "faith" that will be necessary if its empire is to survive and thrive.

However, coming as it does after Tennyson's long gloomy rendering of decline and fall, this brief mystical glance hardly seems, on its own, capable of reviving imperial confidence. It certainly does not seem to restore Arthur's; in his final speech, he implores Bedivere to pray for him and then tells him brokenly,

> "... I am going a long way
> With these thou seest—if indeed I go—
> For all my mind is clouded with a doubt—
> To the island-valley of Avilion
> ....
> There I will heal me of my wounds."
>
> (251–52)

Then his boat disappears.

So, after such tenuousness, it is especially jarring when the epilogue, "To the Queen," turns instantly to shrill expansionist rhetoric. Having just provided an epic parable about the imperial hubris of wandering knights, Tennyson suddenly scolds the Little Englanders by invoking the example of England's "far sons" whose expansive bravery keeps Britain from becoming "a sinking land, / Some third-rate isle half-lost among her seas" (254). Having just shown Arthur, the paragon of imperial faith, losing his religion and his throne, Tennyson abruptly assures Victoria that any kind of disengagement from empire is both a breach of loyalty to the colonized and a kind of apostasy from "the faith that made us rulers" (254). Indeed, at this juncture, "faith" no longer appears as the biblical "assurance of things hoped for" (Hebrews 11:1) but rather as a kind of pathetic wishful thinking—hoping beyond hope that Merlin's blurry prophecy will be fulfilled and Arthur's reign restored (246). To the sympathetic reader, this "faith" might appear as a Platonic noble lie, a necessary empowering self-deception; to the unsympathetic, it is simply a kind of mendacious consciousness.

So, however welcome Tennyson's concluding affirmations were to imperial officials—and for this epilogue he did receive special thanks from Lord Dufferin, Canadian governor-general—the poet himself is admitting that this imperial faith will not bear close scrutiny.[35] In the same epilogue to the queen—while recalling London's tumultuous ovation for Albert on his last public appearance—the laureate states with notable economy the symbiosis of ignorance and power: at the heart of empire there is

>   . . . one isle, one isle,
> That knows not her own greatness; if she knows
> And dreads it we are fallen.
>   (254)

As McGuire writes, "here is a crisis of self-recognition" (391), a psychopolitical double bind. Tennyson leads the imperial imagination toward purifying spiritual introspection; yet that introspection must not look too sharply or deeply in, lest it see through its own empowering illusions—one of which is its belief in purifying introspection. For Seeley, this English "absence of mind" is the empire's atavistic weakness; for Tennyson, it is the empire's secret strength. It is as if the poet were a homeopath prescribing just enough humility to prevent actual humiliation.

Thus in *Idylls of the King*, despite its moments of ideological penetration, we have not so much a prescription for national self-scrutiny as for late imperial self-pity. In the person of Arthur, an ascendant Britain confronts the eventuality of its own decline and begins to lament the ungrateful world and the silent God who will not recognize the empire's sacrificial efforts on their behalf. Early

---

35. Pinion, *Tennyson Chronology*, 134.

in this book, I discussed how Elizabethan Protestants rediscovered Arthurian expansionism, and how in the process they adapted a parallel religion of British Protestant imperialism. In Tennyson's *Idylls*, the curtain rises on the Ragnarök of that religion: as in Arthur's weary and equivocal refrain, "The old order changeth, yielding place to new, / And God fulfils himself in many ways, / Lest one good custom should corrupt the world" (251).

From Binding Tie to Source of Trouble: Toward Post-Protestant Empire in Seeley and Kipling

I have described John Dee and Richard Hakluyt each playing intellectual midwife to this "old order"—that is, to Protestant imaginings of British imperial recovery, relative righteousness, redeeming mission, and authorizing humility— and I have begun to show that Tennyson's younger contemporary John Robert Seeley sought to birth the new. There had, of course, been a "Second British Empire" well before Seeley; however, it is Seeley who first gives extensive articulation to the idea of a more secular and centralized empire, one that is bound together not by metaphysical allegiances but rather by "modern" administration, science, and technology. As a historian, Seeley still recognizes the cultural and social effects of religion, "the strongest and most important of all the elements which go to constitute nationality" (*Expansion* 225). But these effects are clearly subordinate to and dependent on the new binding power of technology, which "has given to the political organism [of the empire] a new circulation, which is steam, and a new nervous system, which is electricity" (74). By implication, the ties that will bind the future empire will be rivets and copper wire.

Significantly, Seeley's focus on mundane material realities at the expense of supposed invisible ones is of a piece with his stated rejection of the imagination —of imperial romance, heroism, and the exotic—in short, with his rejection of appeals to "metaphor . . . as an argument" (*Expansion* 296). So he constructs a rhetorical middle ground for himself by criticizing as extreme not just the anti-imperial "pessimism" of "Little England" but also the "bombastic school" of empire, "lost in wonder and ecstasy at its immense dimensions," that "therefore advocates the maintenance of it as a point of honor or sentiment" (293). Instead, Seeley presents himself as a sort of anti-Dee or anti-Hakluyt: "I have narrated nothing, told no thrilling stories, drawn no heroic portraits" (307). Of course, from the distance of an intervening century, one can perceive Seeley's moderate pose as far more radically expansionist than the "old order" that he rejects; one may also note that his dismissal of metaphor is typical of an emerging technocratic imagination, rife with mechanistic metaphors. However, these ironies should not distract us from the crucial late-Victorian transformation: as religion ceased to be seen as a source of imperial unity or strength, it came increasingly to be regarded as a source of trouble.

The ebbing "Sea of Faith" of which Matthew Arnold had written in 1851 exposed the "naked shingles of the world"; and Seeley's skeptical eye saw there a pullulating mass of conflicting creeds (*Expansion* 76).[36] Among this mass, Christianity was distinguished for Seeley mainly by its being a "fusion of Semitic with Aryan ideas," which gave it some possibilities for reconciling Semitic Muslims and Aryan Hindus in India (278). But by proposing to use Christianity as a kind of intercultural solvent, he is involved in the inherent contradiction of all utilitarian approaches to religion: to treat Christianity (or any faith) as a mere social construction is to deprive it of the very qualities that make it useful for compelling belief and unifying the faithful—that is, the presumption of intrinsic truth and universality. He also implies the faith's inherent instability and a potentially dangerous volatility when its "fusion" turns to fission.

The same conflicts and contradictions are treated with cruel humor in Rudyard Kipling's short tale of foiled evangelism in the Indian jungle, "The Judgment of Dungara" (1888). From its deliberately garbled epigraph—"See the pale martyr with his shirt on fire"—to its mordant conclusion, the story makes light of religious zeal while suggesting the missionary's potential for sparking intercultural disaster.[37] The tale pits the comically wily Athon Dazé, priest of "the naked . . . lazy Buria Kol" and of "the great God Dungara, the God of Things as They Are," against the comically gullible Reverend Justus Krenk, pastor of the Tübingen Mission, and priest of "the God of Things as They Should Be" (122, 126). Significantly, however, the true moral center of the story is "Gallio," the British "Assistant Collector of the countryside" who—like his indifferent Roman namesake in the Book of Acts—"'cared for none of these things'" (124; Acts 18:17).

Gallio is introduced to us as a cheerfully agnostic pragmatist, "a knock-kneed, shambling young man, naturally devoid of creed or reverence," and all the more effective for it. "'When you have been some years in the country,'" he tells the

---

36. Matthew Arnold, "Dover Beach," in *The Poetical Works of Matthew Arnold*, 211, ll. 21, 28.

37. Rudyard Kipling, "The Judgement of Dungara," in *The Man Who Would Be King and Other Stories* (Oxford: Oxford University Press, 1987), 122. All further citations of this edition will be made parenthetically.

shocked newcomer Krenk and his wife, Lotte, "'you get to find one creed as good as another.'" He expresses both affection for his savage imperial charges and suspicion of the Krenks' potentially dangerous missionary idealism: "'I'll give you all the assistance in my power, of course, but don't hurt my Buria Kol. They are a good people and they trust me.'" Having warned the Krenks against the nearly fatal iconoclasm of their predecessor—a Scots Calvinist who "'began hammering old Dungara over the head with an umbrella'" and then demanded "'a wing of regiment'" to rescue him from the ensuing native wrath—Gallio goes about his business: "'I have their bodies and the District to see to. . . . Be gentle with them, Padre—but I don't think you'll do much'" (124–25).

The story's post-Protestant—indeed, post-Christian—moral irony continues as Gallio, whom the narrator tells us has "a longing for absolute power" and a "supreme disregard of human life," daily risks his own mending bridges, killing a tiger, tracking enemy headhunters, and rescuing an exposed native infant. Devoid of any theological reason to do so, he nevertheless performs the works of charity, and without the missionaries' spiritual pride or evangelistic predation. Depositing the abandoned "girl-baby" with the Krenks, he refuses to pass cross-cultural judgment: "The Kols leave their surplus children to die. Don't see why they shouldn't, but you may rear this one." In contrast, the Krenks' response is calculating and figuratively cannibalistic: "'It is the first of the fold,' said Justus, and Lotte caught up the screaming morsel to her bosom and hushed it craftily" (125).

Justus is, for the first and only time, right; the child Nala is the beginning of the mission's growth as her parents come out of the jungle to join her— "'First the Child, then the Mother, and last the Man'" is the Krenks' culturally subversive strategy. As the years pass, other Kols are converted and clothed, and the Temple of Dungara falls into disuse, while Lotte "lightened the Curse of Eve among the women," and Justus "did his best to introduce the Curse of Adam." But the native priest Athon Dazé plots his revenge, feigning conversion while telling his Temple remnant that "'They of the Padre's flock have put on clothes to worship a busy God. Therefore Dungara will afflict them grievously'" (126–27).

Not one to wait on Providence, Athon Dazé engineers the god's judgment with fiendish ingenuity, providing nettle fibers for the unsuspecting Krenk and his converts to weave into dazzling white garments that they don for their chapel dedication in the presence of the venal, pompous district collector himself. As these "shirts of fire" take effect, the converts leap, shriek, strip to the buff, and dive into the river, while Dungara gets the glory. Fourteen-year-old Nala, "naked as the dawn and spitting like a wild-cat," curses the Krenks and their promises of salvation from hellfire—" 'you said that I would never burn!' "—and begs mercy from the God of Things as They Are. Examining the nettle fabric, the bemused Gallio scolds the Krenks, "why didn't you tell me? I could have saved you this. Woven fire!" (127–28).

And indeed it is left to the omnicompetent and long-suffering imperialist Gallio to restore what order he can after this cultural collision. The Tübingen Mission is undone, and the Temple of Dungara is full of vengeful worshipers, but Gallio's unofficial threats protect the Krenks from "the stumpy poisoned arrows of the Buria Kol." Yet even Gallio cannot keep the missionaries fed, and since "man cannot live by grace alone if meat be wanting," the Krenks abandon the chapel and the school to the encroaching jungle and retreat, presumably to Heidelberg, where Justus will "some botany bestudy" (129–30).

It is not known whether Seeley ever read Kipling's little farce (Seeley died in 1895, a year after Victoria knighted him). However much he might have demurred from the story's reliance on image, humor, and irony, he probably would have appreciated its lesson that, when leaving Christian civilization behind, one's knowledge of botany and the native gods, along with a generous supply of quinine and ammunition, are far more valuable than a catechism. So Seeley would likely have agreed also with the tale's endorsement of a nononsense, secular, businesslike imperialism, and with its warning that a zealous salvationism is the unwitting enemy of real progress on the colonial frontier.

There was nothing particularly new in the insight that life in the jungle had a way of loosening religious and civilized bonds; and we have seen that since the empire's beginnings, man-on-the-spot pragmatists out on the colonial margins had often looked askance at holy-minded meddling from the imperial center. However, as Victoria and her reign waned, more and more people at the center were wondering openly how something as fragile and fractured as Protestantism could hold that center in the storm that many saw gathering. Both abroad and at home, both in Greater Britain and in Little England, they were looking for new ties, new ways to connect.

"The End of All Things": Post-Protestant Empire at Home in Forster's *Howards End*

No English book between the century's turn and the First World War says so much so well about the decay of old domestic bonds and the search for new ones as E. M. Forster's *Howards End* (1910). With its famous elliptical epigraph "Only connect . . ." and its publication at the end of the Edwardian decade, the novel gives form to rising English anxiety about social disintegration at home and destruction looming from over the water.[38] The epigraph's primary referent is, of course, the hopeful marriage of "the prose and the passion" enacted by the protagonists Henry Wilcox and Margaret Schlegel—a marriage that, late in the novel, is nearly destroyed by Henry's moral disconnection, his "stupid, hypocritical, cruel" condemnation of Margaret's sister, Helen, for sins disturbingly like his own (148, 243). However, Henry's ethical blindness is not merely personal and domestic; he is also the head of the "Imperial and West African Rubber Company," and the "panic and emptiness" that nearly engulf him and his family are profoundly related to his hollow colonial dynamism (155, 27). "I am not a fellow who bothers about my own inside," Henry says, inadvertently predicting his own undoing (147).

So "Only connect . . ." resonates not just with the personal but with the geopolitical, distantly evoking the ancient Augustinian critique of imperial vastness undoing itself. Indeed, the adverb has at least as much force as the imperative verb: "only" indicts excess, the kind of over-reach that was straining and tearing the national nerves and sinews, threatening to leave Greater Britain immense and paralyzed, like a giant unstrung. The "only" hope for national healing, the paired words imply, is *mere* "connection," as both the means and the end. To Forster, "connecting" in this fundamental way means reconciling mutually necessary opposites—commerce and art, action and reflection, urban and rural, male and female, the city and Bloomsbury, "the prose and the passion"—through intimate personal relations based on chastened self-knowledge. Standing against these new bonds of affection are the old ones of masculine competition, elitist Protestant religion, and imperial gigantism.

Forster came by this attitude honestly: born in 1879 into a Gladstone Liberal family, he was descended on his father's side from members of Wilberforce's Clapham Sect, Protestant evangelicals whose creed, as I have noted, integrated spiritual salvation with social progress at home and, at the most, colonial minimalism abroad. Although Forster had lost the family faith, he had kept its social conscience, and he always remained an uneasy unbeliever, recognizing that a weakened Christian consensus released powerful centrifugal forces in English domestic life.[39]

Indeed, latent fissures had long existed in his own Liberal Party—between Little Englanders who inherited the anti-imperialism of Augustan Tories like

---

38. E. M. Forster, *Howards End* (New York: Signet, 1992), 1. All further citations of this edition will be made parenthetically.

39. Alistair M. Duckworth, *Howards End: E. M. Forster's House of Fiction*, 5–6. See also Duckworth's *The Improvement of the Estate: A Study of Jane Austen's Novels*.

Samuel Johnson, the radicals with their laborite leanings, and the progressive imperialists with their Burkean notions of "trusteeship." These fissures had been opened by the Irish Home Rule Crisis of 1886; and the Anglo-Boer War of 1899–1902 had realized the split, dividing the party in ways from which it never fully recovered—the Liberal imperialists moving toward the now expansionist Tories, and the increasingly socialist radicals splitting off to form the new Labor Party.[40] And the bloody draw in South Africa had domestic consequences far beyond party realignment. Because the empire had long promised upward mobility for the poor, the war's damage to imperial prestige brought social disruption, as deferred class conflict erupted in debate and agitation over the state's providential responsibilities for the poor.

All of these emerging domestic divisions are represented in *Howards End*. Like Jane Austen's *Mansfield Park*—which Forster greatly admired and consciously imitated—the novel plays out its drama of disintegration and renewal in the setting of a country house against the backdrop of overseas colonial possession.[41] Each book shows its thrusting imperial males (Sir Thomas Bertram, Henry Wilcox) nearly ruined by their obtuse neglect of home matters and redeemed through the reintegrative spiritual wisdom of an "outsider" woman (Fanny Price, Margaret Schlegel) who reconstitutes the home as a kind of nonimperial haven. In one important way, however, Forster has improved on Austen by creating a more immediately appealing heroine. Where Fanny is high-minded, timid, and usually silent, Margaret is independent-minded, witty, and admirably outspoken—more like an Edwardian Elizabeth Bennet.

Significantly, Margaret is also an unbeliever, but one who, like Forster, is sensitive to the losses that unbelief involved and appreciative of religion's connecting power. "She was not a Christian in the accepted sense; she did not believe that God had ever worked among us as a young artisan." Yet while Christmas shopping with the ailing Mrs. Wilcox, she is disturbed by the irreverence and chaos of the popular holiday. She felt "the grotesque impact of the unseen upon the seen, and saw issuing from a forgotten manger at Bethlehem this torrent of coins and toys. . . . How many of these vacillating shoppers and tired shop-assistants realized that it was a divine event that drew them together? She realized it, though standing outside in the matter. . . . 'No, I do like Christmas on the whole,' she announced. 'In its clumsy way, it does approach Peace and Goodwill. But oh, it is clumsier every year' " (65). Though standing outside the circle of belief, Margaret sees how necessary is shared faith for social cohesion

---

40. Duckworth, *House of Fiction*, 4.
41. E. M. Forster, *Aspects of the Novel*, 100–101, 112–13; Duckworth, *House of Fiction*, 9.

and worries that these cohesive ties are slackening through sheer oblivion, wondering where all will end. And the novel, as its title announces, is about ends: the end of Protestant religion as a unifier transcending class; the end of the countryside as London encroaches; the end of imperial hegemony as Britain butts up against a unified expansionist Germany; and the end of the "yeomanry," of workers connected to, and nourished by, the land.

These ends converge in the novel's tragicomic and semiallegorical climax: the death of unemployed bank clerk Leonard Bast at the hands of Henry's son Charles Wilcox, and the domestic revolution that follows. In Forster's tableau of the empire's domestic damage, Leonard is the representative "decayed yeoman," "grandson to the shepherd or ploughboy whom civilization had sucked into the town; . . . one of the thousands who have lost the life of the body and failed to reach the life of the spirit" (93). Cut off from the earth by imperially supported industrialization and the accompanying rural decline, Leonard aspires religiously to the status of gentleman, hungrily reading Ruskin and attending public concerts, hoping "to come to Culture suddenly, much as the Revivalist hopes to come to Jesus" (40). But he too has problems with his "inside"; disease and malnutrition have damaged him both in mind and in body; most significantly, he has a fatally weak heart.

In symbolic and literal opposition to Leonard stands Charles Wilcox. For the novel's purposes, Charles is not entirely a "he"—a full-orbed character—but sometimes an "it," the type of the "Imperial": "healthy, ever in motion" in a throbbing, stinking new motor car, "it hopes to inherit the earth. It breeds as quickly as the yeoman, and as soundly; strong is the temptation to acclaim it as a super-yeoman, who carries his country's virtues overseas." But as events show, "the Imperialist is not what he thinks or seems. He is a destroyer" (256).

The indictment of the Wilcoxes is multifarious: their initially comic disconnection from land, as shown early on by their hay fever (3–4); their devouring relationship to both urban and rural space (45, 264); the domestic imperialism of both sons Charles ("Why be so polite to servants? They don't understand it"—20) and Paul (to whom even English field-workers are "piccaninnies"—270); Henry's bad financial advice, which ruins Leonard but which Henry treats with indifference; and Henry's hypocritical refusal to admit any connecting similarity between his past adultery with Leonard's "wife" Jackie and Helen's affair with Leonard (243–44).

This escalating destruction is capped by Charles's role in Leonard's death. The event is richly equivocal: Leonard's diseased heart was bound to fail, but the disease was in a larger sense brought on by "Imperials" like the Wilcoxes who have driven "yeomen" like the Basts from the land. So it is bitterly appropriate that a Wilcox, avenging the pregnant Helen's "honor," should set out as in a farce to "thrash him within an inch of his life" and in the process give the actual coup de grâce (256–57). With perhaps too-poetic justice, Charles is then convicted of manslaughter—by a law that fails to make human connections and thus is "made in his image"—and sentenced to three years in prison (264).

Yet this denouement indicts not only the imperial Wilcoxes but the liberal Schlegels as well. Insulated and intellectual, they naively adopt Leonard as a pet project, thus unintentionally luring him to what will be his destruction; it is their German family sword with which Charles strikes him down; and when Leonard falls, he is buried by a cascade of their books (256–57). It is as if liberalism has inadvertently conspired with imperialism to hollow out old England: liberals offer do-goodism, Teutonic-style ethical culture, and abstraction, rather than real reconnection to sources of strength in land and labor. When Margaret grasps the inadequacy of their liberalism's passive "Imperialism of the air" (23) and makes her own connections, she redeems her marriage, a remnant of her family, and indeed a remnant of Little England at Howards End.

Thus in the wake of disgrace, death, and imprisonment, the novel's last chapter moves beyond tragedy to romance, with Margaret—like Portia, Rosalind, or Paulina—orchestrating the restoration and transformation of her family. She acts with Wilcoxian decisiveness for a Schlegelian purpose: she takes possession of Howards End and realizes its potential as a feminized Eden—centered not in a Tree of Knowledge but on the wych-elm tree and its wreath of pigs' teeth (57) at the heart of the old country, pagan life. So she miraculously fulfills the intuitions of the wisely instinctual Ruth Wilcox, whose intention of leaving the house to Margaret prevails over all the panic and anger of Henry and the children.

It is at the reclaimed Howards End that the imperial Henry, "broken" by Charles's ordeal, is tamed and finally reconciled both to Margaret and to Helen, who bears Leonard's child. This child, who in turn will inherit the house, promises another kind of restoration: he is being raised near the "sacred center of the field" and may grow up a revived yeoman, reintegrating urban and rural, intellectual and practical, male and female (265). In this resurrected Little England, with its back turned on empire, doctrinal Christianity is present, if at all, only as a "wild legend of immortality" (255); yet the dominant tone of forgiveness seems controlled by Margaret's serene sense of providence. Sounding rather like the biblical Joseph reassuring his guilty brothers, she tells the humbly apologetic Henry after he confesses his suppression of Ruth's bequest, "Nothing has been done wrong" (271).

Nevertheless, this concluding pastoral idyll, noted for its dreamlike tenuousness, is portrayed as threatened. As Helen warns, "'London's creeping.'

She pointed over the meadow, over eight or nine meadows, but at the end of them was a red rust" (268). Perhaps worse, the elements are not necessarily kind: "Every summer [Margaret] would fear lest the well should give out; every winter lest the pipes should freeze; every westerly gale might blow the wych-elm down and bring the end of all things" (265). Worst of all, as suggested by the Schlegels' earlier debates with their bombastic German relatives, the clash of Saxon empires may soon bring winds even more dire blowing from the east (23–24). " 'Life's going to be melted down, all over the world,' " predicts Helen, and Margaret is forced to admit the truth of her foreboding. She concedes that "survivals" like Howards End, on strictly modern grounds, "[l]ogically . . . had no right to be alive. One's hope was in the weakness of logic. . . . 'Because a thing is going strong now, it need not go strong for ever,' she said" (268).

To read these words ninety years later, after two largely Saxon world wars, is to see a pair of contradictory truths. The first truth is how pathetically little such hopeful imaginations, or indeed hopeful prayers, could do at the time against armed imperial logic—the worldwide meltdown of life was incalculably worse than Forster could have feared. The second truth is that both of those Saxon empires, and a good many other empires, are dead, and that both tragicomic hopes—in romance and in prayer—have outlived them. The weakness of imperial logic is that it is ultimately self-consuming; though that is no comfort to the other, unnumbered selves consumed in the process.

"Back into the Beast": Post-Protestant Empire Abroad in Conrad's *Lord Jim* and *Heart of Darkness*

About a decade before Forster romanced the end of empire at home, Joseph Conrad was auguring it abroad in *Lord Jim* (1899–1900; 1900) and *Heart of Darkness* (1898–1899; 1902). I already have glanced at the latter in connection with Drake's myth of authorizing Protestant humility. Here I will compare Conrad with Conrad; for the two books—serialized contemporaneously, published close together, and narrated by the same Conradian alter ego Marlow—signal a crucial shift in his and the public's attitude toward religion and imperial loss: *Lord Jim* is a romance with a tragic end, while *Heart of Darkness* is a novella that moves beyond tragedy to horror and sardonic irony.

Of *Lord Jim*, Ian Watt notes that its hero, Jim, belongs more to the nineteenth than to the twentieth century because he "dies for honor."[42] Yet Jim provides an

---

42. Ian Watt, *Conrad in the Nineteenth Century*, 356.

important transition to twentieth-century antiheroics, because, as J. H. Stape writes, this "honorable death" leaves behind "renewed political chaos in Patusan, the final consequence of a blundering imperialist adventurism however well intentioned."[43] Furthermore, Jim represents the increasingly ambivalent relationship between Protestant religion and empire. Originally the product of an English parsonage, Jim was grounded in a "faith invulnerable to the facts."[44]

As we have seen, later Victorian doubt tended to discredit the religious element in Protestant imperialism as irrational, while much religious conscience tended to discredit the imperialist element in it as un-Christian. Jim's "faith" speaks to both sides of this divide. His invulnerability to facts makes his early virtue and confidence a kind of self-deception, which is cruelly exposed by his failure and cowardice when he abandons the *Patna* and its hundreds of Muslim pilgrims in the storm. However, it is Jim's religious conscience that compels him to face his crime and—after his trial, conviction, and expulsion from the merchant service—that drives him to his redemption, and eventual destruction, in Patusan. So Jim's "faith" proves to be both too disappointingly weak and, paradoxically, too dangerously strong.

This faithful quest for atonement carries Jim courageously upriver and into the adoring trust of the oppressed natives of the interior, whom he organizes successfully against their thuggish overlord; and after their victorious struggle he recapitulates the Protestant ritual of authorizing humility by refusing the divine honors offered to him, thus further demonstrating his moral worthiness to rule. Yet this revived moral imperviousness is finally his undoing: he runs afoul of local customs, becoming responsible for the death of his lieutenant, Dain Waris, and so to make another atonement presents himself for execution at the hands of the dead man's father, Doramin. Though he had seemed to be on the verge of creating a new island order with the beautiful half-caste girl Jewel, his sacrificial death instead precipitates further and indeed potentially worse chaos. So while Jim is compared to Jesus by other characters and critics alike, his sacrifice occasions not faith or reconciliation but rather despair and violence. This may be a Conradian cri de coeur regarding religious doubt; it is certainly a comment on the futility of high-minded imperial intervention.

But the profoundly corrupting effects of colonialism receive their most famous treatment in *Heart of Darkness*, with its shattering portrayal of imperial idealism turning, to use Tennyson's phrase, "back into the beast" (*Idylls* 242). We have

---

43. J. H. Stape, ed., *The Cambridge Companion to Joseph Conrad*, 76.
44. Joseph Conrad, *Lord Jim* (New York: W. W. Norton, 1968), 4, 27. All further citations of this edition will be made parenthetically.

seen that Kipling, and Conrad himself, treat the loss of empire elegiacally in "The Man Who Would Be King" and *Lord Jim,* allowing their heroes a measure of tragic grandeur as they fall. But Kurtz's fate is notoriously different. As T. S. Eliot wrote in 1919, Conrad "is . . . the antithesis of Empire . . . his characters are the denial of Empire, of Nation, of Race almost; they are fearfully alone in the wilderness."[45]

Though set in the Congolese empire of Roman Catholic Belgium, *Heart of Darkness* resonates as a grim parody of at least two prototypical Protestant colonial journeys: Stanley's successful inland search for Livingstone and subsequent exploration of the Congo River in the 1870s and, long before, Ralegh's failed quest for the ever-receding El Dorado up Guiana's Orinoco River in 1595. Marlow's initial search for Kurtz as an apostle of light in the heart of Africa, seeking to suppress savage customs (65), alludes unmistakably to Livingstone, less than twenty-five years dead: evangelical missionary, explorer, and opponent of the slave trade. And when Marlow describes the goals of the "Eldorado Exploring Expedition" as being "to tear treasure out of the bowels of the land" (61), he clearly echoes Ralegh's famous description of Guiana as "a countrey that hath yet her maydenhead, never sackt, turned, nor wrought, the face of the earth hath not bene torne."[46] Also, as we have seen, the novella begins by invoking Drake's *Golden Hind,* though in an ironic setting of foreboding and defeat.[47]

However, the novella's anti-imperial credentials have been challenged over the last twenty-seven years on the grounds of its alleged racism. While these challenges—particularly those of Chinua Achebe—are understandable in their objection to perpetuating the "Dark Continent" myth, they miss the story's deeper import: the darkness confronted here is not fundamentally African but Freudian and Darwinian—and human.[48] For instance, Cedric Watts notes that in some ways Conrad's Africans compare favorably with his Europeans, the Africans being "by far the happiest, healthiest, and most vital."[49] Indeed, this savage vitality is what links the Africans to the Europeans' own "vital" and brutal ancestral past: hence the story's powerful opening evocation of ancient Britain as "also . . . one of the dark places of the earth" (29).

As a kind of prologue, Marlow reflects on British savagery and resistance to empire, recalling that the Thames once saw the incursion of Roman triremes,

---

45. T. S. Eliot, *Athenaeum,* May 1, 1919.
46. Ralegh, *The Discoverie of . . . Guiana,* 115.
47. Conrad, *Heart of Darkness,* 29.
48. See Chinua Achebe, "An Image of Africa: Racism in Conrad's *Heart of Darkness*"; and Terry Eagleton, *Criticism and Ideology: A Study in Marxist Literary Theory,* 135.
49. Cedric Watts, "'A Bloody Racist': About Achebe's View of Conrad," 407.

their occupants looking with dread at "the very end of the world, . . . sandbanks, marshes, forests, savages," the strand bristling with native spears and wild threats. "Or think of a young citizen in a toga . . . coming out here . . . to mend his fortunes. Land in a swamp, march through the woods, and in some inland post feel the savagery, the utter savagery, had closed round him,—all that mysterious life of the wilderness that stirs in the forest, in the jungles, in the hearts of wild men. There's no initiation either into such mysteries. He has to live in the midst of the incomprehensible, which is also detestable. And it has a fascination, too. . . . The fascination of the abomination" (30–31). As I have discussed, Elizabethans like Thomas Hariot or Edmund Spenser evoked Britain's savage past in similar ways, in part as a warning against cultural hubris. But the major difference was that these early moderns could contemplate their past savagery with a certain equanimity, hoping in the redeeming power of Christ to conquer the beast within, whereas the modern, Darwinian Marlow has no real hope that in the jungle the civilized mask will not slip from the inner beast. All he has is the modern hope in progress, and in the quarantine that time is supposed to have erected around past evil.

Yet, as Marlow proceeds in memory out of the Thames and eventually up his river of disillusion, his narrative ruthlessly finds the British and European past alive in the African present. In effect, he finds that radical evil is not obsolete, that the past is not even past. So the old colonial romance of the journey as self-discovery is exploded when the self discovered turns out to be the devouring predator under everyone's evolutionary skin, whatever the color. If the story is guilty of racism, its object is the human race.

In the first place, the novella's exotic setting is not—as in Hariot, Ralegh, or Spenser—an Eden, but Eden's demonic other, a jungle "wilderness"; and the jungle's prehistoricity is portrayed in terms not biblical but evolutionary: "Going up the river was like travelling back to the earliest beginnings of the world, when vegetation rioted in the earth. . . . The air was warm, thick, heavy, sluggish. There was no joy in the brilliance of the sunshine. The long stretches of the waterway ran on, deserted, into the gloom of overshadowed distances" (66). Furthermore, the promised wealth that attracts explorers to this setting is not gold—in Drake's legend a glorious, nation-building treasure—but ivory, a kind of bone, sought ravenously by men who lack national or even personal allegiance.

Echoing the old possession myth, the natives of this wilderness do display a kind of ironic savage nobility—though they are cannibals, the riverboat's indigenous crew unaccountably refrain from eating Marlow and his fellow whites. "Why in the name of all the gnawing devils of hunger they didn't have a go at us—they were thirty to five—and have a good tuck in for once, amazes me now when I think of it. . . . Restraint! What possible restraint? Was it superstition, disgust, patience, fear—or some kind of primitive honor?" (75–76). Certainly the cannibals exhibit more restraint—indeed, in the literal sense, are more "religious"—than the craven, trigger-happy European "pilgrims," who lack even the satanic grandeur of the traditional European-as-villain, the conquistador.

But, as noted in chapter three, it is Kurtz who inflicts the story's most wrenching inversion on the possession myth. Having come to the interior as the courageous, high-minded apostle of light, his wholehearted conversion to the darkness reveals that refined ideals of Christian civilization, supposed to be serenely absolute, are frighteningly contingent. The humane imperial "knight-errant" merges with—or, rather, emerges as—the Luciferian imperial Dragon; David defects to Goliath. As we have noted, Kurtz's grasp at godhood contrasts starkly with the frank pragmatism of Kipling's Dan and Peachey. Significantly, in Conrad's tale the object of sacrificial decapitation is no longer a would-be king like Dan who, despite his self-deception, becomes a kind of god through his martyrdom; rather, the sacrificial objects are the god-king's adoring heathen victims, whose severed heads line his path to and encircle his seat of power (96).

So Conrad's book menaces optimistic liberal expansionism by presenting Kurtz's violation of Drake's great taboo—that the man who would be God is not worthy to be king—in terms that are superficially Christian but essentially Darwinian. The beastliness that Marlow discovers and that Kurtz enacts is not—like the Augustinian beastliness in Swift—abominable because it is fallen from an original state of grace; rather, it *is* the original state, the once-and-future darkness that becomes immediately present in any place beyond the reach of women, shame, and the police. We may execrate "the horror" but not exorcise it; it is a fundamental natural force, susceptible merely of suppression, not redemption. Kurtz's outlook is not Calvinism, nor even Calibanism: no one is elect; none can be saved. We can only "exterminate all the brutes" (87), who include, not so incidentally, ourselves.[50]

---

50. English parliamentarian John Bright, in an 1888 speech, said in words that strongly anticipate Conrad's: "For two hundred years, the Judges of England sat on the Bench, condemning to the penalty of death every man, woman, and child who stole property to the value of five shillings; and, during all that time, not one Judge ever remonstrated against the law. *We English are a nation of brutes, and ought to be exterminated to the last man*" (italics mine). In Henry Adams, *The Education of Henry Adams: An Autobiography,* 191.

"Chuck 'em Out": Post-Protestant Empire Abroad in Forster's *A Passage to India*

In 1924, after the Great War had surpassed his worst fears about the meltdown of life, and after two sojourns in South Asia, E. M. Forster turned his literary attentions to the lynchpin of the empire in *A Passage to India*. Significantly, there is a Darwinian darkness at the heart of this book as there is in Conrad's—though in Forster's case, this darkness is in no way beyond the reach of "women, shame, and the police." Indeed, it is when Forster's women encounter primordial darkness in the Marabar Caves that shame and the police intervene with a vengeance, and the book's imperial microcosm disintegrates for lack of a cohesive divine center.

The Marabar Caves resonate literally and figuratively at the core of the novel. It is there that Adela Quested flees her own realization that she is lovelessly engaged to Chandrapore's chief magistrate, Ronny Heaslop, and then disastrously accuses the friendly Muslim physician Aziz of rape; it is there that the Anglican faith of Ronny's mother, Mrs. Moore, collapses in the echoing caverns under the weight of their primordial oblivion; and collapsing along with Protestant religious coherence is the vestigial credibility of Britain's imperial claims. Yet in one of Forster's exquisite ironies the caves are chosen as a destination because they seemed to promise a way to connect. Aziz extravagantly plans the excursion to serve as another and better kind of cross-cultural "Bridge Party," displaying India's Mogul glories and strengthening his tenuous personal ties to his English friends—including not only Adela and Mrs. Moore but also the teacher Cyril Fielding. However, for the English there is something profoundly discordant and disintegrative about the caves, a discordance tied up with the decay of their faith and its connecting, restraining power. Deep under the incalculably ancient Marabar Hills, the caverns are an impassive, indifferent witness to geological time, before the Ganges, before the Himalayas, before religion and spirit and life itself.[51] In short, the Marabar Hills and their caves are older than God.

This conflict between religious coherence and geological witness is strongly implicit when the narrative juxtaposes a conversation about spiritual universals with Mrs. Moore's spiritually shattering experience in one of the caves. The conversation is between Aziz and Adela; she tentatively praises "Akbar's

---

51. *A Passage to India* (New York: Harcourt, 1984), 135–36. All further citations of this edition will be made parenthetically.

new religion"—the Mogul emperor's deliberate syncretism combining Islamic, Hindu, and Christian elements—because it was designed "to embrace the whole of India." Admitting that she is not religious herself, she acknowledges the social—and imperial—utility of "something universal in this country . . . or how else are barriers to be broken down?" (160). Then, speaking more personally, she expresses fears that after marrying the increasingly callous Ronny, she will degenerate quickly into a rude and racially intolerant Anglo-Indian herself. "That's why I want Akbar's 'universal religion' or the equivalent to keep me decent and sensible" (161). Aziz, though charmed by Adela's frankness, feels constrained from even touching on the sexually charged topic of her marriage. Instead, he compliments her as immune to such bigotry, while emphatically warning her against naive universalism: "Nothing embraces the whole of India, nothing, nothing, and that was Akbar's mistake" (160).

It is at this point that the narrative brings Mrs. Moore into the cave. Crushed by the crowd and gasping for air, she experiences a paradoxically nihilist epiphany. Though up to this point she has seemed another of Forster's instinctively wise women—compassionate, relational, and a maker of connections—she is suddenly undone by the echo. "Whatever is said, the same monotonous noise replies. . . . 'Boum' is the sound as far as the human alphabet can express it, or 'bou-oum,' or 'ou-boum'—utterly dull. Hope, politeness, the blowing of a nose, the squeak of a boot, all produce 'boum'" (163). Struggling out into the open, she collapses into a deck chair and feels that the echo has begun "in some indescribable way to undermine her hold on life. . . . 'Everything exists, nothing has value'" (165). Then, with despair creeping over her, "suddenly . . . Religion appeared, poor little talkative Christianity, and she knew that all its divine words from 'Let there be Light' to 'It is finished' only amounted to 'boum'" (166). The unknowing voice of the primeval rock overwhelms her.

If the Darwinian darkness of the caves deprives Mrs. Moore of her psycho-spiritual cohesion, it threatens—and entices—Adela with the removal of her libidinal restraints. As Aziz takes her hand and escorts her alone to a higher cave, she experiences her own epiphany: "She and Ronny—no, they did not love each other." Then, though the narrator tells us that Adela did not admire Aziz "with any personal warmth," and that there "was nothing of the vagrant in her blood," her mind nevertheless runs on the contrast between her cold match with Ronny and the presumed sexual heat of Aziz's relations with his presumedly exotic wife—or wives. In fact, still holding his hand, and "having no one else to speak to on that eternal rock, she gave rein to the subject of marriage," in particular to the fascinating possibility of Aziz's polygamy: "'Have you one wife or more than one?'" (168–69).

Ironically, Adela's moment of release activates Aziz's restraint, as her attempt at intimate connection actually severs their tenuous transracial relationship and precipitates their mutual disaster. "The question shocked the young man very much. . . . 'One, one in my particular case,' he sputtered, and let go of her hand" (169). Bolting into a cave ahead, he leaves her to find her way, and she wanders into another. It is his, and our, last sight of her before she makes her hysterical accusations of rape—a charge that projects back on Aziz her own "crime" of forcing unwanted connection and intimacy. The loneliness of the "eternal rock" at Marabar had temporarily made her forget shame and the police, but she soon remembers the one and calls in the other to protect her from the godless and terrifying freedom of the hollow hills.

Closely related to both of these frightening epiphanies—the English loss of religious connection and religious restraint—is the loss of British imperial credibility. This loss is strikingly anticipated a little earlier in the novel when Fielding drops in, unannounced, to visit the slightly ailing Aziz at home and finds an impromptu microcosm of Chandrapore, and of India, gathered around Aziz's bed. There are the Muslims: Hamidullah, the young lawyer; Syed Mohammed, the assistant engineer; Haq, the police inspector; Rafi, Syed Mohammed's nephew; and Hassan, Aziz's servant. When alone, the Muslims denigrate Hinduism and complain of the English. Then the Hindus arrive: Dr. Panna Lal and his driver, Ram Chand; Lal has been sent by Major Callandar to check whether Aziz is malingering (110–18). After their arrival, the atmosphere becomes more strained until Fielding's sudden entrance.

At first, the Indians respond to the Englishman's presence with "oriental" flattery: " 'It is good of Mr. Fielding to condescend to visit our friend,' said the police inspector. 'We are touched by this great kindness.' " But Aziz, who believes that Fielding "understands" Indians, warns them off this behavior. " 'Don't talk to him like that, he doesn't want it . . . ,' he flashed." The kind of talk that Fielding does want, apparently, is reassuring egalitarian banter. He asks a good-natured, conspiratorial question about Aziz's "shamming," and "the company laughed, friendly and pleased. 'An Englishman at his best,' they thought; 'so genial' " (118–19).

Yet this easiness moves them quickly to uneasy topics. " 'The whole world looks to be dying, still it doesn't die,' " says Fielding archly of Aziz's undefined illness, " 'so we must assume the existence of a beneficent Providence.' " The ensuing exchange is instantly fraught:

> "Oh, that is true, how true!" said the policeman, thinking religion had been praised.

> "Does Mr. Fielding think it's true?"
> "Think which true? The world isn't dying. I'm certain of that!"
> "No, no—the existence of Providence."
> "Well, I don't believe in Providence."
> "But how then can you believe in God?" asked Syed Mohammed.
> "I don't believe in God."

Fielding's frankness sends a shocked thrill around the room, and Aziz is scandalized. Questioned further by the lawyer Hamidullah, Fielding admits that most "'educated thoughtful'" English people are atheists now, "'though they don't like the name,'" and that "'the West doesn't bother much about belief and disbelief in these days.'"

At this juncture Hamidullah presses his emerging prosecution with two crucially paired questions:

> "And does not morality also decline?"
> "It depends what you call—yes, yes, I suppose morality does decline."
> "Excuse the question, but if this is the case, how is England justified in holding India?" (119–20)

Significantly, the suddenly radical query seems like a non sequitur to Fielding; he appears surprised and nonplussed by the unexpected turn from religion to "politics again." His response is as agnostic politically as, he claims, England and the West are religiously. "'It's a question I can't get my mind on to,' he replied. 'I'm out here personally because I needed a job'" (120). Yet now Fielding's informality draws no laughter from the intensely listening Indians.

For Hamidullah's question is no non sequitur to them. They have heard all their lives—from official Englishmen and Indians alike—that "England holds India for her good," and that this good depends on English morality grounded in English religious conviction. While these Indians may not have believed straightforwardly in English Protestant exceptionalism—"what they said and what they felt were . . . seldom the same"—they believed that the English at least believed in it, and their secondhand faith, combined with native disunity and demoralization, had sufficed to maintain their quiescence.

So when Fielding goes on, only half-facetiously, to justify his personal presence in India not on the grounds of English ethical and spiritual superiority but simply because "'I'm delighted to be here,'" it is the Indians' turn to be puzzled. "Unless a sentence paid a few compliments to Justice and Morality in passing," says the narrator, "its grammar wounded their ears and paralyzed their minds" (121). Having long known in their bones that England holds India for England's pleasure, they are still stunned to hear it said, and by "an Englishman at his best."

Hamidullah then intrepidly takes the last step. Having heard Fielding admit to the hollow delights of empire, the lawyer now invites him to name the consequences.

> "And those Englishmen who are not delighted to be in India—have they no excuse?" he asked.
> "None. Chuck 'em out." (121)

These few pages of plausibly breezy and yet portentous dialogue, which find God so conspicuously absent, move all of these characters well beyond where anyone thought he was going: Fielding's offhand expression of unbelief rends the Indians' political firmament, and Fielding himself anticipates their eventual manifesto: "Chuck 'em out" translates quite easily to "Quit India." Yet before any real resistance can begin, there must be an occasion, and Fielding's assertions of divine absence must be confirmed by the antiepiphanies of the Marabar Caves. After the caves, Adela's false accusation of Aziz provides the occasion, and, ironically, the now godless Mrs. Moore provides a kind of divine patronage.

The imperial entropy resulting from divine absence is played out during and after the trial of Aziz. There "English justice" is revealed to be as flawed and partial as the little tribe of frightened Britons circled in their club, clinging to their creed that "God who saves the King will surely support the police" (234). The pivotal moment of the trial comes when Mr. McBryde, the police superintendent and prosecutor, inadvertently mentions Aziz's bad behavior toward "'another English lady'" on the Marabar excursion with Adela. "'He crushed her into a cave among his servants. However, that is by the way.'"

> But his last words brought on another storm, and suddenly a new name, Mrs. Moore, burst on the court like a whirlwind. Mahmoud Ali [one of the defense attorneys] had been enraged, his nerves snapped; he shrieked like a maniac, and asked . . . who was this second English lady.
> "I don't propose to call her."
> "You don't because you can't, you have smuggled her out of the country. . . . She was kept back from us until too late—I learn too late—this is English justice, here is your British Raj. Give us back Mrs. Moore for five minutes only, and she will save my friend. . . . Don't rule her out, Mr. Das . . . oh, Mrs. Moore." (248–49)

However, as her son Ronny smugly points out, Mrs. Moore by now "'should have reached Aden'"; so Mahmoud Ali turns fiercely on Mr. Das, the Indian assistant magistrate trying the case in Ronny's place.

"I am not defending a case, nor are you trying one. We are both of us slaves.... This trial is a farce, I am going." And he handed his papers to Amritrao [the other defense attorney] and left.... The tumult increased, the invocation of Mrs. Moore continued, and people who did not know what the syllables meant repeated them like a charm. They became Indianized into Esmiss Esmoor, they were taken up in the street outside.... To Ronny it was revolting to hear his mother travestied into Esmiss Esmoor, a Hindu goddess.... Suddenly it stopped. It was as if the prayer had been heard, and the relics exhibited. (249–51)

Indeed, as it turns out, the prayer has in a way been heard. Adela, up to this point fortified by "Jehovah and brandy," is called to the witness stand to sacrifice Aziz on the altar of English Womanhood. But once there she has a kind of vision of "something solid and attractive, like the hills" that recalls her to herself. Despite McBryde's leading and bullying, she climbs up out of her psychic fog to shatter his case, admitting that "Dr. Aziz never followed me into the cave" (255). Though all of British Chandrapore rises to stop the proceedings and some to curse her as a traitor, the Indian magistrate stands firm and releases Aziz " 'without one stain on his character' " (256).

As the story continues from this climax—with Aziz deeply embittered at Adela and both Adela and Fielding outcast from the English colony—news arrives of Mrs. Moore's death at sea. But her eternal absence makes her more powerfully present to a whole network of characters whom her memory connects and reconnects. As Fielding observes, "there is about to be an Esmiss Esmoor legend at Chandrapore, . . . and I will not impede its growth" (275). Her devotees are numbered among the indiscriminately adoring Hindu multitude; but she also is invoked as an avatar of inclusivity uniting Hindu, Muslim, Christian, and indeed all who can see past their own particularities. She is revered by Aziz, who "consults" her as an invisible guide in his decision to forgive Adela (282, 359); she is worshiped by the Hindu Professor Godbole, along with countless other spirits in the great "divine mess" (325); she is a sustaining link between Adela and Fielding, who talk over her memory (267–68); and she lives on in her daughter, Stella, whom Fielding, in a concluding surprise, marries (338–40). Like Ruth Wilcox or her spiritual heir, Margaret Schlegel, in *Howards End*, Mrs. Moore seems for many other characters an alternative to failed masculine, local creeds, and the patroness of conciliatory hope triumphing over divisive ethnocentric logic.

Yet even more than in the rather fantastically tragicomic finale of *Howards End*, Forster concludes by suggesting that this tension between logic and hope may not be so happily resolved. The difference between what other characters think about Mrs. Moore and what the reader knows about her bodes ill for any humanist religion of universal inclusion. What we know is that, after being overcome by the echo in the cave, she loses all of her previous desire to connect: "she didn't want to write to her children, didn't want to communicate with anyone, not even with God. . . . She sat motionless with horror, . . . then she surrendered herself to the vision" (166). Indeed, as we also know, she quite willingly abandons Aziz to his fate: neither speaking out against Adela's accusation nor visiting him in jail, she books passage home, glad to have "escaped the trial, the marriage and the hot weather." The only connection that she seems to value when last one sees her is that with Lady Mellanby, wife to the provincial lieutenant-governor, who offers to share her reserved cabin on the return voyage (230). There, we are told, she contemplates the "boum" with "the cynicism of a withered priestess" (231), and there, presumably, she meets her end. Without pushing the analogy too far, we can see something Kurtz-like in the "horror" and alienation of her denouement.

Furthermore, even if we read the resulting cult of "Esmiss Esmoor" as a defensible, if subjective, means of "connecting," the novel's concluding episode strongly suggests that no amount of personal connection, whether mercenary or sincere, is going to stop the disintegration of British India. As Fielding ends his return visit to India by riding horseback with Aziz in the jungle, they argue politics and Fielding finds his friend full of both affection and anger. Even though Aziz has just sent his letter to Adela Quested, forgiving her in the "sacred" name of Mrs. Moore, he is now outspokenly, even belligerently, nationalistic. "'Until England is in difficulties we keep silent,'" Aziz cries, "'but in the next European war—aha, aha! Then is our time.'" Forster follows this threatening piece of prescience—published fifteen years before that war and twenty-three years before Indian independence—with Aziz's moving last words: "'Down with the English anyhow. That's certain. Clear out, you fellows, double quick, I say. We [Indians] may hate one another, but we hate you most. . . . [I]f it's fifty-five hundred years we shall get rid of you, yes, we shall drive every blasted Englishman into the sea, and then'—he rode against [Fielding] furiously—'and then,' he concluded, half kissing him, 'you and I shall be friends'" (361–62). Intriguingly, this speech echoes—I will not say deliberately—both Samuel Johnson and William Blake, those oppositional voices from earlier days of imperial confidence. I have noted how Johnson's imagined Canadian chieftain, like Aziz, looks forward to the day of wrath, when inter-European conflict would provide the occasion for native warriors to "rush down upon [the English, and] force their remains to take shelter in their ships."[52] Yet Aziz has warm dreams of

---

52. Greene, "Great War," 58–60.

reconciliation as well, like Blake's "Little Black Boy," who hopes to join the white child in a millennial embrace, where both will

> lean in joy upon our father's knee:
> And then I'll stand and stroke his silver hair,
> And be like him and he will then love me.[53]

Clearly Fielding wants this embrace. " 'Why can't we be friends now?' " he asks Aziz, "holding him affectionately." But for the present, everything is against their friendship, and it seems that only some great revolution can make their connection possible.

What Fielding and Aziz want doesn't much matter if "the horses didn't want it—they swerved apart; the earth didn't want it, sending up rocks through which riders must pass single file; the temples, the tank, the jail, the palace, the birds, the carrion, the Guest House . . . they didn't want it, they said in their hundred voices, 'No, not yet,' and the sky said, 'No, not here' " (362). In *Howards End*, history and the land are on the side of reconnection, even if economic and imperial logic are not. But in Forster's India, friendship cannot escape the landscape itself, let alone the muddled, god-crazed, and bloody past that it holds. "Nothing embraces the whole of India, nothing, nothing," Aziz had warned Adela; no philosophy, religion, or irreligion, let alone "poor little talkative Christianity."

Savage Laughter: The Last of Protestant Imperialism in Waugh's *Black Mischief* and *A Handful of Dust*

I have been detailing how these earlier modernist writers questioned, subverted, or overtly attacked elements of the Protestant imperial imagination. Forster portrays Protestantism's failure at home to provide the connecting, cohesive power that the nation needs to resist social entropy, and, like Kipling, he recognizes that in the colonies religion is mainly a divisive source of trouble; while Conrad undermines English confidence in their exceptionalist righteousness when compared with European competitors, or indeed with native "savages." Yet neither of these writers gives the lie to Protestant imperialism as corrosively as Evelyn Waugh in *Black Mischief* and *A Handful of Dust*. In George Orwell's essay "Shooting an Elephant," he reflects on a misadventure as a minor official in colonial Burma, confessing that "my whole life, every White

---

53. Blake, *Songs of Innocence and Experience*, 8, ll. 26–28.

man's life in the East, was one long struggle not to be laughed at."[54] Where Kipling, Conrad, and Forster adopt toward declining empire the varied stances of tragedy, horror, or tragicomedy, Waugh delivers on the Orwellian imperialist's worst fears: scathing mockery and savage laughter. This is, in Orwell's terms, the fate worse than death.

Significantly, Waugh's unsparing, frequently hilarious view had much to do with his religious position; while Kipling, Conrad, and Forster were in varying ways and degrees post-Christian, Waugh—the adult convert to Catholicism— was both postsecular and anti-Protestant. So, where the earlier writers at times look back elegiacally to the spiritual élan and unified consciousness of the Elizabethan Protestants who conceived the British Empire, Waugh looks back with scorn. Opening his 1934 biography of the English Jesuit martyr Edmund Campion, Waugh dispenses quickly with Elizabethan glory: it is 1603, and Queen Bess, killer of Campion and persecutor of papists, squats sleepless and dying on the floor, propped by pillows, surrounded by royal bric-a-brac, plagued by guilt, and terrified of death. She rants at the archbishop of Canterbury and refuses his consolations, dismissing him and his Reformed colleagues as mere "hedge priests." Instead, "she had round her neck a piece of gold the size of an angel, engraved with characters; it had been left to her lately by a wise woman who had died in Wales at the age of a hundred and twenty. Sir John Stanhope had assured her that as long as she wore this talisman she could not die."[55] The great Protestant queen is reduced to desperate superstition and witchcraft, and her era is exposed as one of iron and clay.

Waugh found England's true golden age in medieval Catholicism. Born in 1903 and raised in the conventional Anglicanism of the day, he had by 1930 come out of Jazz Age unbelief to embrace the Church of Rome, which he came to regard as the secret soul of the true England, though unforgivably shattered by the Reformation. Waugh's conversion enabled and perhaps compelled him to revisit and reimagine not only the historical sites of Britain's imperial origins but also the literary sites of modernist disillusionment with empire—though this time not as tragedy but as farce. In Waugh's imperial fictions, agents of a debilitated and secularized Protestant progressivism reduce themselves entertainingly to the absurd, and indeed they haven't far to go. Thus Waugh strips away the last of the tragic grandeur with which other writers from Dee and Spenser to Tennyson and Kipling had sought to clothe the death of empire. The earlier and more blatant example of this *reductio* is *Black Mischief* (1932); the

---

54. George Orwell, *George Orwell: A Collection of Essays*, 153.
55. Evelyn Waugh, *Edmund Campion*, 4, 3.

later, more subtle, and finally more devastating example is *A Handful of Dust* (1934).

Both books begin, in a sense, where *Heart of Darkness* ends, assuming the futility of modern secular humanist schemes of colonial improvement, due to the savagery beneath the civilized skins of their representative moderns. R. M. Davis calls *Black Mischief* an "oblique commentary on the dry rot in modern civilization," noting that it marks a turn from Waugh's earlier domestic satire.[56] In *Decline and Fall* (1928) and *Vile Bodies* (1930), Waugh dissects, with astonishing and merciless dexterity, the attractive ennui of his fellow Jazz Age "Bright Young Things." Yet significantly, even these ostensibly lightweight entertainments have larger resonance, the title of the former obviously alluding to Edward Gibbon's monument to Roman imperial collapse, the latter ending in the near future on "the biggest battlefield in the history of the world."[57]

Since the publication of these novels, Waugh had undergone at least two transformative experiences: he had traveled extensively in Africa, and he had been received into the Roman Catholic Church. So *Black Mischief* distills his firsthand observations of imperial deterioration, while his conversion gives him "a new attitude towards it" (Davis 55). The novel tells the story of how Seth, emperor of Azania and self-described "Bachelor of the Arts of Oxford University," seeks to impose modern progress on his culturally divided and barbaric island kingdom—with the help of the charming, mercurial, and mercenary Englishman Basil Seal. Seth (modeled, despite Waugh's circumspect denials, on Haile Selassie of Ethiopia) regards Basil as personifying "all that glittering, intangible Western culture to which he aspired."[58] The reader, on the other hand, is invited to see Basil as the personification of late imperial decadence. A bright and breezy dilettante, he is first seen writing a bad check at his London club, then casually stealing his mother's jewelry to finance his Azanian journey (67, 88). He is, as the Augustinian anti-imperialists would say, quite literally draining domestic resources for foreign adventurism.

Once in Azania, Basil leaps instantly into the role of royal advisor on all things modern, while romancing Prudence Courtenay, the pretty and vapid daughter of the British ambassador. Speaking to the emperor—whom he offhandedly calls "Seth"—Basil reflects on the changing definition of imperial progress:

---

56. R. M. Davis, *Evelyn Waugh, Writer* (Norman, Okla.: Pilgrim Books, 1981), 68. All further citations of this edition will be made parenthetically.

57. Evelyn Waugh, *Decline and Fall;* Evelyn Waugh, *Vile Bodies,* 220.

58. Evelyn Waugh, *Black Mischief* (London: Hutchinson Educational, 1968), 113. All further citations of this edition will be made parenthetically.

"[W]e've got a much easier job now than we should have had fifty years ago. If we'd had to modernize a country then it would have meant constitutional monarchy, bi-cameral legislature, proportional representation, women's suffrage, independent judicature, freedom of the Press, referendums . . ."
"What is all that?" asked the Emperor.
"Just a few ideas that have ceased to be modern." (128)

So instead of promoting old-style liberalism, Basil orchestrates for Seth "the pageant of birth control," which serves Waugh as a set piece on the mutual incomprehension of black and white, East and West.

Advertised by posters contrasting the happy and civilized one-child family with the diseased, deformed, and insane family of eleven, the gala attracts unbounded popular interest. "Nowhere was there any doubt about the meaning of the beautiful new pictures," we are told.

> See: on right hand: there is rich man: smoke pipe like big chief: but his wife she no good: sit eating meat: and rich man no good: he only one son.
> See: on left hand: poor man: not much to eat: but his wife she very good, work hard in the field: man he good too: eleven children: one very mad, very holy. And in the middle: Emperor's juju [the picture of a contraceptive device]. Make you like that good man with eleven children.
> As a result . . . the peasantry began pouring into town for the gala, eagerly awaiting initiation to the fine new magic of virility and fecundity.

At the event itself, modernity is represented by an ox-drawn automobile full of local prostitutes with tennis rackets, typewriters, and telephones, displaying a banner that might well be Waugh's definitive comment on imperial progress: "THROUGH STERILITY TO CULTURE" (146–47).

But it is not enough for Waugh to show colonial modernism spreading its own domestic barrenness to the hinterlands; *Black Mischief* ends with an outrageous send-up of Conradian late imperial romance. As we have seen, *Heart of Darkness* concludes at what would seem the ne plus ultra of irony: first we hear Kurtz's famous last words—"the horror!"—then we hear Marlow's misrepresentation of those words to Kurtz's Intended—"your name"—thus implicating her feminine idealism in "the horror" that Kurtz both envisions and enacts (121). Waugh revisits this famous site by, in effect, collapsing the two episodes as Basil and Prudence are reunited in one act of wildly Swiftian barbarism.

Basil's final meeting with Prudence comes after Seth's overthrow and assassination by the dissolute Viscount Boaz. Prudence escapes from the endangered diplomatic compound in an airplane that is last seen landing with engine trouble. Once Boaz is in turn killed at Basil's orders, Basil then commands the forest tribesmen to "kill your best meat" to give Seth a proper funeral at a place called Moshu, where he goes to eulogize the dead emperor. After delivering his speech, he sits in a daze, surrounded by orgiastic native sex, half-unconscious with their brew, and full of their stew. Then he notices the village headman toying with a woman's hat.

> It was a beret of pillar-box red. Through the stupor that was slowly mounting and encompassing his mind Basil recognized it. Prudence had worn it jauntily on the side of her head, running across the legation lawn [to escape by airplane]. . . .
> "Where did you get that?"
> "Pretty."
> "Where did you get it?"
> "Pretty hat. It came in the great bird. The white woman wore it." . . .
> "But the white woman. Where is she?" . . . Basil shook him violently. "Speak, you old fool. Where is the white woman?" . . .
> "The white woman? Why, here," he patted his distended paunch. "You and I and the big chiefs—we have just eaten her." (228–30)

Basil's colonial romance has ended in the ultimate communion.

Yet upon Basil's return to England, his London friends—all broke and sponging for their next meals—are so utterly jaded that even the prospect of his exotic traveler's tales merely bores them. Sonia Trumpington chatters airily to Basil that she " '[c]an't think what you see in revolutions. They said there was going to be one here, only nothing came of it. I suppose you ran the whole country.' "

> "As a matter of fact, I did."
> "And fell madly in love."
> "Yes."
> "And intrigued and had a court official's throat cut."
> "Yes."
> "And went to a cannibal feast. Darling, I just don't want to hear about it, d'you mind? I'm sure it was all very fine and grand, but it doesn't make much sense to a stay-at-home like me."
> "That's the way to deal with him," said [her husband] Alastair from his armchair. "Keep a stopper on the far-flung stuff."

For generations, the English had put themselves to bed with enthralling "far-flung stuff"; now it only puts them to sleep. Yet conversely, for Basil, life back among the white savages holds little attraction, since he has, to his mind, now experienced the substance of what the London parties are only striving to become: " 'D'you know,' " he reflects, " 'I'm not sure I shouldn't find them a bit flat after the real thing. I went to a party at a place called Moshu . . .' 'Basil. Once for all, we don't want to hear travel experiences. Do try to remember.'" Though the Sonias and the Alastairs neither know nor care enough to connect England's dissipation and economic evisceration with imperial over-reach, they do know that empire no longer delights but bores them. They also sense, to their vague dismay, that the world around them, Basil included, is "turning serious"—deadly serious (232–34).

As extreme as is this foray into cannibalism, Waugh was to produce an even more devastating treatment of the Protestant imperial myth, late colonial romance, and progressive humanism. In his next novel, *A Handful of Dust* (1934), Waugh's contempt for decadent Anglican empire is rendered with his most damaging art. Writing twelve years later, in 1946, he said that the book "dealt entirely with behavior. It was humanist and contained all I had to say about humanism." Clearly, by "humanism" Waugh meant the secular rather than the Augustinian variety—as Martin Stannard notes, "that vision of the world which places man, not God, at the center of existence, and which believes that 'knowledge,' and thus 'progress,' derive from the observation of behavior."[59]

Written during and after Waugh's travels in British Guyana and Brazil, the novel is, as Frederick L. Beaty puts it, about "a gothic man in the hands of savages"—both at home and abroad.[60] It tells of the appropriately named Tony Last, the decent and dull owner of the rural Victorian Gothic Hetton Abbey, and Brenda, his beautiful and dissatisfied wife. After her affair with the vapid and mercenary John Beaver, followed by the death of the Lasts' only child, John Andrew, in an equestrian accident, Tony is shocked by Brenda's demand for a divorce on terms that would force him to sell Hetton. He refuses to meet her demands and instead leaves for South America to join with Dr. Messinger in a Ralegh-like upriver quest for a lost city. When the expedition becomes hopelessly lost and Messinger dies, Tony is first rescued and then held prisoner in the jungle by the insane Mr. Todd, the half-Indian, illiterate son of a renegade English missionary, who forces him to read aloud over and over the novels of Dickens. Given up for dead, Tony is replaced as Brenda's husband by his best friend Jock and is replaced at Hetton by distant Last relatives who turn the estate into a fox farm.

---

59. Martin Stannard, *Evelyn Waugh: The Early Years, 1903–1939* (New York: W. W. Norton, 1987), 378. All further citations of this edition will be made parenthetically.

60. Frederick L. Beaty, *The Ironic World of Evelyn Waugh: A Study of Eight Novels* (DeKalb: Northern Illinois University Press, 1992), 85. All further citations of this edition will be made parenthetically.

Waugh's taxonomy of English domestic savagery dovetails perfectly with his satire of imperial and religious decline in his funniest clerical creation, the Reverend Mr. Tendril of Hetton.

> He was an elderly man who had served in India most of his life. Tony's father had given him the living at the instance of his dentist. He had a noble and a sonorous voice and was reckoned the best preacher for many miles around.
>
> His sermons had been composed in his more active days for delivery at the garrison chapel; he had done nothing to adapt them to the changed conditions of his ministry and they mostly concluded with some reference to homes and dear ones far away.

This arrangement suits the congregation perfectly, since "few of the things said in church seemed to have any particular reference to themselves."[61] The Reverend Tendril's yearly yuletide sermon is especially, though unintentionally, trenchant in its indictment of modern England's domestic viciousness:

> "How difficult it is for us," he began, blandly surveying his congregation, who coughed into their mufflers and chafed their chilblains under their woolen gloves, "to realize that this is indeed Christmas. Instead of the glowing log fire and windows shuttered tight against the drifting snow, we have only the harsh glare of the alien sun; instead of the happy circle of loved faces, of home and family, we have the uncomprehending stares of the subjugated, though no doubt grateful, heathen. Instead of the placid ox and ass of Bethlehem . . . we have for companions the ravening tiger and the exotic camel, the furtive jackal and the ponderous elephant." (79)

Tony, who as lord of the manor sits approvingly in the front pew, had not yet realized that his England has become just such a hostile and spiritually heathen land, devoid of familial love and peopled by social animals every bit as "ravening" and "furtive" as tigers and jackals.

In fact, as Martin Stannard notes, animalism is a major theme in the novel: the opportunistic, home-wrecking Beavers, mother and son; Tory M.P. Jock's obsessive concern for the pigs of his constituency; the boar hunt in which Tony's young son is killed; Tony's card game of "animal snap" after the boy's death with the rodentine Mrs. Rattery; the silver fox farm that takes over Hetton in the end—all remind the reader of "man's primal bestiality" (Stannard 379).

If these characters evoke the jungle under the veneer of domesticity, Mr. Todd has preserved something of English domesticity in the heart of the jungle. He

---

61. Evelyn Waugh, *A Handful of Dust* (Boston: Little, Brown, 1988), 38–39. All further citations of this edition will be made parenthetically.

initially appears as a rescuer when Tony stumbles out of the wild, starving and half-mad with fever. Although Mr. Todd is the son of a man who, like Mr. Kurtz, "went native" and married a savage, he seems more of a Livingstone, a heart not of darkness but of light: surrounded by his affectionate family of "Pie-wie" tribesmen, he has maintained the understated good manners of his missionary father, and, for nursing Tony back to health, he asks nothing but that his "guest" read to him from his treasured cache of Dickens (289–91).

However, just as in England, this civility masks a predatory nature, and a particularly deadly one—the name "Mr. Todd" both suggests the well-mannered but ravenous fox of Beatrix Potter's tales of *Jemima Puddle-Duck* and *Mr. Tod* and echoes the German "Tod" for "death."[62] Tony's slow realization of Mr. Todd's soft-spoken malevolence generates some of the novel's most painful laughter. When Tony discovers the desperate scrawl of a previous "reader" (now dead) folded into the pages of *Martin Chuzzlewit*, he finally grasps his true situation and puts his foot down.

> "I have read for the last time."
> "I hope not," Mr. Todd said politely.
> That evening at supper only one plate of dried meat and farine was brought in and Mr. Todd ate alone. Tony lay without speaking, staring at the thatch.
> Next day at noon a single plate was put before Mr. Todd but with it lay his gun, cocked, on his knee, as he ate. Tony resumed the reading of *Martin Chuzzlewit* where it had been interrupted. (297–98)

Not only is Mr. Todd unfailingly polite; he is also sentimental and banal: as he listens to *Bleak House*, "at the description of the sufferings of the outcasts in 'Tom-all-alones' tears ran down his cheeks into his beard. His comments on the story were usually simple. 'I think that Dedlock is a very proud man,' or, 'Mrs. Jellyby does not take enough care of her children'" (293).

Such Dickensian references are exquisitely chosen to highlight Tony's predicament and to heighten the utter disconnect between Mr. Todd's vicarious emotion and his actual behavior. In *Martin Chuzzlewit*, the naive young hero travels to America where he is defrauded by the Eden Land Corporation and nearly dies of fever, while Mrs. Jellyby of *Bleak House* practices "telescopic philanthropy," supporting missionaries to the distant tribes of Borrioboola-Gha

---

62. Beatrix Potter, *The Tale of Jemima Puddle-Duck;* Beatrix Potter, *The Tale of Mr. Tod*. Waugh elsewhere alludes to children's literature for ironic effect—note, for instance, the epigraph from *Alice through the Looking Glass* and the sustained reference to Edward Lear's "The Owl and the Pussycat" in the last name of Agatha Runcible, both in *Vile Bodies*.

while cruelly neglecting her own family. In both cases, Dickens, the apostle of progressive humanism, is powerless to reconnect Mr. Todd's maudlin imagination to his moral will; indeed, Dickens provides the frame on which Tony will be psychologically racked (Beaty 99–100).

The ironic coup de grâce comes with our last view of Tony, who has just learned that, while he slept in drugged unconsciousness, Mr. Todd has mildly hosted an English rescue party and sent them away convinced of Tony's death. With superb tact, Waugh leaves us to imagine Tony's reaction; the last words belong to his host: "Let us read *Little Dorrit* again. There are passages in that book I can never hear without the temptation to weep" (302).

So in Mr. Todd, Waugh scorns the commonplaces of sentimental moral uplift that gave the empire what legitimacy it had with the English public in its waning decades. Yet Tony—although likable and sympathetic in comparison to these foreign and domestic savages—is himself no very heroic victim, for he is essentially a hollow man too. He has no real defense against the savages because he has not faced radical human evil. He is "gothic" only as in "Victorian Gothic," a style that—like Tennyson's *Idylls*—"invest[ed] a crumbling religion, threatened by scientific skepticism, with visual charm designed to conjure up an age of genuine belief" (Beaty 90). This certainly describes the Arthurian Gothic theme at Hetton, built on the ruins of an authentic abbey (a victim of Henry VIII's Protestant Dissolution, no doubt). Here is revival without essence: Hetton's bedrooms are named for various Arthurian characters, but with Tennyson's spellings rather than Malory's—significantly, adulterous Brenda is in "Guinevere," while Tony is in "Morgan le Fay," implicitly under the enchantment of his boyhood nostalgia and arrested development. There is no room named "Arthur" (14–16; Beaty 91).

There also is no real religion in Tony's life, or rather real life to his religion. He attends church as a part of his routine, posing as "an upright, God-fearing gentleman of the old school . . . Tony saw the joke. . . . 'I only go because I more or less have to'" (36, 37). Later, in the immediate aftermath of his son's death, he says of his uncomfortable and comfortless visit from Reverend Tendril, "'[i]t was very painful . . . after all the last thing one wants to talk about at a time like this is religion'" (158).

So it is appropriate that the failure of Tony's Gothic fantasy of pious domestic happiness sends him questing on an equally hollow colonial adventure. In fact, in compositional terms, the colonial adventure preceded the domestic collapse and called it into being: the novel began life as a short story, "The Man Who Liked Dickens," and Waugh created the earlier "English Gothic" "Du Côté de Chez Beaver" and other domestic episodes in order to get his "gothic man" into his desperately funny jungle exile (Stannard 379–80). Significantly, he retitled the reworked episode of Tony's captivity "Du Côté de Chez Todd," in thematic apposition to that of the devouring Beavers; even more meaningfully, the actual upriver expedition he subtitles "In Search of a City."

This search, as I have noted, evokes both Conrad and Ralegh—alluding to Ralegh's actual Orinoco journey and mimicking Marlow's fictional trip up the Congo (219–20). At first, "the City" appears to Tony as another Gothic fantasy: "all vanes and pinnacles, gargoyles, battlements, groining and tracery, pavilions and terraces, a transfigured Hetton . . . this radiant sanctuary" (222). Like earlier English explorers expecting to find Prester John or the Earthly Paradise or Lost Tribes from Israel (or Wales!), Tony is looking for a purer and truer version of himself in the wild, the familiar at the heart of the Other. And, perversely, he gets his wish, though with a difference: Mr. Todd's squalid little compound burlesques the Lost City, its exotic hidden treasure only a shelf-full of Dickens—a funhouse mirror of English domesticity that is incapable either of reflecting the truth or of improving the viewer. Finally, under Mr. Todd's fatal care, in a fever dream, Tony perceives that "[t]here is no City. Mrs. Beaver has covered it with chromium plating and converted it into flats. Three guineas a week with a separate bathroom. Very suitable for base love." And for a moment the savage laughter yields to piercing pathos: "Listen to me. I know that I am not clever but that is no reason why we should forget courtesy. Let us kill in the gentlest manner" (288).

The Protestant imperial imagination began, as discussed in chapter one, with a dream of Arthurian courtesy, and with the search for a City. John Dee and Richard Hakluyt sought to make themselves *Cosmopolites,* citizens and members of "the whole and only one mysticall citie *universall*" (*PN* 1.16), and thus to recover an ecumenical world citizenship not reliant on papal authority, a political and spiritual catholicity independent of Roman Catholicism. To their Anglo-Welsh imaginations, it seemed reasonable that this universal City should be incarnate in the particular flesh of a recovered Arthurian empire, animated by a reformed English church. More than three and a half centuries later, Evelyn Waugh's renewed allegiance to Rome made him contemptuous of Anglicanism's waning universal claims. At Tony Last's Hetton, English Protestantism is exposed as a laughably parochial affair—in fact not even that, since it cannot give cohesive spiritual life to a parish, let alone to an empire. Waugh, of course, found his universal enduringly particularized in Rome; other post-Protestants—the post-Christian ones—would have to seek their universals elsewhere, or try to do without them altogether.

As the empire grew increasingly secular, a new wave of imperialists and antiimperialists alike scapegoated the English church, which at home reaped the distrust of the nation, and abroad the hatred of proliferating colonial nationalisms and socialisms.[63] So the empire—weakened by over-reach, shattered by two world wars, and unable to keep the colonized either in hope or in fear—by 1945 lacked what it needed most: the cohesive metaphysics to resist the physics of entropy, the collective will even to imagine a resurrection. When Winston Churchill—the last great imperialist—called the Britons in 1940 to defend their home island, they rallied to him like lions; but when that island was secured, and he looked to reassert the empire, he was out of office within two months. "'You can't keep them both,' they explained." So the empire came unbound. Raphael Hythloday and Samuel Johnson were right—in its quest to be the universal City, England had become Nolandia.

---

63. In one notorious instance, Dr. Kwame Nkrumah, the first president of the independent Ghana, directed that his name be substituted for God's in public recitals of the Lord's Prayer, and for that of Jesus Christ in *Hymns Ancient and Modern*. James, *The Rise and Fall of the British Empire*, 590–91.

Afterword ❀ ❀ ❀ ❀ ❀

Moravians in the Moon

> And I saw another Beast coming up out of the earth; and he had two horns like unto a Lamb, and he spake as a Dragon. —*Revelation 13:11*

This book has attended mainly to the colonial center rather than to the margins; it has been concerned primarily with the hegemonic ideology of British Protestant imperialism, not with the consciousness of the colonial subjects. Except in a few instances—the Aztecs' fatal hope in Quetzalcóatl, the Miwoks' worshipful reaction to Drake, Pocahontas's conversion and marriage to Rolfe, Hamidullah's grilling of Fielding in *A Passage to India*—I have not said much about the role of religion in promoting indigenous reception of or resistance to colonization; I have focused instead on the views of the British colonialists and conquerors whose reforming faith bound together the empire, and whose loss of faith led to its dissolution.

One of my reasons for this focus on masters rather than subjects is pragmatic and prudential: the scope of my project is already large, and, to quote Dr. Johnson one last time, "no one wished it longer," least of all myself. However, my other reason is more substantive. Contemporary criticism has had little to say about how Britain's hegemonic imperial center itself began at the colonial margin—that is, about how a smallish island kingdom at the far edge of the medieval *mappamundi* came to draw the world's prime meridian through its own heart. Nor have contemporary critics said much about what we might call "alterity within the hegemonic"—that is, about how anticolonial dissent and resistance arose from *within* English Protestant Christianity. In my first chapters, I have attempted to answer the first question; in my latter chapters, the last.

Still, while I have presented this study as a necessary correction to current emphases, my work also complements some recent work on religion at the imperial margins. Gauri Viswanathan has detailed how Hindu and Islamic India recovered or invented their own spiritual nationalisms that resisted and eventually expelled the British imperial *cultus*.[1] In fact it was what M. A. Jinnah called Mohandas Gandhi's "Hindu revivalism," along with Jinnah's own Muslim League, that ultimately did more than the British conscience to pluck the jewel from the crown—and then split the jewel.[2] Moreover, Viswanathan persuasively critiques the ways in which most postcolonial theory still relies on the inadequate and outworn language of religious "fundamentalism" versus secular "modernity"; indeed, more than fifty years after independence, "fundamentalism" seems to be the rising form of "modernity" in contemporary India and Pakistan.[3] Postcolonial nation building, in modern South Asia as in early modern England, often seems an irreducibly religious enterprise.

Yet this very irreducibility is why Gandhi, for instance, needed British morality as well as Hindu *satyagraha* and World War II to end the Raj and secure Indian independence. Only diamond cuts diamond; Gandhi pierced the well-armored English conscience by appropriating the Christian demeanor of the Suffering Servant and so awakened England's deep-seated revulsion at the notion of attacking the weak and the small. (*Satyagraha* would not have fared so well against the Third Reich.) One should, of course, guard against overpraising English gentlemanliness, but neither should one underrate the importance of English restraint during the devolution of empire. One need only compare the bloody retreats of French, Belgian, and Portuguese colonialism, or the draconian brinksmanship of the waning USSR; Britain went quietly because, by 1945, a majority of Britons were disenchanted with dominion and were eager to shrug off the twin weights of glory and guilt.[4]

---

1. Gauri Viswanathan, *Masks of Conquest: Literary Study and British Rule in India*; see especially chapter 2 on the "pre-evangelistic" uses of English literature in early and mid-nineteenth-century India, and chapter 6 on the ultimate failure and rejection of English literature as a means of Christianizing or anglicizing India.
2. Hector Bolitho, *Jinnah: Creator of Pakistan*, 84.
3. Gauri Viswanathan, *Outside the Fold: Conversion, Modernity, and Belief*; note especially Viswanathan's prefatory discussion of how "even the most innovative historical methods have failed to come up with ways of studying belief systems" without treating them as a "'mere adjunct to political activity'" (xiv).
4. James, *Rise and Fall of the British Empire*, 588–89.

I have described how this deglorification depended significantly on British secularization; the conversion of colonial representatives from Livingstonian apostles to Orwellian apparatchiks made further expansionism seem either laughable or deadening. But British religion played its part too. If the imperial anxieties of Victorian Protestantism had been palliated by hopes of bringing light to the dark places, by the late 1930s Britain's Protestant imagination was undergoing a conversion of its own. Recognizing the Victorian arrangement as Faustian, Anglicanism increasingly turned against its devil's bargain.

This rejection of imperial romance is strikingly represented in the cosmic romances of C. S. Lewis. Like many other conversions, this particular religiopolitical reversal constituted not so much a turn as a return, in this case to the ancient Augustinian critique of conquest and the Christian humanist tradition that it inspired. If More, Swift, and Johnson had all in various ways predicted that England would become Nolandia, Lewis was their latter-day disciple living through the day of wrath, writing in the context of imperial collapse. We have already encountered Lewis the literary critic, but he was probably also the twentieth century's most influential British Christian; and the "mereness" of his Christianity—the revived orthodoxy that he advocated in his apologetics and fiction—spared no place for the pieties of colonial possession.

It is worth noting that among his critical writings, Lewis makes a harsh antiimperial statement in the context of discussing *The Faerie Queene*, which he otherwise admired: "Spenser was the instrument of a detestable policy in Ireland, and in his fifth book the wickedness he had shared begins to corrupt his imagination."[5] And it is significant that in his apologetical writings, Lewis's bitterest declarations against imperialism occur in the context of a work treating smaller-scale, interpersonal relations: *The Four Loves*. Here he writes appreciatively about love of nation as one of the lower forms of affection but then turns scathingly on the ultranational expansionists: "Our habit of talking as if England's motives for acquiring an empire . . . had been mainly altruistic [has] nauseated the world. . . . If there were no broken treaties with Redskins, no extermination of the Tasmanians, . . . no Amritsar, Black and Tans or Apartheid, the pomposity . . . would be roaring farce. . . . If our country's cause is the cause of God, wars must be wars of annihilation. A false transcendence is given to things that are very much of this world. . . . We have shouted the name of Christ and enacted the service of Moloch."[6] If Lewis—like More, Milton, Swift, and Johnson—could be moved by imperialism to something like prophetic outrage,

5. C. S. Lewis, *The Allegory of Love*, 349.
6. C. S. Lewis, *The Four Loves*, 45–46, 48–49.

he also resembled these earlier humanists in conceiving other worlds from which to comment ironically on our own. Thus while the novels in his "Ransom Trilogy"—*Out of the Silent Planet* (1938), *Perelandra* (1944), and *That Hideous Strength* (1946)—are superficially "science fiction," Lewis's primary interest is not in the physics of space travel but rather in its metaphysics.[7] So he imagines a solar system, indeed a universe, in which all the planets have thus far remained unfallen except for poor pagan Earth—Thulcandra, "the silent planet." Yet significantly, it is a symptom of humanity's savagery that it seeks to expand its darkness beyond its terrestrial borders. So out of Earth, and, significantly, out of Britain, comes the trilogy's chief evil agent: an explorer-physicist named Weston.

First on Mars, then on Venus, Weston attempts conquest, by any and all means—shooting some benevolent Martian "natives" while trying to offer others his hostage (a bumbling Cambridge philologist named Ransom) as a human sacrifice. Weston—complete with his pith helmet, revolver, contempt for indigenous life, and belief in his own Darwinian destiny—seems to personify late secular imperialism, a Kurtz seeking the heart of interstellar darkness. Furthermore, in the second novel, *Perelandra*, it becomes clear that, in traveling to Venus, Weston has been possessed not merely by expansionist ambition or megalomania but by Satan himself. Here Lewis displays his debt not only to Conrad and H. G. Wells but also to Milton; this novel was conceived at about the same time that Lewis was completing *A Preface to Paradise Lost* (1942), and the demonic Weston's attempts to seduce the Venusian Eve might well be subtitled "Paradise Retained." For in this rematch the Devil, like Milton's Comus, is undone by the Lady's invulnerable humility—and by the doggedness of Ransom, who though only a bumbling don, nevertheless fights a hand-to-hand death-duel with Weston and emerges victorious, incurably wounded, and spiritually transformed.

The extent of Ransom's transformation, and its relation to Lewis's anti-imperial cosmos, is made clear in the last and weirdest book of the trilogy, *That Hideous Strength*. Weston's attempt at interplanetary conquest may have been defeated, and evil quarantined on Earth, but there an apocalyptic struggle is shaping up in postwar Britain itself: Satan—"the Bent One"—is moving to take possession, quite literally, of the faculty at tiny Bracton College. The only force capable of opposing this "hideous strength"—a modern Babel in the guise of a research

---

7. C. S. Lewis, *Out of the Silent Planet* (New York: Macmillan, 1965); C. S. Lewis, *Perelandra: A Novel* (New York: Macmillan, 1944); C. S. Lewis, *That Hideous Strength: A Modern Fairy-Tale for Grown-Ups* (New York: Macmillan, 1965). Further citations of these editions will be made parenthetically.

institute—is the Pendragon, a *rex futurus* whose return is announced by the sudden reappearance of "Merlinus Ambrosius," and who turns out to be Ransom himself, bleeding from his Perelandran wound like the Fisher King.

Significantly, while Ransom's sufferings have transformed him into a returning Arthurian ruler, he is—unlike Geoffrey's, Malory's, Spenser's, or Tennyson's—a determinedly anti-imperial one: this *rex futurus* comes not only to overthrow the outright Pandemonium at Bracton but also to abolish over-reaching "Britain," with its expansionist legacy of "Mordred . . . Cromwell . . . and of Cecil Rhodes" (*Hideous Strength* 369). Instead, Arthur comes to reassert "Logres," a "Little England" restored to her spiritual simplicity and so content with her island home.

Admittedly, the "Ransom Trilogy" is something of a wild mélange; at times transportingly vivid, at times heavily didactic, it has not aged as well as most of Lewis's other fiction and fantasy. Yet that is part of its significance: completed in 1946, the year after the Labor sweep and the year before Indian independence, it captures the Protestant imagination negotiating a time of tremendous and rapid flux. Amid the ruins of the post-Christian empire, Lewis is pointing the way to a post-imperial Christianity, showing England—and emphatically not "Britain"—its humbling yet healing place not merely in the earth but in the cosmos. So Lewis's imaginary worlds of Sulva, Malacandra, and Perelandra—our Moon, Mars, and Venus—seem designed to answer the spiritual question posed a hundred years earlier by Herman Melville in *White Jacket:* "Are there no Moravians in the Moon, that not a missionary has yet visited this poor pagan planet of ours, to civilize civilization and christianize Christendom?"[8]

Such dissent from universal human hubris provides a sober contrast with the practically universal liberationist language that permeates both colonial and postcolonial studies at present. And indeed, who could not speak emphatically

---

8. Herman Melville, *White-Jacket; or the World in a Man-of-War,* 631. Melville raises this question in the context of a chapter entitled "Man-of-War Trophies"; here he compares an American Indian's bloody prizes of war—his latest victim's red hands painted on his blanket—with two captured men-of-war, one British, one American, representing Anglo-American geopolitical rivalry. He apostrophizes both pagan and Christian:

> Poor savage! And you account it so glorious, do you, to mutilate and destroy what God himself was more than a quarter of a century in building?
> And yet, fellow-Christians, what is the American frigate Macedonian, or the English frigate President, but as two bloody red hands painted on this poor savage's blanket?

Clearly, Melville—like Montaigne with his cannibals—is deflating Christian moral exceptionalism, equating vainglorious imperial warfare with petty "savage" bloodshed; yet, like Swift, he is also drawing attention to universal human evil, savage as well as civilized.

in praise of liberation—any people's liberation—from tyranny, foreign or domestic? Liberty is precious because, as history shows, it has been so terribly rare. Yet to use that perilous phrase again—"as history shows"—recently liberated peoples have frequently been eager to ration the scarce liberty of others, often becoming the most ardent and aggressive expansionists. I am not referring merely to vindictive dictatorial regimes—Spain after the *Reconquista*, Italy under Mussolini, Germany after Versailles and Weimar, Saddam Hussein's Iraq—but to nations with real liberationist pretensions. This book has extensively illustrated one case in point: how marginal England, casting off the political and spiritual bonds of Rome, imagined a reformed nation and then a reforming empire and elected itself the capital of the world.

But other examples are legion: the United States winning independence from Britain and then, within a few decades, pushing its slaveholding "Empire of Liberty" west to the Pacific and south into Mexico; French liberty offered throughout Europe at gunpoint by a provincial Corsican general turned emperor; Red Army tanks protecting socialist democracy from dissent throughout eastern Europe and the Baltic; Jewish death-camp survivors establishing an Israeli homeland and then invading the homelands of Palestine, Syria, Lebanon, and Jordan; India racing to join its former colonial masters in the nuclear club and forcing a dubious claim to Kashmir; China decrying imperialist interference while holding Tibet. Each of these peoples—not to mention the numerous postcolonial nations of Africa, Latin America, and former Soviet Asia—has had its own religious or quasi-religious nationalism, its own nativist celebration of language and culture, its own dark memories of alien oppression and atrocity, and usually its own bright sense of reforming righteousness to whiten its sepulchre. In other words, all of these nations have, more or less, imagined themselves as democratic Lambs while speaking with the voice of imperial Dragons.

Most of this book was written during a decade when, to many, the day of such imperial Beasts seemed past. In a time of unprecedented global peace and freedom it often was easy to believe that perhaps the Internet, or the United Nations, or world trade, or genetics, or Prozac would fundamentally alter the human equation and leash the conquistadorial animal for good. But similar things were being said a century ago about the telephone, the Great Powers, Christian civilization, eugenics, and cocaine—and if the events of August 1914 shattered that modern complacency about progress, those of September 2001 shattered our postmodern hopes for easy globalization. In our current anxious moment a revived western *imperium* seems preferable to the terror and tyranny of *jihad*. But we should not confuse our present necessity with virtue. If the past is any indicator—and in this case the past is barely even past—the next imperial

Beast rising from the earth will present itself as a contemporary liberationist Lamb, speaking our language, our excellent postcolonial language, of peace and self-determination and diversity and interconnection. The crucial question now, as always, is whom we must control or displace, dispossess or destroy in order to reach the City. Again we have need of some Moravians in the Moon.

Bibliography

Achebe, Chinua. "An Image of Africa: Racism in Conrad's *Heart of Darkness*." *Massachusetts Review* 17:4 (1977): 782–94.
Ackroyd, Peter. *William Blake*. New York: Knopf, 1996.
Adams, Henry. *The Education of Henry Adams: An Autobiography*. Boston: Houghton Mifflin, 1946.
Alexander, Michael, ed. *Discovering the New World Based on the Works of Theodore DeBry*. New York: Harper and Row, 1976.
Allen, Michael J. B. "Fitzgeffrey's Lamentation on the Death of Drake." In *Sir Francis Drake and the Famous Voyage, 1577–1580*, ed. Norman J. W. Thrower, 99–111. Berkeley and Los Angeles: University of California Press, 1984.
Andrewes, Lancelot. *A Learned Discourse of Ceremonies Retained and Used in Christian Churches*. London: Charles Adams, 1653.
Anghiera, Pietro Martire. *Decades of the New World*. Trans. Richard Eden. London, 1555. Pollard and Redgrave, *A Short-Title Catalogue of Books Printed in England . . . 1475–1640*, no. 647; hereafter cited as STC.
Anglo, Sydney. "The *British History* in Early Tudor Propaganda." *Bulletin of the John Rylands Library* 44 (1961–1962): 17–48.
Anselment, Raymond A. "'The Church Militant': George Herbert and the Metamorphoses of Christian History." *Huntington Library Quarterly* 41 (1978): 299–316.
Arias, Santa. "Empowerment through the Writing of History: Bartolomé de Las Casas's Representation of the Other(s)." In *Early Images of the Americas: Transfer and Invention*, ed. Jerry M. Williams and Robert E. Lewis, 163–79. Tucson: University of Arizona Press, 1993.
Armitage, David. *The Ideological Origins of the British Empire*. Cambridge: Cambridge University Press, 2000.

Arner, Robert D. "The Romance of Roanoke: Virginia Dare and the Lost Colony in American Literature." *The Southern Literary Journal* 10 (1978): 5–45.

Arnold, Matthew. *The Poetical Works of Matthew Arnold.* Ed. C. B. Tinker and H. F. Lowry. London: Oxford University Press, 1950.

Ascham, Roger. *The Schoolmaster* (1570). Ed. Lawrence V. Ryan. Charlottesville: University Press of Virginia, 1967.

Augustine. *The City of God against the Pagans.* Ed. and trans. R. W. Dyson. Cambridge: Cambridge University Press, 1998.

Austen, Jane. *Mansfield Park.* Ed. Tony Tanner. Harmondsworth: Penguin, 1985.

Axtell, James. *Beyond 1492: Encounters in Colonial North America.* New York: Oxford University Press, 1992.

Baker, David J. *Between Nations: Shakespeare, Spenser, Marvell, and the Question of Britain.* Stanford: Stanford University Press, 1997.

Bale, John. *Select Works of John Bale.* Ed. Henry Christmas. Cambridge: Parker Society, 1849.

Barbour, Philip L. *Pocahontas and Her World.* Boston: Houghton Mifflin, 1969.

Barbour, Reid. "The Caroline Church Heroic: The Reconstruction of Epic Religion in Three Seventeenth-Century Communities." *Renaissance Quarterly* 50 (1997): 771–818.

Barnaby, Andrew. "'Another Rome in the West?': Milton and the Imperial Republic, 1654–1670." *Milton Studies* 30 (1990): 67–84.

Barton, Anne. "Perils of Historicism." *New York Review of Books* (March 28, 1991): 54.

Bascom, Tim. "Secret Imperialism: The Reader's Response to the Narrator in 'The Man Who Would Be King.'" *ELT* 31 (1988): 162–73.

Bass, Jeff D. "The Perversion of Empire: Edmund Burke and the Nature of Imperial Responsibility." *The Quarterly Journal of Speech* 81 (May 1995): 208–27.

Beaty, Frederick L. *The Ironic World of Evelyn Waugh: A Study of Eight Novels.* DeKalb: Northern Illinois University Press, 1992.

Beckett, J. C. "Burke, Ireland, and the Empire." In *Irish Culture and Nationalism, 1750–1790,* ed. Oliver MacDonagh. New York: St. Martin's, 1983.

Behn, Aphra. *Oroonoko, or The Royal Slave.* Boston: Bedford/St. Martin's, 2000.

Bemiss, Samuel, ed. *The Three Charters of the Virginia Company of London. With Seven Related Documents; 1606–1621.* Williamsburg, Va.: Virginia 350th Anniversary Celebration Corporation, 1957.

Bercovitch, Sacvan. *The Puritan Origins of the American Self.* New Haven: Yale University Press, 1975.

Bergeron, David M. *English Civic Pageantry, 1558–1624.* Columbia: University of South Carolina Press, 1971.
Bhabha, Homi K. *The Location of Culture.* London: Routledge, 1994.
Blackburn, Robin. *The Overthrow of Colonial Slavery, 1776–1848.* London: Verso, 1998.
Blackstone, B. *The Ferrar Papers.* Cambridge: Cambridge University Press, 1938.
Blake, William. *Songs of Innocence and of Experience.* Harmondsworth: Penguin, 1995.
Bolitho, Hector. *Jinnah: Creator of Pakistan.* New York: Macmillan, 1955.
Boswell, James. *Boswell's Life of Johnson.* 2d ed. Ed. G. B. Hill. 4 vols. Oxford: Clarendon Press, 1971.
Bourne, Nicholas. *Sir Francis Drake Revived.* London, 1653. Wing, *A Short-Title Catalogue of Books Printed in England . . . 1641–1700,* no. D 84; hereafter cited as Wing.
Boyer, Abel. *The History of the Life and Reign of Queen Anne.* London, 1722.
Brantlinger, Patrick. *Rule of Darkness: British Literature and Imperialism, 1830–1914.* Ithaca: Cornell University Press, 1988.
Brown, Ford K. *Fathers of the Victorians: The Age of Wilberforce.* Cambridge: Cambridge University Press, 1961.
Browning, Robert. *Poems of Robert Browning.* Ed. Donald Smalley. Boston: Houghton Mifflin, 1956.
——. *Robert Browning's Poetry.* Ed. James F. Loucks. New York: W. W. Norton, 1979.
Burke, Edmund. *Burke's Politics: Selected Writings and Speeches of Edmund Burke on Reform, Revolution, and War.* Ed. J. S. Hoffman and Paul Levack. New York: Alfred A. Knopf, 1949.
Butler, Marilyn. *Jane Austen and the War of Ideas.* 2d ed. Oxford: Clarendon Press, 1987.
Byrd, William. *Histories of the Dividing Line betwixt Virginia and North Carolina.* Raleigh: North Carolina Historical Commission, 1929.
Byron, Lord George Gordon. *Lord Byron: The Complete Poetical Works.* Ed. Jerome J. McGann. Oxford: Clarendon Press, 1981.
Calvin, John. *The Institutes of the Christian Religion.* Ed. John T. McNeill. Trans. Ford Lewis Battles. Philadelphia: Westminster Press, 1960.
Camden, William. *Remains Concerning Britain.* Ed. R. D. Dunn. Toronto: University of Toronto Press, 1984.
Cameron, Ian. *Magellan.* New York: Saturday Review Press, 1973.
Campbell, Joseph. *The Hero with a Thousand Faces.* New York: Pantheon, 1949.

Cawley, Robert Ralston. *Milton and the Literature of Travel.* Princeton: Princeton University Press, 1951.

Cicero, Marcus Tullius. *Laelius, On Friendship & The Dream of Scipio.* Ed. and trans. J. G. F. Powell. Warminster, England: Aris and Phillips, 1990.

———. *On Duties.* Ed. and trans. M. T. Griffin and E. M. Atkins. Cambridge: Cambridge University Press, 1991.

Clarke, Samuel. *The Historie of the Glorious Life, Reign, and Death of the Illustrious Queen Elizabeth.* London, 1682. Wing C 4523.

———. *The Life and Death of the Valiant and Renowned Sir Francis Drake.* London, 1671. Wing C 4533.

———. *The Life and Death of William, Surnamed the Conqueror: King of England and Duke of Normandy. Who dyed Anno Christi, 1087.* London, 1671. Wing C 4534.

———. *Marrow of Ecclesiastical History.* Vol. 4. London, 1675. Wing C 4537.

Clayton, Lawrence A. et al., eds. *The DeSoto Chronicles: The Expedition of Hernando DeSoto to North America in 1539–1543.* Tuscaloosa: University of Alabama Press, 1993.

Clendennin, Inga. " 'Fierce and Unnatural Cruelty': Cortés and the Conquest of Mexico." In *New World Encounters*, ed. Stephen J. Greenblatt, 12–47. Berkeley and Los Angeles: University of California Press, 1993.

Collop, John. *The Poems of John Collop.* Ed. Conrad Hilberry. Madison: University of Wisconsin Press, 1962.

Conrad, Joseph. *Heart of Darkness.* Ed. Paul O'Prey. Harmondsworth: Penguin, 1989.

———. *Lord Jim.* New York: W. W. Norton, 1968.

Corrigan, Brian Jay, ed. *The Misfortunes of Arthur: A Critical, Old-Spelling Edition.* New York: Garland, 1992.

Crashaw, William. *[A Newyeeres Gift to Virginea] A Sermon Preached in London before . . . the Lord Warre . . . Febr. 21, 1609* (1610). London, 1610. STC 6029.

Cross, J. C. *Sir Francis Drake and Iron-Arm. As Represented at the New Royal Circus, on Monday, August 4, 1800.* London, 1802. Huntington KD 391.

Crouch, Nathaniel. *The English Hero: or, Sir Francis Drake Revived.* London, 1687. Wing C 7321A.

———. *The English Hero.* London, 172[?]. Wing C 7321A.

Curtin, Phillip. *The Atlantic Slave Trade.* Madison: University of Wisconsin Press, 1969.

Davenant, William. *The Cruelty of the Spaniards in Peru.* London, 1658. Wing D 321.

———. *The History of Sir Francis Drake.* London, 1659. Wing D 327.
Davies, Sir John. *A Discovery of the True Causes Why Ireland Was Never Entirely Subdued....* (1612). Ed. James P. Myers. Washington, D.C.: Catholic University of America, 1988.
Davis, R. M. *Evelyn Waugh, Writer.* Norman, Okla.: Pilgrim Books, 1981.
Dee, John. *General and Rare Memorials pertayning to the Perfect Arte of Navigation.* London, 1577. STC 6459.
———. *The Private Diary of Dr. John Dee, and the Catalogue of his Library Manuscripts.* Ed. James Orchard Halliwell. London: Camden Society, 1842.
Defoe, Daniel. *Robinson Crusoe.* Ed. Angus Ross. London: Penguin, 1985.
Dibble, Sheldon. *History and General Views of the Sandwich Islands' Mission.* New York, 1839.
The Dictionary of National Biography. Ed. Sir Leslie Stephen and Sir Sidney Lee. London: Oxford University Press, 1922.
Donne, John. *The Sermons of John Donne.* Ed. George R. Potter and Evelyn M. Simpson. Berkeley and Los Angeles: University of California Press, 1953–1962.
Drake, Sir Francis, Bart. *The World Encompassed by Sir Francis Drake* (1628). Ed. W. S. W. Vaux. London: Hakluyt Society, 1854.
Drayton, Michael. *Poems.* Ed. John Buxton. 2 vols. Cambridge: Harvard University Press, 1953.
———. *Poly-Olbion. Being the Fourth Volume of His Works.* Ed. J. William Hebel. Oxford: Basil Blackwell, for the Shakespeare Head Press, 1961.
Duckworth, Alistair M. *"Howards End": E. M. Forster's House of Fiction.* New York: Twayne, 1992.
———. *The Improvement of the Estate: A Study of Jane Austen's Novels.* Baltimore: Johns Hopkins University Press, 1994.
Eagleton, Terry. *Criticism and Ideology: A Study in Marxist Literary Theory.* London: Verso, 1976.
Eaves, Morris. *William Blake's Theory of Art.* Princeton: Princeton University Press, 1982.
Eliot, T. S. *Athenaeum.* May 1, 1919.
———. *The Complete Plays and Poems, 1909–1950.* New York: Harcourt, Brace, and World, 1971.
———. *The Sacred Wood.* London: Methuen, 1928.
Elton, G .R. *The Tudor Constitution: Documents and Commentary.* Cambridge: Cambridge University Press, 1960.
Erdman, David V. *Blake: Prophet against Empire: A Poet's Interpretation of*

the History of His Own Times. Rev. ed. Princeton: Princeton University Press, 1969.

Evans, J. Martin. *Milton's Imperial Epic*. Ithaca, N.Y.: Cornell University Press, 1996.

Fallon, Robert Thomas. *Divided Empire: Milton's Political Imagery*. University Park: Pennsylvania State University Press, 1995.

Faragher, John Mack. *Daniel Boone: The Life and Legend of an American Pioneer*. New York: Henry Holt, 1992.

Ferrar, Nicholas. *Sir Thomas Smith's Misgovernment of the Virginia Company*. Ed. David R. Ransome. Cambridge: Roxburghe Club, 1990.

Firth, C. H. "The Political Significance of *Gulliver's Travels*." Reprinted in *Essays Historical and Literary*. Oxford: Clarendon Press, 1938.

Fletcher, Robert Huntington. *The Arthurian Material in the Chronicles*. New York: Burt Franklin, 1973.

Forster, E. M. *Aspects of the Novel*. New York: Harcourt, Brace, and Company, 1927.

———. *Howards End*. New York: Signet, 1992.

———. *A Passage to India*. New York: Harcourt, 1984.

French, Peter J. *John Dee: The World of an Elizabethan Magus*. London: RKP, 1972.

Fuller, Mary C. "Ralegh's Fugitive Gold: Reference and Deferral in *The Discoverie of Guiana*." In *New World Encounters*, ed. Stephen J. Greenblatt, 218–40. Berkeley and Los Angeles: University of California Press, 1993.

———. *Voyages in Print: English Travel to America, 1576–1624*. Cambridge: Cambridge University Press, 1995.

Fuller, Thomas. *The Holy State and the Profane State*. Ed. Maximilian Graff Walten. New York: Columbia University Press, 1938.

Geller, Lila. "*Cymbeline* and the Imagery of Covenant Theology." *Studies in English Literature* 20 (1980): 241–55.

Geoffrey of Monmouth. *The Historia regum Britanniae of Geoffrey of Monmouth*. Ed. Acton Griscom. London: Longmans, Green, and Company, 1929.

———. *The History of the Kings of Britain*. Trans. Sebastian Evans. New York: E. P. Dutton, 1958.

Gibson, Mary Ellis. "Henry Martyn and England's Christian Empire: Rereading *Jane Eyre* through Missionary Biography." *Victorian Literature and Culture* 27 (1999): 419–42.

Gleckner, Robert F. *The Piper and the Bard: A Study of William Blake*. Detroit: Wayne State University Press, 1959.

Gless, Darryl J. *Interpretation and Theology in Spenser.* Cambridge: Cambridge University Press, 1994.
Gosson, Stephen. *The School of Abuse.* Ed. Edward Arber. Birmingham: English Reprints, 1868.
Green, Martin. *Dreams of Adventure, Deeds of Empire.* New York: Basic Books, 1979.
Greenblatt, Stephen J. *Marvelous Possessions: The Wonder of the New World.* Chicago: University of Chicago Press, 1991.
Greenblatt, Stephen J., ed. *New World Encounters.* Berkeley and Los Angeles: University of California Press, 1993.
Greene, Donald J. "Samuel Johnson and the Great War for Empire." In *English Writers of the Eighteenth Century,* ed. John H. Middendorf, 37–65. New York: Columbia University Press, 1971.
Gregerson, Linda. "Colonials Write the Nation: Spenser, Milton, and England on the Margins." In *Milton and the Imperial Vision,* ed. Balachandra Rajan and Elizabeth Sauer, 169–90. Pittsburgh: Duquesne University Press, 1999.
Hakluyt, Richard. *The Principal Navigations, Voyages, Traffiques and Discoveries of the English Nation* (1589). 12 vols. Glasgow: James MacLehose and Sons, 1903–1905.
———. *The Principal Navigations, Voyages, Traffiques and Discoveries of the English Nation.* 2d ed. London, 1598–1600. STC 12626.
Halkin, Léon-E. *Erasmus: A Critical Biography.* Oxford: Blackwell, 1993.
Hall, Kim F. *Things of Darkness: Economies of Race and Gender in Early Modern England.* Ithaca: Cornell University Press, 1995.
Hamilton, A. C., ed. *The Spenser Encyclopedia.* Toronto: University of Toronto Press, 1990.
Hamilton, J. Taylor, and Kenneth G. Hamilton. *History of the Moravian Church: The Renewed Unitas Fratrum, 1722–1957.* Bethlehem, Pa.: Moravian Church in America, 1967.
Hamor, Ralph. *A True Discourse of the Present State of Virginia.* 1615. Reprint, Richmond: Virginia State Library Press, 1957.
Hariot, Thomas. *A Brief and True Report of the New Found Land of Virginia.* 1590. Reprint, New York: Dover Publications, 1972.
Haslop, Henry. *Newes out of the Coast of Spaine.* London, 1587. STC 12926.
Hay, Denys. *Polydore Vergil.* Oxford: Clarendon Press, 1952.
Heizer, Robert F. *Elizabethan California.* Ramona, Calif.: Ballena Press, 1974.
Helgerson, Richard. *Forms of Nationhood: The Elizabethan Writing of England.* Chicago: University of Chicago Press, 1992.

Herbert, Edward. *Occasional Verses of Edward Lord Herbert of Cherbery and Castle-Island.* London, 1665.
———. *The Poems of Lord Herbert of Cherbury.* Ed. G. C. Moore Smith. Oxford: Clarendon Press, 1923.
Herbert, George. *The Works of George Herbert.* Ed. F. E. Hutchinson. Oxford: Clarendon Press, 1964.
Heywood, Thomas. *The Life of Merlin* (1641). London: Lackington, Allen, 1813.
Hobson, J. A. *Imperialism: A Study.* London: J. Nisbet, 1902.
Hodgkins, Christopher. *Authority, Church, and Society in George Herbert: Return to the Middle Way.* Columbia and London: University of Missouri Press, 1993.
Holinshed, Raphael. *Holinshed's Chronicle as Used in Shakespeare's Plays.* Ed. Allardyce and Josephine Nicoll. London: Everyman, 1955.
Hoover, Benjamin B. *Samuel Johnson's Parliamentary Reporting.* Berkeley and Los Angeles: University of California Press, 1953.
Hough, Richard. *Captain James Cook.* New York: W. W. Norton, 1995.
Hovey, Kenneth Alan. "'Wheel'd about . . . into *Amen'*": 'The Church Militant' on Its Own Terms." *George Herbert Journal* 10 (1986–1987): 71–84.
Hulme, Peter. *Colonial Encounters: Europe and the Native Caribbean, 1492–1797.* London: Methuen, 1986.
Hunter, J. Paul. *The Reluctant Pilgrim.* Baltimore: Johns Hopkins University Press, 1966.
James, Lawrence. *The Rise and Fall of the British Empire.* New York: St. Martin's, 1994.
James, William. *The Varieties of Religious Experience.* New York and London: Longmans, Green, 1902.
Jewkes, W. T. "Sir Francis Drake Revived: From Letters to Legend." In *Sir Francis Drake and the Famous Voyage, 1577–1580,* ed. Norman J. W. Thrower, 112–20. Berkeley and Los Angeles: University of California Press, 1984.
Johnson, Samuel. *Johnsonian Miscellanies.* Ed. G. B. Hill. Oxford: Clarendon Press, 1897.
———. *Life of Drake.* In *The Works of Samuel Johnson,* 14: 207–95. Troy, N.Y.: Pafraets Press, 1903.
———. *The Works of Samuel Johnson.* 16 vols. Troy, N.Y.: Pafraets Press, 1903.
———. *The Yale Edition of the Works of Samuel Johnson.* 16 vols. New Haven: Yale University Press, 1958–.
Jones, Emrys. "Stuart *Cymbeline.*" *Essays in Criticism* 11 (1961): 84–99.

Jonson, Ben. *Ben Jonson: The Complete Masques.* Ed. Stephen Orgel. New Haven: Yale University Press, 1969.
———. *Ben Jonson: The Complete Poems.* Ed. George Parfitt. Harmondsworth: Penguin, 1988.
———. *The Complete Plays of Ben Jonson.* Ed. G. A. Wilkes. Oxford: Clarendon Press, 1981–1982.
Jordan, Winthrop D. *The White Man's Burden: Historical Origins of Racism in the United States.* London: Oxford University Press, 1974.
———. *White over Black: American Attitudes towards the Negro, 1550–1812.* Chapel Hill: University of North Carolina Press, 1968.
Kaul, Suvir. *Poems of Nation, Anthems of Empire: English Verse in the Long Eighteenth Century.* Charlottesville: University Press of Virginia, 2000.
Kelly, Ann Cline. "Swift's Explorations of Slavery in Houyhnhnmland and Ireland." *PMLA* 91 (1976): 846–55.
Kenny, Arthur. *Thomas More.* Oxford: Oxford University Press, 1983.
King, John N. *English Reformation Literature.* Princeton: Princeton University Press, 1982.
———. *Spenser's Poetry and the Reformation Tradition.* Princeton: Princeton University Press, 1990.
Kipling, Rudyard. *The Man Who Would Be King and Other Stories.* Oxford: Oxford University Press, 1987.
Knapp, Jeffrey. *An Empire Nowhere: England, America, and Literature from "Utopia" to "The Tempest."* Berkeley and Los Angeles: University of California Press, 1992.
Knoppers, Laura Lunger. *Historicizing Milton: Spectacle, Power, and Poetry in Restoration England.* Athens: University of Georgia Press, 1994.
Lacy, Norris J., ed. *The Arthurian Encyclopedia.* New York: Garland, 1986.
Las Casas, Bartolomé de. *A Short Account of the Destruction of the Indies.* Trans. and introd. Anthony Pagden. London: Penguin, 1992.
———. *The Spanish Colonie, or, Briefe Chronicle of the Acts and gestes of the Spaniardes in the West Indies, called the newe World.* Trans. M. M. S. London, 1583. STC 4739.
———. *The Teares of the Indians.* Trans. John Phillips. London, 1656. Wing C 799.
———. *A Very Brief Account of the Destruction of the Indies.* Trans. F. A. MacNutt. Cleveland: Arthur H. Clark, 1909.
Lawrence, Judiana. "Natural Bonds and Artistic Coherence in the Ending of *Cymbeline.*" *Shakespeare Quarterly* 35 (1984): 440–60.

Leggatt, Alexander. "The Island of Miracles: An Approach to *Cymbeline*." *Shakespeare Studies* 10 (1977): 191–209.
Levi, Peter. *Tennyson*. New York: Scribner's, 1993.
Lewis, C. S. *The Allegory of Love*. Oxford: Clarendon Press, 1936.
———. *The Four Loves*. New York: Harcourt Brace Jovanovich, 1960.
———. "A Note on Jane Austen." *Essays in Criticism* 4 (1954). Reprinted in *Jane Austen: A Collection of Critical Essays*, ed. Ian Watt, 23–24. Englewood Cliffs, N.J.: Prentice-Hall, 1963.
———. *Out of the Silent Planet*. New York: Macmillan, 1965.
———. *Perelandra: A Novel*. New York: Macmillan, 1944.
———. *That Hideous Strength: A Modern Fairy-Tale for Grown-Ups*. New York: Macmillan, 1965.
Lichtheim, George. *Imperialism*. New York: Praeger, 1971.
Lindley, David. *Court Masques: Jacobean and Caroline Entertainments, 1605–1640*. Oxford: Oxford University Press, 1995.
Linton, Joan Pong. *The Romance of the New World: Gender and the Literary Formations of English Colonialism*. Cambridge: Cambridge University Press, 1998.
Litvinoff, Barnett. *1492: The Decline of Medievalism and the Rise of the Modern Age*. New York: Macmillan International, 1991.
Locke, John. *The Works of John Locke*. London: Thomas Tegg, 1823.
Lockyer, Roger. *The Early Stuarts: A Political History of England, 1603–1642*. London: Longman, 1999.
Lunenfeld, Marvin, ed. *1492: Discovery, Invasion, Encounter*. Lexington, Mass.: D. C. Heath, 1991.
MacDougall, Hugh A. *Racial Myth in English History: Trojans, Teutons, and Anglo-Saxons*. Montreal: Harvest House, 1982.
Maley, Willy. "Milton and the 'Complication of Interests' in Early Modern Ireland." In *Milton and the Imperial Vision*, ed. Balachandra Rajan and Elizabeth Sauer, 155–68. Pittsburgh: Duquesne University Press, 1999.
———. *Salvaging Spenser: Colonialism, Culture, and Identity*. New York: St. Martin's Press, 1997.
Maltby, William S. *The Black Legend in England*. Durham, N.C.: Duke University Press, 1971.
Manchester, William. *The Last Lion: Winston Spencer Churchill: Visions of Glory, 1874–1932*. Boston: Little, Brown, 1983.
Mapp, Alf J., Jr. *The Virginia Experiment: The Old Dominion's Role in the Making of America, 1607–1781*. Lanham, Md.: Hamilton Press, 1985.

Margolin, Jean-Claude, ed. *Acta Conventus Neo-Latini Turonensis.* Paris: Librarie Philosophique J. Vrin, 1980.
Marius, Richard. *Thomas More: A Biography.* New York: Knopf, 1984.
Marvell, Andrew. *Andrew Marvell: The Complete Poems.* Ed. Elizabeth Story Donno. Harmondsworth: Penguin, 1978.
Maryland State Hall of Records. The Carmelite Monastery Papers. Mary E. W. Ramey. "Chronicles of Mistress Margaret Brent." Baltimore, 1915.
Maycock, A. L. *Nicholas Ferrar of Little Gidding.* Grand Rapids, Mich.: Eerdmans, 1980.
Maynadier, Howard. *The Arthur of the English Poets.* London: Archibald Constable, 1907.
McColley, Diane Kelsey. "Ecology and Empire." In *Milton and the Imperial Vision,* ed. Balachandra Rajan and Elizabeth Sauer, 112–29. Pittsburgh: Duquesne University Press, 1999.
McDonald, Russ. *The Bedford Companion to Shakespeare: An Introduction with Documents.* New York: Bedford/St. Martins, 1996.
———. "Reading *The Tempest.*" *Shakespeare Survey* 43 (1991): 15–28.
McGuire, Ian. "Epistemology and Empire in *Idylls of the King.*" *Victorian Poetry* 30 (1992): 387–400.
Melville, Herman. *White-Jacket; or the World in a Man-of-War.* In *Redburn: His First Voyage, White-Jacket; or the World in a Man-of-War, Moby-Dick; or, The Whale,* ed. G. Thomas Tanselle. New York: Library of America, 1983.
Middeldorf, John H., ed. *English Writers of the Eighteenth Century.* New York: Columbia University Press, 1971.
Mill, John Stuart. *Disquisitions and Discussions.* London: Longmans, Green, Reader, and Dyer, 1875.
———. *On Liberty: Annotated Text Sources and Background Criticism.* Ed. David Spitz. New York: W. W. Norton, 1975.
Miller, Perry. "The Religious Impulse in the Founding of Virginia: Religion and Society in the Early Literature." *William and Mary Quarterly* 5 (1948): 492–522.
Milton, John. *Complete Poems and Major Prose.* Ed. Merrit Y. Hughes. Indianapolis: Odyssey, 1957.
———. *Complete Prose Works of John Milton.* Ed. Don Wolfe. New Haven: Yale University Press, 1953–1982.
The Misfortunes of Arthur: A Critical, Old-Spelling Edition. Ed. Brian Jay Corrigan. New York: Garland, 1992.

Moffit, Robin. "*Cymbeline* and the Nativity." *Shakespeare Quarterly* 13 (1962): 207–18.

Montaigne, Michel de. *The Complete Essays of Montaigne.* Ed. Donald M. Frame. Stanford: Stanford University Press, 1958.

Montrose, Louis. "The Work of Gender in the Discourse of Discovery." In *New World Encounters*, ed. Stephen J. Greenblatt, 177–214. Berkeley and Los Angeles: University of California Press, 1993.

More, Thomas. *Utopia.* Trans. Paul Turner. Harmondsworth: Penguin, 1965.

Morgan, Edmund S. *American Slavery, American Freedom: The Ordeal of Colonial Virginia.* New York: Norton, 1975.

Morgan, Kenneth O., ed. *The Oxford History of Britain.* Rev. ed. Oxford: Oxford University Press, 1999.

Morton, Thomas. *New English Canaan of Thomas Morton.* Ed. Charles Francis Adams Jr. 1883. Reprint, New York: Burt Franklin, 1967.

Murry, John Middleton. *Jonathon Swift: A Critical Biography.* New York: Noonday Press, 1955.

Nichols, Philip. *Sir Francis Drake Reuiued . . .* London, 1626. STC 18544.

Nietzsche, Friedrich. *The Philosophy of Nietzsche.* Trans. Helen Zimmern. New York: Modern Library, 1927.

Orosius, Paulus. *Seven Books of History against the Pagans.* New York: Columbia University Press, 1936.

Orwell, George. *George Orwell: A Collection of Essays.* New York: Harcourt Brace Jovanovich, 1953.

The Oxford English Dictionary. Ed. James A. H. Murray. Oxford: Clarendon Press, 1888–1933.

Pagden, Anthony. *Lords of All the World: Ideologies of Empire in Spain, Britain, and France c. 1500–c. 1800.* New Haven: Yale University Press, 1995.

———. *Spanish Imperialism and the Political Imagination: Studies in European and Spanish-American Social and Political Theory, 1512–1830.* New Haven: Yale University Press, 1990.

Pagden, Anthony, trans. *A Short Account of the Destruction of the Indies*, by Bartolomé de Las Casas. London: Penguin, 1992.

Pearce, Roy Harvey. "Primitivistic Ideas in the *Faerie Queene.*" *JEGP* 44 (1945): 139–51.

Penzer, N. M., ed. *The World Encompassed and Analogous Contemporary Documents.* New York: Cooper Square, 1969.

Perkins, William. *A Commentarie or Exposition, vpon the fiue first Chapters of the Epistle to the Galatians: penned by the godly, learned, and Judiciall Diuine, Mr. W. Perkins.* Cambridge, 1604. STC 19680.

Pinion, F. B. *A Tennyson Chronology.* Boston: G. K. Hall, 1990.

———. *A Tennyson Companion.* New York: St. Martin's, 1984.

Pitcher, John. *Samuel Daniel, the Brotherton Manuscript: A Study in Authorship.* Leeds: University of Leeds, 1981.

Pollard, Alfred W., and G. R. Redgrave. *A Short-Title Catalogue of Books Printed in England, Scotland, and Ireland and of English Books Printed Abroad, 1475–1640.* London: Bibliography Society, 1926.

Porter, H. C. *The Inconstant Savage: England and the North American Indian, 1500–1660.* London: Duckworth, 1979.

Potter, Beatrix. *The Tale of Jemima Puddle-Duck.* London: Frederick Warne, 1908.

———. *The Tale of Mr. Tod.* London: Frederick Warne, 1912.

Powers-Beck, Jeffrey. *Writing the Flesh: The Herbert Family Dialogue.* Pittsburgh: Duquesne University Press, 1998.

Prebble, John. *The Darien Disaster: A Scots Colony in the New World, 1698–1700.* New York: Holt, Rinehart, and Winston, 1969.

Purchas, Samuel. *Hakluytus Posthumus, or Purchas His Pilgrimes.* 20 vols. Glasgow: James MacLehose and Sons, 1905–1907.

Quinn, David B. "Early Accounts of the Famous Voyage." In *Sir Francis Drake and the Famous Voyage, 1577–1580*, ed. Norman J. W. Thrower, 33–48. Berkeley and Los Angeles: University of California Press, 1984.

Quint, David. *Epic and Empire: Politics and Generic Form from Virgil to Milton.* Princeton: Princeton University Press, 1993.

Rajan, Balachandra, and Elizabeth Sauer, eds. *Milton and the Imperial Vision.* Pittsburgh: Duquesne University Press, 1999.

Ralegh, Sir Walter. *The Discoverie of the Large, Rich, and Beautiful Empire of Guiana.* Ed. Sir Robert H. Schomburgk. 1898. Reprint, New York: Burt Franklin, n.d.

Representations 33 (Winter 1991). Special issue, "The New World."

Roberts, Henry. *A most friendly farewell. . . .* London, 1585. STC 21084.

———. *The Trumpet of Fame.* London: 1595. STC 21088.

Rolfe, John. *A True Relation of the state of Virginia lefte by Sir Thomas Dale Knight in May last 1616.* New Haven: Yale University Press, 1951.

Ronda, James P. *Lewis and Clark among the Indians.* Lincoln: University of Nebraska Press, 1984.

Rosselli, John. *Lord William Bentinck: The Making of a Liberal Imperialist, 1774–1839.* Berkeley and Los Angeles: University of California Press, 1974.

Sahlins, Marshall. *Islands of History.* Chicago: University of Chicago Press, 1985.

Said, Edward. *Culture and Imperialism.* New York: Knopf, 1993.
———. *Orientalism.* New York: Pantheon, 1978.
Sale, Kirkpatrick. *The Conquest of Paradise.* New York: Knopf, 1991.
Scarisbrick, J. J. *Henry VIII.* Berkeley and Los Angeles: University of California Press, 1968.
Scherwatzky, Steven. "Johnson, *Rasselas,* and the Politics of Empire." *Eighteenth-Century Life* 16:3 (1992): 103–13.
Schoeck, Richard J. "Renaissance Guides to Renaissance Learning." In *Acta Conventus Neo-Latini Turonensis,* ed. Jean-Claude Margolin, 239–62. Paris: Librarie Philosophique J. Vrin, 1980.
Scobie, Edward. *Black Britannia: A History of Blacks in Britain.* Chicago: Johnson, 1972.
Seeley, John Robert. *The Expansion of England: Two Courses of Lectures.* Boston: Little, Brown, 1912.
Shakespeare, William. *The Complete Works of Shakespeare.* 4th ed. Ed. David Bevington. New York: Longman, 1997.
———. *The Oxford Shakespeare.* Ed. Stanley Wells et al. Oxford: Oxford University Press, 1988.
Shelley, Percy Bysshe. *Shelley: Political Writings.* Ed. Roland A. Duerksen. New York: Appleton-Century-Crofts, 1970.
———. *Shelley's Poetry and Prose.* Ed. Donald H. Reiman and Sharon B. Powers. New York: W. W. Norton, 1977.
Sherman, William H. *John Dee: The Politics of Reading and Writing in the English Renaissance.* Amherst: University of Massachusetts Press, 1995.
Shuger, Debora. *Habits of Thought in the English Renaissance: Religion, Politics, and the Dominant Culture.* Berkeley and Los Angeles: University of California Press, 1990.
———. "Irishmen, Aristocrats, and Other White Barbarians." *Renaissance Quarterly* 50 (1997): 494–525.
Sims, James H. "Camoens' *Lusiads* and Milton's *Paradise Lost:* Satan's Voyage to Eden." Papers on Milton. University of Tulsa Monograph Series, no. 8, 36–46. Tulsa: University of Tulsa Press, 1969.
Slemon, Stephen. "The Scramble for Post-Colonialism." In *The Arnold Anthology of Post-Colonial Literatures in English,* ed. John Thieme, 45–52. London: Arnold, 1996.
Smalley, William A. *Translation as Mission: Bible Translation in the Modern Missionary Movement.* Macon, Ga.: Mercer, 1991.
Smith, Bernard. "Cook's Posthumous Reputation." In *Captain James Cook and*

His Times, ed. Robin Fisher and H. Johnson. Seattle: University of Washington Press, 1979.

Smith, John. *The Complete Works of Captain John Smith*. Ed. Philip L. Barbour. Chapel Hill: University of North Carolina Press, 1986.

Southey, Robert. *The Poetical Works of Robert Southey*. Boston: Houghton, Mifflin, 1884.

Spenser, Edmund. *The Faerie Queene*. Ed. Thomas P. Roche Jr. New Haven: Yale University Press, 1981.

———. *The Poetical Works of Edmund Spenser*. Ed. J. C. Smith and E. de Selincourt. London: Oxford, 1952.

Stannard, Martin. *Evelyn Waugh: The Early Years, 1903–1939*. New York: W. W. Norton, 1987.

Stape, J. H., ed. *The Cambridge Companion to Joseph Conrad*. Cambridge: Cambridge University Press, 1996.

Stewart, David H. "Kipling, Conrad, and the Dark Heart." *Conradiana* 19 (1987): 195–205.

Stow[e], John. *The Annales of England . . . from the first inhabitation vntill this present yeere 1592*. London, 1592. STC 23334.

———. *Annales, or, a Generall Chronicle of England . . . Continued unto 1631*. London: Ralph Newberie, 1580–1631. STC 23340.

———. *The Chronicles of England, from Brute vnto this present yeare of Christ 1580*. London: Ralph Newberie, 1580. STC 23333.

Strachey, Lytton. *Eminent Victorians: The Illustrated Edition*. New York: Weidenfeld and Nicolson, 1988.

Strier, Richard. *Resistant Structures: Particularity, Radicalism, and Renaissance Texts*. Berkeley and Los Angeles: University of California Press, 1995.

Sugden, John. *Sir Francis Drake*. New York: Henry Holt, 1990.

Swift, Jonathan. *Gulliver's Travels*. Ed. Peter Dixon and John Chalker. London: Penguin, 1985.

———. *The Prose Works of Jonathan Swift*. Ed. Herbert Davis. Oxford: Blackwell, 1957–1963.

Symonds, William. *Virginea [Virginea Brittania]. A Sermon Preached at White-Chappel, in the presence of many, Honourable and Worshipfull, the Adventurers and Planters for Virginia, 25. April. 1609*. London: Printed by John Windet for Eleazar Edgar and William Welby, 1609. STC 23594.

Tacitus. *Agricola, Germany, Dialogue on Orators*. Trans. Herbert W. Benario. Indianapolis: Bobbs-Merrill, 1967.

Tennyson, Alfred Lord. *A Collection of Poems by Alfred Tennyson*. Ed. Christopher Ricks. Garden City, N.Y.: Doubleday, 1972.

———. *Idylls of the King and a Selection of Poems.* Ed. George Barker. New York: Signet, 1961.
Terry, Judith. "Sir Thomas Bertram's 'Business in Antigua.'" *Persuasions* 17 (1995): 97–105.
Thomas, Hugh. *Conquest: Montezuma, Cortés, and the Fall of Old Mexico.* New York: Simon and Schuster, 1993.
Thomas, Keith. *Religion and the Decline of Magic.* New York: Scribner's, 1971.
Thornton, A. P. *The Imperial Idea and Its Enemies: A Study in British Power.* London: Macmillan, 1963.
Tilton, Robert. *Pocahontas: The Evolution of an American Narrative.* Cambridge: Cambridge University Press, 1994.
Tomalin, Claire. *Jane Austen: A Life.* London and New York: Viking, 1997.
Torchiana, D.T. "Jonathan Swift, the Irish, and the Yahoos: The Case Reconsidered." *Philological Quarterly* 54 (1975): 195–212.
Vickers, Brian, ed. *Shakespeare: The Critical Heritage, 1693–1733.* London: Routledge and Kegan Paul, 1974.
Virgil. *Aeneid.* Trans. Robert Fitzgerald. New York: Random House, 1983.
Viswanathan, Gauri. *Masks of Conquest: Literary Study and British Rule in India.* New York: Columbia University Press, 1989.
———. *Outside the Fold: Conversion, Modernity, and Belief.* Princeton: Princeton University Press, 1998.
von Maltzahn, Nicholas. "Acts of Kind Service: Milton and the Patriotic Literature of Empire." In *Milton and the Imperial Vision,* ed. Balachandra Rajan and Elizabeth Sauer, 233–54. Pittsburgh: Duquesne University Press, 1999.
The Voyages & Travels of that Renowned Captain, Sir Francis Drake. London, 1652. Wing V 747.
Wallace, Malcolm William. *The Life of Sir Philip Sidney.* New York: Octagon Books, 1967.
Warren, Michelle R. "Making Contact: Postcolonial Perspectives through Geoffrey of Monmouth's *Historia regum Britanniae.*" *Arthuriana* 8 (1998): 115–34.
Watt, Ian. *Conrad in the Nineteenth Century.* Berkeley and Los Angeles: University of California Press, 1979.
Watt, Ian, ed. *Jane Austen: A Collection of Critical Essays.* Englewood Cliffs, N.J.: Prentice-Hall, 1963.
Watts, Cedric. "'A Bloody Racist': About Achebe's View of Conrad." In *Joseph Conrad: Critical Assessments,* ed. Keith Carabine, 2: 405–18. Sussex: Helm Information, 1992.

Waugh, Evelyn. *Black Mischief.* London: Hutchinson Educational, 1968.
———. *Decline and Fall.* Harmondsworth: Penguin, 1978.
———. *Edmund Campion.* Boston: Little, Brown, 1946.
———. *A Handful of Dust.* Boston: Little, Brown, 1988.
———. *Vile Bodies.* New York: Dell, 1958.
White, Jon Manchip. *Cortés and the Downfall of the Aztec Empire.* New York: Caroll and Graf, 1971.
Whitman, Walt. *The Poetry and Prose of Walt Whitman.* Ed. Louis Untermeyer. New York: Simon and Schuster, 1949.
Williams, A. M., ed. *Conversations at Little Gidding: "On the Retirement of Charles V" and "On the Austere Life."* Cambridge: Cambridge University Press, 1970.
Williams, Glyndwr. *The Great South Sea: English Voyages and Encounters, 1570–1750.* New Haven: Yale University Press, 1997.
Williams, Jerry M., and Robert E. Lewis, eds. *Early Images of the Americas: Transfer and Invention.* Tucson: University of Arizona Press, 1993.
Wing, Donald Goddard. *A Short-Title Catalogue of Books Printed in England, Scotland, Ireland, Wales, and British America, and of English Books Printed in Other Countries, 1641–1700.* New York: Index Society, 1945–1951.
Wiseman, Susan J. *Drama and Politics in the English Civil War.* Cambridge: Cambridge University Press, 1998.
———. "Opera and Colonialism in the 1650s." In *Literature and the English Civil War,* ed. Thomas Healey and Jonathan Sawday. Cambridge: Cambridge University Press, 1990.
Wittgenstein, Ludwig. *Philosophical Investigations.* Ed. and trans. G. E. M. Anscombe. New York: Macmillan, 1953.
Wood, Sarah. *Robert Browning: A Literary Life.* London: Palgrave, 2001.
Wormell, Deborah. *Sir John Robert Seeley and the Uses of History.* Cambridge: Cambridge University Press, 1980.
Wright, Louis B. *Religion and Empire: The Alliance between Piety and Commerce in English Expansion, 1558–1625.* Chapel Hill: University of North Carolina Press, 1943.
Wurgaft, Lewis. *The Imperial Imagination: Magic and Myth in Kipling's India.* Middletown, Conn.: Wesleyan University Press, 1983.
Yates, Frances. *Giordano Bruno and the Hermetic Tradition.* Chicago: University of Chicago Press, 1964.
Young, Philip. "The Mother of Us All: Pocahontas Reconsidered." *Kenyon Review* 24 (1962): 391–415.

Index

Abolition, 196–97, 201; and Johnson, 132, 168, 170, 172; and Burke, 173, 174; and Austen, 185; and Wilberforce, 196–97
Abolition Act of 1807, 196
Abraham, biblical patriarch, 120, 121
Abrahamic model: for Jamestown, 120–21
Acapulco, 60
Achebe, Chinua, 220
Achilles, 41
Acosta, José de, 64, 70–71
Adam, 80, 111, 158, 165, 212. *See also* Milton, John: *Paradise Lost*
Adams, Henry, 222n50
Aden, 227
Ad fontes, 11, 140
Aeneas. *See* Virgil
Afghanistan, 204
Africa, 116, 119, 144, 173, 219–22, 246
Africans: imported to Virginia, 115; and tobacco, 130, 131; evangelization of, 135; compared to Europeans by Conrad, 220. *See also* "Blackamoors"; *Cimarrones*; Moors; Negroes
Aix-la-Chapelle, Peace of, 170–71
Akbar, Mogul emperor, 11, 223–24
Albanact, son of Brutus, 20
Albert, prince consort, 204, 205, 209
Albion: original name of Britain, 15; legendary conquest of, 32; compared to Virginia and Bermuda, 32; mentioned, 41, 124, 125, 137, 178, 179, 183
Alcestis, 31
Alexander VI, pope, 27
Alexander the Great, 87, 100, 108, 140, 171
Algonkians, 123, 129, 136

Allen, Michael J. B., 78, 91
Alterity, 241
Amazons, 40, 42, 43
America. *See* United States of America
American Indians. *See* Indians, American; Native Americans
American Revolution, 104n71, 125n28, 132, 149, 168, 172
Amritsar Massacre, 243
Andrewes, Lancelot, 26
Angles, 122. *See also* Anglo-Saxons
Anglicanism, 8, 112, 174, 223, 231, 239, 242. *See also* Church of England
Anglo, Sydney, 22, 23
Anglo-American colonists, 172
Anglo-Boer War, 215
Anglo-Indians, 195, 224
Anglo-Irish, 164, 174
Anglo-Normans, 19n18
Anglo-Saxons, 203
Anglo-Welsh, 239
Anne of Denmark, wife of James I, 117, 119
Anselment, Raymond A., 152n20
Anti-Catholicism, 3, 6, 7, 11, 16n14, 18, 20, 22, 23, 24, 25, 31, 57, 76, 122, 137, 143–44, 169, 170, 172, 174, 182
Antichrist: pope as, 7, 57, 76. *See also* Anti-Catholicism
Antigua, 186, 187, 189
Anti-heroism, 219
Antihispanicism, 7, 54–76 *passim*, 92, 144, 154, 158, 167. *See also* Black Legend of Spain
Anti-imperialism: Protestant, 2, 7, 142–44; Augustinian, 7, 140–41, 144, 160, 214,

268 Index

232; of Swift, 104–5, 162–66, 188; Roman Republican, 139; and More, 141–43, 188; Catholic, 142–43; Christian humanist, 144, 146, 160, 178, 179, 203, 243; at Little Gidding, 159; and Milton, 160, 161; of Johnson, 167–73, 188; and Austen, 185–90; Victorian, 198; and Browning, 198–202; and Tennyson, 203; and Tory Party, 204; and Forster, 214; and Conrad, 220; and literary Modernism, 230–31; secular, 239–40; and Lewis, 243–45
Anti-miscegenation laws, 130–31, 134, 135
Antipapalism, 26. *See also* Anti-Catholicism
Antipopery. *See* Anti-Catholicism; Antipapalism
Anti-Protestantism, 138, 231, 239
Anti-Romanism. *See* Anti-Catholicism
Apartheid, 243
Apostolic model: for Jamestown, 120, 121, 129
Arabia, 68
Arawaks, 123
Arendt, Hannah, 75
Ariel: claim to Prospero's island, 93–94n41, 94. *See also* Shakespeare, William: *The Tempest*
Aristophanes, 31n39
Arkansas, 84
Armada, Spanish, 33, 38, 39, 56, 87
Armitage, David, 2, 5
Arnold, Matthew, 211
Artaxerxes, king of Persia, 100
Arthur, king of Britain, 11, 12–23, 25, 26, 27, 31, 32–40, 44, 48, 52, 88, 92, 97, 143. *See also* Geoffrey of Monmouth: *History of the Kings of Britain;* Malory, Sir Thomas: *Le Morte Darthur; Misfortunes of Arthur, The;* Spenser, Edmund: *The Faerie Queene;* Tennyson, Alfred Lord: *Idylls of the King*
Arthurianism, 3, 77, 204, 238, 239, 245
Arthur Tudor, prince of Wales, 22, 57
Ascham, Roger, 13, 14, 16, 22, 23, 25, 43
Asia, 148, 151, 223
Atheism, 215, 226–27, 241
Augustan Age, English, 6, 162
Augustine of Hippo, Bishop, 139, 142, 143, 144, 147, 150, 171, 189, 190; influence on Protestant reformers, 13, 19; anti-imperialism of, 140–41; compared with More, Daniel, Ferrar, Milton, Swift, Johnson, and Blake, 178–79. *See also* Augustinianism

Augustinianism, 7, 8, 161, 180, 185, 189, 205, 214, 232, 235, 243
Augustus Caesar, 12, 46, 47, 48, 100, 101
Austen, Jane: attitude toward slavery, 185; influence of Johnson on, 185, 189; anti-colonialism of, in *Mansfield Park*, 185–90; and religion, 188; influence on Forster, 215; mentioned, 8, 138
Authorizing humility, myth of, 191, 210, 218, 219
Avalon, Isle of, 16
Aztecs, 60, 70, 71, 72, 84, 241

Babel, Tower of, 146, 244–45
Babylon, 59, 140
Bacon, Sir Francis, 33
Baker, David J., 3
Bale, John, bishop, 26, 31, 32, 40
Baltic Sea, 246
Baltimore, Lord. *See* Calvert, Cecilius
Baptist evangelism, in Bengal, 195
Barbados, 132, 135
Barnabas, companion of Apostle Paul, 85
Barnaby, Andrew, 64, 73
Barton, Anne, 4, 93–94n41
Bascom, Tim, 110n90
Bass, Jeff D., 174
Baxter, Richard, 100
Beaconsfield, Lord. *See* Disraeli, Benjamin
Beastliness, human, 163–66, 207, 221–22, 236
Beaty, Frederick L., 235, 238
Bede, 31
Behn, Aphra: *Oroonoko,* 8, 133–34
Belgian Congo, 220, 242
Belinus, legendary king of Britain, 15–16, 17
Benedictines, 60
Bengal, 195
Bentinck, Lord William, governor general of India, 195–96, 197
Bercovitch, Sacvan, 152
Bermuda, 32, 68, 78, 95
Bethlehem, 46, 215, 236
Bhabha, Homi, 9, 11
Bible: Hebrew king books, 27–28; 1 Peter, 81; Acts, 85, 211; Philippians, 111; Genesis, 116n4, 120, 121; Luke, 121; Exodus, 130n40; Galatians, 130; John, 189; Revelation, 140; and bard, 179; Bengali, of William Carey, 195; invoked by Byron and Shelley, 197; Hebrews, 209; mentioned, 184

Biblicism: colonial, 8; late Tudor, 19; Protestant, 31; of Miles Philips, 59; and Hakluyt's narratives, 59–60; and founding of Jamestown, 119–24. *See also* Bible

Birth control, 233

"Blackamoors," 134; Elizabethan suspicion of, 114; sometimes distinguished from Arab Moors, 116*n*6; expelled from Elizabethan England, 116–17. *See also* Africans; *Cimarrones;* Moors; Negroes

Black and Tans, 243

"Black beauty," 114, 117–19

Blackburn, Robin, 131–32

"Black legend," of Britain, 8

Black Legend of Spain, 7, 77, 82, 107, 114, 144; and British Protestant imagination, 54–76; as propaganda for England, 57

Blair, Eric. *See* Orwell, George

Blake, William, 8, 73, 138, 197; misunderstood as simple compared with Herbert, 177–78; anti-imperialism of, 177–85, 229; as radical dissenter, as Poetic Genius, as "most perfect Protestant," 178; more bard than prophet, biblicism of, anti-orthodoxy of, 178; "alienism" of, 178; social obscurity of, 178–79; and Christian humanism, 178, 179; and heresy, 178, 179, 180, 184–85; compared with Swift, 179; compared with Johnson, 179, 184, 185; "The Divine Image," 179–80, 182, 184–85; "Little Black Boy," 180–82, 184–85, 229; "The Lamb," 184; *Songs of Innocence* and *Songs of Experience*, 179–85; "A Little Boy Lost" and anti-Catholicism, 182–83; "The Little Vagabond," 183; "London," 184; "The Tyger," 184; excuses French imperialism, 184; compared to Tennyson, 203

"Bloody Mary" 57, 83. *See also* Mary I

Blue Lick, Kentucky, 104*n*71

Boer War. *See* Anglo-Boer War

Bonaparte, Napoleon. *See* Napoleon Bonaparte

Book of Common Prayer, The, 100

Boone, Daniel, 104*n*71

Boston, Massachusetts, 81, 119, 152

Boswell, James, 167*n*47, 168*n*48

Bosworth Field, 47

Bourne, Nicholas, 79*n*3, 100*n*58; *Sir Francis Drake Revived* (1653), 97, 105

Brantlinger, Patrick, 6, 169*n*51; *Rule of Darkness,* 174*n*64, 194, 203

Brazil, 84, 94, 123, 235

Brennius, legendary king of Britain, 15–16

Brent, Giles, 127–28

Brent, Margaret, 127*n*34

Brent, Mary. *See* Kitomagund

Bright, John, 222*n*50

"Bright Young Things," 232

Britain: named for Brutus, 15; revival of name and unifying myth of, 77; sense of relative righteousness, 137; ancient savagery of, 175; Victorian, 208; as savage in Conrad's *Heart of Darkness,* 220–21; post–World War II, 244

British: identity, 7, 124; as degenerate race, 122

British Empire: sixteenth-century origins of, 5, 11, 169; end of, 8, 138, 204, 205, 208–9, 231, 232, 240–42; myth of ancient, 11; Dee's coinage of term, 19–20; first and second, 202, 210; and competition from Russia and America, 203; and competition from Germany, 216; and religious unbelief, 241

British Guyana, 235

British Protestant imagination: and Black Legend of Spain, 54–76

Britomart, 36, 42. *See also* Spenser, Edmund: *The Faerie Queene*

Britons: as chosen nation, 27–28, 122, 162, 240; compared with Virginia "savages" by Hariot, 126; as New Trojans, 124; imperial disenchantment of, 242

Brontë, Charlotte, 195

Brooke, Sir James (the "White Rajah"), 108

Browning, Robert, 8, 197; *Pauline* and Christian liberalism, 198; influences on religion of, 198; self-exile in Italy, 198; "Why I Am a Liberal," 198–99; and anti-imperialism, 198–202; compared with Burke, Johnson, and Donne, 199; "Caliban upon Setebos," 199–202; satirizes natural theology, 200–202; rejection of Westminster Confession, 201; on Prospero and Miranda, 202

Bruce, Robert, 13*n*5

Brute. *See* Brutus

Bruto-Arthurian recovery myth, 114. *See also* Brutus

Brutus, legendary founder of Britain, 16, 17, 21, 23, 29, 32, 34, 36, 45, 48, 78, 124, 125, 128–29; namesake of Britain, 15; division of kingdom, 20. *See also* Geoffrey

of Monmouth: *History of the Kings of Britain;* Spenser, Edmund: *The Faerie Queene*
Brytish Empire, 55. *See also* British Empire
Buckingham. *See* Villiers, George
Buckland Abbey: Drake's estate, 88
Burghley. *See* Cecil, William, Lord Burghley
Burgundy, 141
Burke, Edmund, 8, 138, 193; admired by Johnson as Whig, 173; and chartered rights of man, 173–74; and home rule, Catholic Emancipation, and opposition to slavery, 173, 176; indictment of Hastings, 173, 195; and coherent trusteeship, 173–77; and Protestant conscience, 174; compared with Swift, 174; attacks British Protestant despotism, 174–75; and aftermath of Indian "mutiny," 176; compared with Hakluyt, 177; compared with Wilberforce, 196; compared with Browning, 199; and imperial trusteeship, 215
Burma, 230
Burton, Richard. *See* Crouch, Nathaniel
Burton, Robert, 163
Byrd, William, 8, 135–36
Byron, George Gordon, Lord, 197; "The Destruction of Sennacherib," 198*n16*

Cadwallader, legendary last king of Britain, 15, 20, 29
Caesar, Gaius Julius, 20, 100–101
Caesaro-papism, Catholic, 25–26
Caesars (emperors of Rome), 3, 77, 139, 189
Caliban: as idolatrous heathen, 92–93; compared to Miwok Indians, 93; as noble savage, 93, 94; as displaced colonial oppressor, 93–94*n41*. *See also* Browning, Robert: "Caliban upon Setebos"; Shakespeare, William: *The Tempest*
"Calibanism," 201–2, 206, 222
California, 7, 78, 80, 89, 94, 98, 102; Drake's landing in, 106*n75*, 108
Calvert, Cecilius, second lord Baltimore, 127–28
Calvin, John, 19, 119, 144; on Constantine and Gregory the Great, 24*n25*; *Institutes of the Christian Religion* and Augustine, 143
Calvinism, 212, 222; belief in universal, invisible church, 24; influence on late Tudor Protestants, 26; suppressed by Spain in Netherlands, 57; of John Rolfe, 119; Jacobean, attitudes toward slavery and bond-service, 130, 185; rejected by Browning, 201. *See also* Westminster Confession
Camber, son of Brutus, 20
Cambridge University, 13, 155
Camden, William, 41, 43, 44, 53
Camelot, 16, 206, 207; omitted from *The Faerie Queene,* 34. *See also* Malory, Sir Thomas: *Le Morte Darthur;* Tennyson, Alfred Lord: *Idylls of the King*
Camoëns, Luis de, 66–67, 78
Campbell, Joseph, 18
Campion, Edmund, 231
Canaan: as colonial metaphor, 129, 146
Canada, 6*n13*, 168, 171, 176, 209; dominion status of, 205
Cannibalism: in Defoe's *Robinson Crusoe,* 102–3; in Conrad's *Heart of Darkness,* 221; as farce in Waugh's *Black Mischief,* 234–35
Carey, William, 195
Caribbean, 27, 135, 185, 186, 187
Carlos I, king of Spain. *See* Charles V
Carolingian Empire, 141
Carthagena, 91, 108, 145
Cassibelaunus, king of Britain, 20
Castilians, 60
Castillo, Bernal Díaz del: *Historia Verdadera,* 71
Catholicism, 123, 174, 183, 239, 246; and imperial expansion, 4; Irish, 170, 173, 176; of Waugh, 192, 231; of imperial Belgium, 220
Cavendish, Thomas, 31
Cawley, Robert Ralston, 64*n12*
Cecil, Robert, Lord Salisbury, 204
Cecil, William, Lord Burghley, 31, 87
Cempoala, Mexico, 67, 70
Cervantes, Miguel de, 163
Cham. *See* Ham
Chancellor, Richard, 84, 105
Chapman, George, 144; *Eastward Hoe,* 147
Charlemagne, 18, 100, 141
Charles I, king of Great Britain, 32, 65, 95, 97; execution of, 100*n58*
Charles V, king of Spain and Holy Roman emperor, 141, 143, 144, 145, 147, 149, 151; forbids further American conquest and abolishes Indian slavery, 59; retirement and abdication of, 154, 156–59; compared with King Solomon, 157
Charleston, 81

Charter of rights, 174, 175. *See also* Natural law
Chiapas, Mexico, 55
China, People's Republic of, 246
Chrétien de Troyes, 16
Christendom, 141, 148, 151, 152n20, 153, 160, 245
Christian humanism. *See* Humanism: Christian
Christianity, 224; prepapal, 12; as problematic for empires, 138; and Darwinism, 201; superseded by science, 202–3; as Semitic-Aryan fusion, according to Seeley, 211; as "wild legend" in Forster's *Howard's End*, 217; failure of in Forster's *Passage to India*, 224, 230; post-imperial, 245
Christmas, 215, 236
Cholula, Mexico, 58
Churchill, John. *See* Marlborough, duke of
Churchill, Winston, 110, 240
Church of England: marriage rites of, 115; as scapegoat, 239–40; *Hymns Ancient and Modern*, 240n63
Cicero, Marcus Tullius, 139
Cimarrones, 61, 96, 99
Circe, 207
Circumcision, 121
Circumnavigation: by Drake, 81, 88, 90, 96. *See also* "Famous Voyage," of Drake
City: versus Court, 131; of London, 152. *See also* London
Civil War, English, 131, 160
Clapham Sect, 214
Clarke, Samuel: *Life and Death of the Valiant and Renowned Sir Francis Drake*, 98; popular "Lives" of the great, 100–101; succeeded by Crouch, 101; and authorizing humility, 102
Classicism, colonial, 8, 124–27. *See also* Virgil
Cleveland, John, 128n36
Clive, Robert, 174
Coleridge, Samuel Taylor, 178, 197
Collett, Mary, 154, 156–59
Collop, John: on "black beauty," 117
Color line, 7; Stuart origins of, 128–36. *See also* Racism
Columbian quincentennial, 55
Columbus, Christopher, 22, 57, 58, 67, 68, 149
Conan, legendary king of Brittany, 29
Congo, 219–22. *See also* Belgian Congo

Congo River, 220, 239
Congress of Vienna, 196
Conquistadors, 7, 82; and Milton's Satan, 64–74; worshiped as gods, 83, 85–86n25; as satanic, 222. *See also* Cortés, Hernando
Conrad, Joseph, 7, 8, 78, 85, 106, 111, 175, 218, 222, 233, 239, 244; as post-Protestant, 138, 192; compared to Kipling, Forster, and Waugh, 231
—*Heart of Darkness*, 1, 74, 82, 90; compared to Shakespeare's *Tempest*, 94–95; publication history of, 110n89; and Drake, 110–11; compared to Kipling's "The Man Who Would Be King," 110–11; and post-Protestant imperialism, 219–22; and Stanley and Livingstone, 220; and Walter Ralegh, 220; racism in, 220; and Darwinism, 221–22. *See also* Kurtz, Mr.
—*Lord Jim*, 220; and post-Protestant imperialism, 218–19
Constantine, Roman emperor: British origins of, 12, 15, 17, 24, 40, 42, 48, 52, 53, 124, 139
Constantius, father of Constantine, 40
Constitution, U.S., 132
Contemptus mundi tradition, 159
Conversion, religious, 135
Cook, James, 106–7, 111
Cordelia, legendary queen of Britain, 15, 20. *See also* Shakespeare, William
Cornwall, 20, 29
Cortés, Hernando, 85n22, 141; and Milton's Satan, 56, 64–74; in Cholula, 58; claim to consume gold, 68; worshiped, 84, 85. *See also* Conquistadors
Cosmopolitanism: of Dee and Hakluyt, 18, 19, 239; Protestant, 24
Cotton, Sir Robert, 147–48
Court: versus city, 131
Cowper, William, 107, 185
Cox, Richard, Bishop, 31–32
Coyoacan, Mexico, 69
Crashaw, Richard, 121
Crashaw, William, 121–22, 123, 126,128, 175
Cree Indians, 173
Crimean War, 8, 108, 193
Cromwell, Oliver, 7, 97, 98n52, 174, 245; and war with Spain, 65–66; compared to Milton's Satan, 67n19; and failed "imperial republic," 73; Western Design of, 66, 67n19, 160; Caribbean War of, 170. *See also* Western Design

272 Index

Cromwell, Richard, 98
Cromwellian regime, 73, 179
Cross, J. C.: *Sir Francis Drake and Iron-Arm*, 107–8
Crouch, Nathaniel: *The English Hero: or, Sir Francis Drake Reviv'd* (1687), 98, 101–2
Cultural materialism, 5, 95. *See also* Cultural poetics; New historicism
Cultural poetics, 4, 159. *See also* New historicism
Cvnobelinus, 46. *See also* Cymbeline
Cymbeline, legendary king of Britain, 15, 45–46. *See also* Shakespeare, William
Cyrus the Great, king of Persia, 100, 101

Da Gama, Vasco, 66–67, 78
Dagon, Philistine deity, 139
Dale, Sir Thomas, governor of Virginia, 115, 119, 120, 123, 125*n*26, 127
Dampier, William, 102
Daniel, Hebrew prophet, 59, 140
Daniel, Samuel, 8, 159; *Epistle to Prince Henry*, 138, 147–52; heroism redefined by, 150; compared to Blake, 178–79
Dare, Virginia: and Pocahontas, 125*n*28
Darien disaster: satirized by Swift, 162–63
Darwin, Charles, 201, 207. *See also* Darwinism
Darwinism, 8, 110; and Conrad, 192, 220, 221–22; and Forster, 192, 223, 224; and Christianity, 201–2, 207; and Tennyson, 203, 207
Davenant, William, 107–8; *The Cruelty of the Spaniards in Peru*, 66, 98*n*52; *History of Sir Francis Drake*, 97–100
David, king of Israel, 160, 222; compared to Geoffrey of Monmouth's Arthur, 28; typological reading of, 31; Drake as compared to, 83, 87, 96; and Jamestown, 120, 129
Davies, Sir John, 123–24, 128
Davis, R. M., 232
DeBry, Theodore, 116, 126
Dee, Arthur, son of John Dee, 30
Dee, John, 7, 11, 12, 17, 19, 20, 23, 24, 25, 30, 36, 40, 53, 55, 125*n*28, 148, 231; as coiner of term *British Empire*, 13–14; as Protestant, 13–14, 30–31; as Merlin, 13–14, 18, 30–31; *Private Diary*, 14*n*8; *General and Rare Memorials*, 14, 27; cosmopolitanism of, 18, 239; and Erastianism, 26; and Protestant humanism, 30–31; and imperial recovery, 210

Defoe, Daniel: *Robinson Crusoe*, 7, 82, 102–4, 105; on claiming California for England, 102*n*66
Denmark, 16
Dennis, John, 134
Deptford, 87
De Soto, Hernando: worshiped, 84, 85
Despotism: British Protestant, attacked by Burke, 174–75; with barbarians, legitimated by Mill, 193; liberal, in India, 196; Browning on, 199
Destiny, imperial: British myth of, 3, 6; British sense of, 77; denied by Johnson, 169, 170
Devil. *See* Milton, John: *Paradise Lost*; Satan
Devonshire, 60
Diana, goddess of the moon, 15, 16
Dibble, Sheldon, 107
Dickens, Charles, 235, 237–39 *passim*
Diocletian, 170
Disraeli, Benjamin, 174, 204
Dissent, radical religious: and Blake, 178, 179, 180, 184–85
Dissolution of the monasteries, 32
Dominicans, 58, 60
Doña Marina, Cortés's translator and concubine, 71
Donne, John, 78; "Sermon to the Virginia Company," 155–56*n*28; and Protestant conscience, 174; Browning compared with, 199
Doubt, religious: and Tennyson, 204, 206, 207; of later Victorians, 219
Doughty, Thomas, 81, 86*n*27, 96, 107
Dover, 80
Drake, Sir Francis: "white legend" of, 7, 78–82, 109–10, 114; circumnavigation of, 27, 81, 107; and Arthur, 27, 92, 97; pious restraint of, 36, 85–86*n*25, 98, 109; alliance with Cimarrones, 61, 98; impact on English literature, 78, 82; refuses godhead, 79–80, 84–85, 92, 105, 106; execution of Doughty, 81; and Foxe's *Actes and Monuments*, 83*n*16; as David, 83, 86, 87, 96; early accounts of, 83, 86–91; in West Indies, 83, 90–91, 107; and Protestantism, 84, 85, 86, 92; and other travelers' tales, 85*n*22; compared to Paul and Barnabas, 85; compared to conquistadors and to Hawkins and Grenville, 85–86*n*25; and Elizabeth I, 87–88, 90, 90–91; and Spenser's *Faerie Queene*, 88–90; death of, 91; compared to

Moses, 91; as *El Draque*, 91n37; legends about, 91, 102, 108; antihispanicism of, 92; reputation of, 92, 95–102, 107–8; and Shakespeare's *Tempest*, 92–95; as Adam, 96, 111; compared with Defoe's Crusoe, 103–4; recast by Johnson, 105; compared with Swift's Gulliver, 105; and late Augustan sensibility, 105; and Conrad's *Heart of Darkness*, 110, 220; parody of Christ's *kenosis*, 111; authorizing humility, myth of, 137, 218; mentioned, 1, 14, 31, 56, 60, 106, 145, 221, 241. *See also* Cross, J. C.: *Sir Francis Drake and Iron-Arm;* Davenant, William: *History of Sir Francis Drake;* Johnson, Samuel: *Life of Sir Francis Drake*

Drake, Sir Francis, Bart.: Drake's nephew, 79n3; *The World Encompassed by Sir Francis Drake*, 96–98, 105

Drake's Bay, 78–79

Drayton, Michael: "Ode. To the Virginian Voyage," 68; *Poly-Olbion*, 124; classicism of, and intermarriage, 126–27; mentioned, 128

Druids, 26

Dryden, John, 134

Dublin, 56, 124

Duckworth, Alistair, 215nn39,40

Dufferin, Lord, Frederick Temple Hamilton-Temple-Blackwood, governor-general of Canada, 209

Dutton, Sir Richard, 132

Duvian: sent by Pope Eleutherius, 24n25

Eastern Europe: Dee's travel to, 31
East India Bill of 1783, 175, 176
East India Company, 173, 174–77, 195
East Indies, 81, 147
Eaves, Morris, 184
Ector, Sir, 16
Eden, Garden of: as colonial metaphor, 62, 80, 111, 146, 149, 151, 154, 156–58, 159, 160, 237; compared to Mexico in Milton's *Paradise Lost*, 64–74 *passim;* Nova Albion as, 92; feminized in Forster's *Howards End*, 217; replaced by wilderness in Conrad's *Heart of Darkness*, 221. *See also* Milton, John: *Paradise Lost*

Edward, Black Prince of Wales, 100
Edward I, king of England, 13n5, 19n18
Edward VI, king of England, 83n16, 143
Edwardian era, 213–14
Egypt, 59

Eichmann, Adolph, 75
El Dorado: myth of, 1, 7; Ralegh's quest for, 61, 62; parodied in Conrad's *Heart of Darkness*, 220; mentioned, 147. *See also* Guiana; Ralegh, Sir Walter

Election, divine, 202. *See also* Calvin; Calvinism; Westminster Confession

Eleutherius, pope, 24n25

Elijah, 29, 30, 31

Eliot, T. S.: "Little Gidding," 154–55; on Tennyson, 203; on Conrad, 220; mentioned, 177, 178, 179

Elizabeth I, queen of England: Welsh blood of, 12; tutored by Ascham, 13; and imperial prophecy, 17–18; and Dee's "crystal," 18; and *The Misfortunes of Arthur*, 33–34; in Spenser's *Faerie Queene*, 36, 38, 39, 90; Spanish threats to, 56; excommunicated, 56; imprisons Ralegh for secret marriage, 63; as virgin liberator of Guiana, 63; knights Drake, 87; death of, 92, 231; superstitions mocked by Waugh, 231; martyred Edmund Campion, 231; mentioned, 6n13, 11, 19, 27, 31, 32, 57, 65, 80, 82, 83, 86, 90, 96, 100, 101, 110, 144, 145

Elizabethan England: as postcolonial, 25
Elizabethan era, 11, 12, 169
Empire, of King Arthur, 239
"Empire," embarrassment of, for late Regency and early Victorians, 194–97
"Empire of Liberty": French, 178; of United States of America, 246
England, Little. *See* Little England
English remnant, myth of, 125n28
Erasmus, Desiderius: Las Casas compared to, 58; *De Libero Arbitrio* and anti-Protestantism, 143n13; and Christian humanism, 163; as ironist, 163; mentioned, 83n16, 143, 167n47

Erastianism: and Dee, 26
Esau, 116n4
Ethiopia, 232
Europe: as ruined by American gold, 148–49, 152–53, 157–58
Evangelicalism: and Austen's *Mansfield Park*, 185n81; and early Victorians, 192; revival of, 193, 194–97; alliance with utilitarianism, 193, 195; and abolition of slave trade and slavery, 196–97; and Forster, 214; mentioned, 8

Evangelism: by Drake at Nova Albion, 84–85; as motive for colonization, 86,

121–22, 136, 150, 153, 155, 158, 163; of slaves, 132, 135; imperialist opposition to, 132–33, 155, 195; failure of at Jamestown, 156, 159; in Bengal, 195; in Kipling's "Judgment of Dungara, 211–13
Evans, J. Martin, 66, 70, 73
Eve: women of Guiana compared with, 63; and Doña Marina, in Milton's *Paradise Lost*, 71; Pocahontas as, 127; curse of, 212; on Venus in Lewis's *Perelandra*, 244; mentioned, 165. *See also* Milton, John: *Paradise Lost*
Evolution, 201, 207. *See also* Darwinism
Exceptionalism, moral: British Protestant, 3, 6, 7, 226; defined, 77–78; Elizabethan, 144; of Ralegh, 154; rejected at Little Gidding, 158; mocked by Johnson, 169, 170; of Johnson's Prince Rasselas, 171; and Blake, 182, 184; attacked by Conrad, 230; Christian, 245n8
Expansionism, imperial: decline of, 193; revival of, 197, 210–11; late Victorian, and Tennyson, 203; menaced by Conrad's *Heart of Darkness*, 222; mentioned, 199. *See also* Imperialism

Fagan: sent by Pope Eleutherius, 24n25
Falkland Islands, 168
"Famous Voyage," of Drake, 82, 87. *See also* Circumnavigation: by Drake
Faustus. *See* Marlowe, Christopher: *Doctor Faustus*
Ferrar, Nicholas, 129, 138, 153; anti-imperialism of, 154–60, 190; career before Little Gidding, 155–56; compared to Blake, 179
Ferrar, Nicholas, Sr., 155
Ferrex, son of Gorbodog, 20
Final Solution, 166
Firth, C. H., 164
Fitzgeffrey, Reverend Charles, 91, 102
Flanders, 16
Fletcher, Francis, Drake's chaplain, 79, 80, 86n27, 88; journals from circumnavigation, 90, 96
Florida, 61
Forster, E. M., 8; as post-Protestant, 138, 192, 214, 230, 231; *Aspects of the Novel*, 215n41
—*Howards End*, 213–18, 228; and Augustinian anti-imperialism, 214; compared to Jane Austen, 215; compared to Shakespearean romance, 217; compared to Kipling, Conrad, and Waugh, 231
—*A Passage to India*, 223–30, 241; Aziz compared to Johnson's native chieftain, 173; compared to Conrad's *Heart of Darkness*, 223; and separating power of landscape, 230
Foxe, John, 83, 183
France, 39, 57, 162, 175, 177; Johnson on, 170
Francis I, king of France, 143, 149
Franciscans, 60
Franklin, Benjamin, 119n16
Franklin, Sir John, 110
Free Trade: and Lord Palmerston, 194
French and Indian War, 172. *See also* "Great War for Empire"; Seven Years' War
French Empire, end of, 242
French Revolution, 178
French romance, 32
Freudianism, 220
Frobisher, Martin, 14
Fuller, Mary C., 62, 159
Fuller, Thomas, 97, 98, 100
Fundamentalism, religious, 242

Gandhi, Mohandas, 242
Ganges River, 223
Gaul, 16, 29. *See also* France
Geller, Lila, 45, 46
"General Bobs." *See* Roberts, Frederick Sleigh
Geneva, 26
Genocide: and Spenser in Ireland, 41
Gentlemen's Magazine, 167
Geoffrey of Monmouth, 14–17, 24n25, 33, 40, 44, 245; *History of the Kings of Britain*, 12, 14–17, 23, 27–28, 29, 38, 45–48, 124, 206; and *Historia regum Brittaniae*, 28n33; appropriated by Protestants, 31; and Heywood's *Life of Merlin*, 32; compared to Tennyson, Spenser, and Malory, 205
German, 16, 216, 217, 246
Ghana, 240n63
Gibbon, Edward, 232
Gibraltar, Straits of, 141
Gibson, Mary Ellis, 195
Gilbert, Sir Humphrey, 31
Gildon, Charles, 134–35
Gladstone, Mary, 207
Gladstone, William, 207, 214; as "Murderer of Gordon," 199; as friend of Tennyson, 204

Glastonbury Abbey, 11, 13, 20
Gleckner, Robert F., 184
Gless, Darryl, 38
Glorious Revolution, 98, 131
Gogmagog: defeated by Brutus, 128–29
Gold: American, 56–57, 61, 80, 147; colonial hunger for, 57, 68, 80, 147, 149, 152–54, 156–57, 169; Ralegh's search for, 61–64; and Milton's Eden, 68; and ivory in Conrad's *Heart of Darkness*, 221
Golden Hind, Drake's flagship, 1, 78, 87, 110
Golden Rule, 172, 182, 193
Goliath, 222; Spain as, 83, 87, 107
Gómara, Francisco López de, 64, 67, 69, 70, 85n22
Goneril, daughter of Lear, 20
Gonzalo, 5. *See also* Shakespeare, William: *The Tempest*
Gorbodog (Gorboduc), legendary king of Britain, 15, 20
Gordon, General Charles, 110, 199
Gorlois, 16. *See also Misfortunes of Arthur, The*
Gosson, Stephen: *School of Abuse*, 43
Gothic, Victorian: in Waugh's *Handful of Dust*, 235, 238
Grail Quest, 16, 23; omitted from *Faerie Queene*, 34; in Tennyson's *Idylls of the King*, 205–6
Gravesend, 129
Gray, Thomas, 162
Great Britain, 12, 52, 245n8, 246; and Little England, 168
"Greater Britain": proposed by Seeley, 203, 213–14
Great Taboo, 82; violated by Shakespeare's Prospero, 94; violated by Cook, 106–7; violated by Kipling's characters, 108–9; violated by Conrad's Kurtz, 222
Great Terror of 1794, French, 178
Great War. *See* World War I
"Great War for Empire": Samuel Johnson opposed to, 168. *See also* French and Indian War; Seven Years' War
Greece, 15, 197
Green, Martin, 6, 82n13, 169n51
Greenblatt, Stephen J., 3, 55, 93–94n41, 159, 164n41, 200; on Doña Marina, 71n24
Greene, Donald J., 6n13, 168nn47,48, 169–70, 172
Greenland, 14, 16
Greenwich Palace, 33

Gregerson, Linda, 162
Gregory the Great, pope, 24n25
Grenville, Sir Richard, 85–86n25, 145–46
Guaraní, 84, 94
Guatemala, 60
Guenevere. *See* Guinevere
Guiana, 123, 144, 147, 154, 156–57, 159; Ralegh in, 61–64
Guilpin, Edward, 128n36
Guinevere (Guenevere), wife of Arthur, 16, 17, 23, 37; omitted from Spenser's *Faerie Queen*, 34. *See also* Geoffrey of Monmouth: *History of the Kings of Britain*; Malory, Sir Thomas: *Le Morte Darthur*; Tennyson, Alfred Lord: *Idylls of the King*; Waugh, Evelyn: *A Handful of Dust*
Gulf of Mexico, 54
Gulliver: worship of Houyhnhnm master, 104–5; as Yahoo, 104–5, 165–66. *See also* Swift, Jonathan: *Gulliver's Travels*
Gunpowder Plot: and Merlin, 32

Haile Selassie, emperor of Ethiopia, 232
Hakluyt, Richard: *Principal Navigations*, 2, 14, 88, 92, 157; as antiquarian, 13–14; claims England's right to Arthur's empire, 14, 210; *Divers Voyages*, 14, 88; cosmopolitanism of, 18, 239; prefers Geoffrey of Monmouth over Malory, 23; Protestant bias in citing *History of the Kings of Britain*, 24; Welsh blood of, 30; and liberation of New Spain, 59–61; publishes Miles Philips, 59–61; publishes John Sparke, 74; publishes first account of Drake's circumnavigation, 87–88; employed by Walsingham, 88; and English textiles, 88n32; as literary imperialist, 90; early twentieth-century republication of, 110; and Protestant conscience, 174; compared with Burke, 177; and England's relative righteousness, redeeming mission, and authorizing humility, 210; mentioned, 7, 11, 12, 17, 19, 31, 40, 55, 56, 57, 79n3, 81, 82, 86, 96, 105, 144, 145, 146, 148
Hakluyt Society, 108
Halkin, Léon-E., 143n13
Hall, Kim F., 114–15, 117, 119, 128
Ham, son of Noah, 155
Hamor, Ralph, 115, 120
Hannibal, 100
Hariot, Thomas: *Newfound Land of Virginia*,

88; evokes Britain's savage past, 221; mentioned, 31, 126, 175
Haslop, Henry, 87*n*30
Hastings, Warren, 195; Burke's indictment of, 173, 174–75, 176
Havana, 91, 167
Hawaii, 106–7
Hawkins, Sir John: flouts Line of Tordesillas, 27; enslaves Sabies, destroys Sambula, 75; mentioned, 31, 85–86*n*25, 91
Hay, Denys, 41
Heidelberg, 213
Helena, mother of Constantine, 17, 40
Helgerson, Richard, 3, 55
Henrician Reformation, 32
Henry VII, 22, 29, 47
Henry VIII: and Katherine of Aragon, 16*n*14, 57; neglects Matter of Britain, 23; Supreme Head of English Church, 26, 37; and Polydore Vergil, 40; and More's *Utopia*, 143; mentioned, 32, 48
Henry of Navarre, 42
Henry Stuart, prince of Wales. *See* Stuart, Henry
Henry Tudor. *See* Henry VII
Herbert, Sir Edward, Lord Herbert of Cherbury, 117
Herbert, George: "The Church Militant," 138; and westward expansion, 152–53; cyclical vision of, 152*n*20; *The Temple* in Harvard College Library, 152*n*20; friend of Ferrar, 153, 155; *A Priest to the Temple*, 153*n*21; and Protestant conscience, 174; compared with Blake, 177–78; mentioned, 8, 128*n*36
Hercules, 44; as type of Christ, 31. *See also* Pillars of Hercules
Heroism: redefined by Daniel, 150; redefined by Milton, 160; and Conrad's *Heart of Darkness*, 218–19
Herod the Great, 100
Hesperides, 149
Heylyn, Peter, 64*n*12
Heywood, Thomas, 32
Himalayas, 223
Hinduism, 195–96, 224, 228, 242
Hindu Kush, 108, 109, 125
Hindus, 211, 228
Hispaniola, 58, 68
Hispanophobia. *See* Antihispanicism; Black Legend of Spain
Historicism, 3, 4. *See also* New historicism
Hobbes, Thomas, 41

Hobson, J. A., 110
Hoel, king of Brittany, 17
Holinshed, Raphael, 32, 33*n*44, 45–46
Holy War: against Native Americans, 129, 208
Homer, 91
Home rule: American, 173; Irish, 176; Indian, 176
House of Commons, 29, 167, 176
House of Lords, 131, 176
Houyhnhnmland: and Drake's Nova Albion, 104–5; compared to Prospero's island, 166. *See also* Swift, Jonathan: *Gulliver's Travels*
Hovey, Kenneth Alan, 152*n*20
Hudibras, legendary king of Britain, 15
Hughes, Thomas, 33
Hulme, Peter, 116*n*4, 125*n*26, 133
Humanism, 140–41; protestant, 22, 23; anti-imperialism of, 157, 185, 188, 189; failure of to oppose empire, according to Said, 188, 192; secular, satirized by Waugh, 232, 235; progressive, 238; and alternate worlds, 244
—Christian: anti-imperialism of, 8, 138, 141, 144, 146, 147–52, 192, 203, 205–7; and Behn, 133–34; and More, 133–34, 163; and Swift, 133–34, 163; and Johnson, 133–34, 173; and Daniel, 147–52; of Milton's Jesus, 161; and Erasmus, 163; and Rabelais, 163; and Montaigne, 163; and Cervantes, 163; and Burton, 163; failure of against colonialism, 194; and Tennyson, 203, 205–7; mentioned, 11, 167*n*47, 178, 179, 180, 186, 193
Hunter, J. Paul, 103*n*67
Hussein, Saddam, 246
Hussites, 168
Huxley, Thomas, 201
Hythloday, Raphael, 141–42, 143, 147, 189, 240. *See also* More, Sir Thomas: *Utopia*

Iceland, 16
Imperialism: Iberian, 2, 85; secular, 8, 210–11, 232, 239–40; Spanish, and origins of British Empire, 55–57; Augustine on, 140; More's Raphael on, 141–42, 189–90; Daniel on, 148–49, 150, 190; Johnson on, 170–71, 186; French, excused by Blake, 184; in Austen's *Mansfield Park*, 186–89; Christian, 208; liberal, 215; Anglican, 235, 239; post-Christian, 245
—Post-Protestant: in Forster's *Howards End*,

213–18; in Conrad's *Lord Jim*, 218–19; in Conrad's *Heart of Darkness*, 219–22; in Forster's *Passage to India*, 223–30
—Protestant: as "reformed," 85; competition with Protestantism per se, 86; satirized by Waugh, 230–39; as hegemonic ideology, 241
Imperial recovery, 144, 239; British myth of, 114; and Reformation, 124; and early Tudors, 124; Elizabethan hopes of, 191; and Dee, 210; and Hakluyt, 210
Incas, 62, 64n12
Index Librorum Prohibitorum, 31
India: Mogul glories of, 11, 223; da Gama's sea route to, 67; "Mutiny" of 1857, 108, 176, 193; Burke and, 173, 174–77; ancient civilization of, 175; as Crown colony, 176; disintegration of British control in, 229; independence of, 242, 245; Anglicization and Christianization of, 242n1; mentioned, 6n13, 109, 138, 168, 171, 192, 195–96, 197, 204, 224, 226, 227, 230, 236, 246
Indians, American, 136; love of poetry, according to Sidney, 43–44; as equal with whites, 121–22, 126; Welsh-speaking, legends of, 125n28; removal of, 156. *See also* Native Americans
Indigenous Americans. *See* Indians, American; Native Americans
Infanta of Spain, 95
Innogen, wife of Brutus, 47
Inquisition, Spanish, 60, 84
Intermarriage: with Arawak of Guiana, proposed by Ralegh, 123, 124; with Irish, proposed by Davies, 124; of Kipling's Daniel Dravot, 125; never outlawed in England, 134; outlawed in English colonies, 135–36; by ancient Romans, 136; by French in America, 136, 170; advocated by Johnson, 168; and Waugh's Mr. Todd, 237. *See also* Miscegenation
Internationalism, Protestant, 31. *See also* Cosmopolitanism
Interregnum, 131, 160
Inys Brydain: Welsh name for Britain, 20
Iraq, 246
Ireland: as Irena in Spenser's *Faerie Queene*, 39; British Crown's claim to, denied by Johnson, 168; parliament of, 168n48; home rule of, opposed by Burke, 176; as part of "Britain," 176; Spenser's "wickedness" in,

according to Lewis, 243; mentioned, 16, 41, 42, 44, 124, 150, 162, 173, 174
Irish, 165, 170; Swift's Yahoos as, 164
Irish Home Rule Crisis of 1886, 215
Islam, 67, 224, 242
Israel, biblical, 146, 160–61, 239
Israel, State of, 246
Italy, 15, 128, 197, 246
Ivan the Terrible, Czar of Russia, 84

Jacobean era, 11, 52. *See also* Tudor-Stuart era
Jacobins, 176
Jacobites: Johnson and, 168
Jamaica: Cromwellian conquest of, 66, 98; slavery in, 132, 170
James I, king of Great Britain: consolidates Scots and English crowns, 21; claims descent from Arthur, 21, 52; as *rex futurus*, 29, 52; invokes Merlins, 29; renames kingdom "Great Britain," 29; attends Shakespeare's *Cymbeline*, 45; claims descent from Constantine, 52; "détente" with Spain, 65, 92; hostility to Puritanism, 92; execution of Ralegh, 92; welcomes Pocahontas, 115–16; dissolves Virginia Company, 156; hatred of tobacco, 156; mentioned, 95, 117, 118, 147, 152, 155
James VI, king of Scotland, 12. *See also* James I
James, Lawrence, 135
James, William, 110
James Peninsula, 130
James River, 130, 135
Jamestown: as "New Troy," 21, 53; and Protestant biblicism, 119–24; and Abrahamic model, 120; and Davidic model, 120; and apostolic model, 120; lack of English wives at, 127; Massacre at, 129, 155–56; criticized by Daniel, 149; failure of evangelism at, 155; mentioned, 95, 147, 152, 154
Jazz Age, 231, 232
Jefferson, Thomas, 119–20n16, 125n28
Jefferson family, 135
Jehovah: resemblance of Jupiter to in Shakespeare's *Cymbeline*, 46; rejected by Blake, 178; and Byron, 197; mentioned, 107, 121, 146, 228
Jenkins, Captain Robert, 167
Jerusalem: restored by Cyrus, 101
Jesuits. *See* Jesus, Society of

Jesus, Society of, 127, 231
Jesus Christ: birth of, and Shakespeare's *Cymbeline*, 12, 45–46; return of, 13; cited ironically by Las Casas, 58; "heathens" as enemies of, 120, 121; as Roman citizen, according to Orosius, 140*n5;* directs French Great Terror, according to Blake, 178; cited by Shelley, 198; Conrad's Jim compared with, 219; mentioned, 31, 111, 112, 122, 155–56*n28*, 189, 201, 202, 207, 216, 221, 240*n63. See also* Milton, John: *Paradise Regain'd*
Jesus of Lubeck: slave ship of Hawkins, 75
Jewkes, W. T., 78
Jews, 160, 161, 180, 198*n16*, 246; as chosen nation, 27–28
Jihad, 246
Jinnah, M. A.: and Muslim League, 242
Job, biblical, 29
Johnson, Samuel: dislike of Shakespeare's *Cymbeline*, 52; as Tory, 105, 168, 173, 185; *Life of Sir Francis Drake*, 105–6, 107; anti-imperialism of, 106, 167–73, 184–85, 188, 190, 214–15, 229; anti-slavery of, 132, 168, 170, 172; *Rasselas*, 134, 171–72; as satirist, 167; compared to More, 167, 168; compared to Swift, 167, 168; and Christian humanism, 167*n47*, 173; as arch-conservative, 168; opposed to "Great War for Empire," 168; *The Patriot*, 168; radicalism of, 168, 170; *Taxation No Tyranny*, 168; religion of, 169; on origins of British Empire, 169; on imperialism, 170–71, 186, 188; as Augustinian, 171, 185; and American Revolution, 172; *The Idler*, 172; and Native American patriotism, 172–73; admiration of Burke, 173; on end of empire, 173; compared with Blake, 179; influence on Austen, 185; contrasted to Mill, 193; compared with Browning, 199; compared with Tennyson, 203; compared with Lewis, 243, 244; mentioned, 6*n13*, 8, 138, 240, 241
John the Baptist, 203; Dee as, 30
John the Divine: Revelation to, 140
Jones, Emrys, 46, 52
Jonson, Ben: *Masque of Blackness*, 8, 117–19; *Masque of Beauty*, 118–19; on religion and empire, 137, 138–39; *Eastward Hoe*, 147
Jordan, Kingdom of, 246
Jordan, Winthrop D., 114–15, 116*n6*
Joseph, biblical patriarch, 59, 217
Joseph of Arimathea, 20
Joshua, biblical conqueror, 129
Jove, 45, 139, 144
Judaism: problematic for empires, 138
Julius Caesar. *See* Caesar, Gaius Julius

Kalm, Peter, 132–33
Kashmir, 246
Katherine of Aragon, 16*n14*, 57
Kaul, Suvir, 5–6
Kealakekua Bay, Hawaii, 106–7
Keats, John, 197
Kelly, Ann Cline, 164
Kenosis: Drake's parody of Christ's, 111
Kentucky, 172
Kenyatta, Jomo, 173
King, Henry, 128*n36*
King, John N., 38, 83*n16*
Kipling, Rudyard: "The Man Who Would Be King," 2, 82, 108–10, 111, 125, 220, 222; compared to Conrad, 110–11, 230–31; "The Judgment of Dungara," 211–13; on religion as source of colonial trouble, 230–31; compared to Forster and Waugh, 230–31; as post-Christian, 231; and tragic grandeur of empire, 231; mentioned, 7, 8, 78, 106
Kitchener, Horatio Herbert, Earl Kitchener of Khartoum, 6, 110
Kitomagund, Pascataway princess, 127–28
Knapp, Jeffrey, 3, 55
Knoppers, Laura Lunger, 73
Kurtz, Mr., 2, 90; compared to Shakespeare's Prospero, 94–95; and Drake's imperial legend, 111; impersonates a god, 111, 222; Marlow's search for, 220; mentioned, 233, 244. *See also* Conrad, Joseph: *Heart of Darkness*

Labor Party, 215, 245
Lake Poets, 197
Lancelot, 16, 23; omitted from *Faerie Queene*, 34. *See also* Malory, Sir Thomas: *Le Morte Darthur;* Tennyson, Alfred Lord: *Idylls of the King*
Landscape, eroticization of, 63, 70
Lapland, 16
Las Casas, Bartolomé de, 7, 56, 58, 64, 65–66, 70, 74*n27*, 75, 83, 85*n22*, 164; and Spain's "Black Legend," 55, 57; *Brevissima relación* and translations, 59, 83*n15*, 98*n52;* imperialism of, 144–45

Laski, Albert, 31
Lavinia. *See* Virgil
Lawrence, Judiana, 45, 52
Laws of Hywel Dda, 30
Lear, Edward, 237n62
Lear, legendary king of Britain, 15, 20. *See also* Shakespeare, William
Lebanon, 246
Lee family, 135
Leggatt, Alexander, 46
Leland, John, 26, 32, 40
Le Morte Darthur, 13, 22. *See also* Malory, Sir Thomas
Le Testu, Huguenot pirate, 61
Levi, Peter, 204
Lewis, C. S. (Clive Staples), 8, 146, 185; *The Four Loves,* 243; influences upon, and anti-imperialism of, 243–45; *A Preface to Paradise Lost,* 244; Protestant imagination in "Ransom Trilogy," 244–45; and Arthurian matter, 244–45
Lewis, Meriwether, 125n28
Leyenda blanca, 114
Leyenda negra, 56, 72, 78, 93, 114, 158, 172, 183. *See also* Black Legend of Spain
Liberalism: in India, 196; and Tennyson, 204, 205; of Forster's Schlegels, 217; as satirized by Waugh, 233
Liberal Party, 194, 199, 214, 215
Liberation movements, colonial: predicted by Johnson, 168, 172–73
Libertarianism, 192
Libyans, 136
Lichtheim, George, 174n64
Lilliput: Johnson refers to, 167
Linton, Joan Pong, 3
Lisbon, 183
Literary Magazine, 169, 170, 171
Little England, 168, 210, 213, 214, 245; Howards End as, 217
Little Gidding community, 138; *Conversations* of 1631, 154–60; "Little Academy" of, 156
Livingstone, David, 110, 220, 243
Locke, John, 2, 133; *Fundamental Constitutions of Carolina,* 132, 135
Lockyer, Roger, 151n18
Locrine, son of Brutus, 20
Logres, 245
Lollards: and Merlin's prophecies, 31
London, 66, 91, 111, 129, 159, 232, 234; as new Rome, 3; as "New Troy," 15, 124;

visited by Pocahontas, 114; encroachment of, in Forster's *Howards End,* 216, 217–18
"Lost Colony," 125n28, 146. *See also* Roanoke Colony
Lost Tribes, myths of, 239
Louisbourg, Canada, 171
Louvain, 141
Lovelace, Richard, 128n36
Low Countries, 141. *See* Netherlands
Loyola, Saint Igatius of, 119–20n16
Lucifer, 222. *See also* Milton, John; Satan
Lucius, legendary king of Britain, 24n25
Lucius, Roman procurator of Burgundy, 17
Lud, legendary king of Britain, 15
Lulbegrud River, Kentucky, 104n71
Luther, Martin, 57, 143
Lutheranism, 24
Lyonesse, 207

Machiavelli, Niccolò, 41, 196
Madoc, legendary Welsh prince, 14n8, 125n28
Magellan, Ferdinand, 84, 85, 94
Magellan, Straits of, 81, 85n22, 96
Magna Carta, 175
Majorca, 60
Maley, Willy, 89, 162
Malinali, 71
Malinche, La, 71
Malintze, 71
Malory, Sir Thomas, 16, 18, 206, 238, 245; *Le Morte Darthur,* 12, 22; and Geoffrey of Monmouth, 23, 205; and Tennyson's *Idylls* and Spenser's *Faerie Queene,* 205, 208
Maltby, William S., 65, 83
Marin County, 80–82, 85, 91, 111
Marlborough, duke of, John Churchill, 162
Marlow, 1, 218. *See also* Conrad, Joseph: *Heart of Darkness;* Conrad, Joseph: *Lord Jim*
Marlowe, Christopher, 101; *Doctor Faustus,* 1, 30
Maro, Publius Vergilius. *See* Virgil
Maroons. *See* Cimarrones
Marshall family, 135
Marston, John: *Eastward Hoe,* 147
Martyn, Henry, 195
Marvell, Andrew: "Bermudas," 68, 78
Marxism, 189. *See also* Cultural materialism
Mary, Blessed Virgin, 33, 38
Mary I, queen of England, 42, 57, 143; and

Merlin, 32; as Adicia in Spenser's *Faerie Queene*, 38, 39
Maryland, 127–28, 131
Mary Stuart, Queen of Scots, 42, 92
Mary Tudor. *See* Mary I
Massachusetts, 119, 160, 176
Matoaka, 115. *See* Pocahontas
"Matter of Britain," 7, 12, 17–20; and Reformation England, 11, 13, 23, 24, 25–27, 31; compared to other foundation myths, 21. *See also* Arthur; Arthurianism; Bruto-Arthurian recovery myth; Brutus; Geoffrey of Monmouth
Mauritania, 116
Mayans, 60
McColley, Diane Kelsey, 64, 73
McGuire, Ian, 203–4, 206, 209
Melchizedek, 31
Melville, Herman: *White Jacket*, 245
Merlin, 12, 18, 15, 16, 18, 20, 36, 40; as Elijah, 30; and Dee, 30; and Protestantism, 31–32. *See also* Geoffrey of Monmouth; Lewis, C. S.: Protestant imagination in "Ransom Trilogy"; Malory, Sir Thomas; Spenser, Edmund: *The Faerie Queene*; Tennyson, Alfred Lord: *Idylls of the King*
Mexico, 55, 58–60, 123, 149, 169, 246, 156; and Milton's Eden, 64–74 *passim*; conquest of, 141
Meyers, Debra, 128n35
Milford Haven, 29, 47
Mill, John Stuart, 192, 193
Millenarianism: of Blake, 197
Miller, Perry, 119n16
Milton, John, 5, 8; *Paradise Lost*, 7, 56, 64–74, 75, 165, 177, 194, 244; *Paradise Regain'd*, 36, 66, 73, 138, 160–62; Satan compared to Cortés, 56, 64–74; and anti-imperialism, 64–65, 66, 73–74, 160–62, 190, 243–44; and *Purchas His Pilgrimes* and *Brief History of Moscovia*, 64n12; and anti-hispanicism, 64–65; *Latin Manifesto*, 65; compared to Cromwell, 67n19; *The Readie and Easie Way to Establish a Free Commonwealth* and *The Second Defense of the English People*, 73; *Samson Agonistes*, 73; *Eikonoklastes*, 162; *History of Britain*, 162, 194; and Protestant conscience, 174; compared to Blake, 179; *Comus*, 244
Minotaur, 125n26
Mirrour for Magistrates, 32
Miscegenation, 8; of Pocahontas and John Rolfe, 115; and religious syncretism, 120–21; forbidden in Virginia, 130–31. *See also* Intermarriage
Misfortunes of Arthur, The, 33–34
Mississippi River, 84
Missouri River, 125n28
Miwok Indians, 85, 88n32, 89, 97, 106; and Drake, 79–82, 241; compared to Spenser's satyrs, 90
Mixed marriage. *See* Intermarriage; Miscegenation
Modernism, colonial: in Waugh, 233
Modernism, literary, 230–31
Modernity, secular, 242
Moffit, Robin, 45
Mogul Empire, 11, 223, 224
Moloch, 243
Moluccas, 80
Monasteries, dissolution of, 13
Montaigne, Michel de, 163, 201, 245n8
Monterey, California, 81
Montezuma, Aztec emperor, 64, 67, 68, 70–71, 84
Montrose, Louis, 62, 159
Moors, 64, 74, 116, 134–36
Moravian Brethren, 8, 168, 245, 246
Mordred (Modred), Arthur's son and nephew, 16, 17, 37; omitted from Spenser's *Faerie Queen*, 34. *See also* Geoffrey of Monmouth; Lewis, C. S.: Protestant imagination in "Ransom Trilogy"; Malory, Sir Thomas: *Le Morte Darthur*; *Misfortunes of Arthur, The*; Tennyson, Alfred Lord: *Idylls of the King*
More, Sir Thomas, 8, 146, 167n47, 173; *Utopia*, 134, 138, 141–43, 147, 170, 171, 186; and anti-imperialism, 138, 141–43, 188; "Nolandia" (Achora) of, 142n10, 144, 170, 186; *Responsio ad Lutherum*, 143n13; and Christian humanism, 163; and Johnson, 167, 171; compared to Blake, 178–79; Lewis as disciple of, 243, 244
Morgan, Edmund S., 135n57
Morgan, Kenneth O., 13n5, 204n28
Mortlake: home of John Dee, 18
Morton, Thomas: *New English Canaan*, 130
Mosaic Law, 130
Moscow, 84
Moses, 31, 91, 146
Mozambique, 68
Muses, 167n47
Muslim League, 242
Muslims, 211, 219, 228. *See also* Islam

Mussolini, Benito, 246
Mychallus, 167*n47*

Napoleon Bonaparte, emperor of France, 106, 178, 246
Napoleon III, emperor of France, 194
Napoleonic Wars, 8, 107, 108, 193. *See also* Napoleon Bonaparte
Nathan, Isaac, 198*n16*
Nationalism: English Protestant, 7, 11, 23, 26, 26, 31, 32, 52; undermined by Blake, 179, 182; postcolonial, 240, 242
Native Americans, 136, 245*n8;* extermination of, 57–59, 129–30; Milton's Adam and Eve as, 70; supposed descent from Trojans, 125; Spanish butchery of, 143–44; Johnson's sympathy for, 172. *See also* Indians, American
Native Canadians, 172–73
Natural law, 175, 196
Natural selection, 202. *See also* Darwinism; Evolution
Natural theology, 200–202
Nazis, 166
Nebuchadnezzar, king of Babylon, 59, 100, 140
Neeley, Alexander, 104*n71*
Negroes, 132, 136, 172. *See also* Africans; "Blackamoors"; *Cimarrones;* Moors
Negro insurrection: toasted by Johnson, 168
Nelson, Admiral Horatio, 106
Nero, emperor of Rome, 170
Netherlands, 39, 42, 57, 141
New Albion. *See* Nova Albion
New England, 73, 119, 125, 152
New historicism, 5, 95, 159
New Spain: Hakluyt's appeal for "liberation" of, 59–60, 61. *See also* Spanish Empire
New Testament, Urdu, 195
Nicholas I, czar of Russia, 194
Nichols, Reverend Philip, 86*n26,* 90–91, 98; *Sir Francis Drake Reuiued* (1626), 95–96, 97
Nkrumah, Kwame, 240*n63*
Noble savage myth, 12, 52, 70; and Shakespeare's *Cymbeline,* 45; and Spenser's satyrs, 88–90; and Shakespeare's Caliban, 93, 94; and Swift's Yahoos, 104–5; and Pocahontas, 115–16; and Jonson's *Masque of Blackness,* 119; and native Americans, 126; and ancient Britons, 126; and Behn's *Oroonoko,* 133

Nombre de Dios, Panama, 61, 91
Norman conquest, 15
North Carolina, 62, 125*n28,* 145. *See also* "Lost Colony"; Roanoke Colony; Virginia
Nova Albion, 78–81, 84, 86, 87, 88, 90, 91, 92, 94, 95, 96, 98, 102*n66,* 104, 105–6, 108, 137

Odysseus, 60
Ohio, 172
Opechancanough, brother of Powhatan, 129
Opera, and Puritans, 66
Orientalism, 171
Orinoco River, 61, 62, 239
Orkney Islands, 16
Orosius, Paulus, 139–40
Orwell, George, 230–31, 243
Othello, 114, 134. *See also* Shakespeare, William: *Othello*
Ottoman Empire, 197. *See also* Turks
Oxford University, 232

Pacific Ocean, 157, 246
Pagden, Anthony, 74
Pakistan, 242
Palestine, 153, 246
Palmerston, Lord, John Henry Temple, 194
Panama, 91, 96; Drake's early raids on, 61, 98; and Darien disaster, 162–63
Papacy, 2, 13, 140, 143. *See also* Catholicism; Pope; Vatican
Paradise, as colonial metaphor, 81, 127, 239. *See also* Eden, Garden of
Parliament, 167, 196. *See also* House of Commons; House of Lords
Parthia, 160
Pascataway Indians, of Maryland, 127–28
Paul, the Apostle, 85, 111
Pax Britannica, 194, 196
Pax Romana, 139
Pequot War, 129
Perkins, William, 130
Peru, 64*n12,* 66, 149, 156, 169
Peter, the Apostle, 81, 121
Philip II, king of England and Spain, 38–39, 42, 57, 80, 83
Philips, Miles, 54, 57, 59–61
Philips, John, Milton's nephew, 64–66
Pigafeta, Antonio, 85*n22*
Pilate, Pontius, 189
Pillars of Hercules, 141, 149
Pitt, William, 171–72, 176

Pizarro, Francisco, 64*n12*
Plato, 156, 209
Plymouth, England, 86, 88
Plymouth, Massachusetts, 81
Pocahontas, 7, 120, 121, 135, 136, 155; marriage to Rolfe, 53, 115, 241; visit to London, 114; welcomed by King James as royalty, 115–16; as noble savage, 115–16; and biblical Rebecca, 115–16; conversion of, 115–16, 122–23, 241; renamed "Rebecca," 116, 123, 124; compared to Virgil's Lavinia, 116, 126; and Virginia Dare, 125*n28*; compared to Kitamagund of Maryland, 127–28; as American Eve, 127; death of, 129; Peace of Pocahontas ends, 129. *See also* Matoaka; Powhatan
Pompey the Great, 100, 102
Pontiff, 71–72. *See also* Catholicism; Papacy; Pope; Vatican
Poole, England, 60
Pope: as equal to other bishops, 24; as usurping foreign prince, 26; excommunicates Elizabeth I, 56; as antichrist, 57
Popocatepetl, Mount, in Mexico, 69
Porrex, son of Gorbodog (Gorboduc), 20
Portugal, 66, 87
Portuguese Empire: and Line of Tordesillas, 27; and slave trade, 74, 76; end of, 242
Potter, Beatrix, 237
Postcolonial: Tudor-Stuart England as, 7, 11, 242; Norman England as, 15
Postcolonial theory, 5, 25
Post-Protestant imperialism, 138, 192, 238; in Kipling's "Judgment of Dungara," 212; in Forster's *Howards End*, 213–18; in Conrad's *Lord Jim*, 218–19; in Conrad's *Heart of Darkness*, 219–22; in Forster's *Passage to India*, 223–30
Powhatan, Chief, 126, 129. *See also* Pocahontas
Powhatan Confederacy, 123
Preracism, colonial, 8, 115, 116–19, 128. *See also* Racism
Prester John, 125, 239
Priam, king of Troy, 17–18
Prince Albert. *See* Albert
Prospero, 92, 130; and Dee, 30; as colonial oppressor, 93–95; as magus, 94; compared to Drake, 94–95; compared to Conrad's Mr. Kurtz, 94–95; compared to Swift's Houyhnhnms, 165–66. *See also* Browning, Robert: "Caliban upon Setebos"; Shakespeare, William: *The Tempest*
Protectorate, 97, 98. *See also* Cromwell, Oliver; Cromwellian Regime; Western Design
Protestantism: Tudor-Stuart, 2, 3; and imperial expansion, 4; and anti-imperial opposition, 4; Victorian, 8, 243; and British imperial religion, 111; relation to Protestant imperialism, 114, 138, 191–92; Elizabethan, 210; end to binding power of, 216; and imperial ambivalence in Conrad's *Lord Jim*, 219; mocked by Waugh, 231
Protoracism, colonial, 8, 116, 119; and classicism, 128–29; and Judeo-Christian tradition, 128–29. *See also* Racism
Purchas, Samuel: *Purchas His Pilgrimes*, 64*n12*; 82*n13*, 92, 136
Puritanism, 73, 125*n26*, 160. *See also* Cromwell, Oliver; Cromwellian Regime; Milton; Protectorate
Puritans, 26, 66, 81, 92, 119, 131

Quakers: and abolition, 174
Quebec, 171, 172
Quetzalcóatl, 241; impersonated by Cortés, 70–71; Cortés worshiped as, 84
Quinn, David B., 87–88
Quint, David, 64, 73

Rabelais, François, 163
Race: Tudor-Stuart attitudes toward, 114
Racism, 179, 180–82; Stuart origins of, 128–36; in *Heart of Darkness*, 220. *See also* Color line
Ragnarök, 210
Rainolds, Henry, 128*n36*
Raj, British, 108, 227, 242
Rajan, Balachandra, 161
Ralegh, Sir Walter (1552–1618), 1, 6, 7, 14, 31, 92, 128, 144–47, 149, 154, 156–57, 158, 159, 235; and Spenser, 37–38, 88–89; in Guiana, 61–64, 123–24; on "liberation" of New Spain, 64; and intermarriage, 123–24, 126; *Discovery of Guiana*, 154, 159–60; parodied in Conrad's *Heart of Darkness*, 220–21; and Waugh's *Handful of Dust*, 239
Raleigh, Sir Walter (1552–1618). *See* Ralegh, Sir Walter
Raleigh, Sir Walter (1861–1922), 82*n13*; on Hakluyt's "prose epic," 110
Ramusio, Giovanni Battista, 85*n22*
Randolph family, 135
Rastell, John, 23, 40
Reconquista, 74, 114, 246

Red Army, 246
Reformation, Protestant, 2, 6, 7; and "Matter of Britain," 11, 13; and imperial recovery myth, 124; Waugh's views on, 231
Regan, daughter of Lear, 20
Regency period, 194
Religion: binding power of, 6–8, 191–92, 214–18 *passim*, 221–22, 223, 225, 241; of British Protestant imperialism, 111; and subordination of native Americans, 129–30; as domestic guardian in Austen's *Mansfield Park*, 188; as source of colonial trouble, 210–13, 230; in Forster's *Howards End* and *Passage to India*, 214–18, 223, 225, 228–29; in Conrad's *Lord Jim* and *Heart of Darkness*, 218; of Mogul emperor Akbar, 224; and imperial credibility, 225–26; Kipling on, 230; in Waugh's *Handful of Dust*, 238; and postcolonial nation-building, 242
Renaissance, 6, 14. *See also* Humanism
Restoration era, 73, 131
Returning king myth, 12–21, 97
Revett, Eldred, 128n36
Rex futurus: Spenser's Arthur as, 36; myth of, 40, 204; in Lewis's *That Hideous Strength*, 245
Rhodes, Cecil, 245
Richard III, king of England, 22, 29
Rio de Janeiro, 84
Roanoke Colony, 126, 145–46
Roanoke Island, 95
Roberts, Frederick Sleigh, Lord Roberts of Kandahar ("General Bobs"), 110
Roberts, Henry, 83, 87, 91
Rolfe, John, 7, 114, 120, 123–24, 125n28, 135, 241; marriage to Pocahontas, 53, 115–16; Calvinism of, 119; as Theseus, 125n26; as Aeneas, 126, 128; and color line, 129
Rolfe, Rebecca. *See* Pocahontas
Rolfe, Thomas, 129, 135
Roman Catholicism. *See* Catholicism
Romance: in Forster's *Howards End*, 217; colonial, 234, 235, 242
Roman Empire, 12, 41, 124, 138, 139–40, 148, 150, 162, 194, 206, 208, 232, 246; and Arthur, 16–17; and British claims to, 16–17, 20, 24; and Ciceronian "protectorate," 139; in Milton's *Paradise Regain'd*, 161
Romanitas, 43, 46, 48
Roman Republic, 139

Romantic poets, 178, 197
Rome, 2, 3, 12, 14–16
Romulus, 29
Round Table, 16, 34
Royal Navy, 196–97
Rush, Benjamin, 125n28
Ruskin, John, 216
Russia, 16, 84, 203. *See also* Union of Soviet Socialist Republics
Rymer, Thomas; *Short View of Tragedy*, 134

Sabies, West African tribe, 74–76
Said, Edward, 6, 169n51, 192; *Orientalism*, 171; *Culture and Imperialism*, 174n64, 186–89, 193
Saint Augustine, Florida, 145
Saint Julian, South American port of, 96
Salamanca, University of, 142
Salisbury. *See* Cecil, Robert, Lord Salisbury
Samboses, West African tribe, 74, 75
Sambula, West Africa, 74–75
San Diego, 81
Sandwich Islands. *See* Hawaii
Sandys, Sir Edwin, 155n26
San Francisco, 81
San Juan De Ullua, 61, 145
San Salvador, 68
Santo Domingo, 145
Satan, 80, 97, 194, 244–45; in Milton's *Paradise Lost*, 64–74, 222; *See also* Milton, John: *Paradise Lost;* Milton, John: *Paradise Regain'd*
Sati, 195–96
Satyagraha: Gandhi and, 242
Savage, domestic, myth of, 235, 236, 238; and Spenser's Artegall, 40–42
Savagery: in Conrad's *Heart of Darkness*, 220–21; in Waugh's *Mr. Todd*, 237
Savages, 40, 245n8; of Virginia, 126; and equality with whites, 121–22, 126, 129, 136; ancient British, 175. *See also* Noble savage myth
Saxon race, 8. *See also* Racism
Saxons, 15, 20, 47, 122; empires of, 218. *See also* Anglo-Saxons
Scandinavia, 16
Scatology: in Swift's *Gulliver's Travels*, 163–64, 166
Scherwatzky, Steven, 171–72
Schoeck, Richard, 14
Scotland, 2; failed conquest of Edward I, 13n5; and Dorien disaster, 162–63; Johnson on, 168

Index

Scots, 162–63, 168, 212
Scythia, 43
Scythians, 41
Secularism, 192, 202, 243
Seeley, John Robert, 8, 194, 209, 213; *Ecce Homo*, 202; *The Expansion of England*, 203, 210–11; anti-religion views of, 210–11
Sejanus, Lucius Aelius, 139
Selkirk, Alexander, 102
Semites, 211
Sennacherib, 197
Setebos, Brazilian deity, 94. *See also* Browning, Robert: "Caliban upon Setebos"; Shakespeare, William: *The Tempest*
Seven Years' War (1756–1763), 6n13, 172. *See also* "Great War for Empire"
Seville, 58–60, 83n15, 84, 91, 183
Shakespeare, William, 5, 53, 78, 128; *The Tempest*, 7, 50, 93–95, 146; *Cymbeline*, 7, 12, 25, 44–53, 146; *King Lear*, 20; *Hamlet* and *Antony and Cleopatra*, 45; *Much Ado about Nothing*, 49; *The Winter's Tale*, 49, 50, 217; *Othello*, 49, 134–35; *Pericles*, 50; *The Merry Wives of Windsor*, 147; *Richard III*, 207; *The Merchant of Venice* and *As You Like It*, 217
Shaw, George Bernard, 52
Shelley, Percy Bysshe, 197, 198n16
Sherman, William H., 11n2, 14, 27, 30
Shield of Arthur, 33, 38–39
Shuger, Debora, 4, 5, 41
Sidney, Sir Philip, 31, 151; *The Defense of Poesy*, 43–44
Silvius, father of Brutus, 15
Slave Coast, African, 74–76
Slavery: abolished in New Spain by Charles V, 59; African and Mexican, 60; chattel, opposed by Jacobean Calvinism, 130; expansion of in southern colonies, 130–36; opposed by Johnson, 132, 168, 170, 172; early English, 144; opposed by Jane Austen, 185; abolition of, and evangelicalism, 196–97
Slaves: African, 61, 172; loss of religious freedom, 132; evangelization of, 135; West Indian, 186
Slave trade, 130; abolition of, 185, 196–97
Sleeman, Captain William, Anti-Thug Superintendent, 196
Slemon, Stephen, 25
Smalley, Donald, 200, 201

Smart, Christopher, 170
Smith, John, captain, 119n16; *Historie of Virginia*, 115
Smith, Sir Thomas, 154, 155, 156
Socialism, 215, 240
Society for the Propagation of the Gospel in Foreign Parts, 136
Socrates, 141, 154, 156, 157
Solomon, king of Israel, 157, 171
South Africa, 215
South America, 81, 235
South Asia, 167, 242. *See also* India
Southey, Robert, 197; *Madoc*, 125n28
South Sea Bubble, 162, 163
Soviet Union. *See* Union of Soviet Socialist Republics
Spain, 38, 39, 78, 83, 102n66, 129, 137, 139, 141, 145, 169, 183, 246; Black Legend (*leyenda negra*) of, 7, 54–76, 77, 82, 107, 114, 144; threat to Reformation, 24; and Arthur, 29; White Legend (*leyenda blanca*) of, 74, 114; decline of, 147, 148–49; mentioned, 6. *See also* Black Legend of Spain; Spanish Empire
Spaniards, 54–76 *passim*, 80
Spanish Empire, 55–57, 60–61, 74, 77, 150, 158, 160, 163, 170. *See also* Black Legend of Spain; Spain
Sparke, John, 74–76, 144
Spenser, Edmund, 2, 5, 29, 49, 53, 78, 88–89, 245; *View of the Present State of Ireland*, 41
—*The Faerie Queene*, 7, 124; compared to Malory's *Le Morte Darthur* and Geoffrey of Monmouth's *History of the Kings of Britain*, 34, 36; and Protestant *sola gratia*, 37–39; compared to Milton's *Paradise Lost*, 65, 72; and imperialism, 90; compared to Tennyson's *Idylls of the King*, 205; compared to Conrad's *Heart of Darkness*, 221; colonial "wickedness" of, according to Lewis, 243
Stanhope, Sir John, 231
Stanley, Henry Morton, 110, 220
Stannard, Martin, 235, 236, 238
Stape, J. H., 219
Stewart, David H., 110n90
Stow, John, 32–33, 38, 45–46
Strauss, David Friedrich, 202
Strier, Richard, 9
Stuart era, 65; racism, origins of, 128–36. *See also* Racism; Tudor-Stuart era
Stuart, Henry, prince of Wales, 138, 147–52

Stuart, Mary, queen of Scots, 10
Sugden, John, 80, 85–86n25, 96n47
Swift, Jonathan, 5, 8, 105, 134, 146, 162, 163, 164, 167, 179, 233, 243, 244, 245n8; influence on Johnson, 167n47; "A Modest Proposal," 166; anti-imperialism of, 188, 190
—*Gulliver's Travels*, 82; and Christian humanist tradition, 104, 165, 222; and noble savage myth, and Drake, 104–5; as anti-imperial satire, 104–5, 162–66
Symerons. *See* Cimarrones
Symonds, William: against intermarriage at Jamestown, 120–21, 123, 126, 127
Syria, 246

Tacitus, Gaius Cornelius, 12, 43, 44
Taj Mahal, 11
Tamerlane, 100, 101
Tartars: invasion of India, 175
Tasmanians: extermination of, 243
Temple, Henry John. *See* Palmerston, Lord
Tennyson, Alfred Lord, 219, 231, 245; expansionism of, 192, 203–4, 205; and imperial trusteeship, anti-imperialism, and Darwinism, 203–4; sometime Liberal and friend of Gladstone, 204; as Poet Laureate, 209; *Idylls of the King*, 138; and imperial anxiety, 203–10; as metonym and metaphor for empire, as neo-Arthurian, 203–4; on loss of empire, compared to Spenser's *Faerie Queene*, 205; and Waugh's *Handful of Dust*, 238; mentioned, 8
Tenochtitlán, Aztec capital: compared to Eden, 69; destruction of, 71–72; Cortés worshiped at, 84
Ternate, Sultan of: Drake deals with, 81
Terra Australis Incognita, 81
Tesky, Gordon, 37–38
Texcoco, Lake, in Mexico, 69
Thames River, 111, 220–21
Third Reich, 242
Thomson, James, 162
Thornton, A. P., 194
Thornton, Henry, 196
Throgmorton, Elizabeth, 61
Thugi, 195–96, 197
Tiberius Caesar, emperor of Rome, 139, 161
Tibet, 246
Tilton, Robert, 120
Tlaxcala, Mexico, 67
Tobacco, 155, 155–56n29; cultivation of, and Rolfe, 129; and African labor, 130; 131; hated by James I, 156; as emblem of colonial vanity, 158
Tomalin, Claire, 185
Torchiana, D. T., 164
Tordesillas, Line of, 27
Toryism, 134, 138; and radicalism of Johnson, 168, 171, 173, 185; anti-imperialism of, 193
Tory Party, 163; and imperialism under Disraeli and Lord Salisbury, 204; Augustan, 214–15; and late Victorian expansionism, 215
Tower of London, 151
Trail of Tears, 129
Translatio imperii, myth of, 48, 77, 140, 153; from Rome to Britain, 12; and Spenser's *Faerie Queene*, 40–44; and Shakespeare's *Cymbeline*, 44–53; mentioned, 3, 7
Trinity College, Cambridge, 30
Trojans: legend of British descent from, 12, 15, 124, 126; rejected by Camden, 41; as ancestors of Native Americans, 125; mentioned, 17, 20, 52. *See also* Arthur; Arthurianism; Bruto-Arthurian recovery myth; Brutus; Geoffrey of Monmouth
Troy, 15, 16, 21, 127, 139
Troynovant: legendary original name of London, 15, 17, 124; Jamestown as, 53
Trusteeship, imperial, 138, 146, 174, 192, 193; and Roman Empire, 139; and Herbert, 153; ironies of, and Burke, 173–77, 215; and Tennyson, 203, 204; and Liberal Party, 215; mentioned, 8
Tübingen, 211, 213
Tudor-Stuart era: and Protestantism, 3; and intertextuality, 5; and imperial recovery myth, 12, 124. *See also* Stuart era
Turks, 74, 180. *See also* Ottoman Empire

Union, Act of, 163
Union of Soviet Socialist Republics, 193, 242, 246
United Nations, 246
United States of America, 80, 107, 193, 237; nineteenth-century rivalry with British Empire, 203, 245n8; as slave-holding "Empire of Liberty," 246
Urdu language, 195
Uther Pendragon, legendary king of Britain, 15, 16, 17, 34–35. *See also* Arthur; Geoffrey of Monmouth: *History of the Kings of Britain*; Malory, Sir Thomas: *Le Morte Darthur*; *Misfortunes of Arthur, The*;

Spenser, Edmund: *The Faerie Queene;* Tennyson, Alfred Lord, *Idylls of the King*
Utilitarianism: alliance with evangelicalism, 193, 195; and Christianity, 211; mentioned, 8

Van Sype, Nichola, 80
Vatican, 2, 11, 67. *See also* Catholicism; Papacy
Vaux, W. S. W., 79n3, 80n9
Venice, 134
Vergil, Polydore, 12; doubts Arthur's existence, 23, 40; imperialism of, 40; and Shakespeare's *Cymbeline*, 48
Versailles, Treaty of, 246
Vespucci, Amerigo, 14
Victoria, queen of Britain, 193, 209, 213
Victorian era: later, 8, 176; in India, 138; early, and evangelicalism, 192, 194; and religious doubt, 219; mentioned, 3, 6, 108, 198, 208, 211, 213, 243
Villiers, George, duke of Buckingham, 97
Virgil, 128; *Aeneid* contrasted with Geoffrey of Monmouth's *History of the Kings of Britain*, 27, 116; "Messianic Eclogue," 31; *Aeneid* as model for intermarriage at Jamestown, 124–26; and anti-imperialism, 139
Virginia, colonial, 8, 21, 53, 68, 73, 114, 130; as new Albion, 32; as religious undertaking, compared with Massachusetts, 119; as paradise, 127; miscegenation criminalized in, 130–31, 132, 135, 147, 149, 158, 176; planters in oppose evangelization of natives, 195
Virginia, Commonwealth of, 135
Virginia Company, 129, 153; failure of, 154–56; dissolution of charter of, 155–56, 158
Virginity: as colonial metaphor, 62–63, 147, 159, 220
Viswanathan, Gauri, 242
Vitoria, Francisco de, 142–43, 144
Vizilopuchtli, Aztec city of, 69
Von Maltzahn, Nicholas, 162
Vortigern, legendary king of Britain, 29, 31, 32

Wales: conquered by Edward I of England, 13n5; Lost Tribes of, 14n8, 125n28, 239; home to Geoffrey of Monmouth, 15; ancestral home of Tudor monarchs, 22; as ancient British remnant, 43–44; savagery of, according to Johnson, 168; mentioned, 12, 29, 30, 47, 231
Wallace, William, 13n5
Walsingham, Sir Francis, 31, 87, 88
War of Jenkins' Ear, 167
War of the Spanish Succession, 162
Warren, Michelle R., 15
Waterloo, 196, 197
Watt, Ian, 218
Watts, Cedric, 220
Waugh, Evelyn, 8, 146; as anti-Protestant, 173, 231; as Catholic convert, 192, 231, 232; mocks Protestantism, 230–39 *passim;* satire of secular humanist imperialism in *Black Mischief* and *A Handful of Dust*, 230–39; as post-secular, compared to Kipling, Conrad, and Forster, 231; *Edmund Campion*, 231; evokes and parodies Conrad's *Heart of Darkness*, 232–33, 239; end of empire in *Decline and Fall* and *Vile Bodies*, 232; travels of in Brazil and British Guyana, 235; "The Man Who Liked Dickens" as origin of *A Handful of Dust*, 238; mentioned, 2
Weimar Republic, 246
Wells, H. G., 244
Western Design: of Cromwell, 65–66, 160
West Indies, 83, 86, 90, 96, 98, 147, 156, 186, 189
Westminster Confession, 201. *See also* Calvinism
Whiggery, 134, 135, 162, 164, 171
Whig Party, 162, 163, 173
Whitaker, Alexander, 123
White, John, governor of Roanoke Colony, 146
Whitgift, John, archbishop of Canterbury, 31
Whitman, Walt, 179, 184
Wilberforce, Samuel, bishop, 201
Wilberforce, William, 196–97, 214
William the Conqueror, 100, 101
William III, king of Great Britain, 168n48
Winthrop, John, 119
Wittgenstein, Ludwig, 9
Wolfe, General James, 171
Wordsworth, William, 178, 197
World War I, 213, 223, 240
World War II, 240, 242
Wounded Knee, 129
Wright, Louis B., 3, 4, 84
Wurgaft, Lewis, 6, 169n51

Wyatt, Sir Francis, 129

Xenophobia: Tudor-Stuart, 114, 117

Yahoos: and noble savage myth, 104–5; as Irish, 164; as degenerate Englishmen, 164–65*n43;* and Shakespeare's Caliban, 165. *See also* Shakespeare, William: *The Tempest;* Swift, Jonathan: *Gulliver's Travels*

Ygraine (Igerna), mother of Arthur, 16

Young, Philip, 127

Yucatan Peninsula, 54, 60

Permissions

I gratefully acknowledge permission to quote from or reproduce the material indicated:

—Tate Britain Gallery, Sir John Everett Millais's *The Boyhood of Raleigh,* © Tate, London 2002, used as the frontispiece.
—From Augustine, *City of God against the Pagans,* ed. and trans. R. W. Dyson (Cambridge: Cambridge University Press, 1998). Reprinted with the permission of Cambridge University Press.
—From *Culture and Imperialism* by Edward W. Said, copyright © 1993 by Edward W. Said. Used by permission of Alfred A. Knopf, a division of Random House, Inc.
—From *Howards End* by E. M. Forster, copyright 1910. Used by permission of Dutton Signet, a division of Penguin Putnam.
—Excerpt from *A Passage to India* by Edward Morgan Forster, copyright 1924 by Harcourt, Inc. and renewed 1952 by E. M. Forster, reprinted by permission of the publisher.
—From Thomas More, *Utopia,* trans. Paul Turner (Harmondsworth: Penguin, 1965). Reproduced by permission of Penguin Books Ltd.
—"The Uses of Atrocity: Satanic Spaniards and Hispanic Satans from Las Casas to Milton," which appeared in *Mediterranean Studies* 8 (1999): 175–92, and which now appears substantially as chapter two of this book. Reprinted by permission of Ashgate Publishers.
—"Stooping to Conquer: Heathen Idolatry and Protestant Humility in the Imperial Legend of Sir Francis Drake," *Studies in Philology* 94 (1997): 428–64, which now appears substantially as chapter three of this book. Reprinted by

permission of *Studies in Philology* (published by University of North Carolina Press).

—"The Nubile Savage: Pocahontas as Heathen Convert and Virgilian Bride," *Renaissance Papers* 1998: 81–90, which now appears as a section of chapter four in this book. Reprinted by permission of *Renaissance Papers* (published by Camden House).

OHIO UNIVERSITY LIBRARY
Please return this book as soon as you have finished with it. In order to avoid a fine it must be returned by the latest date stamped below. All books are subject to recall after two weeks or immediately if needed for reserve.

JUN 16 2005

RECEIVED

JUN 1 0 2008

JUN 03 2008

CF